PLEASURE
THE BOURGEOIS EXPERIENCE
VICTORIA TO FREUD

VOLUME V

PETER GAY is a Sterling Professor of History Emeritus at Yale University. In addition to the *Bourgeois Experience* series, he is the author of the best-selling *Freud: A Life for Our Time*, and a two volume study of the Enlightenment, of which the first, *The Rise Of Modern Paganism*, won a National Book Award. He lives in Hamden, Connecticut.

More from the reviews:

'His huge and boldly ambitious survey of bourgeois experience in the nineteenth century [ranges] across several European countries and North America...The central subject according to its author is "the highly ambiguous engagement of the bourgeoisie with the avant-garde" More broadly, it deals with the bourgeoisie's attitudes to high culture as a whole: literature, music and the visual arts. Perhaps its most fascinating section is devoted to Manchester, where Gay traces the development of musical taste, mainly through the enterprise of a small but influential class of assimilated German Jewish businessmen; their enduring legacy is the Hallé Orchestra, whose eponymous founder was born Karl Halle in Germany, acquired the acute accent at the end of his surname during his time in France, and died, a grand old Lancashire institution as Sir Charles. *Pleasure Wars* is wide ranging, not only geographically but in theme; there are potted essays on French art critics and literary critics, early modernist architecture, even on the lives and policies of the Kings of Bavaria...most ambitious, interesting and original.'

RICHARD JENKYNS, *TLS*

'Gay – nothing if not the consummate cosmopolitan – wields two favourite weapons – one familiar, the other less so. The old one is omniscience. He appears to have read everything and by consequence, one of the great delights of this undertaking is that alongside masterly discussions of mainstream topics you suddenly run across a learned disquisition on, for example, the price of pianos. The other sword is psychoanalysis, of which Gay is a great champion...Whereas psychoanalysis has formerly been used to diagnose the Victorian malady (to show how repressed they were), in Gay's hands it is a tool for plumbing hidden depths. Dusted down and polished up in the earlier volumes, the bourgeoisie now shine out as men of passion and principle, integrity and independence, surprisingly aware about their inner conflicts, their passions and prejudices and sexually upfront rather than uptight. In short, were they not, in one of Gay's many nice phrases, "conventionally unconventional"? Free to examine their record with a fresh eye, Gay finds much to respect. Far from being mammon-worshipping Philistines who preferred facts to fantasy, engines to expressionism, the middle classes were deeply committed to the coexistence of wealth and culture, believing it was commerce's mission to enhance civilization. "By the gains of Industry we promote Art," proudly proclaimed the founders of the Birmingham Art Gallery. The complex relations between avant-garde artists and their plutocrat patrons are here astutely explored'

ROY PORTER, *Sunday Times*

'The first two volumes [of *The Bourgeois Experience*] cover sensual life and theories of love; the third aggression. Volume Four, concerns the intense middle-class preoccupation with self. This final, fifth volume deals with the trade, both personal and commercial, in the values of art...The pleasure of Gay's work lies in what the author has called "a conversation and a collaboration.'

JAD ADAMS, *Guardian*

BOOKS BY PETER GAY

The Bourgeois Experience: Victoria to Freud
Volume IV   The Naked Heart (1995)

The Bourgeois Experience: Victoria to Freud
Volume III   The Cultivation of Hatred (1993)

Reading Freud: Explorations and Entertainments (1990)

Freud: A Life for Our Time (1988)

A Godless Jew:
Freud, Atheism, and the Making of Psychoanalysis (1987)

The Bourgeois Experience: Victoria to Freud
Volume II   The Tender Passion (1986)

Freud for Historians (1985)

The Bourgeois Experience: Victoria to Freud
Volume I   Education of the Senses (1984)

Freud, Jews and Other Germans:
Masters and Victims in Modernist Culture (1978)

Art and Act: On Causes in History—Manet, Gropius, Mondrian (1976)

Style in History (1974)

Modern Europe (1973), with R. K. Webb

The Bridge of Criticism: Dialogues on the Enlightenment (1970)

The Enlightenment: An Interpretation
Vol. II   The Science of Freedom (1969)

Weimar Culture: The Outsider as Insider (1968)

A Loss of Mastery: Puritan Historians in Colonial America (1966)

The Enlightenment: An Interpretation
Vol. I   The Rise of Modern Paganism (1966)

The Party of Humanity: Essays in the French Enlightenment (1964)

Voltaire's Politics: The Poet as Realist (1959)

The Dilemma of Democratic Socialism:
Eduard Bernstein's Challenge to Marx (1952)

Pleasure Wars

The Bourgeois Experience
VICTORIA TO FREUD

VOLUME V

PETER GAY

FontanaPress
An Imprint of HarperCollins*Publishers*

Fontana Press
An Imprint of HarperCollins *Publishers*,
77-85 Fulham Palace Road,
Hammersmith, London W6 8JB

1 3 5 7 9 8 6 4 2

First published by Great Britain by
HarperCollins *Publishers* 1998,

Copyright © Peter Gay 1998

Peter Gay asserts the moral right to
be identified as the author of this work

ISBN 0 00 686369 8

Set by Rowland Phototypesetting Ltd,
Bury St Edmunds, Suffolk

Printed in Great Britain by
Caledonian International Book Manufacturing Ltd, Glasgow

FOR
RUTHIE

Contents

"Bourgeois," I observed, "is an epithet which the riff-raff apply to
what is respectable, and the aristocracy to what is decent."
— "Anthony Hope," [pseud. Sir Anthony Hope Hawkins],
Dolly Dialogues, *1894*

Der heuchlerische Anschein, mit dem alle bürgerlichen Ordnun-
gen übertüncht sind, wie als ob sie Ausgeburten der Moralität
wären—z. B. die Ehe; die Arbeit; der Beruf; das Vaterland; die
Familie; die Ordnung; das Recht. Aber da sie insgesamt auf die
mittelmässigste Art Mensch hin begründet sind, zum Schutz
gegen Ausnahmen und Ausnahme-Bedürfnisse, so muss man es bil-
lig finden, wenn hier viel gelogen wird.
—Friedrich Nietzsche, Nachlass

Bourgeois, vous avez—roi, législateur ou négociant—institué des
collections, des musées, des galeries. Quelques-unes de celles qui
n'étaient ouvertes il y a seize ans qu'aux accapareurs ont élargi
leurs portes pour la multitude. Vous vous êtes associés, vous avez
formé des compagnies et fait des emprunts pour réaliser l'idée de
l'avenir avec toutes ses formes diverses, formes politique, industrielle
et artistique. Vous n'avez jamais en aucune noble entreprise laissé
l'initiative à la minorité protestant et souffrante, qui est d'ailleurs
l'ennemie naturelle de l'art.
—Charles Baudelaire, Salon de 1846

Pleasure Wars

Introduction
Definitions

In the Victorian decades, the name *bourgeois* was at once a term of reproach and a source of self-respect. Although many members of the middle class took pride in their status, it was leavened with a good deal of uneasiness; for them, an age of confidence was also an age of anxiety. Moderating between the aristocracy's persistent claims to preeminence in politics, society, and high culture and an increasingly restive working class pressing for a living wage and the vote, to be "middling" took hold less as a compromise than as a widely supported bourgeois ideology.

This was the style of thinking that the French critic Emile Faguet explored looking back in 1890 on the career of François Guizot—prolific historian, educational reformer, briefly prime minister under King Louis Philippe during the July Monarchy. Guizot, he wrote, not without justice, "invented the party, the government, and the doctrine of the *juste milieu.*" During the years he wielded influence, Faguet noted, the bourgeoisie interpreted and expressed the national will. The lower class can feel but not speak; the upper class can speak but, too remote from public life, has nothing of value to say.[1] Radicals did not thank him for it, but Guizot's political stance informed most middle-class politicians in the nineteenth century, though not without facing severe criticism.

By the time Queen Victoria ascended the throne, in 1837, the bourgeoisie had long defined itself as a distinct social class, although commentators continued to spar with one another about details. Its name and its sense of identity could call on the authority of tradition. Free imperial German cities or Dutch metropolitan centers, Hamburg or Amsterdam, had been dominated for generations by a patriciate that wanted no aristocratic *de* or *von* to decorate their names and that decried ostentation as vulgar. Middle-class plutocrats might ache to erase the stigmata of trade, but many good bourgeois took visible pride in their status as *Bürger.* There were magnates ill at ease in their palatial houses —mansions too aristocratic for them.* And Alfred Krupp, the most energetic in the family clan of Germany's foremost armament manufacturers, declared that he would "rather be the first among industrialists than the last among knights."[2] His attitude was anything but eccentric among confident Victorian bourgeois.

From the age of the Reformation onward, portraits of commercial men, even of moneylenders, had spoken of an unapologetic ease in their rank; the road from portraits by Holbein to those by Degas is straight and short. In the age of the Enlightenment, social commentators like Addison and Voltaire singled out the pacific, unheroic, trading middle class for praise. And a virtual epidemic of town hall building raced across European and American cities after mid-nineteenth century; from the 1850s on, literally scores were built, some of them very grand, in Munich and Manchester, Berlin and Paris and smaller towns elsewhere. They document not merely the multiplying functions of urban bureaucracies but also the bourgeoisie's claims to high esteem and even power, and at times defiance of its noble "betters."

Admittedly, in every country except perhaps in France, political leaders of the nineteenth-century bourgeoisie showed themselves downright diffident and opportunistic in the struggle for political preeminence. Again and again they allowed themselves to be co-opted for dubious rewards.[†] Even the Eng-

---

* Lea Mendelssohn-Bartholdy (wife of the banker and mother of the composer) wrote to her son-in-law Wilhelm Hensel on January 4, 1826, "I find our palace-like house too sumptuous throughout, not bourgeois enough, to be heartily happy with it." Felix Gilbert, *Bankiers, Künstler und Gelehrte* (1975), 65.

† The self-betrayal of the Victorian bourgeoisie was a common feature of nineteenth-century politics, even in France. There, in the early 1830s, the brilliant artists, historians, philosophers, and journalists who had earlier mounted a vigorous critique of the restored Bourbons were spoiled by success; the revolution of 1830, in part *their* revolution, brought them into prominent positions. Out of power, they wanted to overthrow the Bourbon regime; once more or less in power, they were determined to save its Orléanist successor. The German *Bürgertum* traded idealism for realism. In Prussia, in the mid-1860s, its progressive leadership, advocating a liberal regime and German national unity, scuttled liberalism in favor of nationalism and embraced Otto von Bis-

lish middle classes, firmly set, it would seem, on their way to hegemony, recorded failures—or, perhaps better, almost deliberate refusals to succeed—in taking
power. As late as the 1890s, Friedrich Engels was astonished at what he thought
the meekness of prosperous English merchants and manufacturers as they
capitulated to the gentry and the landed aristocracy in Parliament. Despite all
this, the growing prominence of the bourgeoisie in the production of wealth,
the arena of politics, and the shaping of social habits was beyond dispute. When,
around 1840, Heinrich Heine called his time an "industrial, bourgeois age," he
was voicing a generally held perception.[3]

In 1836, narrowing this claim to his own country, the French travel writer
and public servant Michel Chevalier announced that "today it is universally
recognized that the middle class rules in France."[4] He too, like Heine, could
count on his readers' assent. Was not King Louis Philippe, the embodiment of
his regime with his ubiquitous umbrella, little more than the executive agent
of a bourgeois financial elite? Had French nobles not fled to their landed
estates and left the work of governing to bankers, entrepreneurs, and publishers? In this fostering climate, reaching far beyond France, historians found it
hard to resist elevating into a commonplace the image of a bourgeoisie rising
steadily through the centuries, an explanation that, explaining too much, actually explained very little.

But it proved hard to confine the bourgeoisie to a simple definition. Reasonable observers of contemporary society acknowledged that if the bourgeoisie was a reality rather than a construct devised to save time and mental
effort, it was necessarily subtly stratified, often distinctly rent into mutually hostile cliques. They could cite persuasive evidence that it was not *the* bourgeoisie
that was struggling for, or had reached, the pinnacle of power, but a select few.
After mid-century, the marquis Massimo d'Azeglio, painter, novelist, prime
minister of Piedmont, noted that in his country "the hierarchical instinct dominates the whole of society," exhibiting the narrowest divisions between ranks.
Hence "the social distinctions generally carried by terms such as nobles, bourgeoisie, people and plebs and which are elsewhere sufficient to describe social
gradations, here in Piedmont are quite inadequate and make it necessary to use
a whole series of sub-categories," intelligible only to someone who has lived
in the country for a long time.[5]

D'Azeglio's analysis was astute enough, but he was wrong to suppose that
matters were simpler elsewhere. Any rapid outline of the nineteenth-century

---

marck's tough, unconstitutional policies for the sake of a unified Germany. In mid-nineteenth-
century Russia no one expected much from the small urban merchant class, but its capitulation
to the reactionary czarist autocracy was more heartfelt than the Westernizing minority among
them had hoped for.

bourgeoisie can be no more than a charcoal sketch that neglects finer shadings. This much we can securely say: each country divided its middling strata according to a variety of markers—source of income, size of property, place of residence, level of education. The French had their grande, bonne, and petite bourgeoisie, a ranking that was duplicated almost everywhere. And everywhere, too, a compact undisputable bourgeois was surrounded by less sharply defined and more problematic outcroppings. Substantial businessmen and manufacturers, members of the professions—lawyers, physicians, professors, middling bureaucrats—were unmistakably at home in the bourgeoisie. If they were anxious, as many of them were, it was never about their class identity but about maintaining with their limited income the prestige they thought proper to them. In contrast, at the top, capitalists eager to procure the station of gentleman and perhaps a patent of nobility had far deeper anxieties to cope with. So, at the bottom of the pile, did lowly clerks and independent craftsmen, mortally afraid of sinking into the mass of the proletariat.

It was perhaps inescapable that the language of social observation should try to accommodate these realities by coining illuminating oxymorons. At first confusing but meaningful phrases like "merchant princes" or "captains of industry" or *"l'aristocratie financière"* and "labor aristocrats" on one side, or on the other the sneer of German Social Democrats at clerks and petty bureaucrats, "proletarians with stand-up collars—*Stehkragenproletarier,*" survived the tests of usage. What was one to make of the name "bourgeois proletarians" except to admit that recognizable social groups fitted that description? The bourgeoisie, in short, was at once sizable and differentiated—in Emile Zola's words, "a vast class reaching from the common people to the aristocracy."[6] Not surprisingly, contemporaries imposed a certain order on this chaos by picturing it as a pyramid.

This image remained serviceable through the long century from the rise of Napoleon to the outbreak of the First World War. The middling and upper reaches of the middle class grew impressively in numbers and power, the petty bourgeoisie in numbers alone: with the passage of decades, the pyramid came to look particularly distended in its lower segments. The Germans gave these hapless thousands a name and after a time a political identity of their own: *Mittelstand.* In France it was that adroit politician Léon Gambetta, one of the founders of the Third Republic, who recognized the changed shape of things by famously asserting that *nouvelles couches,* small merchants and white-collar workers, were knocking on the doors of power.

The burgeoning new middle class desperately insisted on its identity: it was *not* part of the proletariat. No one was more bourgeois than a miserably paid post office clerk. Too often life in this subclass was shadowed by financial worries and status anxiety. Lowly civil servants or bookkeepers often earned less than skilled artisans, and while their occupation was usually more secure than that of factory workers, a grave illness or a reversal in their employer's fortunes loomed as ever-present hazards. Even without these calamities, petty bourgeois had to watch over their budgets as over a sick child: attentively, patiently, and, if one was so disposed, prayerfully.

Part of bourgeois identification, then, was a negative one. The very financial and emotional insecurity of the *nouvelles couches* worked to underscore the image of a single, recognizable bourgeois self-image. It was precisely because most of them clustered around the lower edges of the pyramid that they were all the more intent on upholding middle-class morality and middle-class styles of living, even though their showy alliance with more prosperous bourgeois was often subverted by sharp conflicts of interest. They could be more ostentatiously respectable than their betters, more severe with their family about table manners, just as calculating and manipulative to keep their children from marrying inappropriate suitors. Shabby gentility was a harsh taskmaster.

Whatever the psychological risks, the expansion in the number of clerks employed in department stores and government offices, insurance companies and banks was dramatic. In the quarter century between 1882 and 1907, in Germany alone, while there was a slight decrease among owners of factories and mines, factory workers doubled and white-collar workers multiplied sixfold. Similar startling statistics described developments in other countries; even if they gave no special name to the phenomenon of the lower middle class, they too had their *Mittelstand*.

The reasons for this drastic reshaping of the bourgeois pyramid are obvious enough. With historic strides in transport and communications, improved access to capital formation, the easing of credit, and the introduction of expensive machinery, only the most determined defender of the old ways could overlook the savings inherent in large-scale operations. The principal resistances to expanding factories, banks, insurance companies, and railroad lines were emotional ones: the reluctance to take on heavy debt or the cherished tradition of the family firm. Just as strongly held sentiments secured the survival of the small neighborhood store in face of that irresistible modern invention—the department store: the opportunity to buy on credit, the pleasure in combining a little gossip with local shopping, the easy familiarity with owner and clerk. Sooner or later the logic of modern capitalism won the day. The new giants of manufacturing, commerce, and service industries, not to forget governments laden with unprecedented duties, generated an insatiable appetite for typists, secretaries, bookkeepers, sales personnel, and, late in the century, telephone operators. Demand generated supply; the campaigns of major Western powers to wipe out illiteracy and open sound primary and secondary schools to the children of the lower orders produced the recruits essential to late-nineteenth-century enterprise.

Fundamental changes in the bourgeois pyramid were both cause and consequence of revolutionary innovations across all of Victorian society. As inventions speeded travel and the mails, identified diseases and modernized production, the shock of the new became the signature of the age. And it was not solely politics and religion, technology and urban life that were forced to respond. The arts, music, and literature, the themes of this volume, proved equally volatile. Maps to conduct, policy—and taste—like guides to good manners or efficient household management threatened to become obsolete before revised editions had been drawn up. The population explosion radically altered the dimensions of the market and introduced unanticipated warfare between employers and employees; millions migrated from country to city or across the ocean, swelling hamlets into towns and cities into vast agglomerations not seen since ancient Rome. After 1859, the year of Charles Darwin's *Origin of Species,* which aroused envenomed controversy, the bourgeoisie would never be the same. In this heady atmosphere, since the luxuries of high culture never float untouched above the workaday world, upheavals in taste were only to be expected. It seemed natural, almost predictable, that what late Victorians would learn to call modernism, that disrespectful revolt against academicism and conventionality, would be born in their time.

As early as 1831, in an arresting series of essays, John Stuart Mill had mused on the feeling of impermanence that haunted the spirit of his era: "The first of the leading peculiarities of the present age is, that it is an age of transition." No earlier time, it seemed to him, had come close to matching the swiftness, intensity, and range of current subversions. Hence he warned against trivializing the situation: "Mankind have outgrown old institutions and old doctrines, and have not yet acquired new ones." Theirs was a time of "intellectual anarchy." Yet, matching the assurance buoying up other men of hope, Mill was not alarmed. Considering the "discredit into which old institutions and old doctrines have fallen," he was persuaded that this discredit was "perfectly deserved." * The new

---

* J. S. Mill, "The Spirit of the Age, I," *Examiner* (January 9, 1831), in *Collected Works,* ed. J. M. Robson et al., 33 vols. (1963–91), XXII, 230, 231. This perception became a commonplace. In 1847, the well-known American phrenologist O. S. Fowler prefaced his book on self-culture with the excited observation that "improvement is the practical watch-word of the age. Since the Revolution"—he meant, of course, the French Revolution—"men have probably made more numerous and valuable inventions and discoveries in machinery, agriculture, and the means of human comfort and luxury, than ever before since the Creation." He professed himself uneasy that they had not made similar progress in their moral and intellectual faculties—in other words, that not

could come into its own only after the old had died, but the old was surely dying. Mill's testimony is particularly poignant since he had experienced the beneficent touch of the modern in his own life: he would never cease being grateful to the romantic poetry that had saved him from the ravages of a relentless and debilitating depression.

Mill's verdict bespeaks a certain reveling in change, and that in itself was a modern way of thinking. The nineteenth century seemed to be ratifying the way of Goethe's Faust with the opening phrase of the Gospel of John. Usually translated to read, "In the beginning was the Word," it was turned by Faust into a tribute to activism: "In the beginning was the Deed." Throughout most of history the term "innovation" had been a term of reproach; the demonstration that a religious belief, a cultural habit, a literary canon could show venerable credentials was a compelling plea in its favor.* But among Victorians, respect for long-lived ways was under assault. Traditionalists continued to rest their claims to authority on the remote origins of their dogmas, and made the presumed superiority of the past into an ideology. But they suffered defeat after defeat at the hands of scientific reasoning, more interested in tangible results than in the patina of antiquity, and of painters and composers driven to experiment with untried departures. There had always been buccaneers breaking the patterns of dull routine, but in providing a battery of realistic hopes, the nineteenth century lent the double ideal of resourcefulness and autonomy new prestige and, with that, released a flood of energies.

Historians, politicians, editorial writers, and cultural prophets made change their business. Inevitably their responses varied. Carlyle was tormented by living in a time of upheavals, Tocqueville analyzed it, Marx saluted it. In the name of Restoration, Metternich attempted to undo the rush of history after the defeat of Napoleon, while a decade later the Saint-Simonian champions of an industrial society labored to hurry its pace. In the arts, too, long-accepted standards were in danger as unprecedented openings were freely canvassed; Richard Wagner, with his Music of the Future, was only one among the mutineers. And, as this book will show, lovers of music, literature, and painting beset by uncertainties and open to innovation mirrored the preoccupations of their culture.

Defying the surviving nostalgia for more perfect—and largely imaginary—

---

enough of them shared his faith in phrenology. But as to the essential fact of vast changes he had no doubt. *Self-Culture, and Perfection of Character Including the Management of Youth* (1847), iii.

* That is why for many centuries innovators disguised their radical inventions as minor readjustments: the emperor Augustus masked the imperial regime he was inaugurating as a mere modification of the institutions of the old Republic; the first printers used typefaces that made their books appear to be handwritten, and such proceedings have been typical through the ages, right into the nineteenth century.

times, Victorians found the temptations of the new more and more appealing. The volcanic eruption of energy generated by the passion for progress mobilized the efforts necessary to prevail over tenacious human defenses against change, to venture the untried in preference to staying with the familiar. Spirits dismayed by the instability of the age were fighting a losing battle, but they remained highly audible. The great historian and cultural conservative Jacob Burckhardt spoke for them all. "Everybody wants to be *new*," he wrote in 1843 with palpable disapproval, "but nothing else."[7]

Contradicting their reputation for aversion to risk taking, in short, nineteenth-century bourgeois were in the vanguard of transforming the worlds of work and leisure in private and public life alike. The Victorian age was a time of entrepreneurs as much as of rentiers. Critics of the bourgeoisie who perceived the middle classes ridden by tightfisted bankers, merchants, and patrons of the arts could adduce some hard proof, especially before mid-century: the reluctance of French entrepreneurs to welcome strangers to their firm, the failure of Dutch capitalists to take advantage of improved technologies, the persisting appeal of accepted hierarchies in the arts. Often enough it was only after troubling hesitation that the temper of conservative bourgeois moved toward a degree of daring.

It would be irrational to slight the dividends scattered by the spirit of initiative and experimentation. Marx's thesis that the point of philosophizing is to change the world and not merely to interpret it has been much quoted, but it was telling nineteenth-century readers nothing they did not already know. While grandiose, rigid philosophical systems survived the scorn of the Enlightenment and at least in Germany prospered anew, while legal theorists held fast to ritualistic deductive jurisprudence, the empiricist impulse tightened its grip over Western culture. One of its most characteristic agents was Auguste Comte's positivism; a French version of practical philosophizing exported to Britain and elsewhere in the 1840s, it professed to ground its propositions in experience rather than in metaphysics and welcomed moves toward a science of society. Until Comte turned his philosophy into an absurd quasi-religion, a retreat from reason that alienated his most intelligent followers, he saw the road to true knowledge signposted with exacting investigations of, and respect for, realities.

Realities! "They kiss the dust before a fact." Ralph Waldo Emerson was speaking of Englishmen, with their "supreme eye to facts" and a "logic that brings salt to soup, hammer to nail, oar to boat; the logic of cooks, carpenters, and chemists, following the sequence of nature, and one on which words make no impression." Yet this temper was not confined to the English, notorious though they were for their antimetaphysical disposition. It reverberated in

Oliver Wendell Holmes, Jr.'s memorable declaration of 1881, in *The Common Law*, "The life of the law has not been logic: it has been experience." In their programmatic statements, scientists of the mind and of society took care to present a severely professional posture, eager as they were to legitimate themselves as engaged in a credible discipline by commending close observation and quantitative precision in place of the disembodied generalizations that had served their predecessors so ill. They scorned what the English psychologist Alexander Bain called the *"rusted lock of metaphysics."* There was much work to be done before empiricism could rest on its laurels, but what philosophers were calling "a thirst for facts" was in the ascendant.[8]

All change is traumatic, even change for the better. The very gratification of wishes generates dislocations; as Freud once pointed out, humans resist giving up a pleasure they have once enjoyed and dislike waiting for the dividends that later, greater pleasures might bring. Hence all nineteenth-century progress was pursued by anxiety at times repressed and only reluctantly recognized—some of it, of course, like worries over the social cost of urbanization, perfectly justified. And that anxiety invaded matters of taste, as self-appointed experts sent contradictory signals. The tension between the modern lust for, and the fear of, originality gave the Victorian middle-class mind good grounds for uneasiness.

Even weddings, presumably a happy event, could extort a heavy emotional toll. Victorian middle-class brides wept as they were compelled to desert the parental home that had so affectionately enveloped them.* Nor were men immune; they could be more nervous than their sheltered brides. The evidence is spotty, but it appears that while impotence in early marriage was probably less of a hazard to wedded bliss than frigidity, it *was* a hazard. Besides, however fond a groom might be of his future wife, marriage called on him to forfeit his irregular hours and the dissipations he had savored as a bachelor, to say nothing of the duty to perform creditably in bed.† Untested satisfactions are tri-

---

* To give but one instance: in early August 1835, on her wedding day, Fanny Anne Burney, a young Englishwoman, recorded in her journal how *"very, very painful"* she was finding it to part from her family. She was suffering with innumerable respectable bourgeois women. August 8, 1835, in *A Great-Niece's Journals, Being Extracts from the Journals of Fanny Anne Burney* (Mrs. Wood), ed. Margaret S. Rolt (1926), 61.

† The anecdotes that portray Victorian males deserting the manliness their demanding culture held out to them as an ideal, and yielding to anxiety, have an aura of plausibility. On his wedding day, the painter John Millais, very much in love with his bride, Effie Gray, who had escaped a pathetic, unconsummated six-year marriage with John Ruskin, was agitated almost beyond bearing. After the ceremony, as the couple took a train to their honeymoon, he broke down and, his bride reported, "cried dreadfully," so that she had to comfort him and bathe his face with eau de cologne. Mary Lutyens, *Millais and the Ruskins* (1967), 262–63.

umphs over carefully cultivated resistances, and in the nineteenth century there seem to have been many such Pyrrhic victories.

This diagnosis does not draw on hindsight; contemporary observers frequently dilated on the mental costs of their highly mobile culture. For physicians and preachers, clandestine erotic activities like masturbation ranked high among the pathologies of sexual maturation they thought only too distinctive of their civilization. To disentangle confusions about such maladies—or, rather, to redirect the anxieties that had qualified them as maladies in the first place—was Freud's contribution to the ongoing debate. But a solid majority among students of mental malfunctioning, including writers of fiction, pointed the finger directly at their industrializing, urbanizing times and blamed what they called "attacks of nerves" on the adjustments that the nineteenth century had been forcing on its populations.

Thus the Goncourt brothers described their century as one of "activity, febrility, prodigious production"—in a word, they blamed the age of energy itself for making people feverish and tremulous. Others dwelt more concretely on the overwork imposed by machine civilization or "the hustle and bustle" of modern urban life. In 1879 (to give but one instance from a vast literature) the essayist Frederic Harrison, a leading English positivist, agonized over "that rattle and restlessness of life which belongs to the industrial maelstrom wherein we ever revolve."[9] In defense against this anxiety-provoking climate which threatened chaos, Victorians, entrepreneurs prominent among them, devised their obsessive routines: a nail-biting devotion to numbers, a surrender to timetables, a fussy punctuality.* This is the blight that Max Weber memorably named the iron cage in which the spirit of capitalism imprisoned its joyless beneficiaries. As usual, the Victorian age produced opposite responses to a single cause: restlessness as much as rigidity.

Understandably, specialists in mental ailments took the lead in attempts at psychosocial analysis. Until the end of the century, the reigning psychology was heavily physiological and lent itself to establishing links between nervousness and contemporary conditions; a person was doomed to suffer from nerves not only through "bad heredity" but also through physical jolts like an injury sustained in a railroad accident. The American physician George M. Beard, who

---

* Here is one instance: Charles Kingsley, the muscular Christian, writing to his wife in 1843 about domestic arrangements: "We must have a regular rule of life, not so as to become a law, but a custom. . . . Family prayers before breakfast; 8:30 to 10, household matters; 10 to 1, studying divinity, or settle *parish* accounts and business . . . between 1 and 5, go out in all weathers, to visit sick and poor and to teach in the school; in the evening we will draw, and feed the intellect and the fancy. . . ." Charles Kingsley, *His Letters and Memories of His Life,* edited by his wife, 2 vols. (1877; 16th abridged ed., 1888), I, 78.

coined the term "neurasthenia," secured an international reputation by turning such vague assessments into a law governing his time: "Modern nervousness is the cry of the system struggling with its environment."[10] Long before the end of Victoria's reign, this plausible caricature of the hardworking middle classes caught like so many sorcerer's apprentices in the snares of their own ingenuity had become a common lament. The age seemed to be generating too many stimuli to be safely and sanely absorbed. And the arts, with long-accepted styles under sustained attack, were no exception.

Creative spirits were not exempt from the nervousness of their time, in fact displayed some poignant patients. Thinking of himself and his fellow painters, van Gogh told his sister-in-law Jo half a year before his suicide in 1890, "We are all of us more or less neurotic."[11] This was far too sweeping a verdict, yet there is evidence that van Gogh's contemporaries thought it probable that painters or poets, given their exposed position in a time of change, were exceptionally vulnerable to mental breakdowns. Yet even good bourgeois, whose involvement in avant-garde culture was remote and intermittent, saw themselves as principal victims of vertiginous change, certainly more sensitive somehow than those placed above and those below them on the social scale. Editorials bemoaning moral decay, warnings by physicians or divines against the scourge of "self-pollution," politicians showing anxiety over foreign competition or falling national birthrates, a widespread anxiety over anxiety, all beyond rational calculations, lent a noticeable undertone of uneasiness to nineteenth-century bourgeois culture.

The blight of neurasthenia appeared to be exacerbated by the waning of traditional authority. We can see now that whatever specters the timid painted on the wall, late-Victorian middle-class culture was nowhere near anarchy. Millions still attended religious services. Habits of deference were fading slowly. The patriarchal legal rights of husbands over their wives and fathers over their children, though no longer unchallenged, were still largely in place. So were the old bourgeois preachments in behalf of hard work and honest dealings. Yet time-honored powers of state, church, morals—and the arts—seemed to be under siege or at least open to question.

The strains bedeviling the middle classes could be borne more easily when there was some realistic expectation of social betterment, if not always from class to class, at least from one level in the pyramid to the next. Interestingly enough, not everyone hailed evidence of social mobility as an unmixed blessing. In 1905, Arthur Graf von Posadowsky-Wehner, Germany's undersecretary of the interior, told members of the Reichstag that no country was so strongly inclined to foster upward mobility as their own. But, though it underwrote

Germany's intellectual and economic prosperity, he warned, "nervous haste" had entered political life and threatened great dangers. Under certain circumstances, Germany's "haste and nervousness" might even lead to self-destruction.[12] This curious diagnosis was more than aristocratic disdain for social climbers; fear of mobility was part of the litany of anxiety so familiar to the Victorians. Naturally the upwardly mobile were bound to take a less alarmist view, at least consciously.

After all, appearances could become facts, cherished facts. Sales clerks working in French or German department stores, usually from working-class backgrounds, were co-opted into the lower reaches of the bourgeoisie as their superiors instructed them how to dress and deal with customers. What the managers wanted was not a few polite stock phrases but a cast of mind, a courtesy and self-restraint that the middle classes had trained themselves to make into second nature. Not to have to change clothes at work, except perhaps to add a green eyeshade or sleeve protectors, reinforced the sense of newfound dignity. That, too, is why petty bourgeois took so much touching pride in their more or less dreary houses; their programmatic domesticity only underscored their distance from the masses. "After my work in the City," that archetypal clerk Mr. Charles Pooter, the English "Nobody" invented by George and Weedon Grossmith, noted in his diary, "I like to be at home. What's the good of a home, if you are never in it? 'Home, Sweet Home,' that's my motto."[13] Nothing could offer more vivid a contrast to the working classes, who notoriously lived in the pub, the beer hall, the café.

That is why those among them who shared the political ideology of their employers were almost bound to see the newly organized working-class parties, addicted to revolutionary rhetoric, as the enemy. In 1909, the English Liberal politician C. F. G. Masterman put it tersely: "The rich despise the Working People; the Middle Classes fear them," and he had the petty bourgeoisie in mind.* He could have said the same thing a quarter of a century earlier, and about many countries.

---

* Masterman, *The Condition of England* (1909; ed. J. T. Boulton, 1960), 58 [ch. 3]. This fear, though overdone and another symptom of "neurasthenia," had its realistic side. The centuries-old habit of paternalism was in decline as working-class parties equipped with political programs and campaign tactics demanded no favors but, rather, a drastic reorganization of economic life and redistribution of political power. The widely exposed exploitation of the working population that had marred early-nineteenth-century capitalism was being slowly brought under control by legislation after decades-long campaigns for reform, fiercely resisted and as fiercely supported by bourgeois. More independent-minded lower-middle-class conservatives, like self-respecting working poor, no longer found deference acceptable. Nor could they accept what William Morris called "the swinish luxury of the rich." Fiona MacCarthy, *William Morris: A Life for Our Time* (1995), 210.

Alarmist rhetoric apart, for a young man—and, very gradually, a young woman—escaping from the working-class world by securing a job in an office or a department store was a moment of real liberation. Heady fantasies about clothing and entertainment became realistic wishes. And no doubt, despite the accompanying anxieties many in the new middle class found rewards in social ascent: a relatively stable existence complete with an orderly marriage and, for the devout, regular church attendance, a cozy family dwelling, a chance for advancement after drawn-out faithful service to one firm.

Yet, even if personal experience showed them that the myth of mobility had a certain substance, most in the middling orders discovered that entertaining the vision of climbing very high on the ladder was chasing a mirage. Even in the United States, idealized at home and abroad as the almost literally Golden Land—the Germans called it "the land of unlimited possibilities"—social mobility all too often meant trading a life of hardship in one locality for another farther west. But not all the stories about the climb from rags to riches, the mainstay of a proliferating success literature, were pure invention. Victorian bourgeois had enough tales both spectacular and true to encourage them.

Still, the success literature of the age, which spawned extravagant daydreams, was more self-deluding fiction than tough-minded reportage. Its prolific authors stressed the cheerful side at the expense of gloomier examples in a very complicated story. A lapsed American cleric, Horatio Alger, perpetrated more than a hundred vastly popular novels, all of them essentially alike, celebrating, as one of his series has it, "Pluck and Luck," with luck a principal key to success. And that jaunty term "self-made man" eloquently attests to irrepressible Victorian optimism. It was, as one might expect, an American coinage, characterizing someone who had come from nowhere to conquer his world without the push of inherited wealth, advanced education, or distinguished forebears, owing everything to his energy, competitiveness, and sheer talent. By the early 1860s, as the bracing fable of worldly affluence wrested from adverse circumstances became an established motif in capitalist countries, the term had been adopted as a title of self-improvement books.[14] In the United States, where it enjoyed more justifiable support than elsewhere, it was embroidered or invented by political candidates fond of regaling their listeners with tales of a humble birth in a log cabin.

Even though the myth of America the paradise of opportunity enshrined more than a token of reality, many immigrants were forced to shed their illusions after living and laboring in their new home for some years. Most of the two and a half million East European Jews who settled in the United States

between 1880 to 1914 to escape pogroms, the dying shtetl, and long-term con-
scription into the czarist army remained on a low level of subsistence or rose,
when they rose at all, to a pinched, petty bourgeois existence. They lived, as it
were, through their children, who made careers as writers, editors, physicians,
lawyers, and professors, as big entrepreneurs and, sometimes, as big gangsters.[15]
And rather like these immigrants, great bankers, industrialists, and other movers
and shakers found that the doors they wanted to force would open only to
their sons or grandsons, far more polished, far better educated, and socially far
more acceptable. With rare exceptions, the odor of money faded only with the
passage of generations.

In Europe, as in America, bridging the gap between childhood travail in
obscure neglect and ostentatious plenty became familiar enough to find its way
into fiction. The repellent, aptly named Bounderby in Dickens's *Hard Times,*
"banker, merchant, manufacturer," the most powerful figure in Coketown,
never tires of telling everyone that he had been born in a ditch, and a wet ditch
at that. But he is exposed and shamed as the son of lower-class but honest parents, who has pensioned off his mother on condition that she keep away from
him.[16] Significantly, "self-made man" rapidly made its way to the Continent as
a welcome loan word.

But there were gulfs that no measure of disciplined self-education or effron-
tery could cross. The contrast between someone who could rightfully call himself a gentleman and someone who could not was virtually beyond erasing; the
preoccupation with suitable marriage partners, to which the fiction of the age
amply attests, often drew fine distinctions, by no means all financial. Yet, it is
necessary to remember that not all of the Horatio Alger literature was a riot of
the imagination. There were newcomers to ride the crest of industrialization.
Thousands had heard, and not only in France, of the brothers Eugène and
Adolphe Schneider, whose father had been a provincial notary but who within a single generation made themselves magnates in steel production and coal
mining and achieved social exclusiveness no less than political influence.

Intellectual and artistic gifts built bridges. Adolphe Thiers, lawyer, journalist,
editor, popular historian, cabinet official under the July Monarchy, and prime
minister early in the Third Republic, was born into destitution—his father was
a ne'er-do-well of many trades. Karl May, who came from a poverty-stricken
weaver's family in a miserable German village in Saxony and who as a young
man spent several years in prison as a thief and an impostor, made himself
around the turn of the century, with his facile pen and unsurpassed gift for
brazen lying, into Germany's favorite and richest storyteller. The Danish inven-
tor of modern fairy tales, Hans Christian Andersen, whose origins were even
more unpromising than Karl May's, became the pet of great nobles and royal-

ty, literally a household word across Europe, all with his luxuriant imagination.
Still more to the point, Andrew Carnegie, the greatest tycoon of them all,
immigrated as a little boy to the United States from Scotland with his impov-
erished working-class family. Napoleon's overworked slogan of careers open to
talent beckoned spirited and ambitious young men through the century. But
the figures leave little doubt: to succeed in industry, business, or politics it
helped to have well connected parents and a good education.

Exemplary erudition and a position of distinction in the sciences, the arts,
or the church could provide access to a select society at which most bourgeois
could not realistically aim. Two hierarchies competed with each other. One in
which wealth and inherited or acquired status were subtly intertwined, and
another that let a bourgeois climb the steep, slippery hill toward fame and fortune through his abilities alone. The Germans, interestingly enough, distinguished between the property-owning bourgeoisie—*Besitzbürgertum*—and the
cultivated bourgeoisie—*Bildungsbürgertum*—groups that overlapped but were
far from identical. In the end, the two hierarchies could coalesce as prestige
brought coveted dividends. Eminent scholars and scientists were presented
with distinguished medals, honorific titles, and lavish pensions. France treated
its great healer Louis Pasteur, and Germany its own Pasteur, Robert Koch, as
national treasures. And the German practice of ennobling not just bankers and
makers of cannons but also rare heroes of the pen and brush further violated
tradition: the historian Leopold Ranke became Leopold *von* Ranke in 1865;
the painter Adolph Menzel, Adolph *von* Menzel in 1898.

The Victorian bourgeois world, then, contained pockets of opportunities for
advancement that resembled, if they never quite equaled, contemporary wish
dreams. In England, Unitarian ministers, many of them drawn from straitened
circumstances, served congregations enjoying a station higher than their own,
and were assimilated, as it were, to their rank. And they were not alone. To
complicate matters further, standards for social status derivable from size of
income or property enjoyed no undisputed authority. Of course, money mattered, and mattered mightily, but not money alone. When circumstances were
propitious and connections smoothly cultivated, bourgeois magnates might
buy, or marry—which could be much the same thing—entrée to exclusive
clubs, even to nobility. But they had to reckon with the resistance of those
already in place, eager to kick away the ladder on which their own ancestors
had once climbed. Snobs never forgot, or let anyone else forget, the fatal distinction between old and new social status.

Even as the bourgeoisie recruited new numbers in the Victorian decades, it
remained in a minority in the cities, largely swamped by the poor, whether

subdued or restless. (Urban historians have shown that the Victorian bourgeoisie amounted to about 10 or 12 percent of the total population.) And this
exposed position only strengthened its ties through shared disdain and anxieties. Granted, this self-differentiation from other classes, this secure possession
of middle-class ways of thinking and feeling, was sufficiently imprecise. It had
something to do with respectability, though not that alone, since it was the
standard that upper segments of the working classes also hoped to achieve.
Other ideals were more distinctly bourgeois: probity in commercial dealings,
fidelity to one's spouse, self-control in expenditure, the need for privacy, the
gospel of work, the love of beauty. Good taste was a badge craved by those who
could, and often by those who could not, afford it.

At the core of this middle-class self-idealization lay the family. To hear its
apologists describe it, with minor local variations the Victorian family was the
privileged agency for the transmission of values, the setting of boundaries, the
source of homely pleasures. It served the husband as a retreat from the cruel
worlds of business, politics, or professional life. It assigned to the wife the cir-
cumscribed but authoritative domestic sphere. It made responsible human
beings out of the children, those little savages. And—though this, obeying the
bourgeois passion for privacy, was rarely even hinted at—it reserved a secret
place for legitimate love, including sexual enjoyment for husband and wife·
alike. Sentimental genre paintings illustrated these functions of family life (all
but the sexual one) as though they were flawless, exemplary: no strains, no tensions anywhere as they show bourgeois around the piano, listening to the father
reading aloud, leaping with joy (family dog included) as he comes home, or
watching as mother, all tender maternity, nurses her new baby.

As we shall see, in Victorian times and ever since, antibourgeois polemicists
have poured ridicule on this self-portrait as saccharine and mendacious, and
insisted that, far from embodying their family ideals, bourgeois regularly violated them all. No doubt the Victorian bourgeois family had much to answer
for. The high value placed on the father's legal supremacy could work as an
alibi for paternal tyranny; the respect paid the mother might mask the exploitation of her vulnerability and a supercilious denial of her intellectual competence; the discipline thought proper for children was in the wrong hands a
rationalization of sadistic impulses and a way of handing down parental neuroses to new generations. The haven could become a prison house.

The historian of the Victorian bourgeoisie is bound to note that the makers of these incompatible portraits were both right—in part. In general, taking
into account individual, regional, national, and confessional variations, the average middle-class family was not so vicious as its detractors contended, not so

pure as its admirers liked to think. Whatever the truths about this diverse phenomenon, the family was an emblem of what bourgeois wanted to be, or
thought they were: a model that united middle-class men and women in the
conviction that this blessed institution was really unique to them, an essential
ingredient in their self-portrait.

In the end, the definition of the Victorian bourgeoisie must depend as much
on self-perceptions, however wishful, as on solid economic facts. It was their
vision of the regulated will, of energy channeled, that helped to set the bourgeoisie apart from other classes. Though expending unexampled energies on
translating their wishes into actuality, Victorians recognized that power can be
abused, knowledge turned to evil purposes, and that impassioned improvers
(utopian zealots who, far from disappearing, flourished in the century of fact)
could be more fanatical, more alienated from realities than traditionalists hostile to the most modest adjustment in laws and practices.

In short, the will struck Victorian bourgeois as an immensely powerful but
potentially destructive force. In the 1860s, the eminent English alienist Dr.
Henry Maudsley lauded it as "the highest force in nature, the last consummate
blossom of all her marvellous efforts," which "represents the exquisitely and
subtly adapted reaction of man to the best insight into the relations in which
he moves." Yet he took care to add that he meant not the will let loose but the
"well-fashioned will."[17] It seemed beyond dispute that without firm guidance,
the passions (which is another word for energy) will act imperiously, insatiably,
and, avid only for their gratification, selfishly in the extreme.

Thus the task of mastering the will's raw, blind urges ranked high on the
Victorians' pedagogic agenda. They thought self-restraint essential to the formation of good character, that harmonious assemblage of traits, endlessly
debated as the most valuable but most elusive aim of education. At home or at
school, in churches or in the newspapers, adults spent untold hours on the
question. Concrete manifestations of the will in the marketplace were controversial. Were John D. Rockefeller's stratagems for amassing a vast fortune a welcome expenditure of energy or a perversion of it? Were strikes a legitimate
weapon for achieving a living wage or a disruptive combination of greedy
workingmen? Were the clashing imperialist ventures of the great powers an
admirable grasp of the national destiny or a barbaric exploitation of Africans
and Asians? No consensus could be expected; the answers depended more on
political positions than on empirical information. But on the larger issue, the
need to tame the will, the Victorians could agree. They thought that it could
go wrong in two ways: by excess or by deficiency. Idleness or lassitude were
hazards to personal happiness and social concord little less than lawlessness or

sexual excess. In either incarnation, the untamed will took center stage in the bourgeois theater of anxiety.*

The cure, nearly all bourgeois might agree, could not be found in the aristocracy; it seemed too idle, too arrogant, too corrupt. And the lower orders? In August 1883, Freud wrote to his fiancée, Martha Bernays, responding to her description of the noisy, exuberant behavior of working men and women at a fair: "One could show that 'the people' are quite unlike us in the way they judge, believe, hope, and work. There is a psychology of the common man that is rather different from ours." The "rabble" freely give way to their impulses while good bourgeois train themselves to resist the pressures of the drives. And this "gives us the quality of refinement." Bourgeois feel things more deeply than the poor, who are too helpless, too exposed to misery, to practice renunciation. Why don't we get drunk? Because the discomfort and shame of a hangover give us more pain than drinking gives us pleasure. Why don't we fall in love with someone new every month? Because every separation tears away a piece of our heart. "And so we make more of an effort to keep suffering away from us than to procure pleasure for ourselves."[18] In the wisdom and the bias of these musings, much of what it meant to be a bourgeois in the Victorian age stands revealed, much of its luster and its travail.

Clearly, then, the most efficient, if not the most expeditious, way of defining the bourgeoisie in all its varieties is to watch it in action. But before we resort to instances, we need one more definition, that of "Victorian." *The Oxford English Dictionary* informs us that the adjective first turned up in 1839, two years after Queen Victoria's accession to the throne, and promptly proliferated to grace coins, medals, carriages, plums, pigeons, and water lilies. These early tributes were domestic or diplomatic courtesies, but by the early 1870s "Victorian" had developed into the shorthand name for an age presided over by the British monarch like a benign and mournful household icon, esteemed for her unblemished reputation, her exemplary domestic felicity shattered by Prince Albert's premature demise, and her pitiable, unceasing grief. But then, years before her own death in 1901, the accolade was radically metamorphosed into an insult; those savaging the age reduced "Victorian" to a synonym for unequaled hypocrisy, prudery, and bad taste.

Then and later, Victorianism mobilized supporters among historians who, controlled by professional respect for facts, offered more nuanced assessments. Collectors of antiques charmed by nineteenth-century quaintness, too, had

---

* In its own uncompromising way, Schopenhauer's elevation of the voracious will as the ubiquitous driving force, though it took decades to find followers and never dominated the nineteenth-century sensibility, featured precisely what the Victorians feared.

kind words for the age. And, incensed by their slanderers, loyal bourgeois coun-
terattacked, denouncing the denouncers as ignoramuses and sensationalists. But
none of these appreciative heirs of Victorianism have done much to restore its
reputation, as critics kidnapped precisely the characteristics in which the nineteenth-century middle classes had taken pride. What bourgeois valued as their
good sense was taken for a stolid lack of imagination; their practicality, for vulgar self-satisfaction; their ready tears, for sentimentality rather than authentic
feelings; their dutiful regular life, for a slavery to schedules—rationalism gone
mad. In the battle for public opinion, the most bellicose anti-Victorians, amply
supplied with ever-repeated anecdotes about lustful husbands and frigid wives,
canting churchgoers and unscrupulous capitalists, carried the day. To many
minds the Victorian decades came to stand, and still stand, as a time of greed,
lies, and kitsch.

In the narrow, cold mentality of Victorian bourgeois, we have been told, not
even their increasingly vocal commitment to romantic love was heartfelt; they
tamed romantic transgressions of propriety out of recognition into the deadly
virtues of earnestness and conformism. Preachers of virtue in public, bourgeois
were apparently secret devotees of vice. In 1848, Marx and Engels accused
them of making marriage a sham, busy seducing one another's wives. In the
Communist Manifesto, the two were, to be sure, writing as partisans with a radical political agenda, but their disdain would echo through the century. Some
thirty years after, in *Pot-Bouille,* Zola lent color to these sensational charges
with tales of adultery among worthy *citoyens;* in that novel, the preferred stage
for gross sexual escapades was a Parisian apartment house pervaded by "the
deadly quiet of a bourgeois drawing room, carefully closed in, letting in not a
whisper from the outside."[19] Zola conjured up an unappetizing sight: scheming
bourgeois surrounded by tasteless things in a self-congratulatory haze that
enabled them to plead ignorance of the havoc they wrought at home and in
the workplace.

Just which version of "Victorianism," the compliment, the condemnation,
or some mixture of the two, best epitomizes the age, especially in the domain
of taste, will emerge in the chapters that follow. Here we may briefly note the
intricacies of the epithet. Its turnabout of signification is only one of them; to
blur matters further, "Victorianism" did not coincide with the queen's reign.
There had been Victorians, we might say, decades before Victoria, late-eigh-
teenth- and early-nineteenth-century moralists as severe, celebrants of home
life as unctuous, as any the mid-century would muster. And a quarter century
before the end of her reign, by the 1880s, the anti-Victorian campaign was well
launched; by then delicacy, prissiness, and overstuffed interiors were in fact far
less prevalent and far more contested than they had been three or more decades

earlier. Even faultless Victorians were growing uneasy with their own evasiveness: in the mid-1880s, after reading the biography of George Eliot that her
husband, J. W. Cross, had just published, Gladstone protested, "It is not a Life at
all. It is a Reticence, in three volumes."[20] Roughly from the 1840s to the 1870s,
then, the Victorianism of the hostile caricature seemed most conspicuous, but
its roots went back half a century and more.

The quintessential manifestation of Victorianism came in 1851, with the
Great Exhibition in London, its displays extravagant and its appeal overwhelming. The sheer accumulation of physical objects at the Crystal Palace
trumpeted the religion of progress, as only a small tribe of censorious aesthetes
issued dissenting opinions. Crowded with devices promising ever-greater
power over nature, furnishings boasting intricate ornamentation, works of art
celebrating heroic conduct and moral purity, the exhibition seemed ideally
suited to demonstrate just how utility can be ennobled by taste. It was at once
a sign, a promise, and an engine of improvements in which all might share—
utterly Victorian in its resolute conviction that material inventiveness can assist
spirituality.

One perceptive observer was Charlotte Brontë. Spending a month in London, she went to the Crystal Palace five times, dragged along by well-meaning
friends. She was impressed intellectually more than stirred emotionally, but she
knew that she was witnessing a remarkable event. "It is a wonderful place—
vast, strange, new, and impossible to describe," she wrote her father in early
June. "Its grandeur does not consist in *one* thing, but in the unique assemblage
of *all* things. Whatever human industry has created you find there." To her dazzled view "magic only could have gathered this mass of wealth from all the
ends of the earth—as if none but supernatural hands could have arranged it
thus, with such a blaze and contrast of colours and marvellous power of
effect."[21] And the similarities among national products were as striking as the
contrasts: English and Belgian exhibitors showed almost identical engines;
American sculptured nudes resembled little less naked German Amazons.

The confluence of taste at the exhibition that Charlotte Brontë observed
suggests that we may profitably expand "Victorian" from its original British
context to the civilized Western world. Cultural historians have already natu-
ralized it in the United States: they speak of Victorian America without fear of
being misunderstood. Other countries, too, fit the pattern without procrustean
efforts. Not that distinct cultures were being homogenized; on the contrary, in
an age of nationalism, patriots took pride precisely in what separated their
beloved country from the others. But, just as trade, far-flung for centuries, was
moving toward an interdependent world economy, ideas, inventions, and works
of art or music crossed frontiers with little impediment.

One experience that Victorian bourgeois had in common, if with differing nuances, was of course the memory of the French Revolution, which shaped European, and to some extent American, political consciousness for half a century. The astonishing spread of the railroad net in England stimulated ventures on the Continent and in the United States; late in the century, German social legislation heartened foreign observers to push for analogous reforms at home. And, as we shall see, culture high and low, too, was impressively cosmopolitan. English and French romantic poets and philosophers borrowed from their German fellows; operas traveled with ease across Europe; in an age of international exhibitions, painters and sculptors profited from the example of foreign artists; French Naturalist literature left its impress on novelists and playwrights from Scandinavia to Italy. At least for the affluent, the culture of consumption reached from London to Milan, not to forget Paris and Chicago. Anxieties, too, did not respect national boundaries: the panic of divines, teachers, physicians, and parents over the evil of "self-pollution" was a transcontinental epidemic of collective hysteria, as cajoling or bullying anti-masturbation tracts were quickly reprinted and widely translated. Even revolutions, as the year 1848 attests, were for export.

One marked cross-national quality of Victorianism will receive intensive attention in the next chapter: its exposure to antagonistic propaganda, which, for all its local variations, essentially sang a single tune. After the 1870s and 1880s, drawing on a sizable, incendiary stock of abuse and adding new accusations, Zola in France, Shaw in Britain, Strindberg in Sweden, Ibsen in Norway and Germany, echoed by a small army of committed followers, aimed shafts at the comfortable classes, at those princes of cant, paragons of conventionality, sworn if devious antagonists of higher motives, vulgarians in the arts and letters—in a word, the bourgeoisie. Once modernist artists of all genres joined forces to intensify antibourgeois aggression, these denunciations became common property. Their popularity is beyond question, their merits remain to be examined.

BOURGEOIS EXPERIENCES, V

Bourgeoisophobes

Throughout virtually all of recorded history, the makers of high culture were fully integrated into their society. Painters and sculptors, composers and architects, storytellers, poets and playwrights were the willing servants of power, of state and church alike. They gave beautiful, often memorable expression to shared fundamental values and convictions. Even historic exiles like Dante or Machiavelli retained their loyalty to the larger community from which they had been expelled; even in times of irreparable conflict like the Reformation, when writers and artists lent their talents to the contending parties, they thought of the enemy, of the other, as the outsider. Then, toward the end of the eighteenth century and the beginning of the nineteenth, this tacit, durable cultural compact was radically subverted. Artists in all genres increasingly made society itself the target of their scorn.

They thought they could do no less. Did not the nineteenth-century bourgeoisie love money and hate art? Was it not so different from the old honorable, public-spirited patriciate as to be in effect a new class? The few bankers or merchants who displayed good taste or supported museums were too exceptional, or their motives too dubious, to discredit this sweeping characterization. Hence creative spirits felt duty-bound to detest the bourgeoisie and to adopt an aggressive stance that gave them pleasure as they mobilized to rescue the sacred cause of honest art, honest music, and honest literature. And so, as the Victorian century went its way, painters, composers, and the rest formed avant-gardes to fight lively and implacable pleasure wars in which they confronted the dominant, hopelessly conventional middle class with all the energy at their command.

This is the modernist myth that has continued to shape our perception of the Victorian middle classes' attitude toward the higher things. To call it a myth is not to denigrate it as a fantasy woven together from fragments of imaginary grievances. There was, as will emerge, a measure of truth in it. But it was none the less self-serving and partisan, greatly oversimplifying a tangled array of cultural interactions. Clarity about matters of taste was the last of the qualities about which the age had any right to boast. Hesitations, mixed motives and mixed feelings, unexpected alliances and tensions, attacks of hubris and anxiety reduce the portrait of Victorian society as permanently split between two adversaries to a caricature.

1. Gustavus Flaubertus

Denunciations of the middle classes were, of course, not new. For all the kind words thrown them across the centuries from the time of Aristotle on, they had long had articulate vilifiers. There had been, and continued to be, open season on middling people—traders, shopkeepers, moneylenders—centuries before there was a well-defined bourgeoisie. Jesus, who, Scriptures report, drove the money changers and pigeon sellers from the temple and pronounced himself doubtful about the chances of a rich man's entering heaven, reinforced a tradition that would prosper through the ages. But none were more strident than nineteenth-century antibourgeois, none more tendentious than Gustave Flaubert.

In late December 1852, Flaubert wrote his closest friend, the poet Louis Bouilhet, a charming note of thanks for some Latin verses. Borrowing the manner of Rabelais and Montaigne, two of his favorite writers, he imitated sixteenth-century spelling in a playful reply at once mocking and erudite. It was as though he were snatching a moment of relaxation from the agony of literary creation, the laborious progress of an ambitious first novel to be titled *Madame Bovary.* And consistent with the style he had adopted, he signed himself in Latin: "GUSTAVUS FLAUBERTUS, Bourgeoisophobus."[1]

The missives that Flaubert normally sent out from his hideaway, his mother's house at Croisset, near Rouen, to his friends, his beloved sister, Caroline, and his promiscuous mistress the minor poet Louise Colet, were didactic, scatological, dripping with disenchantment. But if his bearish humor in the letter to Bouilhet was uncharacteristic for the adult Flaubert, his hatred of the bourgeoisie was not. A visceral distaste for the safe middle runs like a leitmotiv through his writings published and unpublished. Though couched in an imaginative bouquet of vituperation, the lesson he meant to impart was always the same: one must not become like *them!* In 1855, with *Madame Bovary* almost completed, he seconded Bouilhet's cultural pessimism: "Yes! this is on the whole a rotten century! And we are in a shitty mess! What makes me indignant is the *bourgeoisisme* of our fellow writers! What merchants! What dull imbeciles!"² He found nothing more disheartening than middle-class decorousness; looking about, he was horror-stricken to observe how easy it was to slide down the greasy slope to bourgeoisdom, a fate he thought literally worse than death.

Flaubert developed this phobia early in life and never outgrew it. Even as a schoolboy, he had dashed off sarcastic outbursts against "stupid" people and "stupid" ideas. As a perceptive adolescent, he recognized that he was given to provocations and shocking poses, as he peppered his letters with sallies against royalty, the church, and the boring, repellent world in general. A youthful satanist, he cultivated lurid fantasies professing a taste for novels by that "honorable writer" the marquis de Sade, claimed to admire prostitutes, declared himself capable of crime, dreamt of deflowered virgins, and aimed to grow into a destroyer of good morals. But he reserved his utmost spleen for the bourgeoisie. As he told his sister, Caroline, in July 1842—he was twenty—the more he provoked bourgeois, the more content he felt. Decades later he wrote his admired *"chère bon Maître"* George Sand, "Axiom: Hatred of Bourgeois is the beginning of all virtue."³

There was much scurrility in between, and its ferocity never slackened. In early 1843, a reluctant law student in Paris, Flaubert described to his sister some acquaintances he disliked, their visits to restaurants and their theatergoing, as "provincial bourgeois coming to Paris to amuse themselves. What stupid grocers!"⁴ The epithet he used—*épiciers*—was a supreme sneer. At times Flaubert's antibourgeois nausea grew physical in its intensity. As late as 1872, encountering three or four bourgeois in his native Rouen, he was sickened by "the spectacle of their vulgarity, their frock coats, their hats, what they said and the sound of their voices." They all, he wrote, "made me want to vomit and to cry at the same time. Never since I have been in this world have I been choked by such disgust." He was mourning Théophile Gautier, sure that his friend had died of suffocation caused by his prolonged exposure to "modern stupidity." Three days later, still harping on Gautier, he told his friend the playwright Ernest Feydeau that he was getting ready to burst, he was about to vomit. "It will be copious and bitter."⁵

Flaubert's case against his middle-class contemporaries ran to many, mutually reinforcing counts. Bourgeois are commonplace, cowardly, colorless, censorious, sentimental, devious; their pleasures are abominable, their moments of happiness squalid, their political opinions foolish; they have no inkling of the inner life and are so obsessive in their habits that they fall ill when they go to bed at an unaccustomed hour. They are of course materialistic from head to toe, lacking all sense for the exotic, the adventurous, the extraordinary.

In 1867, Flaubert reported to George Sand from Rouen that he had come upon a camp of Gypsies—*Bohémiens*—whom he had noticed twice before, "always with new pleasure. It was wonderful to see how they aroused the *Hatred* of bourgeois, even though they were harmless as sheep. I had the crowd look askance at me by giving them a few sous.—And I heard some pretty Philistine comments." He found it easy to explain this hatred for a handful of innocent vagrants: it "has to do with something deep and complex. We find it among the whole *party of order*. It's the hatred felt for the Bedouin, the Heretic, the Philosopher, the recluse, the poet.—And there is fear in that hatred. This exasperates me, since I am always for the minorities." Later observers might call that hatred a typical bourgeois defensive maneuver, transforming fear into rage. As cheerleader for a mutinous avant-garde, Flaubert was "driven wild" by these middle-class traits. When in *Lui,* her transparent roman à clef, Louise Colet coarsely revenged herself on Flaubert for making her unhappy, the most wounding insult she could imagine was to call him a "well-read bourgeois."[6]

In the onslaughts Flaubert launched against fellow Rouennais, he portrayed them as though interchangeable, all of them privates in a vast army of lumpen bourgeois. In truth, as historians studying Flaubert's native city have shown, they were a far more differentiated lot. In the 1850s, the years of *Madame Bovary,* Rouen was bustling with some 100,000 inhabitants. As capital of its *département,* it was home to high government officials and ecclesiastical personages. The urban profile was dominated by a lofty cathedral partly dating back to the fourteenth century, signpost of a lasting, if by now endangered, religious tradition; modern bourgeois lived and worked or enjoyed an idle retirement in its shadow. It was this cathedral that Monet famously painted in different weathers, and that was William Morris's favorite exemplar of French Gothic; for its sake he visited "Rouen, glorious Rouen" twice.[7]

Certainly Emma Bovary admired the city. On one of her visits to Rouen for an assignation with her lover Léon, she was dazzled by its closely crowded brick houses, ships at anchor, foundries roaring and factory chimneys coughing up trails of brown smoke. A prominent center of trade and diversified manufacturing, its principal industry was cotton, in which Rouennais made, and at times lost, massive fortunes. There were other ways to get rich in the city: in the wine and cattle trade or the export and import business, or comfortably living as a rentier after decades of shrewd investments. Achille Cléophas Flaubert, Gustave's father, an eminent if scientifically conservative surgeon and director of a local hospital, had invested in real estate and proved sufficiently clever (or fortunate) to leave his son enough to embark on a career as a fulltime writer.[8]

As in all cities, in Rouen the bourgeoisie was distinctly in a minority. Only a quarter among local households could afford two servants—always a sensitive indicator of wealth and status—and most of these were classic *petit bourgeois*. Five percent boasted three and only 2 percent four or more in household help; the ladder of affluence, matching those in other Victorian cities, was steep and, with every rung, increasingly vertiginous. Less than roughly one in ten Rouennais could be counted as prosperous bourgeois.[9] Small shopkeepers were lucky if they took in some 2,000 francs a year; many had less and only a few of them more. Rentiers, a substantial population in Rouen, drew on the average some 7,000 to 8,000 francs annually; in tandem with high government functionaries and thriving members of the liberal professions, the caste of landed proprietors could count on about 30,000. The mercantile and industrial elite, men of great fortunes, including a handful of millionaires, clustered at the top.[10]

Although the broadly flowing tidal Seine made Rouen into a port providing daily contacts with the outside world, its culture lived mainly from local resources—classical lycées, professional schools, literary societies. Like most bourgeois, the better-off Rouennais usually kept their diversions domestic, with receptions, charades, evenings of poetry recitals. The well-educated, it seems, spent much of their leisure doing strenuous reading, sampling even advanced, risqué authors like Maupassant and Zola, to say nothing of their own celebrity, Flaubert. And in 1880, the year of Flaubert's death, they added an imposing new museum for paintings hitherto inadequately housed and poorly exhibited in the city hall. If connoisseurs derided some of its supposed "old masters" like its vaunted four "Raphaels" as mediocre copies, its large rooms crowded landscapes, nudes, portraits, history paintings together, with contemporary French schools strongly represented and some of its Italian and Dutch masters even authentic.[11]

With touching fidelity, leading citizens—bankers, lawyers, bureaucrats, naval officers—supported a brave literary periodical, the *Revue de Rouen*. While it repeatedly faded away, it was just as repeatedly revived as though its three hundred subscribers needed it to tell them what they really liked. Reading circles, domestic music making, exhibitions of new paintings, most of them from the region, added color to Rouen's cultural landscape. And it could proudly point to a handful of impassioned collectors, of watches and faience, of china and even pictures.

Probably the most interesting among them was the magnate François Depeaux, amateur yachtsman, munificent philanthropist, fervent local patriot anxious to enhance Rouen's name. For well over two decades he had poured substantial profits from trading in cotton and outfitting ships into an odd assortment of relatively inoffensive academic paintings and of Impressionists, an unconventional departure for his conventional city. Although an expensive divorce forced him to dispose of some valued pictures, he never stopped buying. In a touching address to his fellow citizens in 1909, he modestly disclaimed any right to speak as an art critic but eloquently celebrated his holdings as *"the modern music of painting."* And he expressed his gratitude to the artists: "Let us thank the Impressionists for having taught us to *see Nature better* and therefore to *love it better.*"[12]

The occasion for this little speech was Depeaux's donation of fifty-three treasured paintings, about a fifth of his collection, to the city. It was an event worth celebrating by the mayor, the city council, and the local newspapers: modernism finally had found a place in Rouen, however modest.[13] True, six years earlier, goaded by Rouennais of immovable academic tastes, the city had rejected Depeaux's very similar offer—how this would have amused Flaubert! But Depeaux's two overtures and their contrasting fates are of interest to the historian as a fine instance of the complexities besetting bourgeois tastemakers, complexities we shall often encounter throughout these chapters. This much is clear: Rouen's citizens were not all the money-ridden souls who would label the arts, as Flaubert's *Dictionary of Accepted Ideas* has them do, as "quite useless, since they can be replaced by machines, which manufacture the same things even more quickly."[14]

Flaubert's mock dictionary became an inexhaustible hunting ground for bourgeoisophobes; he drew it from his *sottisier,* a lovingly gathered bouquet of inane opinions intended to supply material for the second volume of his last, unfinished novel, *Bouvard and Pécuchet.* The *Dictionary* exposed middle-class lovers of culture as shamelessly unapologetic for yawning their way through a musical evening: "CONCERT. Well-bred pastime." Their didacticism was unrelieved, untouched by flights of the aesthetic imagination: "NOVELS. Corrupt the masses"; hence "only historical novels can be tolerated because they teach history." Flaubert's bourgeois were the kind of misbegotten creatures who could define "LITERATURE" as "pastime of the idle" or the "BOOK" as being "always too long, whatever it is about."[15] How could one expect a discerning palate from such barbarians?

Undeterred by mere facts, Flaubert imported his phobia into his fiction. *Madame Bovary* traces, from an impersonal distance laced with crushing irony, the sexual victimization and eventual suicide of the overeducated daughter of a well-to-do farmer. After recording the protagonist's wretched love affairs and dismal end, the book concludes with the triumph of the supreme bourgeois in the novel, the local pharmacist, Monsieur Homais. The smooth progressive slogans that this brazen careerist likes to spout give rationalism a bad name, but the state rewards him for being precisely what he is. "He had just received," the novel closes, "the Cross of the Legion of Honor."

Some twenty years later, Flaubert started on *Bouvard and Pécuchet,* which focuses on the misadventures, at once hilarious and pathetic, of two ordinary clerks. Having come into money, they devote their free time and ample funds to undergo an invariably disastrous education in agriculture, archaeology, religion, the sciences, the arts, rational housekeeping, and sexual seduction. Flaubert made the very profession of these two friends, copyist, a trade to which they return at the end, an obvious hit at the unproductive bourgeoisie. Bouvard and Pécuchet were the bourgeois who spouted the commonplaces Flaubert had collected in his *Dictionary.*

That dictionary concentrates Flaubert's loathing for the class that he thought was running, and ruining, his country. But all this mayhem leaves a question: it is all very funny, but is it reportage or slander? No reader of Flaubert's *Dictionary,* his letters, or his novels can overlook the intemperance of his language. A psychoanalyst would rightly point to all this unrelieved, emotion-ridden bluster as a sign of some inner maladjustment. Yet many interpreters have taken Flaubert's fiery barbs or sarcastic parodies as well-informed, trustworthy bulletins from a front he had scouted with care. That Flaubert was the son of a local celebrity and of the most conformist of doting mothers—he even nicknamed her "la bourgeoise"—lent his denunciations from the inside all the more authority.[16] Since they did capture certain facts of contemporary middle-class life, Flaubert's neurosis has been read as the private correlative of a cultural neurosis, that infectious and dangerous modern malady called bourgeoisdom. Freud would later analyze that middle-class affliction as springing from unwarranted embarrassment before the sexual drive, and Flaubert would no doubt have agreed. But, more interested in denunciation than in diagnosis, he preferred to call it names: mediocrity, mendacity, deadly virtuousness.

Yet our glimpses of the real Rouen suggest that Flaubert's judgments do not deserve all this credit. On occasion he undercut his argument with observations that make his emotions less revealing than at first appears. Bouvard and Pécuchet, those votaries of science and platitudes, acquire a certain stature as Flaubert has them learning from their failures and sucking wisdom from the venality and ingratitude of those they had meant to benefit. As they grow less gullible about human nature and even consider suicide, Flaubert hints that he has grown rather attached to them. Writing to his friend Turgenev, who had closely followed the making of the novel, he called Bouvard and Pécuchet "my two idiots." They were at least *his* idiots. Their quest had not been simply ludicrous: "A lamentable faculty developed in their minds, that of recognizing stupidity and no longer tolerating it."[17] And so, Bouvard and Pécuchet almost function as Flaubert's surrogates in his campaign against the idiocies of his time.

His uncontrolled hatred could dull Flaubert's social tact and provide moments of involuntary humor. In 1879, near the end of his life, accepting an invitation to the Charpentiers for dinner, he was unable to repress a gratuitous slur: "The absence of bourgeois reassures him on his prospects. For he has now reached a point of such exasperation that when he finds himself with persons of that species he is consistently tempted to strangle them, or rather to hurl them into the cesspool (if one may express oneself thus), an action whose consequences would be embarrassing to the publishing house of Charpentier, which is close to his heart, children and bow-wows included."[18] It apparently had not occurred to him that he was writing to *his* publisher, who was also publishing Zola, Huysmans, and other noncanonical writers, or that Georges Charpentier and his wife, Marguerite, were friends of Renoir and collectors of Monets. Nor that his hosts, complete with children and dogs, were bourgeois whose avant-garde taste invalidated his gross and rancorous mockery.

This way of using his favorite term of abuse with no regard for sociological rigor throws further doubts on Flaubert's reliability as a witness. His loathsome bourgeoisie was a state of mind rather than a recognizable social class, and "bourgeois" an all-purpose epithet. In the summer of 1861, shortly after completing his strange, sanguinary novel about Carthage, *Salammbô,* he professed to be looking forward to irritating the archaeologists and being unintelligible to the ladies. He hoped people would call him a pederast and a cannibal. *Salammbô,* he told Ernest Feydeau, "will annoy the bourgeois, that is to say, everybody."[19]

There is bravado in this pronouncement, but its vagueness robs it of all point. In fact, when Flaubert told George Sand that the hatred of bourgeois is the beginning of virtue, he defined the key word in a way quite useless for social analysis: "I include in the word 'bourgeois' the bourgeois in a smock as much as the bourgeois in a frock coat." As a self-designated cultural aristocrat, he derived his right to malign the bourgeoisie from his membership in a small civilized minority of which his correspondent was also a member: "We, and we alone, are the People, or, to put it better, the tradition of Humanity." He was unalterable in his imprecision. "I put *messieurs* the working people into the same bag as bourgeois," he told Sand in April 1871, as the upheavals of the Paris Commune were at their most intense. "One should chuck them all into the river together."[20]

He had been saying this sort of thing all along. As early as 1852, he had told Louise Colet that nowadays the bourgeois "is all humanity, the 'people' included." This irresponsible usage did not remain hidden from his contemporaries. In 1884, the novelist and shrewd essayist Paul Bourget observed that Flaubert had conducted a "war" against the " 'bourgeois,' " a word that "in his mouth—

that of an impenitent romantic—became a synonym for the worst villainies."[21]
Flaubert the hater of the bourgeoisie was not doing sociology; he was
indulging his pugnacity. Freud coined the suggestive phrase "the narcissism of
minor difference" to indicate why neighbors, whether individuals or nations,
view the Other with particular distaste to let them give free vent to their
aggressions. Surely Flaubert's differences with his fellow Rouennais were drastic enough, but he distorted them far beyond what the facts warranted.

Flaubert's obtuseness about the Charpentiers shows that he was not open to
corrections from experience; he had chosen the psychiatric term "phobia" for
better reasons than he knew. A phobia is a bleak stratagem designed to avoid
greater misery; the mental anguish phobics undergo is less cataclysmic than the
anxiety against which this defense insulates them. Their sufferings are their
armor. Flaubert was haunted by conflicts deeper than the disharmonies that
assail the most fortunate of mortals. His hermit-like devotion to literature
coexisted with fantasies, at times realities, of rough sexual experimentation; his
stern rejection of public opinion was paired with an extraordinary sensitivity
to it; his severe antiromanticism was, as Bourget had already seen, a way of
warding off a seductive romantic streak.

Thus Flaubert's disavowal of his own class looks like a response to the fear
that he had not really escaped it. He was, it seems, projecting onto his fellow
bourgeois qualities he detected in himself, making enough noise to drown out
his anxiety. No one embodied the middle-class gospel of work, or the middle-
class ideal of sacrificing oneself for one's family, more intensely than Flaubert.
No dandy, no bohemian would have tolerated his hopelessly bourgeois conduct for a moment. Even going on strike against the legal career on which he
had so reluctantly embarked was like a rebellious bourgeois adolescent braving
his family; later, he repudiated any ambition to join the local Academy of Arts
and Sciences, of which Dr. Flaubert had been vice-president. Louise Colet's
vindictive name for him—well-read bourgeois—was not entirely off the mark.

None of this psychologizing reduces Flaubert's phobia into a mere symptom. However distorted by hidden conflicts, however ill-defined the name
"bourgeois" under his pen, the fact that Flaubert fastened on that particular
curse word hints that the cultural malaise he saw all around him might really
be endemic in the class he so inexactly designated and so furiously denounced.
For the historian, particularly the historian favorably disposed to psychoanalysis, perceptions are facts as hard as the most brutal reality; they, too, have consequences in the world. Even though avant-garde attacks on the Victorian
bourgeoisie were florid in rhetoric, deficient in evidence, and malicious in
intent, it does not follow that they had no objective grounds.

2. Six-Pack Philistines

The history of bourgeoisophobia has never been written. When it is, we have seen, it will have to begin in ancient history. But late in the eighteenth century the prosecutors of merchants and their ilk added new grievances and spoke with new urgency.* The roots of Victorian bourgeoisophobia can be traced to the Sturm und Drang, which with humorless intensity trumps Molière's satire on the *bourgeois gentilhomme*. Goethe's Werther is probably the first modern alienated soul, probably the first to assert that the uneducable bourgeois, that embodiment of order and mediocrity, will never grasp, let alone share, the passionate commitments of the artist and the lover. And the author of *Werther* returned to the disagreeable philistine more than once right to the end of his life. In 1830, two years before his death, Goethe told Johann Peter Eckermann (who faithfully took it down) that any worthwhile writer was bound to have society make a martyr of him. Byron, who with his early death had escaped the philistines and their hatred, was, he thought, only the latest instance.[1]

Goethe's inconstant admirers, the German romantics, those gifted ancestors of late-nineteenth-century modernists, widened the split between proper burghers and rebellious creative spirits. The bourgeoisie that these challengers of respectability were battling, they told the world, was obscenely devoted to its pursuit of profit and comfort. Perhaps the most compelling romantic model for other antibourgeois was that versatile and alcoholic genius E. T. A. Hoffmann—painter, composer, judge, teller of haunting, uncanny tales. Generations of the avant-garde would be indebted to him for inventing the character that served them as an emblem for their crusade: Kreisler, the mad musician. This leading man among some of Hoffmann's most accomplished fictions is saner by far than his mundane audiences, who chat their way through sublime compositions and whose cherished mental balance amounts to a pathetic lack of spiritual refinement. This was the figure that Robert Schumann and, later, Johannes Brahms adopted to underscore their contempt for the middle classes' mortal failures of civilized perception.

Later in the century, as antibourgeois propaganda gained wider circulation, other Germans took up the cry. Writing in March 1882 to his patron Conrad Fiedler, an eminent and wealthy art critic, the painter Hans von Marées spoke

---

* They were encouraged by the observations of cultural critics as different from one another as Rousseau and Adam Smith, the poets and playwrights of the German Sturm und Drang, Schiller and Novalis. All of them had made much of the fact that modern civilization with its irresistible specialization was producing fragmentary human beings, sadly inferior to the wholeness of the ancient Greeks.

derisively of "bourgeois narrow-mindedness." A varied array of self-appointed spokesmen for higher cultivation, including the great surgeon and accomplished amateur pianist Theodor Billroth (Brahms's good friend) and the literary historian Rudolf von Gottschall, identified *Bürger* as asleep to the bracing currents of modern art and as people who read nothing but newspapers and take good care to be close to their beer at all times. Detlev von Liliencron, known for his novellas about war and Teutonic virtues, grimly called the phrase "the golden middling road" a "comfortable word for the philistine ... a repellent, cold, cowardly word." And the nationalist historian Heinrich von Treitschke thought it necessary to sneer at prosperous French bourgeois—only at the French of course—as exemplars of cowardice, vanity, greed, coarseness, heartlessness, arrogance, and a total inability to govern. Haunted by social anxiety, he wrote, the dictatorial empire of Napoleon III had saved the bourgeois, as it were, from themselves. Bourgeoisophobia attracted a motley assortment of recruits, chauvinists little less than cosmopolitans.[2]

This was the atmosphere in which Nietzsche invented the devastating name *Bildungsphilister*—cultivated philistine—a formulation in which he took some pride.[3] It designated what we have learned to call "middlebrow," unpoetic beings for whom thrift meant meanness; delicacy, prudishness; gentility, evasiveness; good taste, defensive aversion to depth and originality in the arts. Nietzsche portrayed the *Bildungsphilister* as a coward, not moderate as he liked to boast but mediocre to his bones, a pedant who chattered learnedly about history or aesthetics and heartlessly maligned anyone who dared to be an outsider in "healthy" middle-class society—in short, an educated person whose vaunted cultivation was a sham: pseudo-culture.

Other Germans, attempting to emulate Nietzsche's verbal ingenuity, improvised combinations like "six-pack philistine—*Weissbierphilister*," but none of them could match Nietzsche's ability to think through the implications of his coinage.[4] For in his quest for the heroic man, Nietzsche stigmatized the obedient, passive, supremely uncreative bourgeois as a "herd animal" who had been to the university and occupied positions of leadership in the academy, business, and government. After his death in 1900, Nietzsche, whether soundly interpreted or distorted—his slashing, aphoristic style invited misreadings—who philosophized with the hammer, the thinker everyone quoted and many actually read, was conscripted as a general in the army of bourgeoisophobes.

Aggressive as they sounded, German haters of the bourgeoisie were outdone by the French. Observers of the Orléanist dynasty, which had come to power in 1830, were convinced that the bourgeoisie had taken charge of the country—bad news, they thought, for creative spirits. In 1836, in his energetic, rather depressed autobiographical novel, *Confession of a Child of the Century*, Alfred de

Musset spoke for a generation of wounded and outraged talents. To be a child of the early nineteenth century was to be stricken with its malady, *ennui,* and crushed by the burden of bourgeois dishonesty. The young "were delivered over to vulgar pedants of all sorts," of *cuistres* who were beyond a doubt impeccably middle-class.[5]

Others readily seconded Musset, among them Heinrich Heine, in permanent exile in Paris from 1831 on. Reviewing the Salon of 1843, he wondered whether perhaps "the spirit of the bourgeoisie, of industrialism, which now penetrates all of France's social life," had left its mark on the arts of drawing and painting. He believed that it had. The painted Christs and emperors, saints and statesmen shown at the exhibition all looked to him like brokers who have just lost a sizable sum on the stock exchange. And those portraits! They had an expression as though the sitters had thought only about how much this picture would cost them.

No less sarcastic, Théophile Gautier, poet, novelist, essayist, critic of art and theater, expended his impressive fluency denouncing what he called the hypocrisy swamping his age. Praising the merciless caricatures of middle-class types that were the specialty of Henri Monnier, popular actor and pitiless cartoonist, Gautier found them uncannily lifelike. "His bourgeois—and no one has painted them more truly, not even Balzac—bore you like real bourgeois with inexhaustible floods of clichés and solemn asininities. This is no longer comedy; it is stenography." Monnier's drawings seemed like illustrations for Flaubert's *Dictionary of Accepted Ideas.* Late in the century, a celebrated saying attributed to Guy de Maupassant made the rounds: "Three things dishonor a writer: *La Revue des deux mondes,* the Légion d'honneur, and the Académie Française." Official success was artistic failure.[6]

Important characters in Balzac's *Human Comedy* lent substance to this indictment. "All of Balzac's bourgeois, with two or three exceptions," wrote Zola in an appreciative retrospect, "are egoists, ambitious folk, beasts keen and patient after the spoils." Balzac had observed them well, Zola added: "The French bourgeoisie is too much the shopkeeper, too deeply sunk into its fat."[7] Even Victor Hugo, that long-lived romantic, joined the voices excoriating the bourgeoisie once he turned leftward after the February Revolution of 1848. In private and in public, he expressed his disillusionment with a middle class that had failed to awaken to its higher mission. To him, the bourgeois, far from heading the great procession of progress, was but a greedy belly.

This venom did not lessen with the years. Around 1880, the year Flaubert died, the French avant-garde was made up of a cadre of bitter, highly self-conscious poets, painters, novelists, and critics. In that year, Zola struck back at the novelist and critic Jules Barbey d'Aurevilly, that curious amalgam of religious

conservative and blasphemous melodramatist—Zola called him a "hysterical
Catholic"—whom he had long detested for his superior bearing and his unfor-
tunate sallies against writers Zola admired. "In the course of time," he wrote,
"d'Aurevilly has become terribly provoking by patronizing people as bour-
geois. We are all bourgeois. Goethe, bourgeois! Diderot, bourgeois! Eh, monsieur, bourgeois yourself! because 'bourgeois' is an insult! yes, bourgeois, and,
what is more, provincial bourgeois!" Once launched, Zola would not stop,
savoring the epithet much like a boy calling a schoolmate he detests the same
name over and over. "You, monsieur, have the manias, the tics, the religions of
that horrible bourgeois class, which cannot do anything simply and which
dresses up in its Sunday best when it is eating a melon. Bourgeois! bourgeois!"
Zola accused Barbey d'Aurevilly of being half a century behind the times and
of knowing nothing about modern art. "In truth, I tell you, you show the confusions, the ignorance of a bourgeois, the obstinacy and the repetitiousness of
a bourgeois. Bourgeois! bourgeois!"[8]

Nor was Zola's attempt at annihilating his literary enemy, among the most
intemperate rhetorical bombardments ever discharged against Victorian bourgeois, merely a posture for public show. "To speak of the bourgeoisie," Zola ful-
minated in an unpublished note, "is to draw up the most violent indictment
one can launch against French society."[9] To hear these enemies of bourgeois
supremacy tell it, they were engaged in a crusade to save culture from the middle classes. Even the subtle Marcel Proust could not resist this temptation.
Meeting Marguerite Charpentier, that adventurous art collector, he called her
a "ridiculous, philistine bourgeoise," a comment as cruel as it was unjust.[10] But,
then, neither kindness nor justice ranked high in the bourgeoisophobes' choice
of weapons.

One reason they left so little room for geniality, let alone compromise, was
that tensions between the bourgeoisie and those phobic to it were not confined to aesthetic matters. Quarrels over the arts became quite directly quarrels
over politics. The extreme right and the extreme left concluded unintended,
ill-assorted alliances. Zealous materialists on the one hand and nostalgic
monarchists, fanatical nationalists, and votaries of utopian antimodern schemes
on the other shared their hostility toward the bourgeoisie. The French reactionary Charles Maurras was typical: at once cranky and persuasive, he spent
his life agitating against the bourgeois French Third Republic; so was the idiosyncratic—and, across his career, chameleon-like—German economist Werner
Sombart, who in some of his incarnations regarded modern capitalism, which
he virtually identified with the bourgeoisie, as the nemesis of freedom and
individuality. By the end of the nineteenth century, these peculiar amalgams of
beliefs and aversions included large doses of that poisonous brew anti-Semi-

tism: for some political bourgeoisophobes the modern Jew was bourgeoisdom incarnate, bourgeoisdom at its worst.

Perhaps most impressive of all was the famous Danish literary critic and prolific biographer Georg Brandes, known to history as the man who discovered Nietzsche. In his time, his strongly held opinions shaped the minds of readers and listeners across Europe; his lectures, reviews, essays, histories, and lives of Shakespeare, Goethe, and Caesar were translated into the major languages and read with admiration. Brandes was a modern Caesarist, committed to the Great Man theory of history, who saw only little men around him. The bourgeoisie was "the ruling Caliban." His correspondence yields sallies that at times rival Flaubert's. In 1873, writing to his brother, he voiced a savage aversion from which he never retreated. "One can never sufficiently imagine the philistinism of the Danish middle class, its impenetrable resistance to enlightenment and clarity, its cowardice and stupidity." Thirteen years later, he generalized his contempt, "I detest bourgeois society."[11]

In the parade of bourgeoisophobes, Karl Marx must occupy a conspicuous place, not just for a virulence that equaled anything Flaubert or Brandes could mobilize to blast the hated middle class but for the worldwide influence that his caricature came to exert late in the century. Not long after his death in 1883, when Marx's ideas were spreading beyond strictly Marxist circles, left-wingers used the dismissive epithet "bourgeois" to define historians, economists, philosophers, or politicians they could safely consign to the wastebasket.

But Marx's attitude (and this set him apart from his more primitive allies) was complicated by a remarkable tension, one that permitted him to pay the bourgeoisie some left-handed tributes. It all depended on whether Marx the philosopher of history or Marx the political agitator was speaking. Viewing the grand sweep of social evolution, Marx granted that the modern bourgeoisie had been entrusted with an epochal mission.[12] True, it had fulfilled its great assignment and was on the verge of being defied and defeated by that universal class—the proletariat. But to play the role that history had delegated to it, and to play it well, he wrote, had been no mean achievement. It had created a world economy, built enormous cities, and freed millions from the idiocy of rural life.

Almost inevitably, it was the polemical thrust of Marx's assaults on the bourgeoisie that people would remember. Modern bourgeois were moneymaking machines, fiercely attached to their self-interest. Though canting about individualism, morality, and the beauties of family life, they systematically violated all their pieties. Declaring their devotion to political democracy, they were actually partisans of authoritarian Bonapartism, which would protect them against the just demands of the working class. Preaching charity and magnanimity, they were in fact calculating and selfish. Professing religious sentiments, they used their churchgoing habits as a mask for the most mean-spirited conduct. The vaunted bourgeois family was a business arrangement. Husbands saw their wives as fountains of income and instruments for making children. Not satisfied with sexually exploiting the proletarian women in their power, bourgeois cheerfully seduced one another's wives. This kind of talk satisfied aggressive impulses, gave those who believed it a welcome sense of superiority, and had all the charm of the higher gossip.

There was something new about the vehemence of the bourgeoisophobes. The account with which this chapter opens had some truth to it. Since the ancient Greeks, patrons—kings, bishops, nobles, patricians—had treated artists as servants, privileged to be sure, but as servants none the less. A giant like Michelangelo might mutiny against a benefactor, even a pope, and suffer few of the expected penalties. But he was not called "divine" for nothing; exceptional enough to be thought unique, he left no legacy of independence. Seventeenth-century painters like Velázquez or playwrights like Racine had been courtiers, and not ashamed of their position. It was in the age of the Enlightenment that Alexander Pope, Samuel Johnson, Voltaire, and a few like-minded spirits in their wake worked with some success to liberate themselves from dependence on condescending patrons and deliver themselves over to the uncertain mercies of the marketplace. But these brave souls did not see themselves, or want to be seen, as outsiders. Even satirists worked within the system.

Then, for the first time in history, romantics intimated that a society divided between producers and consumers of high culture was a realistic possibility. With dizzying hubris, Shelley elevated the vocation of the poet above that of priest and statesman; Beethoven, though still tied to commissions from aristocratic amateurs, gruffly tried to establish his right to live his life and do his work as he pleased. Thus the conviction spread that the supremely gifted must for the sake of their consecrated task distance themselves from the public that fed them. It was a strenuous ideal, but as it gained credibility, antibourgeois coteries, the party of the geniuses, secured ever new recruits.

Not without hesitations and ambiguities. As will emerge, the autonomy that nineteenth-century painters, writers, or composers claimed was often achieved not in the face of bourgeois but with their aid. In defying authority, mid- and late-nineteenth-century artists pushed the romantics' yearning for aesthetic self-realization to its limits, but they rarely recognized, let alone acknowledged, how much they owed to middle-class support as they fought for their place in the sun. The implacable avant-garde remained unrepentant: to succeed with the public was to fail as an original spirit, to achieve popularity was to suffer a curse for which the true artist must apologize. As Detlev von Liliencron wrote, his rhymes dripping with sarcasm: it is hard for the poet to evade fame. If he cannot secure the favor of the masses in his lifetime, posterity will praise his heroic way of starving to death.* In a word, to sell was to sell out.

One of the most grating affronts Victorian bourgeois had to endure was the charge that their pretensions to cultivation were laughable, their taste bad. Though familiar for centuries, this disdain grew more sweeping, more irascible as middle-class music lovers and art collectors were caricatured wallowing in trash, debasing art into entertainment, or displaying their acquisitions with the uncouthness of social climbers. In 1834, Alfred de Vigny assailed bourgeois society with a drama about that spectacular eighteenth-century suicide Thomas Chatterton, the doom-haunted young English poet and forger, transforming his protagonist into a hero destroyed by a heartless and prosaic world. It was the account, he wrote, of "a spiritual man stifled by a materialistic society" marked by avarice and low calculation.[13]

He found ready support for his indiscriminate generalizations: "We are a prudish nation and enslaved to routine," the French poet Leconte de Lisle lamented in 1861, "born enemies of art and poetry," at once licentious and moralistic, ignorant yet excessively vain. He must have liked the sound of this accumulation of adjectives, for three years later he returned to it. The "multitude"—de Lisle of course meant the bourgeoisie—enamored of equality, was suffering from "an instinctive horror of art." The French middle classes, it seemed to him, were incurable. "Neither their eyes nor their ears or their intelligence will ever perceive the divine world of Beauty."[14]

What about one of these poor creatures who actually professed advanced taste? Bourgeoisophobes did not hesitate. He must be disparaged for impure motives; middle-class sentiments about art or literature must be unmasked as sordidly utilitarian.† In 1835, in the preface to *Mademoiselle de Maupin,* an ener-

---

* "So leicht entgeht der Dichter nicht dem Ruhm; / Kann er die Gunst der Massen nicht erlungern. / So preist die Nachwelt doch sein Heldentum, / Dass er verstand, heroisch zu verhungern." Liliencron, *Der Mäcen* (1889), in *Sämtliche Werke,* 15 vols. (1905–8), V, 313.

† In 1889, in an involuntary and striking revelation, an American offered a utilitarian reason for the flaws of utilitarianism: "In America, more than anywhere else, is music needed as a tonic, to cure the infectuous and ridiculous business fever which is responsible for many causes of premature collapse. Nowhere else is so much time wasted in making money, which is then spent in a way that contributes to no one's happiness—least of all the owner's." Americans take pride in being preeminently practical, but the inability to take pleasure is supremely impractical. "Our so-called 'practical' men look upon recreation as something useless, whereas, in reality, it is the most useful thing in the world. Recreation is re-creation—regaining the energies lost by hard work. Those who properly alternate recreation with work, economise their brain power, and are, therefore, infinitely more practical than those who scorn or neglect recreation." Anon., "Theatres v. Music Halls," *Musical Times and Singing Circular,* XXX (December 1, 1889), 713–14, quoting a "Mr. Finck."

getic manifesto celebrating art for art's sake, Théophile Gautier had already
offered the antibourgeois rationale with tart economy: "Nothing is truly beautiful unless it cannot be used for anything; everything that is useful is ugly
because it is the expression of some need, and those of man are ignoble and
disgusting, like his poor and infirm nature."[15] Like de Lisle, he had the bourgeoisie in his gunsights; its ostentatious consumption of culture, he, Gautier,
and their fellows asserted, far from existing for its own sake, attested to a well-
rehearsed social dexterity. Wealthy families would hang select paintings on their
walls to impress guests, take a box at the theater or the opera to be seen consuming refinement, acquire a piano to have a mantrap in the house.

The bourgeois piano proved an especially savory target, giving rise to spiteful remarks. As early as 1808, more than a decade before Flaubert was born, the
Vienna correspondent of the *Leipziger Musikzeitung* had already taken this sarcastic tack: "To give an idea of the extent of dilettantism here, every refined
girl, talented or not, must learn to play the piano, or to sing; first, it is the fashion; second, it is the most convenient way of displaying oneself prettily in society and thus, if fortune smiles, to make a striking match." By 1840, there were
something like twenty thousand pianos in Paris alone.[16] Most marriageable
amateurs at the keyboard were still confined to the upper middle class, for in
those decades, this aid to charming self-display remained rare and expensive.

Offspring of earlier keyboard instruments, the pianoforte had begun to
secure an identity of its own after the 1770s, and from the early nineteenth century on, with decades of experimentation and a flood of patented improvements ahead, it came to approximate the pianos we know today. The first
pianofortes were designed for public performances, but, in a move characteristic for this age of tinkering, piano makers built smaller instruments calculated
to fit spaces more compact and budgets less capacious than those a concert
grand would require. In 1828, a Broadwood, made by England's best-known
manufacturer, cost anywhere from 36 to 172 guineas, depending on size, materials, and detailing. The most expensive model was an upright grand in a rose-
wood case—it would have swallowed up more than a year's income of a
respectable lower-middle-class family.[17] Significantly, Broadwood and other
British piano makers priced their product in a denomination that carried an
aura of distinction normally reserved to prices charged for race horses, paintings, and the services of eminent physicians.

Yet owning a piano was the dream of petty bourgeois everywhere; in 1851,
the year of the Great Exhibition, the *Cyclopaedia of the Industry of All Nations*
praised the firm of Collard for offering pianos so reasonably priced that they
were within the reach of "the public of small means—the needy clerk, the
poor teacher, the upper class mechanic."[18] This report was more an expression

of hope than a report on reality: financing a piano on the installment plan, which took hold in the second half of the century and foisted flimsy specimens on naive consumers, attests that a reliable piano long remained the preserve of the well-to-do. But, suavely ignoring the genuine pleasures it provided, bourgeoisophobes incorporated the piano mania into their portrait of the uncivilized middle classes. It allowed them to condescend to petty bourgeois for aching to emulate their betters, and the prosperous for driving their daughters into neurosis. Actually many nineteenth-century private journals recorded delighted domestic music making. Hardly a day went by that the young Gladstone, whose agreeable voice made him welcome at musical evenings around the piano, would laconically note in his diary, "music" or "concert" or "singing."

These pleasing scenes did little to reduce widespread disgust with parental aspirations and mindless practice sessions for tone-deaf young ladies. Music, complained the report of the English Schools Inquiry Commission of 1868, "is equally demanded of all girls, however little taste they may have for it." In 1884, the English periodical *Musical Opinion* reported that there were no fewer than 424 German piano makers employing 7,834 workmen and turning out about 73,000 instruments a year. These impressive numbers would only have incensed Flaubert; respectable families found the piano, he cynically noted, "indispensable in a drawing room," and he did not cite love of music as a reason for making it indispensable.[19]

3. Confusing Confrontations

The confrontations that pitted makers of Victorian tastes against one another were as confusing as they were numerous. Alliances of opinion formed and dissolved, members of one camp fraternized with members of the other. Van Gogh, an artist as alienated from middle-of-the-road fashions as the age produced, admitted to "an absolutely unlimited admiration for Meissonier," the supreme academic painter, and this crossing of presumably impenetrable battle lines was far from rare.[1] No standard went unchallenged among the Victorians, no secession existed long without being accused of timidity.

Nor was it always possible to identify a style as radical or reactionary: in the romantic era, the Nazarenes meant to revolutionize German painting by taking early Italian art as their model; at mid-century the English Pre-Raphaelites left the impression (as their name indicates and their critics believed) that they meant to secure the future honesty and seriousness of English art by embracing a style from a distant past. Wagner aimed at blessing the world with the

Music of the Future, but Brahms, a composer whom the Wagnerites decried as
out of date, produced music that its first listeners considered difficult, unduly
modernist.

In this fluid situation, in which name-calling usually took the place of reasoned debate, denunciations of the bourgeoisie actually functioned as a screen
concealing the anti-academics' true target. Rebels striking for independence
were rising up against a cluster of privileged styles, against the restrictive—they
thought, paralyzing—canons governing all the arts. The issue, as we shall see
over and over, was one of aesthetic conscience to be sure, but of economic survival no less. However pure the bourgeoisophobes' motives, the practical point
of the avant-gardes' manifestos was quite simply to survive and, if they did not
despise it too much, to change the taste of the paying public. Canonical sculptors and composers, novelists and dramatists had their work selected by a variety of legitimizing agencies—endorsed by dealers and bureaucrats, protected
by critics and museum directors, favored by civilized music lovers or gallery-
goers who, as it were, voted with their feet and their wallets.

Still, the rebels' effort to change the public's mind, though admittedly ardu-
ous, was not an unmanageable task. Secessionists were bound to notice what a
few observant thinkers like David Hume had long known: the canons they
most detested were not immutable. Take painting: official culture favored by the
art establishment preached the neoclassical realism taught by the academy, but
its margins were flexible. In France, government-sponsored salons could appropriate the feathery landscapes of Camille Corot, the quick, proto-Impression-
ist brush stroke of Thomas Couture, even, after years of relative neglect, the
fresh air painters of the Barbizon school. Théodore Rousseau, the most eminent among them, had made a modestly successful career in his lifetime, and in
1873, six years after his death, one of his canvases was auctioned off for 35,000
francs, too late for him but not for art.[2] In short, during the Victorian years, as
throughout history, newcomers, with varying success, besieged the door of the
official pantheon to claim admission.

They did so across frontiers. Beethoven conquered the German-speaking
countries first, then England, and, later, a French musical public reluctant to jet-
tison its belief in the superiority of operatic to orchestral music. John Constable was more highly esteemed by Eugène Delacroix than by the Royal
Academy of Art, Gustave Courbet in Munich more than in Paris. The highly
original Scottish architect and designer Charles Rennie Mackintosh found
stronger resonance among rebellious Secessionists on the Continent, notably
Vienna, than at home. Some tastes remained firmly anchored in their native
soil; German anal humor, for example, which greatly amused the educated in
its country of origin, traveled badly, and so did the preoccupation of German

painters with profundity and death. But in general, the market for innovation was wide open as currents ran fairly freely across European and, soon after, American capitals of high culture.

In short, although the advocates of reigning canons represented them as the embodiment of good taste, they could never permanently exclude all new recruits; these canons proved less authoritative than academicians, swollen with commissions and hung with medals, liked to believe. No doubt, there was a sizable portion of realism in the rebels' cursing the powers that be for neglecting and underpaying them. How realistic depended on just how the avant-garde dealt with pressures to conform and on the penalties for nonconformity. And this in turn depended on the most varied social habits of adaptation. When in 1897 Léonce Bénédite, curator at the Luxembourg Museum, tried to define what united the Impressionists, he praised their autonomy, their impatience with routine, their resistance to official tastes—all admirable but negative qualities. The exhibitions that the Impressionists mounted from 1874 on were not called the Salons of the Independents for nothing.

Where, then, does the truth about Victorian bourgeois culture lie? This much should already be plain: whatever this truth, simplicity cannot be one of its qualities. Significantly a few—only a few—exceptionally perceptive Victorians recognized this crucial fact of Victorian life. Toward the end of the long nineteenth century, in 1903, Thomas Mann's novella *Tonio Kröger* managed to hint at the intricacies that will take center stage as we proceed. It is late summer, September; Tonio Kröger is sitting in a Danish spa and writing to his friend in Munich, the painter Lisaweta Iwanowna, replying to a startling comment she had made about him some months before. A professional writer, he had passionately and at length declared his love of life, his yearning for the "bliss of the ordinary," from which his vocation—he called it his curse—had exiled him forever. This was a troubled modernist speaking, mouthing the familiar cliché of the artist alienated from middle-class culture yet miserable about his separation from the class into which he had been born. Lisaweta Iwanowna had had no patience with this vociferous self-torment and called Kröger to his face "quite simply a bourgeois—*ganz einfach ein Bürger,*" and then, retreating just slightly, "a bourgeois gone astray—*ein Bürger auf Irrwegen.*"[3]

Kröger adopts his friend's diagnosis of his torn nature and explains his Hamlet-like self-consciousness by heredity: a north German father, correct, thorough, inclined to melancholy, and an exotic mother, beautiful, sensual, and impulsive. "What resulted was this: a bourgeois who got lost in art, a bohemian homesick for his respectable upbringing, an artist with a bad conscience." It is "my bourgeois conscience that lets me see in all art, in all extraordinariness, and in all genius something profoundly equivocal, profoundly disreputable, profoundly dubious." Still, he cannot abandon his calling and concludes with a sigh, "I stand between two worlds, at home in neither of them, and hence I am having a bit of a hard time."[4]

Bound as we are to reject Kröger's biological determinism, we may build on his acknowledgment of the artist's ambivalence toward nineteenth-century bourgeois culture. It calls attention to a pervasive, almost defining paradox haunting that culture: the coexistence of strains and cooperation between self-proclaimed avant-gardes and their reputed mortal foe, the bourgeoisie. Kröger's uneasy middle-class conscience is an instructive document for its time, a subtle hint far more useful to the historian of Victorian culture than Flaubert's single-minded acrimony.

Obviously Mann's post-Victorian diagnosis came too late for Flaubert's benefit. But that does not release Flaubert from responsibility for propagating the image of a scarecrow that has gravely, though not irreparably, damaged our interpretation of Victorian bourgeois culture. For, quite apart from the palpable realities of Rouen, he could have consulted an attentive contemporary to correct his social astigmatism—if he had been interested in correcting it—a witness he professed to admire: Charles Baudelaire. Writing in the mid-1840s, when Flaubert was a young, still unpublished author, Baudelaire, almost as important a critic as he was poet, championed the middle class with a vigor one might have expected from a self-interested banker or industrialist rather than, what with his drugs and his mistresses, from a principled outsider. That scornful epithet "the *bourgeois*," Baudelaire urged in his Salon of 1845, is "impertinent"; redolent with the argot of the studios, "it should be erased from the dictionary of criticism," especially since "there are so many bourgeois among artists."[5]

Baudelaire knew that this brave defense of the much derided middle class, offered without a touch of sarcasm, put him at odds with his *confrères;* to them, after all, "that inoffensive being" the bourgeois, "who would like nothing better than to love good painting," had long been anathema. But Baudelaire did not let himself be intimidated. In the following year, he dedicated his Salon to the bourgeoisie. Was it not the majority in numbers and intelligence? He addressed it directly: "You are the natural friends of the arts," some of them rich, some of them scholars. Whether king, legislator, or businessman, "you have founded collections, museums, galleries." And some of the treasures "monopolized" by the few only a few years before, "you have made accessible to the masses." When bourgeois are happy and satisfied, he concluded, society too will be happy and satisfied.[6]

No doubt, Baudelaire's dedication was a wish lending wings to facts. But it remains, for its time and its author, an astonishing attempt to rescue the middle classes from the opprobrium they were suffering, and continue to suffer to this day. With its energy and lucidity, the dedication raises a most unlikely prospect, one against which untold numbers of avant-garde propagandists have labored for perhaps two centuries: the bourgeois as a possible backer rather than the sworn adversary of unconventional, even, after the 1880s, modernist taste.

ONE

The Political Economy of Art

Taste is the arbiter of choice, and in the Victorian decades aesthetic choices imposed heavy burdens of decision making on the bourgeoisie. So domestic an industry as furniture design, spreading its offerings before the middle-class buying public, displayed a riot of styles all the way from primitive to contemporary. So did architecture: Greek, Roman, Gothic, and Renaissance revival; Jacobean, Queen Anne, German rustic, French provincial, and Biedermeier echoes of the more recent past, to say nothing of imaginative forays like pseudo-Chinese, jostled one another in showrooms or trade magazines, each style minutely subdivided and temptingly named. And bourgeois lusting for something new, perhaps unique, could always explore eclecticism.

"Tasteful" furniture and houses were vivid instances of nineteenth-century embarrassments of riches available to the middle classes; there were many others. The prosperous, even bourgeois with an upper-middling income, found leisure and money to read and to fill up a glassed-in case with books, attend concerts or the theater, visit museums, perhaps buy a picture or two. Newly founded or drastically enlarged institutions were designed to serve, and slyly to create, their tastes: concerts with annual subscriptions, orchestras with a stable corps of musicians, athenaeums displaying art and artifacts, well-publicized exhibitions of industrial and domestic objects, a mushrooming tribe of art dealers, impresarios launching virtuosos or new playwrights, battalions of critics advising readers just what they really ought to enjoy. The self-satisfied notion that it was enough to know what one liked, already under attack by Kant late in the eighteenth century, retreated before the more strenuous ideal that taste, at least good taste, was a kind of knowledge. And all this activity fostered the business of culture in unexampled varieties and with unexampled profits.

I. Battles of the Budgets

Predictably the Victorian century, this supreme age of movement, was exposed to drastic shifts in the arts. They raised perplexities less grave, to be sure, than the sufferings dealt out by child labor, technological unemployment, persistent poverty, the vagaries of the business cycle, or incompetent medicine. But to most makers of high culture their quandaries mattered as if their life, or at least their livelihood, were at stake. Though still hesitantly, the arts and letters, embedded in a wider world, took their chances on continual surprises. "What strikes one right away?" asked Alfred de Musset reviewing the Paris Salon of 1836. "Nothing homogeneous, no common thought at all, no schools, no families, no link among artists either in their choice of form or subject matter. Each painter presents himself isolated, and not only each painter but sometimes even each picture by the same painter. Most often, the canvases publicly exhibited have neither mothers nor sisters." All, in short, was "caprice."[1]

Only a decade later, walking through the Salon of 1845, the great French critic Théophile Thoré noted the same phenomenon, if in a far more positive spirit: "We find French painting without system and without direction, given over to individual imagination." But he was not complaining: "Surely this is not an evil, since originality is the precondition of art." Reflecting on the exhibition, he exclaimed with almost visible elation, "What diversity!"[2] His comment was symptomatic for one party in the pleasure wars; this kind of aesthetic individualism, not glimpsed since the Renaissance and eventually surpassing it with its radicalism, still found strenuous opposition in conservative circles. Originality implied unpredictable and not always welcome changes of unknown dimensions.

Through the age, patrons of high culture were caught up in the jungle of discordant opinions and witnessed—at times provoked—noisy conflicts. Their preferences and their quarrels were clouded by pervasive anxieties: diagnosticians of Victorian society, we know, experienced their time as exceptionally unsettled, and they included in the roster of things that made them nervous what people did with whatever leisure time and surplus cash they could muster. In 1904, in an exhaustive survey of art in nineteenth-century Europe, the German art historian Friedrich Haack isolated the events that, he thought, had produced its unique character, citing chiefly the French Revolution and the current of stylistic free trade it had released. Together these two had broken down the dictatorship over taste that institutions like the state, the nobili-ty, and the church had enforced for centuries. We may add that it was the mas-sive entry of bourgeois into the market of cultural consumption, coupled with the rising social status of those who produced what these buyers craved, that had made the old consensus all the more problematic. Bourgeois choices responded to a variety of impulses; the geography of taste and the geography of politics and culture were inextricably intertwined.*

They are indeed hard to disentangle. Nineteenth-century students of cul-ture like Hippolyte Taine were interested far more in the social than in the psy-chological determinants of the arts. It was Freud who, in an essay of 1908 on creative writers and daydreaming, laid bare the unconscious dimensions in the making of literature and the equally unconscious ties linking its producer with its consumers. Decades earlier, some critics had already perceived that the arts win acceptance to the extent that they give pleasure and—which is less banal—that pleasures are spread across a wide palette. Reviewing the Salon of 1846, Baudelaire, citing Stendhal, noted a little extravagantly, "There are as many sorts of beauty as there are habitual ways of seeking happiness."[3] This plu-ralistic view of aesthetic enjoyment directly contradicted the neoclassical dis-pensation of an ultimate, lawful uniformity in the appreciation of high culture. But it won growing support through the century, and would prove a mainstay of late-nineteenth-century modernism. Desire, it seemed, like beauty, was many things to many people.

To translate desire into action usually means that a conflict has been resolved, one inclination has bested its rivals. Cultivation battles regression; lev-els of aesthetic appetite coexist and compete with one another.† What is more, the stylistic preferences of painters, conductors, or museum directors, *their* choices, cannot help leaving their mark on the publics they touch. But, though all these elements have substantial roles to play, among the Victorians no less than at any other time, the supreme determinant was of course money—or the lack of it.

A look at what John Ruskin called the political economy of art should sort out middle-class publics for the higher things and the levels of expenditure at which they were compelled to operate. Nineteenth-century Germany, with its boast of being the land of writers and thinkers, supplies particularly instructive

---

* This issue deserves a chapter of its own, and will get it; see the detailed treatment just below.
  † The psychoanalytic view of human nature leaves no doubt that pleasures coexist on many levels, depending largely on what one brings to them.

informants.* In 1872, Max Liebermann was paid 3,000 marks for *Die Gänserupferinnen.* One of his first important canvases, it depicted a group of peasant women plucking geese in a barn. Liebermann, then twenty-five, was on his way to becoming Germany's most controversial painter; escaping from the academic doctrines that dominated German art schools and ateliers, he had absorbed the lessons of Frans Hals and the Barbizon school on long study trips to Holland and France. The purchaser, the railroad magnate Bethel Henry Strousberg, at the time a multimillionaire with baronial tastes, obviously did not have to lose sleep over the price.

The vast majority of Germans did not enjoy this luxury. From the 1850s, independent craftsmen, perhaps with a shop and an apprentice, could reckon on making some 1,500 marks a year, sometimes a little more and often a little less. The *Gänserupferinnen* would have cost them two years' work. Engaged in ferocious struggles over their middle-class identity, they found their economic position particularly vulnerable to the vagaries of the market. Modest merchants and innkeepers or teachers in elementary schools felt less panic about their status and were marginally better off. But theirs, too, was a life that imposed long hours of work and made most acquisitions beyond necessities quite unthinkable. As in other countries, in Germany these *Kleinbürger* distinguished themselves from the working class through formality of dress, correctness of speech, firmness of moral admonitions, and a longing to be thought cultured, all matters by which they set great store and drummed into their children. Above these millions of families toiling to make ends meet, incomes mounted into the clouds. The German financial pyramid, matching pyramids abroad, was exceedingly wide at the bottom and exceedingly narrow at the top.

That is why German bachelors intent on settling themselves for life devoted much time and calculation hunting for an heiress, or at least a substantial dowry. There was nothing clandestine about this search for security: prosaic advertisements in the personal columns of the newspapers frankly disclosed the wish for a widow with a fortune, or one presiding over a prospering retail store. The Germans had a word for it, *Einheirat,* which essentially meant marrying a trust fund or a business with a woman attached to it. Other *Bürger,* though, more timid or more scrupulous, rejected this unmitigated materialism. Making do without such booty, they took as much pleasure as they could from the titles—Commercial Councillor, Privy Councillor—that German governments

---

* This self-definition, which first gained currency after 1800, captures a glowing sense of Teutonic preeminence in high culture. It was not pure self-congratulation, though, but barely masked a flight into art and literature to provide a refuge for *Bürger* shut out from political participation. In any event, the most relevant question remains just how much culture Germany's fellow citizens of their *Dichter und Denker* could actually afford.

lavished on the deserving and the long-lived. *Gymnasium* teachers, who made around 2,000 marks a year or a bit more, were honored less with pecuniary rewards than with the resounding title of Professor, which at least rhetorically assimilated their modest position to that of their far more prosperous "colleagues" at a university. No wonder that insisting on being addressed by their honorifics acquired such an emotional charge in that country.

Middle-level officials and reasonably thriving merchants, professional men, and university *Professoren* reached incomes of around 6,000 marks. This was the level, some ten times the pay of all but the most skilled factory workers, that most German bourgeois thought the pinnacle of the living standard to which they could aspire without engaging in self-deluding fantasies. In the 1890s, in his last years as Munich's highly respected chief conductor, Hermann Levi drew precisely that salary.* No one at this rank could hope to buy a major painting unless he had a private fortune, counted a generous artist as his close friend, or collected obsessively by sacrificing everything else to his fixation.

Beyond these solid burghers was the stratosphere: the magnates who could buy pretty much whatever they fancied. Ministers of state in Prussia earned 30,000 marks a year (plus a free apartment), and even that was dwarfed by the astronomical incomes of a clan small in numbers and large in influence. This was Strousberg territory, the *Grossbürgertum* made up of bankers, industrialists, businessmen, and heirs to the fortunes their fathers had made. Their forays into spending resembled adult gratifications of childhood wishes: they acquired castles, built mansions, bred racehorses, collected Renaissance medals, endowed museums, or led lives of leisure and corruption on Capri and other luxurious southern spas. And a few of them, like the Berlin banker Joachim Wagener, put together a major collection of contemporary paintings.†

If these tycoons did not have to ask what a painting cost, households counting on around 6,000 marks a year, though impeccably respectable and dwelling in the upper reaches of the *Bürgertum*, were often beset by money worries. In

* This was scarcely munificent; and since the 1870s, Levi had been drawing 5,000 marks a year for his services to the state. No doubt, he eked out his income with visiting stints. In early 1869, while still *Kapellmeister* in Karlsruhe, he was offered the position as one of three chief conductors of the court orchestra in Vienna at 2,500 gulden—well over 4,000 marks—a year. Writing to his friend Brahms, he asserted that he could not live in Vienna on that salary, especially since he had no private fortune of his own. Since all he could do was wave his baton (he did not see himself giving lessons, a resource for other underpaid musicians), he would need at least 4,000 gulden a year. Brahms replied that one source of added income might be starting a choral society, but he advised against accepting the offer. Hermann Levi to Johannes Brahms, April 19, [18]69; Brahms to Levi, April [18]69, *Johannes Brahms im Briefwechsel mit Hermann Levi, Friedrich Gernsheim sowie den Familien Hecht und Fellinger*, ed. Leopold Schmidt (1910), 43–47.

† For Wagener and his collection, see below, pp. 182–85.

many ways they seemed little better off than fellow Germans earning half that sum, since they were oppressed by expenditures their status forced upon them, victims more than beneficiaries of a conspicuous consumption they found well nigh compulsory. Their living quarters were expected to speak affluence: the piano to bear the label of a choice maker, the cuisine appetizing and ample, the stationery engraved, the servants visible. But the stylishness of their ambiance, supposedly a social and financial guarantor, was often a façade for some trying corner cutting. The wine, the cigars and candy, the holiday arrangements that went with their rank were not inexpensive.

Nor were the children: their parents' standing kept them out of the labor market for years after working-class or petty bourgeois youngsters had begun to make their living. The financial exactions of university life could become onerous; students found it hard to resist the blandishments of exclusive fraternities, costly outfits, and lavish parties, draining their father's coffers with their monthly allowance and special subventions. In some status-conscious families, even a sensible son could eat up more than a quarter of its total expenditures.[4] Daughters, too, did not come cheap. They were supposed to display themselves stylishly dressed at receptions and balls and trained for suitable marriage partners with music and painting lessons from professionals who commanded substantial fees. And behind all this loomed the expense for the dowry. What price taste in these households?

It was very high. In nineteenth-century Germany, paintings by reputable or young, promising artists were reserved to a fairly, but not entirely, exclusive club. In 1859, Anselm Feuerbach sold *Dante and the Noble Ladies of Ravenna,* typical of his monumental, classicizing canvases, to the grand duke of Baden for 3,000 gulden. To hear the self-pitying painter tell it, he was insufficiently appreciated and insufficiently remunerated, but the more than 5,000 marks he got for his *Dante* was a respectable sum. Yet it was far from being a record in the central European art bazaar. The fashionable Austrian salon artist Hans Makart, whose outsized, decorative, sensually overloaded scenes were much in vogue before he died in 1884, got 14,000 marks for his *Juliet's Death,* which milked an affecting scene for more than it was worth. And Franz von Lenbach, Germany's best-known and highest-priced portraitist in the last third of the century, friend of Bismarck and companion of kings, princes, and industrial barons, commanded between 6,000 and 12,000 marks for his portraits, expertly drawn and, with their brooding chiaroscuro, remotely suggesting Rembrandt. One can see how Lenbach could build a princely residence for himself in Munich paid for largely with his fees.

The prize capitalist among German artists was Anton von Werner, the quasi-official painter to Prussia and the empire. His strongest point was the crowded historical composition: a conference of Prussian strategists during the war with France, tense moments of battle, and, most famously, festive occasions like the unveiling of a monument to Richard Wagner or the opening of the Reichstag by Emperor Wilhelm II. Werner's gift for rendering likenesses in paint was almost uncanny; painstaking sketches made it possible to recognize even marginal participants. The time and effort it took Werner to complete his monumental machines went into the prices he could demand, as did his ability to "correct" the episode for the sake of dramatic impact or political message. The government bought *In a Rear Billet before Paris,* to be hung in the National Gallery, for 16,000 marks. Completed in 1894, twenty-four years after Werner had sketched Prussian officers in the salon of a requisitioned French house, singing, playing the piano, peacefully lighting the fire and smoking their pipe, the painting secured its popularity through photographs, photogravures, and picture postcards.

The best-known of his group portraits, which Werner produced in several versions, depicts Prussia's king Wilhelm being proclaimed emperor of Germany by the grand duke of Baden on January 18, 1871. Werner had been invited to witness this historic event in the Hall of Mirrors at Versailles. The emperor, in heroic posture, confronts Bismarck, who, in his dazzling white uniform, is the true focus of the painting. The first version cost the grand duke of Baden 60,000 marks, a sum no other German painter could approach and very few private individuals could have mustered.[5]

Set against such amounts, usually solicited with little hesitation and met with barely a murmur, Liebermann's *Gänserupferinnen* begins to look like a bargain. In fact, the prices reached in 1873 at an international exhibition in Munich, the liveliest fair for paintings in Germany, which attracted a well-heeled clientele, averaged more than 2,000 marks, confirming that Liebermann's price was not extravagant for its time.[6] These figures document the obvious: the most prestigious artists were well beyond the means even of bourgeois in the much envied middling strata. Peaks of high culture remained for the most part the domain of what the nineteenth century liked to call "cultural aristocrats," a sport for an elite within an elite. But, as the keen interest in high-priced paintings at exhibition attests, that elite was expanding. Well-to-do bourgeois—importers, publishers, department store owners—seemed desperate to spend money for what they had come to consider a kind of necessity. Still, the *Gänserupferinnen* would have cut deeply into Hermann Levi's bank account, taking half a year's salary; a professor teaching in a *Gymnasium* would have had to drudge more than double that time.

2. Affordable Masterpieces

Unlike their betters, most burghers made do with reproductions of master-pieces, or modern drawings and etchings available at under 1,000 marks, some-times at much less. Compelled to husband their resources, they were bound to shy away from giving costly hostages to fortune. We have the 1889 budget of a hardworking public servant living in Berlin with a cheerful wife who knew how to make do with what she had, and three teenage children; the eldest, a nineteen-year-old daughter, held a part-time job painting flowers, which enabled her to buy her own clothes. The father's salary was 5,450 marks a year, and this reduced the family to low-cost entertainments: reading out loud after supper—one sees the wife and daughter busy sewing or knitting—walks and excursions, a rare visit to the theater. In 1889, they went to the *Schauspielhaus* just once. All together these investments in high culture cost no more than 62 marks, little more than one percent of the father's salary. The party they gave once a year was an extravagance: it added up to around 80 marks; and they set aside about half that sum for the father's weekly congenial get-togethers with fellow bureaucrats. So tight a budget left very little, if anything, for art.[1]

The domestic economy of this family is exemplary for the middling German middle classes, as for the *bonne bourgeoisie* in France and elsewhere. No wonder that a daughter at the piano with the others grouped around to provide vocal support was the diversion of choice for Europe's (and America's) average bour-geois in the nineteenth century. Music certainly had its charms, for amateurs as much as for professionals. Yet the comforting sense that one need not go into debt for such civilized entertainments remained a valued ingredient in this sociable domesticity. So much money had to be spent on so much else.

It is worth reiterating that the economic dimensions of high culture were not decisive for the making of taste. Families having to content themselves with impromptu musicales were not necessarily indifferent to the quality of their preferences. To judge from readily available sheet music, the lieder their resi-dent virtuoso—usually the lady or a daughter of the house—shared with her family were often by Schubert; the pieces she performed as a soloist often by Schumann or the early Beethoven. Yet not even these evenings were without their expenditures. Sheet music was fairly costly and had to be acquired pru-dently; around 1890, a *Romanze* by Anton Rubinstein for four hands cost two marks; Franz Liszt's piano version of Berlioz's *Symphonie fantastique,* four times that sum.

Yet culture trickled in, with the mysteries of art and literature, like that of music, unlocked by reasonably priced publications. The bookcases in bourgeois households were likely to display, in addition to popular editions of the classics with garish spines—Shakespeare in Britain, Molière in France, Goethe and Schiller in Germany—biographies of composers, painters, or poets. Late in the century, they were enriched by didactic texts on individual artists or schools of art. Once launched, this genre practically exploded, as enterprising publishers issued series of affordable volumes aimed at exposing proper bourgeois to the higher knowledge. Their prose was exclamatory and their paper gray-brownish, their appraisals were unctuous and their illustrations vile, but they assuaged a ravenous thirst for self-education. One successful series, collectively titled "The Artist's Book"—*Das Künstlerbuch*—offered slender, generously if crudely illustrated studies of favorite German painters; published by the house of Schuster and Loeffler of Berlin and Leipzig at a moderate three marks, they were printed in editions of 1,000, with each additional thousand proudly noted on the title page. More ambitious monographs, on paper less drab and reproductions less foggy, were naturally more expensive. So, of course, were the leatherbound editions of the masters.

In a word, it would be naive to equate money with taste. A manufacturer could obviously spend a great deal more on cultural goods than his bookkeeper, an attorney more than his clerk. But this says little about what the manufacturer or the attorney would do with the cash he set aside for culture. The bookkeeper and the clerk might have discriminating (and, in fantasy, expensive) tastes, laboriously polished after years of uncomfortably standing in the back of the top balcony at the opera house or the theater, visiting museums on free Sundays, and collecting cheap reproductions. Since there were those among middling, even among petty bourgeois who had a genuine feeling for what they saw, heard, or read, taste became a source of frustration for those knowledgeable enough to want what they could not have. This is where astute merchandisers met them halfway by introducing modern techniques of popularizing culture. Lowering the fences separating aesthetic craving and aesthetic fulfillment, they tried to meet the needs of those yearning after the real thing by cajoling them into being content with a simulacrum.

At times, bourgeois spent good money to get that real thing. In 1828, Paganini gave a series of sensational recitals in Vienna, making the violin sing in ways thought impossible before. Mathias Perth, a court official, attended one of the sold-out performances, so overcrowded that scores fainted and had to be carried from the hall. Duly impressed, he noted in his diary, "It cost me a lot of money. I was dripping with sweat, but I heard him, and in order to get an idea of his playing, one must hear him. The effect on each listener of the tones he coaxes from the violin is indescribable." Paganini was, to Perth's infatuated mind, the Napoleon of violinists. No wonder he was reported to have earned more than 30,000 gulden during his visit—$6,000 in 1828 dollars—but Perth, who probably made about a tenth of that sum a year, did not envy him.[2] He had strained his resources to hear this diabolical miracle worker, and he was glad he had spent the money.*

Obviously, the key to widespread pleasure was differential prices that reflected differential quality. Those who found the painting they coveted out of reach could buy an engraving or (in the second half of the century) a photograph of it, or perhaps clip an illustration from their family weekly. In the Victorian century, art, literature, and music were inching their way toward a consumer culture that provided for everyone with money to spare, no matter how little, a culture of book clubs, massive supplies of reproductions, reduced admission fees catering to students or impecunious families. The instruction of popular guides to culture supplied cherished benefits as they directed grateful readers to aesthetic delights on their honeymoon or their infrequent holiday trips to distant museums. Faithfully consulting their Baedeker, that handy cicerone to the tourist—itself something of an investment, averaging six marks—they could revel in paintings, drawings, sculptures, and buildings they had only glimpsed in reproductions remotely hinting at the original.[†]

The docility of most bourgeois tourists before the masterful tone of their guidebooks, leaving only a few mutinous spirits to strike out for independent judgments, demonstrates the helplessness felt by the majority, coupled with a longing to share, however humbly, in Beauty. In 1853, on their honeymoon, the prosperous Lübeck wine merchant Heinrich Leo Behncke and his wife, Caroline, took in the renowned picture gallery in Dresden. "Raphael's great Madonna long captivated us and filled us with enthusiasm," he noted. "Not far from the Raphael Madonna hung Correggio's *Holy Night;* the shepherds stand

---

* Virtuosi in the performing arts offered an exception to the almost unbreakable rule among the Victorians that when women were in the world at all, they would earn less than men. Respectability helped—and so did P. T. Barnum's adroit publicity. Jenny Lind, "the Swedish Nightingale," was renowned for her charities and the purity of her life as much as for the purity of her voice. Her celebrated 1850 concert series in the United States under Barnum's management netted her $150,000 (and her manager more than three times that). And the pianist Clara Schumann, a widow with an impeccable reputation and seven children (several of whom strained her resources with health problems and gambling debts), gave recitals across Europe for substantial fees, even without the guidance of a Barnum.

† The 1898 Baedeker to southern Germany cost five marks; that to Berlin and environs, only three marks; but the volumes for more "exotic" places like Egypt, Spain and Portugal, Palestine and Syria, twelve marks each.

near the Christ child and the mother, with her great love, filled with the bliss of which only a happy mother is capable, bends down and regards the child. A stream of light that comes from the child illuminates the mother, and her angelic features dazzle the shepherds and shows in the distance Joseph, Maria's husband." Strolling through the museum, the couple allowed one painting after another to "captivate" them. Behncke thought Holbein's Virgin with child "lofty and magnificent, most beautiful!" In contrast, he frowned at canvases by Rubens and Jacob Jordaens as "indecent and not very appealing." Then, "filled with lasting impressions," the couple took their midday meal.[3]

Behncke's verdicts sound only too familiar; his expressive adjectives, sec-ondhand. But his sensibility was representative for his time and station, and his responses, though untrained and unsophisticated, were apparently altogether authentic. The common accusation that they must have been just another instance of middle-class cant is unhistorical. While many bourgeois did not have the right words for art or music, they had, often enough, the right feel-ings.* Like most bourgeois, indeed like academic critics in his time, Behncke paid particular attention to the subject matter of a painting and insisted on its respectful handling by the artist; spiritual elevation was a principal reason for aesthetic approval. That is why Behncke could not warm up to Rubens or Jor-daens, not even to their sacred scenes: their coarseness insulted his religious sentiments. However one may judge the Behnckes' taste with the benefit of hindsight, there is little doubt that they, and thousands of their fellow bour-geois, aspired to possess in some way goods which, they had been taught and firmly believed, made life gracious and lifted it above mundane routine.

Surpassing expectations, the age of inventions devised an extraordinary array of techniques to bring paintings to middle-class multitudes. Some manufactur-ers did not scruple to make the questionable promise that they would match the emotional impact of the original. From lithography early to photogravure

---

* In his semi-autobiographical novel, *The Way of All Flesh,* Samuel Butler savagely lampooned the inauthentic appreciation of nature and art of a principal character, George Pontifex, for whom he invented a diary that included a record of his travels to the Continent for the sake of his cul-tivation. "I remember seeing at Battersby in after years the diary which he kept on the first of these occasions. It is a characteristic document. I felt as I read it that the author before starting had made up his mind to admire only what he thought it would be creditable in him to admire, to look at nature and art only through the spectacles that had been handed down to him by gen-eration after generation of prigs and impostors. The first glimpse of Mont Blanc threw Mr. Pon-tifex into a conventional ecstasy," while the pictures at the Uffizi "threw him into genteel paroxysms of admiration." *The Way of All Flesh* (1899; introd. William Lyon Phelps, 1916), 15, 17 [ch. 4]. But there seems to me nothing meretricious about the Behnckes' "conventional ecstasy." They expressed their feelings as best they could.

late in the century, a rapidly expanding industry produced a wealth of illustrations, publicized them in the press, and distributed elaborate catalogs. By around 1880, there were no fewer than thirty publishers in Germany offering photographs to householders clamoring to embellish their rooms.[4]

Not without controversy. From its earliest days in the 1830s, photography had generated a flood of excited comment and portentous prophecies that did not recede for decades. In the words of Nadar, the most famous photographer of mid-century France, the invention had caused "universal stupefaction." Duly stupefied, the prognosticators took the most extravagant positions. Photography would be the death of art or its salvation, a mortal competitor for the portraitist or his obedient servant, the triumph of vulgarity or an instrument of cultivation. There was general agreement that the kind of pictures once seen in the houses of the rich alone would soon appear in those of ordinary bourgeois. And as usual, the democratization of culture brought anxious and angry protests. In 1867, Barbey d'Aurevilly (the writer, we recall, who had aroused Zola's wrath by patronizing Goethe and Diderot) defined photography as "that democracy of the portrait, that equality before the object, brutal and mendacious, that art of *quatre sous,* put within reach of an egotistical beggars' world in a century of bargains and shoddy goods."[5] That was snobbery, but Barbey d'Aurevilly was right to point out that photography "cheapened" culture—which meaning of that verb remained open.

While traditional genres of reproduction—engravings, etchings, woodcuts—had to contend with heavy competition from their inexpensive and efficient modern challengers, they survived. Art-loving Victorians could enjoy standard favorites from Albrecht Dürer to Angelica Kauffmann, Botticelli to Gainsborough and Goya, all without leaving their easy chair. Yet the alarm of self-appointed guardians of good taste grew with the expansion of the fashion for graphic surrogates: Barbey d'Aurevilly was not alone.

Not to be intimidated, middlebrows struck back. In 1884, with the jovial, heavy-handed metaphors so well adapted to its petty bourgeois subscribers, the *Gartenlaube* celebrated the "modern art industry" for turning "the lovely luxury of the richest into the common property of all burghers, so that a sense of beauty and thoroughly cheerful domesticity rises from the first floor to the attic and descends to the cellar, shutting the mouth and paralyzing the fist of crudity and ugliness."[6] The art industry did no such thing; it neither silenced nor disarmed anyone, and the clan of pedagogues devoted to raising the public's taste found it necessary to intensify their mission to the middling and lower bourgeoisie. The quantity of art in people's houses was surging, but what of the quality?

Wrestling with the craving of bourgeois for instruction, books of advice on

manners and on home furnishings issued warning against unworthy imitations.
Some even rejected the more respectable ones—they belonged, this stern wisdom held, not on the wall but in a portfolio to be produced on special occasions. The question of choice remained acute. Should one buy modern
etchings of genre scenes designed for the purpose of mass distribution, or a
well-made reproduction of a Rubens or a Raphael? In 1868, in his authoritative *Hints on Household Taste,* Sir Charles Eastlake, painter, connoisseur, director
of the National Gallery, firmly laid down a rule that most discerning bourgeois
could endorse: choose "the humblest type of Turkey carpet or the cheapest
hearthrug from Seinde, and be sure it will afford you more lasting eye-pleasure
than any English imitation."[7] The truth lay in original objects—and might even
turn out to be affordable.

Surviving illustrations of nineteenth-century bourgeois interiors suggest
that this counsel had only limited impact. Reproductions of old masters ranging in price and quality became cherished decor. Among these reminders of
mastery, Dürer's hands folded in prayer, Leonardo da Vinci's *Last Supper,*
Raphael's *Sistine Madonna,* or a Rembrandt self-portrait held pride of place.*
Their grip on the middle-class imagination emerges from the moody, revealing recollections of the poet and novelist Rudolf Binding, the son of a law professor at the University of Leipzig. One day around 1880, he sat in his parents'
reception room and mused on it with fresh eyes as though he had never been
there before. He saw uncomfortable and showy chairs and couches, heavy curtains, all the furniture loaded down with fringes, tassels, knots. Red velvet and
plush were everywhere; the upholsterer, Binding thought, had triumphed. All
available surfaces were laden with family photos, many in plush frames. And the
pictures to which the family had resigned themselves (or which they really
treasured) were well-produced "colored reproductions of the great wall paintings by Raphael and Michelangelo," imported from England.[8] Even if the
Binding family would have admired Liebermann's *Gänserupferinnen,* which is
unlikely, they would have been unwilling, probably unable, to invest so much
cash in art.

Nor could they have managed copies of masterpieces, oils that matched
their models in size, color, materials—and appearance—as closely as talent and
practice could make them. To buy one required an income in the upper reaches of the middle classes. In 1862, the powerful and affluent French politician

---

* A watercolor done around 1859, showing the study of the eminent *Germanist* Wilhelm
Grimm in the year of his death, displays several small pictures, life-size busts of Athena, Goethe,
and Schiller, and, most prominent of all, a large reproduction of the *Sistine Madonna.* Only the
chalk-white busts mark Grimm's study as that of a scholar; the rest, especially the Raphael, look
like the kind of adornment one might see in any solid bourgeois household.

Adolphe Thiers, temporarily between high government posts, showed an interviewer around his apartment in Paris. It was laden with works of art, and Thiers told his visitor that while his "small fortune" did not permit him to collect on the scale "of our greatest financiers," he could indulge his love of art with more modest, but apparently none too modest, expenditures. He had amassed an impressive collection of Rembrandt etchings and Dürer woodcuts, and a few copies—some of them full-size—of the old masters.[9]

Copies from the Italian, Dutch, or Flemish masters had long been the most desirable substitutes for the originals, and the Victorian century begot a veritable industry devoted to paintings of paintings. A highly paid surgeon like Theodor Billroth, a German teaching and practicing in Vienna, could adorn his music room with respectable copies of Correggio, Caravaggio, and Rubens.[10] Copyists became a familiar sight to the museumgoer with their folding chair, portable easel, and intense stare. Their drudgery was by no means reserved for dilettantes; it formed a common element in the training of aspiring artists in academies and private ateliers. When in 1850 Edouard Manet applied for permission to copy in the Louvre, he did so as the pupil of Thomas Couture, and in his apprentice years he did Tintorettos, Rembrandts, Bouchers. Around the same time, that artistic and political enthusiast Gustave Courbet copied the Dutch and Spanish painters he valued most: Rembrandt, Hals, Velázquez, Ribera. When Madame Morisot took her three talented daughters to the Lyonnais artist Joseph Guichard for instruction in painting, his first piece of advice was to have her apply for a permit to let Berthe, the most clearly gifted of the sisters, work in the Louvre.[11]

A few detractors denounced the practice as deadening ancestor worship. Edmond Duranty, novelist and anti-academic critic, made a fierce mock confession in 1856: "I have just come from the Louvre. If I had had matches I would have set fire to that catacomb, without remorse, firmly convinced that I would have served the cause of the art to come." Several decades later, Camille Pissarro echoed these incendiary intentions: "the necropolises of art," he said, should be burned to the ground.[12] Yet the Impressionists, all but Monet and Sisley, dutifully did their copying and found it useful, at times even inspiring. Mainly concentrating like their more conventional brethren on Rubens and the great Venetians, they schooled their eye, improved their technical facility, and paid their tributes to greatness. Cézanne, in awe of Delacroix's genius, copied and adapted his work some twenty-two times, and busied himself with an El Greco.[13] Whatever Pissarro might say, copying could be a road to innovation.

It could also be a road to pecuniary success. A copyist who managed to render a classic with striking fidelity was destined to make a reputation. His was so honorable a practice that his name would be highly visible, a source of pride rather than embarrassment.* At times painters copied themselves, on demand. Arnold Böcklin's *Isle of the Dead* of 1880, a nocturnal, portentous seascape that he had painted for a young widow who asked for a picture to dream by, proved so fashionable that Böcklin himself did four further versions. Predictably, this enigmatic and moody *Toteninsel* soon featured in countless bourgeois households in engravings or photogravures—copies on a lower level.

Making copies cost money, then, usually less than the copyist hoped for and more than most *Bildungsbürger* could manage. Yet, even when artists were dissatisfied with their stipends, they rarely minded the assignment; after all, it sent them to Paris, to Madrid, or, best of all, to Rome. The young Franz Lenbach spent three instructive years in Italy from 1864 on, copying Titians, Tintorettos, Giorgiones for the German collector Count Schack. In the summer of 1865, one of his cultivated friends from Munich, Rosalie Braun-Artaria, came upon Lenbach in the Uffizi at Florence, doing a Rubens self-portrait for Schack, and exclaimed over the "magnificently successful copy, which stood like a second original beside the first." A prodigiously rich northerner settled in Munich, Schack could play the Maecenas, commissioning promising painters to stock his treasure trove with plausible versions of old masters; he was said to have about 100,000 marks a year, of which he frugally spent only one-sixth, leaving the rest for art. He guaranteed Lenbach a stipend of 1,000 gulden for the first year, 1,400 for the second, and 2,000 for the third, sums that would relieve any young artist of financial worries. But with time the chore lost its charm for Lenbach; in 1868, he informed his patron from Madrid that he had had enough. He wanted to focus on his own "productive aims."[14]

Other copyists were no less skillful and no less busy. Henri Fantin-Latour, known for his precise flower pieces and his painted homages to fellow artists, made himself available to supply collectors with faithful replicas. His "true teachers," noted Adolphe Jullien, his friend and biographer, in 1909, "were in the Louvre." Everyone called him, Jullien noted, "the painter par excellence of the middle class and bourgeois society, some to praise him, others to make fun of him."[15] Among the best clients of these copyists were Americans intent on giving the small private museums they had founded some glimpses of immortal works of art. The Athenaeum at St. Johnsbury, Vermont, for one, has amid other excellent, clearly identified copies, Thomas Waterman Wood's version of Rosa Bonheur's *Plowing on the Nivernais.*[16] Thus local art lovers intent on seeing masterpieces could save themselves a trip to Europe.

* The Century Club in New York has a full-scale copy of Correggio's *Antiope*, identified on the label as dating from 1809, after the painting in the Louvre, by John Vanderlyn, then a prominent American history painter living in Paris. On the label his name appears far larger, far more prominent, than that of Correggio.

Reproductions in varied techniques, then, satisfied a sizable spectrum of more or less substantial burghers. The most astute entrepreneurs addressed several of these markets on the same occasion. Even three-mark tracts on art advertised collections of engravings by prominent German painters at fairly high prices, most of them inaccessible to the bulk of their readership.[17] In 1880, Otto von Leixner, journalist, essayist, poet, and editor, used as the frontispiece for a collection of studies on aesthetics a collotype of Angelica Kauffmann's painting of a vestal virgin, and advertised engravings of it at 150, 30, or 25 marks, promising the "artistic rendition" to be "a masterpiece which does justice to the beauty of the original in every respect."[18] He did not specify what differentiated the engravings he was offering from each other, but it must have been a matter of quality and size alike.[19]

The Photographische Union in Munich resorted to the same technique. In 1899, it advertised a three-volume set offering a selection of "the most outstanding works of the master" Arnold Böcklin, the Swiss painter whom German art lovers had begun to embrace a decade or more earlier for his virile mermen and hefty mermaids, and for cryptic nocturnes like the *Isle of the Dead*. The sets cost a generally prohibitive 100 or 200 marks each. But those interested in a single Böcklin could ask the publisher for a price list of photogravures or photographs. And in the same year, people with modest means intent only on being introduced to Böcklin's muscular, rhetorical art could buy a sixty-page essay by Professor Dr. Max Lehrs for 1 mark 50. A small shopkeeper needed to put in only about three hours to acquire this informative little monograph. We have seen it before: the culture industry had learned to have something for everyone.

The cost of music made the same accommodations. Except for socialites who took a box to satisfy their gregariousness or pursue sexual adventures, concertgoers came for a musical experience they had usually had before. Conductors and soloists had, of course, distinct predilections and might smuggle into programs unfamiliar, hence difficult, numbers. But they also tacitly allowed subscribers some say in the making of programs. Audience-tested symphonies or concertos, arias or sonatas, became staples of the repertory because there was a demonstrable clamor for them. They were popular because they were popular. And nineteenth-century merchants of culture tailored concerts and recitals, just as they did pictures, not just to some all-purpose taste but more precisely to the size of their customers' purses. Whether conventional or venturesome, concert managers developed a scale of ticket prices to gratify the social elite and the middle-income bourgeois without forgetting the student or the petty clerk.

Munich, proud of its high culture, provides some suggestive examples.* On June 10, 1865, for the world premiere of Wagner's *Tristan und Isolde* at the Nationaltheater, the ticket for the most desirable boxes went for 15 gulden (about 25 marks), a sum at which even a professor might balk, especially if he wanted to take his family. But for poverty-stricken Wagnerites there was the lowly "Parterre" at 48 kronen (about 1 mark 20) or, still more modest, the "Galerie," which cost a mere 24 kronen, or some 60 pfennig. Tickets for "ordinary operas" were pitched at prices more affordable than those of most Wagner performances; and by the 1870s, on royal command, selected nonsubscription evenings had lowered prices still further.

Even Wagner became relatively accessible: on February 13, 1886, the Munich opera put on a *Flying Dutchman* "at reduced prices," ranging from 4 marks to 60 pfennig. The management thoughtfully discriminated among the beneficiaries entitled to such reductions: on January 10, 1886, it mounted a matinee of Charles Gounod's *Romeo and Juliet* for the fund benefiting the company's widows and orphans with tickets from 1 mark 50 down to 50 pfennig. The latter price was reserved for students at Munich's two universities and students at the Academy of Fine Arts; and, responsive to the pupils at the Royal School of Music and secondary school students, the management put their admission at 40 pfennig. It was in this spirit that the Munich Philharmonic Orchestra, founded in 1893, staged affordable evenings with the highest-priced ticket set at 1 mark—which would cost a lowly bureaucrat less than two hours' exertion.

The theater, too, regularly featured nonsubscription performances at especially modest rates: in January 1886, the Nationaltheater offered *The Merchant of Venice* with tickets no higher than 2 marks 50, the lowest-priced seat costing a mere 30 pfennig. In general, and not only in Germany, plays both classic and modern were more affordable than operas, to which, for all their managers' efforts to attract the impecunious, a certain aristocratic aura continued to cling long after the titled had been reduced to a small minority in the audience.[20] In contrast, the theater became a favorite middle-class entertainment, each country of course identifying its pleasures in its own way. French plays about the demimonde or adorable courtisans, which filled Parisian houses, did not seem appropriate for Germany unless they had treacle poured over them.

The fervor of missionaries agonizing over the level of German culture was, as we have seen, aimed at all social strata. But while graduates of the *Gymnasium,* even of the university, might need guidance in distinguishing the authentic from the meretricious, the segment the reformers worried over most was the

---

* I shall offer a detailed analysis of Munich's culture in "The Geography of Taste."

Mittelstand. This sizable segment of the German middle orders has had an even worse press than the bourgeoisie as a whole. It has been accused of indulging in the politics of *ressentiment* with devastating consequences, and of living contentedly in an aesthetic desert with no wish to emulate their betters.

But this is simplistic and heartless. Simplistic because the petty bourgeoisie was not a monolithic entity; heartless because try as they might, denizens of the *Mittelstand* found it exceedingly hard to overcome the handicaps built into their economic lot. Only the most determined could gather up the leisure and the energy after a hard week's toil, or for that matter the money, to haunt museums, or follow compositions in the concert hall with a score, let alone travel to improve their hazy acquaintance with what they had long prized from a distance. Their perpetual fear of social descent haunted them. Those who saved their meager assets for culture, then, were making a distinct choice of how they wanted to live, favoring beauty over beer, self-improvement over self-indulgence. Yet despite these creditable exceptions, German cultural pedagogues had a point in detecting among Germany's *Kleinbürger* an identifiable taste in which few could take pride. Their most valued teachers, family weeklies like the *Gartenlaube* or its Catholic counterpart, *Daheim,* did nothing to stretch their aesthetic imagination.

In abundantly illustrated numbers, these periodicals and their imitators pursued a safe cultural agenda. When they spoke of art, they polemicized against the "naked realism" of painters like Courbet, who to their mind extolled the ugly at the expense of the comely. When they reported on an international exhibition, they would congratulate themselves on how well their compatriots had performed in the face of a world that thought them barbarians. These great fairs struck them as fights to the finish in which Germans went all out to win the wars of art—decisively. Covering the German paintings represented at the 1878 Parisian World's Fair for the *Gartenlaube,* Fritz Wernick observed that, organized in an amazingly short time and crammed into a small suite of rooms, the offering had incontestably "become the most beautiful of all the art exhibitions." The superiority of German generalship had been demonstrated once again on the battleground of painting and sculpture. In Paris (which, no one could forget, German armies had entered as a victorious enemy only seven years before), "our Germany has secured a brilliant victory with the smallest army." The gathering of German paintings had "struck like a bomb."[21]

This chauvinist tone was maladroit, to be sure, yet it usefully reminds the historian once again that nationalist fervor could be as potent in the politics of culture as in any other domain. But in a patriotic mood or not, family magazines were resolutely set against any touches of modernism, which, with some striking exceptions, was a cosmopolitan venture. They defended academicism by featuring a full-page engraving of a conventional painting or two in every issue and, late in the century, handed out portfolios as premiums. Their art ran to the sentimental, the humorous, or the pious. Anecdote was king.

Examples abound. At an outdoor feast a shy Italian beauty, eyes lowered and hands clasped, waits for a swain, no less bashful, fingering his hat, to ask her to dance. A schoolboy wearing a guilty expression—he has doubtless been caught fighting or with his hand in the cookie jar—stands before the principal, who, birch rod in hand, is about to administer painful justice. A pair of putti flutter above the head of a mother smiling rapturously at her infant. In a well-stocked cellar, two or three corpulent, bibulous monks taste the wine they are supposed to be bottling. Christ takes in the bustle of a modern city, his expression at once compassionate and troubled. A kitten and a puppy fight peacefully over a ball of wool. A mighty stag bestriding a hilltop utters his mating call. Kaiser Wilhelm and his consort sit together stiffly on a sofa, incarnating in their dignified way the German family ideal. Or the kaiser stands alone, wearing one of his elaborate uniforms and leaning on a sword, glowering at the viewer as if to enforce a rush of patriotic emotion.

For *Bürger* who chose to frame such decorative items, the Nazarenes, let alone the Expressionists, might as well never have painted. The makers of modernist culture retaliated with impatience and disdain; they read these flights from strenuous pleasures as symptoms of middle-class ignorance and invincible sloth. In 1829, Berlioz had a "naive" conversation with François Adrien Boieldieu, composer of smooth, highly successful comic operas, who advised him to compromise with the bland taste of the day rather than insist on writing outlandish pieces that even trained musicians could not follow. Recalling this encounter years later, Berlioz suggested that Boieldieu was only voicing French tastes dominant at the time. The "*gros public* wanted relaxing music," he wrote in his *Mémoires;* it wanted music "a bit dramatic" and "colorless," quite "free of extraordinary harmonies, unusual rhythms, new forms, unexpected effects"— music that "demanded from its interpreters and its listeners neither major talents nor close attention." Since then, Berlioz added, things had only got worse.[22]

He was speaking for resentful serious Victorian composers, painters, playwrights, novelists. One other pronouncement among many belongs here, for it strikingly echoes the tone of Berlioz's biting scorn for the middlebrow customers in the marketplace of culture. In 1855, the celebrated violinist Joseph Joachim wrote his close friend Johannes Brahms, "The public *en gros*" consists of "people addicted to entertainment," people who badger true artists with their "crude expectations."[23] Technical finish, that witness to proficient craftsmanship and modest claims on aesthetic intelligence, ranked high among these strata of the public. No wonder that aristocrats of the brush and pen thought the democratizing tendencies in the arts synonymous with the triumph of vulgarity; no wonder that representative spokesmen for the self-selected bourgeois elite, sensitive and educated enough to grasp the intentions of controversial artists, found themselves reiterating the alarms they heard from the geniuses they idolized.

Their laments were not mainly the condescension of upper-middle-class snobs: the bourgeois masses (which, we know, included sizable portions of the educated) did need to cultivate a receptivity to unfamiliar sights and sounds, to acquire the experience and train the mental suppleness necessary to welcome the innovative rather than remain mired in the commonplace.* To appreciate the finest in art and music is a trial for human nature: it calls for the hard work of breaking the cake of custom for the sake of discriminating pleasures running counter to the pressure for simplicity and mere relaxation in rare leisure hours. Cultural conservatism came naturally, like all conservatism; the avant-gardes were boldly defying a prominent ingredient in human nature, the fear of the unfamiliar.

3. Limits and Possibilities

It would be easy to duplicate from other sources this sketch of economic and aesthetic hierarchies; the limits set and the possibilities open to bourgeois purchasers of high culture showed remarkably similar profiles everywhere, from Scandinavia to the Mediterranean. Even Americans, nervous about the lower middle class, set aside the ideology of the open frontier and of classless equality; straining to raise their countrymen's taste to an acceptable level, they largely followed the European model.

A canvass of the cultural temptations for the British middle classes tells much about these family resemblances. The most effective adjustment to the financial capacities of all ranks in Britain was, of course, as it was elsewhere, a range of prices for roughly similar experiences. In 1848, a teapot designed by

---

* This was no secret to the nineteenth century. As early as 1810, Bettina von Arnim, a lively, intelligent, politically progressive critic of her culture and a self-invited friend of the great, told Goethe that she found it odd to see music being considered incomprehensible: "Hence that rage against what has not yet been heard, not only because it was not understood, but also because it was not even known. Humans stand before music like a sawhorse; the familiar they can stand, not because they grasp it, but because they are used to it, like the donkey with its daily burden." Bettina von Arnim to Goethe, [Christmas 1810], *Werke und Briefe,* ed. Gustav Konrad and Joachim Müller, 5 vols. (1959–63), V, 103.

the painter Richard Redgrave and manufactured by James Dixon and Sons of
Sheffield could be purchased for 20 guineas in silver, £2 in silver plate, and 16s.
in a tin alloy called "Britannia-metal," which looked like silver.[1] Organizations
providing operas or dramas found this strategy perfectly congenial. The King's
Theatre, appropriately renamed Her Majesty's Theatre after Queen Victoria's
accession, was the principal opera house in London until 1847, when Covent
Garden opened as its rival. Her Majesty's Theatre could accommodate an audience of roughly 2,500, with 900 places taken up by the boxes, and 800 each by
the pit and the gallery. Naturally the boxholders, who occupied the most
sought-after places, were the targets of the managers' special solicitude. But less
affluent opera lovers could find seats in the pit and the gallery ranging from
10s. 6d. down to 3s.[2]

These ticket prices for opera sound reasonable enough, but even the most
modest place in the gallery meant a substantial outlay for a lower-middle-class
London family, rather more than it was likely to find comfortable. The local
theater was easier on the purse: the lowest-priced ticket for a play at the Drury
Lane was one shilling, and in 1846 the newly decorated Sadler's Wells Theater
advertised a gallery seat for Shakespeare's Henry IV, Part One at six pence. This
was manageable but still wanted thinking about; for the petty bourgeoisie thrift
was not just a moral ideal but a fact of life. Dickens recognized this predica-
ment from the beginning of his career. Most three-volume novels of his time
cost a guinea and a half, and this induced him to have his major novels published in nineteen monthly installments—the last a double number—costing
one shilling each, that is to say a pound for the whole, the expense spread over
a year and a half.

That was the sort of levy on the purse to which those condemned to rigorous economies could respond. A shilling was also the price of admission to
Madame Tussaud's waxworks, complete with a tour of the Chamber of Hor-
rors. And from 1844 on, music lovers could buy, for the same amount, a number of the Musical Times and Singing-Class, which conveniently included the
notes to an anthem or a part-song in each issue.[3] When a middle-class family
earned around £150 a year—and thousands barely did—this was the kind of
pleasure in which they might safely indulge.

In fact, in a society with a rapidly growing appetite for their services, clerks
had even after long service very little to spare once they had met the necessities of respectable living. In his posthumous Autobiography, Anthony Trollope
recalled that in 1834, at nineteen, his starting salary as a clerk in the General
Post Office was £90 per annum, and he smiled wryly in retrospect at the
thought that he had been expected to live on that, no matter how unpreten-
tiously, without help from his family. By 1841, his pay had risen, along with his

responsibilities, to £140. When he went to Ireland for the post office in that year, his income, based on a combination of fees and salary, dramatically multiplied to £400. Even this, although most middle-class young Britishers thought they could marry on it, far from satisfied Trollope.

But, then, he made greater demands on life than most: he wanted to keep a good house over his head, insure his life, educate his two boys, and "hunt perhaps twice a-week," and he could not accommodate all this until he earned £1,400 a year, nearly half of it from publishers, a sum that a successful physician or attorney would have found almost lavish.[4] If in 1841, years before he became a highly paid novelist, he had wanted to hear an opera at Her Majesty's Theatre, he would have had to invest five or six hours' work for a good seat in the pit.

If he had wanted to buy a painting, however, even Trollope the novelist would have had to think twice. At English auctions old masters, knocked down to private collectors or museums, ran from £300 to £3,000 and for an exceptional gem even more. Some seventeenth-century Dutch paintings, unless they were securely assigned to Rembrandt or the popular Hobbema, proved to be bargains: in 1844, the National Gallery acquired a Gerard Dou self-portrait for just over £150, the sum at which a British subject began to pay income tax.[5] The best-known of contemporary painters, too, fetched prices that would give middling bourgeois pause. True, William Morris bought Ford Madox Brown's *The Hayfield* for a reasonable £40, but Landseers went for around £300, Turners for £250 to £400, about a year's top salary for reliable clerks after many years of loyal service, or three to four months' work for a rising physician. The 3,000 guineas that Queen Victoria paid in 1863 for William Frith's *Marriage of the Prince of Wales* defined him as an artist for the rich.

But quite like other countries, Britain provided remedies for art lovers who craved a masterpiece old or new but found their urges outrunning their means. The country had long trained distinguished practitioners in the craft of copying: in etchings and engravings, lithographs and other modern techniques. "Original works of art, whether in oil or water-colours are only within reach of the wealthy," wrote Sir Charles Eastlake, among his other accomplishments a trusted cicerone to good taste, in 1872. "But photographs and good wood-engravings are procurable at a moderate cost, and are far more serviceable than chromo-lithography in the development of household taste."[6] The trade in reproductions flourished mightily: in 1859, the London dealer Ernest Gambart bought the rights to engrave Frith's large canvas *Derby Day* for £1,500 and followed it up the year after with the rights to Holman Hunt's *Christ in the Temple* for a staggering £5,500.

Plainly there was much money to be made in the business, especially since the absence of international copyright permitted pirates to put out reproductions and save themselves the royalties. In 1891, Luke Fildes sold a large painting, *The Doctor*, to the sugar magnate Sir Henry Tate for £3,000. In a disheveled attic that proclaims poverty, on a pallet improvised with some chairs and pillows, a sick girl lies under a blanket; seated near her, chin in hand, a kind-looking bearded physician leans forward as he studies his patient intently. The canvas—according to its defenders a triumph of sentiment over sentimentality—was a natural for the engraver, and copies were sold by the untold thousands in Britain and the United States, the latter enjoying freedom from the hardship of paying for the rights. And for those who could not afford, or would not bother, to buy an engraving there was the pleasure of looking: in 1860, Hunt's *Christ*, on view at the German Gallery in London for a shilling a person, is reported to have earned some £4,000.[7]

For all the varieties in bourgeois tastes, most of them held few surprises.* Most but not all; although the income of collectors was usually proportionate to the prestige of the artists they fancied, that prestige was never quite secure. Not even Rembrandt escaped carping criticism. The Victorian century, that age of debates, offered irresistible opportunities for disputes over taste to play themselves out in the press, at auctions, in museum acquisitions, or with private collectors. Fashions in beauty, even in the classics, shifted across the century as critics rediscovered major but virtually forgotten artists.† And the international quality of the art market, with French dealers mounting shows in the United States, English painters finding buyers among Germans, Russian collectors going to Paris, made for unexpected confrontations. It is a commonplace, confirmed by the Victorians again and again, that new styles arouse opposition

* Among others, John Ruskin, speaking of two English watercolorists he admired, Samuel Prout and William Hunt, recognized the impact of status on taste; their art, he wrote in 1879, "seemed admirable, though not pretending to greatness, and we felt to be delightful, though not provoking enthusiasm, in the quiet and little diverted lives of the English middle classes." Their "drawings of this simple character were made for these same middle classes, exclusively; and even for the second order of the middle classes, more accurately expressed by the term *bourgeoisie*. The great people always bought Canaletto, not Prout, and Van Huysum, not Hunt." While their "bright little water-colours" would look "pert in ghostly corridors, and petty in halls of state," they "gave an unquestionable tone of liberal-mindedness to a suburban villa," and worked cheerfully in a "moderate-sized breakfast-parlour opening on a nicely-mown lawn." Once one has got over Ruskin's condescending tone, one may use this statement as a fair description of the range among middle-class buyers of art. *Notes by Mr. Ruskin on Samuel Prout and William Hunt* (1879–80), in *The Works of John Ruskin*, ed. E. T. Cook and Alexander Wedderburn, 39 vols. (1903–12), XIV, 373–74.

† As we shall see, astonishingly, Vermeer was one of them.

before the culture-loving public first makes peace with them and then, after fervently adopting them, wonders how it could ever have failed to recognize these masters. Thus the passage of time and the tides of taste transformed unsalable works of art into treasures fetching astronomical prices.

Toward the last decades of the century, middle-class taste seemed to be on the move, following more or less reluctantly impulses given by innovative architects, painters, composers, playwrights. In the 1860s, Eastlake's *Hints on Household Taste* had carried the flag of the small, brave band fighting what, despite visible improvement, it never tired of lamenting as the middle classes' deplorable fondness for false glamour. Enjoying several editions in Britain, and at least seven in the United States, the book assailed the gulf that had opened up between the theory of design and the fashion for artifacts that householders saw and handled every day. Popular taste, Eastlake asserted, was "commonplace," seduced by the latest fad, indiscriminately enamored of what insinuating salesmen called "elegant" or "striking," and pathetically ignorant of "the faculty of distinguishing good from bad design in the familiar objects of domestic life."[8] The best hope, he hinted, was a book like his, lavishly illustrated, mercifully untechnical, and refreshing in its opinionated choice of examples.

In 1866, in a history of modern taste the Austrian writer Jakob von Falke also dwelt with visible abhorrence on the kitsch that passed for art. His *History of Modern Taste* proved almost as compelling for central European readers as Eastlake's *Hints on Household Taste* had been in Britain and the United States. But fourteen years later, in a new edition, he was cheered to report "fresh and active new life." As he saw it, the Great Exhibition of 1851 at the Crystal Palace had laid bare the "misery to its full extent," and its lessons, absorbed mainly by the British, had led to a welcome renovation.[9] The private art associations that had first sprung up around 1800 in several countries and multiplied in the nineteenth century—by 1896 there were ninety of them, with around 100,000 members across Germany—participated in the didactic enterprise with exhibitions and auctions that featured selected reproductions. These societies of dilettantes explicitly aimed at wider elements among the cultivated public that were fortunately affluent enough to make use of the instruction they provided.

Despite these heartening developments, skepticism about bourgeois taste survived, even grew. A critic of the middle class like Eastlake was himself soon under fire for his reactionary, Gothicizing designs. Conflicts over beauty lasted unabated well beyond the 1880s and could engage the passions of publics larger than art critics or a handful of patrons. The Arts and Crafts movement in Britain, Art nouveau in France, the Werkbund in Vienna, struggling late in the nineteenth century and early in the twentieth to purify the aesthetic landscape, were so many reproaches to prevalent bourgeois taste. Each of them made scathing remarks at the middle classes' mundane surroundings, their furniture, cutlery, china, curtains, floors and walls, down to the hardware on doors and windows.

Eastlake's strictures on the self-satisfied and uninformed members of the middle classes who "know what they like" sounded severe enough until William Morris began to write and lecture. "Apart from the desire to produce beautiful things," he wrote in 1894, two years before his death, "the leading passion of my life has been and is hatred of modern civilization." He loathed its "contempt of simple pleasures which everyone could enjoy but for its folly" and its "eyeless vulgarity." The "quasi-artistic of the middle classes" were hoping to "make art grow when it has no longer any root." Hence, as a designer and later in life as a socialist, he found himself in "practical conflict with the philistinism of modern society."[10] No one doubts that Morris was a remarkable designer, and he stood as a model of probity and originality; yet—and he was painfully aware of the paradox—his products did little for the lower segments of the middle classes: they were far too expensive for them. And an uncritical acceptance of his diagnosis of bourgeois life has proved almost as damaging as a naive reading of Flaubert; however valuable Morris's work, however valiant his crusade against the evils of capitalism, he nourished the legend of an irreparable split between the aesthetic avant-garde and the anti-aesthetic bourgeoisie, a legend that has long survived him.

This myth found particularly obstinate support in France, where conflicts over high culture were fought out with exceptional virulence fed by pervasive political acrimony. But even in that country, cultural entrepreneurs were not in the business of pitting avant-garde purists against bourgeois philistines. Far from despising their potential lower-middle-class customers, they priced their offerings to lure them into the opera house or the concert hall, into buying low-cost reproductions of classic paintings or graphic works explicitly made for the market. In Paris, and to a lesser extent in the provinces, the nineteenth-century artistic and musical fare was as rich and as controversial as it was anywhere, probably more stimulating. Neoclassical painters feuded with romantics, academic painters felt the sting of critics committed to the Barbizon landscapists and, later, the Impressionists.

In Paris, the stakes were just as high in music. Operagoers, we know, took to the press to defend their cherished entertainment against the invasion of sober-sided Germans, and demanding concerts faced the appealing competition of operettas. The capital had a hall for every genre of music: operas, oratorios, symphonies, quartets, sonatas, operettas, and "light" classics for jaded or unsophisticated spirits. Once the city of Giacomo Meyerbeer, Paris became the

city of Jacques Offenbach, and it remained hospitable to magicians like Nic-
colò Paganini and Liszt and to dedicated conductors like François Antoine
Habeneck, the tireless champion of Beethoven.

As everywhere, in France prices were pitched to specific levels. When, in
1840, Hector Berlioz devoted a concert to his compositions, the price of
admission ranged from two francs to ten. During the empire of Napoleon III,
the top ticket to a single seat at the opera was twelve francs; it was to meet the
needs of the relatively impecunious that the Conservatoire launched, in 1861,
the Concerts populaires de musique classique, at which the best seat cost five
francs—two days of a laborer's wages.

These spreads inadequately reflect the gap between rich and poor in France:
the pyramid of income, even when picturing only bourgeois, was far steeper
than this. After the 1850s, a schoolteacher earned on the average some 1,500
francs a year, which sufficed—just—for an unpretentious way of life. A salary
of 2,000 francs, the top for his profession (unless he was appointed a school
principal and rose to 3,000 francs), was also the ceiling for an elite of skilled
craftsmen: a printer might take home about 1,800 francs. After devoting years
to compiling an unblemished record and attracting affluent regular customers,
sales clerks in the grandiose new department stores and the elegant specialty
shops that had survived the onslaught of the *grands magasins* could count on
3,000 francs, including commissions. Clerks in the Ministry of Finance, who
drew better than average salaries among bureaucrats, started at 1,900 francs a
year and could double that and a bit more after rising through the ranks. Their
earnings of 4,000 to 5,000 francs roughly matched that of a thriving small
shopkeeper.[11]

That level, which most Frenchmen could only envy, was the starting point
for engineers employed by the railroads or by mine owners, though at the summit of their careers they could count on anywhere between two and five times
that: the severe training at the Ecole Polytechnique paid off handsomely.
Lawyers, physicians, higher clerics had 8,000 francs at a minimum, depending
in part on where they lived, and at best ten or twelve times as much. High-
ranking public servants took home salaries from 12,000 (a prefect) to 25,000
francs (a presiding judge in a court of appeals), figures that successful businessmen and the most comfortably situated among the rentiers, a tribe strongly
represented in France, matched and often surpassed.

Exceptional talents had their own ways of making money. While obscure
orchestra musicians, who were easily replaced, might earn no more than 1,000
to 1,200 francs a year, a virtuoso—an acclaimed pianist, violinist, or soprano
—could command that much for a single performance; it was possible, if
exceedingly rare, for a star to be offered a contract guaranteeing 30,000 francs

a year.* Still in his twenties, in the short span between 1821 and 1828, Adolphe
Thiers, who we know had started from the humblest of circumstances, earned
125,000 francs with his journalism and his monumental *History of the French
Revolution,* a project he would follow up with the even bulkier, no less profitable, *History of the Consulate and the Empire.* And Victor Hugo estimated that
in the first half of his literary career, from 1817 to 1845, he had made about
550,000 francs—almost 20,000 a year. Only the financial aristocracy of industrialists, bankers, rentiers, and speculators, who disposed over half a million
francs a year or more, could condescend to such numbers.

Naturally these capitalists were in a position to buy everything in sight.
What of government clerks or middling merchants? None of them thinking of
having their wife or daughter polish their piano playing would have solicited
the services of Chopin or Liszt, who in the 1830s charged twenty francs a lesson. The customary fee for such instruction, one franc (plus twenty-five cen-
times if the teacher came to the house) would have had to do.[12] As for art, *bon
bourgeois* would read in the newspapers about astronomical prices for Salon
favorites and be entitled to speculate that affordable versions might soon
become available. In the late 1860s, Zola made the point tersely with some sardonic comments: Gérôme, that favorite among academic artists, whom we shall
meet again, "paints a picture so that this picture can be reproduced through
photography or engraving and sell thousands of copies. Here the subject is
everything, the painting is nothing: the reproduction is worth more than the
work itself."[13] Ordinary French bourgeois disposed to social satire could frame
a Daumier clipped from *Charivari,* to which he contributed regularly; if they
preferred sentimental or religious pictures for their walls, they could cannibal-
ize other illustrated periodicals.

There was a time in the 1870s when moderately well-to-do Frenchmen
could have aspired to an Impressionist without going deeply into debt: few
wanted these subversives. Paul Durand-Ruel, the Impressionists' favorite dealer, a combination of commercial manipulator and principled lover of modern
art, first bought Sisleys and Renoirs for 200 to 300 francs and tried to sell them
at a reasonable markup; Pissarros could be had for less than that. As late as 1881,
Monet agreed to deliver twenty-two paintings to Durand-Ruel for 300 francs
apiece.[14] A government clerk in mid-career would have had to work about a
month and a half to raise this sum. A few of the leading figures among the anti-
academics—mainly Manet, Degas, Caillebotte, and Cézanne—had private
financial resources, but most of the Impressionists needed to make their living

* In the Vienna of the early nineteenth century, a leading lady could count on 5,000 gulden a
year, while an ordinary musician in the opera made (after ten years' steady service) less than 500
gulden. Alice M. Hanson, *Musical Life in Biedermeier Vienna* (1985), 20–21.

by their art. Bogged down in poverty in their early years, they would borrow money from Durand-Ruel to buy materials and free time, fortunate to have a dealer endowed with an unfailing eye for new art and a shrewd sense for its commercial possibilities. Willing to wager on their future reputation, he would send the Impressionists the small sums for which they regularly importuned him.

In helping these unknowns, Durand-Ruel helped himself even more. In 1866, reviewing the annual Salon in Paris, Emile Zola, Cézanne's school friend and for some two decades the Impressionists' energetic champion, predicted that "in fifty years" the price of Manet's provocative canvases would rise fifteen or twenty times.[15] To Durand-Ruel's delight, this forecast proved conservative. One day in 1873, he recalled in his candid, businesslike reminiscences, he visited Manet and bought all he saw in the studio, twenty-three pictures, for 35,000 francs. In the years ahead, he sold most of his Manets, then bought back some of them for resale at a vast markup. In the end, he grossed about a million francs. He could not have done so without the American collectors who were entering the European market, men and women whose bank accounts and willingness to pay seemed unlimited.* But in the 1870s and even the 1880s, an Impressionist would have been a possible luxury for the middling middle classes.

The years of bargains did not last long. If in 1881 Monet had to be satisfied with 300 francs, three years later he could already demand double or four times that much. In 1897, at a London sale, Pissarro reported to his painter son Lucien, Monet sold "a dozen things, five or six of them first-rate"; one went for 21,000 francs. The celebrities among academic artists had been realizing such spectacular prices for decades. At this very sale, Pissarro noted, a Daubigny brought 72,000 francs, while "an admirable Corot, a marvelous landscape which reduced the Daubigny to nothing," made only 7,000 francs. "This sort of thing," he commented bitterly, "is incomprehensible!"[16]

To the Impressionists, Jean Léon Gérôme's success was even more irritating. His polished, coolly sensual canvases stood for everything they held in contempt; a colorist especially accomplished doing the flesh tones of female nudes, he had his early painting *Cock Fight* go to the Luxembourg Palace for 20,000 francs. In 1863, Thoré disparaged Gérôme's "meticulously finished miniatures," but plainly French officialdom and art lovers with ample disposable cash had other views.[17] Gérôme garnered every award open to the academy, the state, and private citizens—gold medals at salons, lucrative government commissions, bids from insatiable collectors. With this came influence as he sat on one

* "American prices" became a widely used epithet in Europe.

weighty jury after another: a bully pulpit as professor at the Ecole des Beaux-Arts and a compelling voice in French artistic politics.

Pissarro dismissed Gérôme as an "idiot," as "the last straw!"[18] His animus requires no explanation: he and his friends had a long-standing grievance against this star of the salons and his companions in fame and fortune—William Bouguereau, Alexandre Cabanel, Ernest Meissonier—whom reviewers almost automatically mentioned in his company. In thirty years of hard work, Pissarro had earned little more than they had with a single canvas—more than once. Bouguereau got over 20,000 francs for *The Secret,* which the American department store pioneer Alexander T. Stewart commissioned from him. That was almost a two years' salary for a prefect. Cabanel demanded, and obtained, similar prices, and Meissonier, at the height of his career, once received 70,000 francs for a canvas. Compared with that coup, the 20,000 francs that Napoleon III paid for Meissonier's *The Brawl* in 1855 as a gift for Queen Victoria appears downright modest, always presuming the buyer could command the resources of the emperor, or of that magnate among magnates Alexander Stewart, reputed to be one of the three richest men in the United States.[19] True enough, these millionaires had their day and made a difference. But middling and lower bourgeois still had their facsimiles and their fantasies.

❧ TWO ❧

The Geography of Taste

There was one bourgeoisie in the nineteenth century, but it showed a dozen faces and took diverse paths to taste. It might have an identifiable intellectual and emotional style, as Freud told his fiancée, but the variations within this common characteristic were marked.* The education of Parisian bourgeois in art did not match that enjoyed by Berlin's *Bürger,* and, as the following pages will show, Manchester's way of cultivating the pleasures of music or painting would have been unrecognizable in Munich. There was nothing arbitrary or accidental about this diversity. True, Victorian high culture had dynamics of its own; as we have suggested, international exhibitions, peripatetic collectors, traveling art dealers, mobile conductors and virtuosi made it increasingly cosmopolitan and increasingly autonomous. Still, taste was embedded in cultural habits, political institutions, and attitudes to authority that left their imprint. It had, in short, its distinctive geography.

I. Dividends from Commerce

In June 1848, Hermann Leo, a prosperous calico printer in Manchester, went to London to offer the German piano virtuoso Charles Hallé an agreeable, and he hoped irresistible, invitation. Leo was, in Hallé's judgment, "not only a very amiable man, but a most enthusiastic amateur of music and a great connois-

---

* We may think of the bourgeoisie as a closely knit but diverse family.

seur." Like other artists and performers, Hallé had been driven from France by
the February Revolution. Born Carl Halle in Westphalia in 1819, he had for the
past dozen years carved out a notable career in Paris, having slightly adjusted
his name to fit his altered circumstances.

But in the turmoil of early 1848, his repute as a concert pianist, efficiency
as an organizer of chamber music soirees, and friendships with Liszt and
George Sand bought no bread. Hence Hallé, who already enjoyed something
of a reputation in London musical circles, chose to try his luck among them.
Though he was busy performing at musicales and looking for pupils, his
prospects were precarious. The city was swarming with soloists, conductors,
composers from the Continent, all of them competent professionals. "O
damnable Revolution!" Hallé wrote to his parents from London late in April.
"The competition is very keen." He gloomily predicted that the refugees
would "probably end by devouring one another."[1]

In this anxious moment, Leo's offer was welcome. Speaking for like-minded Mancunians, he portrayed his city as "quite ripe *to be taken in hand*" by a
musician as versatile and seasoned as Hallé, "the fittest man to stir the dormant
taste for the art."[2] As a first inducement he offered him a sufficient number of
well-paying pupils, and Hallé accepted, justly persuaded that he was in truth
the right man to awaken Manchester to undimmed musical glories. His wife,
Désirée, enthusiastically agreed to the move; to her, Mr. Leo was "our good
angel," whose wife, "good Mrs. Leo," saw to it that their rented house was
flooded with flowers.[3] It was the auspicious launching of a long, singular track
record.

The sponsors so intent on importing Hallé to take Manchester in hand,
merchants and manufacturers all, had educated and exacting musical palates;
their city had not been a desert before his arrival. Yet it was falling pitifully
short of the professional musicianship that Leo and his friends had come to
expect. Several of these demanding amateurs were, like Leo, cultured capitalists
from the German-Jewish immigrants to Manchester. They and their children
were often widely traveled and exposed to lofty standards of music making at
home. For some of these newcomers, acculturation to English ways involved
abandoning their faith. When Chopin visited Manchester in 1848, he stayed
with "the kind Schwabes" and gave a recital at their house. Salis Schwabe,
Chopin wrote, was one of "the first manufacturers" of Manchester, "a friend of
Cobden and himself a great Free Trader. He is a Jew, but a protestant"; in fact,
both Schwabes had turned Unitarian.[4] Whatever their denomination, these
bourgeois asked for more than Manchester had to offer.

Mancunians who enjoyed such cosmopolitan experiences could draw comparisons, not all of them invidious. Late in January 1848, C. A. Seymour, a gift-

ed violinist, revived quartet concerts that had been inactive for four years. Much to "the delight of musical amateurs," the *Manchester Guardian* noted, the total of fifty subscribers, all that Seymour's house could comfortably accommodate, was quickly reached. A subscription to four concerts cost a guinea or fifteen shillings, clearly for the select few. In the same month Seymour, who far from resenting the newcomer made Hallé a fast friend, also conducted one of eight concerts by the Harmonic Society, and drew some fifteen hundred listeners. Also in January, Louis Jullien, the ingenious French entrepreneur whose traveling band mixed Beethoven with popular songs, offered, in the magnanimous report by the *Guardian*'s music critic, a "varied, brilliant, and interesting" concert to an audience of four thousand.[5]

This is only a sampling of more extensive fare. Manchester had the usual choral groups and one regular orchestra, the Gentlemen's Concerts Society, which took itself seriously as a purveyor of respectable programs and, for decades, as an educator in much needed civility.* But the uncouth manners of the audience were not its chief anxiety; by the 1840s, the quality of the orchestra, all of the players local talent, had noticeably deteriorated. When, in September 1848, Hallé joined it for the first time, taking the solo part in Beethoven's *Emperor* Concerto, he was appalled and almost canceled his engagement: "The orchestra! oh, the orchestra!" he recalled. "I was fresh from the 'Concerts du Conservatoire,' from Hector Berlioz's orchestra, and I seriously thought of packing up and leaving Manchester, so that I might not have to endure a second of these wretched performances. But when I hinted at this my friends gave me to understand that I was expected to change all this—to accomplish a revolution, in fact, and begged me to have a little patience."[6] Hallé's friends, all prosperous bourgeois, did not think small.

Nor did Hallé let them down. He started with a season of chamber music concerts and refused to be dismayed by the yawning empty seats in the hall. Gradually he built up acceptance for Beethoven's and Mendelssohn's quartets: it helped that the "best" Manchester society liked to be seen at his evenings. Among the first subscribers was Hermann Leo. This was in 1849; in the same year, Hallé was appointed permanent conductor of the Gentlemen's Concerts orchestra. Quickly, ruthlessly, he weeded out mediocre players, went to London to audition superior musicians, and engaged the best he could find, includ-

---

* On April 5, 1803, the managers of the society found themselves obliged to "animadvert upon the loud conversation with which several preceding performances have been embarrassed. Such a deviation from propriety cannot be permitted." Michael Kennedy, *The Hallé Tradition: A Century of Music* (1960), 4.

ing exiles from the Continent. In 1852, he took on yet another assignment, conductorship of a new singing group, the St. Cecilia Choral Society. Hallé did prodigious things for music in Manchester by insisting on having his own way. No one was more artful in playing that time-honored card—the threat to resign.

All this activity was prelude to an orchestra of his own. That came in 1857, following a major exhibition of art treasures modeled on its ancestor of 1851 at the Crystal Palace. Opened by Prince Albert, visited by Queen Victoria, attended by more than a million visitors, it was enlivened with daily concerts by a respectable fifty-man orchestra, the inevitable Hallé its conductor. His successes generated enthusiastic proposals from music lovers to keep the ensemble together, and after the exposition closed, in October, Hallé enlarged his pick-up band and undertook to offer regular seasons from then on.

On January 30, 1858, Hallé's Grand Orchestral Concerts had their premiere before "a scanty audience." The program, exhausting in the nineteenth-century manner, included Beethoven's First Symphony, Weber's Concertstück with Hallé at the piano, overtures by Rossini, Auber, and Weber, Berlioz's ballet music for *The Damnation of Faust*, selections from Verdi's *Il Trovatore*, an excerpt from a Mozart symphony, and Hallé playing three of Mendelssohn's Songs without Words—much digestible but all of it serious music. It was a copious banquet of culture for the holders of reserved seats, who paid 2s. 6d.; all the more satisfying to those who took a chance of finding an unreserved seat at 1s.—somewhat more than two hours' work for an average clerk. And, though hardly a bargain for those with modest incomes and though top admission prices rose drastically, the concerts remained a relatively affordable pleasure. In the late 1880s, a subscription to a twenty-concert season cost five pounds, well within reach of substantial citizens; and for the impecunious, the shilling admission remained in place as it had for decades.* As in other major cities, in Manchester high culture was slouching toward democracy.

The Hallé orchestra, it is worth underscoring, was a private venture; its owner mounted his weekly offerings during the fall and winter seasons at his "own risk and peril." The risk proved bearable; the peril soon faded. Manageable as the admission charges were, they did not make the Hallé orchestra a philanthropic organization. After the first season, its owner's profits were a derisory 2s. 6d., just enough to cover one reserved seat; by 1866, in its ninth

---

* It is symptomatic of Hallé's hold on his audience that ticket prices could rise through the years without alienating it. Within a few seasons, a reserved single seat, "cushioned," had tripled to 7s. 6d., a price maintained for the rest of Hallé's life. But the 1s. general admission ticket was preserved unaltered. By 1890, with on the average 1,800 listeners, some 350 to 400 had these cheapest seats in the "body of the hall."

year, they exceeded £2,000. Local pride in Hallé's property mounted with each passing year. "No provincial town except Manchester, we venture to think," wrote the *Manchester Guardian*, "is in a position to make such an experiment."[7] The paper modestly neglected to point out that its notices and articles about forthcoming programs had done their share in elevating the city's musical literacy.

Hallé's experiment never lost its glow. When he died in October 1895—Sir Charles Hallé since 1888—three long-standing friends undertook to guarantee the future of his orchestra and pay possible losses out of their own pockets. They were James Forsyth, Henry Simon, and Gustav Behrens, the first Hallé's business manager and proprietor of a well-known music shop, the second a rich industrialist, the third a shipping magnate with heavy investments in cotton exports. Both Simon and Behrens were scions of the assimilated German-Jewish minority that had been so consistently engaged in Manchester's high culture.[*] Without these bourgeois patrons, the Hallé orchestra would probably have gone under.

In November 1883, after a triumphant concert in Manchester, Vienna's celebrated conductor Hans Richter, whose range embraced Wagner and Brahms, wrote to his wife, "We can be especially proud of conquering this city, for the Manchester public consider themselves the best and most critical public in England."[8] Thoroughly familiar with the English musical scene, Richter had every right to pronounce on Manchester's taste: Hallé had schooled his audiences well. Taken together, his programming was an exemplary lesson in how to bring along Manchester's sizable elite intent on improving its tastes yet loyal to its war horses and somewhat reluctantly reconciled to novelty.[†] Except when evening-filling works like Mendelssohn's ever-popular *Elijah* or Saint-Saëns's far more provocative *Samson and Delilah* were on the program, Hallé made his concerts a smorgasbord of overtures, symphonies, fantasias, arias, violin and piano sonatas—the last regularly performed by the conductor himself. His ped-

---

[*] "The Jewish contribution to Manchester's economic and cultural life has been a large one. Commercially the Jewish community helped Manchester to reach out to the markets of the world. Culturally its activities brought the arts of Europe more freely into the life of the city." Of course, the author adds, "there were many German immigrants in the city who were not Jewish." W. M. Crawford, "A Cosmopolitan City," *Rich Inheritance: A Guide to the History of Manchester*, ed. N. J. Frangopulo (1962), 116.

[†] In his tribute to Hallé, Michael Kennedy writes that "slowly and relentlessly he undertook his noble task of educating a musically illiterate public." *Hallé Tradition*, 65. This is justly generous to Hallé but somewhat too severe on Manchester's listening public.

agogic strategy was transparent: something for everyone in the hall garnished with samples from the likely staples of the future.

Hallé's unshakable confidence in his own taste lent individuality to his programming. He was active in promoting the compositions of Berlioz, a friend from his Paris days—his debut as the conductor of the Hallé orchestra, we recall, had included a selection from the dramatic legend *The Damnation of Faust*. In 1879, far from shocked by Berlioz's dazzling orchestral effects—the *Guardian* reviewer described the composer's mind as "singularly unconventional, if not absolutely eccentric and fantastic"—Hallé led the first complete performance of the *Symphonie fantastique* in Britain.⁹ And *The Damnation of Faust* appeared no fewer than fourteen times during his tenure. Nor was he slow to introduce new compositions: Brahms's Third Symphony, first performed in Vienna in 1883, reached the Hallé the year after; in November 1893, the orchestra played the Intermezzo from Leoncavallo's *Pagliacci,* an opera premiered in Milan the previous year.

At the same time, Hallé controlled his experimental bent with a measure of prudence, taking care to retain the good will of the public he served by surrounding, if never quite swamping, risky novelties with uncontroversial favorites. Tchaikovsky's Fifth Symphony, first played at St. Petersburg in 1888, had to wait five years before he gave it a hearing at the Free Trade Hall. And he bowed openly, almost ostentatiously, to the requests of subscribers. In 1870, "in consequence of the large numbers who have been unable to obtain admission in former years," he decided that Handel's *Messiah,* the unmatched attraction that would be done fifty-five times in the Hallé decades, should be performed twice on succeeding evenings rather than once as before.¹⁰ After years of intimate association between Manchester's audiences and Manchester's conductor, it became pointless to ask whether Hallé was imposing his preferences on the city's middle classes or suavely responding to their pressure: his programs added up to the kind of high-level compromises that speak of a true community of tastes among cultivated Victorians.

Hence no one grumbled at having Beethoven entrenched as the mainstay of the Hallé orchestra's repertory, with his symphonies, concertos, and overtures each offered a dozen times and more. Yet this did not keep Hallé from testing the ranges of his audiences with the works of living composers. He tried to remain studiously neutral between Brahms and Wagner, giving each sufficient opportunities to present his case, as it were, at the Free Trade Hall. Granted, the more showy Wagner held the upper hand: since Manchester had no opera company, Hallé mounted concert performances of the third acts of *Lohengrin* and *Tannhäuser,* and there were few seasons when such Wagnerian crowd pleasers as overtures to his operas were absent from the program. Yet

Brahmsians had little to complain about: between 1858 and 1895, sixty-two compositions by Brahms entered the orchestra's repertory.*

Some of the moderns whom Hallé brought to Manchester—Antonín Dvořák, Henri Vieuxtemps, Emmanuel Chabrier—still feature in concert halls a hundred years later; others like Joachim Raff or Louis Théodore Gouvy and English composers like Hubert Parry or Sterndale Bennett are now the preserve of the specialist. Yet Hallé's policy, his flexible solidity kept alive by his successors, was by its nature unstable. In October 1905, Gerald Cumberland, then a young music critic, pleaded in a letter to the *Manchester Guardian* that it was time to drop the *Messiah* or *Elijah,* or perhaps both. "The performance of these oratorios has become a tradition—almost a superstition. They are no longer musical works; they have become religious services." *Elijah,* though rich in beauties, was drenched in "shallow philosophy and mawkish sentiment"; its "authentic spirit of Philistinism" must strike educated listeners as "stale and unprofitable." After all, "we have in our literature and our pictorial art emerged from the smugness and self-sufficiencey of the mid-Victorian age."[11] Philistine! The dread word had been spoken; after the turn of the century, Manchester's bourgeoisophobes were deriding as sadly out of date the consensus that Hallé had taken such pains to forge. But for fifty years, Mancunians had found it a salutary synthesis of the familiar and the fresh.

In the decades that Hallé presided over Manchester's musical culture, its leading citizens provided his orchestra with an imposing array of companions: that impressive exhibition of 1857 from which the Hallé orchestra grew, free libraries, new museums, centers of higher learning, and a massive, self-confident neo-Gothic town hall, a symbol of bourgeois pride it took ten years to build. But these monuments to culture and self-confidence did not rise in isolation. Manchester had long been a byword for its smoke and slums, its materialism and political violence. It was a city that emphatically demonstrated the impact of industrialization. Only the most determined myopia could venture to deny some disturbing facts. The class struggle had apparently long been, and

---

* Between 1858 and 1895, Beethoven's Fifth Symphony was on the program eighteen times; the violin concerto seventeen times; the *Emperor* Concerto sixteen times, beating the Fourth Symphony by a single presentation. The clear favorite was the *Pastorale,* with twenty-three performances. At the same time, Hallé paid devoted attention to Beethoven's minor works—including the egregious "Battle Symphony," generally known as *Wellington's Victory,* performed twice in 1858. In all, 143 compositions of Beethoven's were performed during Hallé's regime. The number of performances is taken from a handwritten repertory of Hallé's offerings and a handwritten account of income and expenditures, both in the Henry Watson Music Library, Manchester, and a three-volume compendium (copious but not quite complete) bound together as *Programmes: Hallé's Concerts.*

remained, more palpable in Manchester than anywhere else—it was after a visit
to the city that Disraeli coined his much quoted slogan of the two nations, rich
and poor. At a time of exploding urban populations, Manchester was in the
forefront: between 1801 and 1831, it doubled from 70,000 to 142,000 and
showed every sign of strong further growth, a token of progress and misery to
come. By 1890, it had over 700,000 inhabitants, the city swollen with natural
increase, working-class Irish immigrants, merchants from Germany, and new
residents from the neighboring countryside.

Visitors foreign and domestic responded to Manchester with excited and
incompatible appraisals. Their letters, pamphlets, and books spread the image of
the city as documenting the dubious blessings of the industrial age, usually
emphasizing the dubiousness rather than the blessing. "Manchester is the chim-
ney of the world," exclaimed Major-General Sir Charles James Napier in 1839,
where "rich rascals" confront "poor rogues, drunken ragamuffins and prostitutes." He could not contain himself: "What a place! the entrance to hell realized." Two years later another traveler, W. Cook Taylor, called the city
"essentially a place of business, where pleasure is unknown as a pursuit and
amusements scarcely rank as secondary considerations." No wonder that "every
person who passes you in the street has the look of thought and the step of
haste."[12] The common notion that nervousness follows upon the hustle and
bustle of industrial civilization had an early rehearsal in Manchester.

Whether bourgeois were nervous or not, the working classes were the most
conspicuous casualties of industrialization. But with the passage of years, Manchester's need to attack social problems began to dominate its political agenda.
Among the first to victimize the lower orders, Manchester's manufacturers, mill
owners, businessmen, and shopkeepers were also among the first to sponsor
investigations into the scandal of living in the slums and working in the factories; in the 1840s, moving from research to action, the city issued reforming
ordinances aimed at improving living conditions, including its poorest quarters.
Private philanthropy, too, began to respond. In 1844, the *Manchester Times,* a
radical journal, expressed the hope that Manchester "would become an inspir-
iting example to every city and town in the kingdom in this great work of civic
reform."[13]

To outspoken critics, these reforms were disguised, wholly inadequate acts
of expiation. In 1845, the year after the *Manchester Times* hailed Manchester as
a model of reform, Friedrich Engels stigmatized middle-class philanthropy as
"the bourgeoisie's brutal greed taking a hypocritical, civilized form."[14] Still, for
all of Manchester's highly visible destitution, undignified haste, aggressive moneymaking, and class combat, some observers glimpsed in this theater of bound-
less enterprise something superb. The warehouses, justly celebrated landmarks

with their bulky solidity, at once utilitarian and representative, were too imposing to be overlooked. Even Thomas Carlyle, the most eloquent and, down to
mid-century, the most compelling critic of industrial capitalism, detected in
Manchester a "precious substance, beautiful as magic dreams" concealed within "its cotton-fuzz, its smoke and dust, its tumult and contentious squalor" and
its "noisome wrappage."[15] He could not withhold grudging admiration from
the raw energy, the bursting vitality, of the place.

For novelists, too, modern Manchester offered tempting themes. The most
interesting among them, Elizabeth Gaskell, who anatomized Manchester from
the standpoint of an active Unitarian minister's wife, laid bare the city's social
plight in her widely appreciated *Mary Barton* of 1848. But seven years later, in
North and South, she paid tribute to the complexities of an emerging society
by contriving a match between Margaret Hale, the daughter of a genteel, inef-
fectual cleric, and the manufacturer John Thornton, the incarnation of the Victorian bourgeois will: strong, rough, fiercely determined in his urge to conquer
his domain, yet decent at heart. To her mind the young industrial North, Manchester and its companions in modernity, had much to offer. Even Carlyle
could see that.

But, while Carlyle hoped that the "soot and despair" of Manchester were
"not the essence of it," neither he nor other social critics perceived the city as
richly endowed in high culture.[16] Yet even for the years before 1848, this perception was ill informed. Manchester had its Gentlemen's Concerts, however
mediocre; the active Literary and Philosophical Society, established more than
forty years before; a promising recently launched newspaper, the *Manchester
Guardian,* which addressed itself to the trading middle classes; the Portico
Library, according to its founders an amalgam of "a news-room and library on
an extensive and liberal plan." This library, founded decades before the accession of Queen Victoria, prospered in her reign and had been, typically, the
brainchild of two merchants. Owned by its members, it was governed by cler-
gymen, lawyers, physicians, and businessmen.[17]

The principal supporters of such institutions were nothing less than self-
conscious. In 1835, at a meeting called to found the Manchester Athenaeum
Club for the Advancement and Diffusion of Knowledge, one speaker urged
that it was badly needed, since "the great and rapidly increasing community of
Manchester is felt to be inadequately supplied with the incentives to, and the
means of, intellectual cultivation."* Quickly subscribing £10,000, the founders

* In 1834, when Worcester opened a hall devoted to high culture, it called the building
"Athenaeum," a label that burghers would attach to similar edifices across Britain and the United States. The exhibition that inaugurated Worcester's Athenaeum was a show of recent paintings
by local artists, sponsored by the Worcester Institution for the Promotion of Literature, Science

promptly undertook to meet the needs they had identified.[18]

Berlioz says somewhere, and found approving echoes in his age, that a commercial city has little time for culture. But once Manchester's merchants and
industrialists could afford to set aside time and energy to think beyond the
walls of their shop, they wanted it to be a haven as much for civilized pleasures
as for profits.* True, down to the 1840s exposed to rowdy Chartist agitation for
political reform, some prominent Mancunians took an interest in art largely as
a practical agent of social peace. "When there is reason for presuming that the
contemplation of the more noble works of art may contribute in no small
degree, to elevate and purify the sentiments of a people," proclaimed a catalog
for an exhibition of paintings in 1831, "the subject at once assumes a sort of
national importance."[19] The trust of Manchester's reform-minded bourgeois in
the soothing powers of paintings, sculptures, and concerts was touching—or
was, as radicals had it, a self-serving way of evading real issues: wages, housing,
safety, health, working hours. But from the true believers' perspective, aesthetic choices and ethical goals were not necessarily incompatible.

The elite that made decisions about matters of taste in Victorian Manchester
was open to newcomers, but remained a handful of men best situated to translate private bouts of conscience or a taste for the higher things into public
action. Yet though one needed to be rich to found a great library or finance a
major university, a Mancunian with a few disposable shillings could vote on the
musical repertory on offer at the Free Trade Hall or choose from a rich selection of what later generations would call a tasteful or a tasteless print to hang
on the wall. Defying the sour predictions of bourgeoisophobes, the results were
far from uniformly embarrassing; philistines and anti-philistines alike could
congratulate themselves on the impact of middle-class taste on Manchester's
way with the arts, ranging all the way from naive to sophisticated.

Nor were all the merchants and manufacturers of Manchester ignorant

---

and Fine Arts. The "Address," serving as a preface for the catalog, likened "Athens, in the splendid era of Pericles, with its 30,000 free citizens," to Worcester, "with its 25,000," a distant resemblance perhaps but one that, once evoked, made Worcester's citizens feel like members of a
historic, self-confident troop. Paraphrase of address in *John Constable's Correspondence,* ed. R. B.
Beckett, 6 vols. (1962–68), V, 59.

* This timetable should not be taken too literally. As early as the 1790s, Thomas De Quincey
testified that the Manchester merchant class often "applied a very considerable portion of [its]
expenditure to intellectual pleasures" such as pictures and, "in a large measure, to books." Grevel
Lindop, *The Opium-Eater: A Life of Thomas de Quincey* (1981), 5.

grubbers after money: Hallé's sponsors proved that.* As early as 1831, their city boasted four weekly newspapers and several privately managed institutions like the Natural History Society and the Mechanics Institution. Two years later, local bankers and industrialists inaugurated the widely copied Manchester Statistical Society. Its members were not dilettantes, they wrote in their first annual report, being associated not merely "for the purpose of collecting facts" but also "to assist in promoting the progress of social improvement in the manufacturing population by which they are surrounded."[20] The investigations the society mounted and the reports it issued—candid, sober, informed, humane—demonstrate that this was not self-serving rhetoric. They were powerful incentives to reform.

All these things were true of Manchester's high culture, and more; yet admittedly, before Hallé came, most public activities were derivatives of its commercial and industrial interests. The Chamber of Commerce, an undisguised lobby, was established in 1820; it was followed in 1839 by the Anti–Corn Law League, founded to make the ideal of free trade government policy by urging the elimination of import duties on a variety of goods, not just on grain. A rugged engine of political propaganda, it would extend its influence across the country. There is something symbolic about the fact that Free Trade Hall, the monumental building named after the crusade of the Anti–Corn Law League, should house the concerts of the Hallé orchestra—symbolic but after mid-century, we have seen, to Mancunians a natural merger between commerce and culture.[21]

The cardinal fact about these institutions, whatever their purposes, was that their origin was private, their governance autonomous. "Everything in the exterior appearance of the city attests the individual powers of man, nothing the directing power of society," Alexis de Tocqueville noted in 1835 with mingled bewilderment and admiration. "At every turn human liberty shows its capricious creative force."[22] This force would enrich the high culture of Manchester, dragging the taste of its middle classes away from the seductions of the easy and the conventional. Late in the century, Oliver Elton, translator, schol-

---

* It will not do to idealize all these local worthies. On September 2, 1883, C. P. Scott, editor of the *Manchester Guardian,* described to his wife the formal opening of the Manchester City Art Gallery. In the evening, at supper, he complained, the only distinguished guests were C. T. Newton of the British Museum, Holman Hunt, "who was the only great artist, and Sidney Colvin, the only distinguished art critic." They were casually seated across the room, with Hunt being placed between H. M. Cundall, "the veriest understrapper . . . in charge of our loam potteries," and the aged alderman Goldschmidt, "who passed a note to his opposite neighbour with the intelligent interrogatory, 'Who or what is Mr. Holman Hunt?' " J. L. Hammond, *C. P. Scott of the Manchester Guardian* (1934), 49–50.

ar, drama critic in Manchester, defined this energy as "private enterprise and patriotism."[23]

The history of Manchester University testifies to local resourcefulness. It was founded in 1846 with a legacy of around £100,000 by John Owens, who in his will barred any religious tests for faculty or students. At first named after its most generous patron—there were to be others—it was rebaptized Victoria University in 1887. But the new name of the university was ornamental not substantive; its financing, like its liberal spirit, were pure Manchester.

Quite as emphatically, another notable institution, the John Rylands Library, was a private creation. Founded in 1890 by Mrs. Enriqueta Rylands in memory of her husband and dedicated nine years later, the arresting red neo-Gothic building housed one of the world's choicest collection of early books. And in his inaugural address, worth reporting at some length, the Reverend Dr. Fairbairn, principal of the Congregationalist Mansfield College at Oxford, once more preached the creed of the Manchester bourgeoisie. John Rylands had been "a typical Manchester manufacturer, merchant and citizen. He loved the city where he had made his wealth, the trade by which the city achieved its name, and the honesty which was the honour of its sons."[24]

For Fairbairn, as for Rylands or Owens before him, trade was a source of pride because it was an agent of civilization. "This library will add to the dignity and the fame of this city. It will stand as the creation of the widow of a man who added to the munificence of the merchant a profound admiration of learning and of letters. It stands as a monument of one who lived and made his wealth and fulfilled his duties in our very midst, and it adds another example to the already vast cloud of witnesses who testify to the princely munificence of the merchant to literature and art."[25] He was invoking the beneficent bourgeois trinity—work, wealth, citizenship—that the antibourgeois camp was so strenuously deriding. We shall soon see that this was not the kind of speech they were giving in Munich.

Significantly, Fairbairn linked Manchester to great commercial cities of the past. "It is noteworthy that the most famous library of the ancient world, whose loss was a permanent impoverishment of the human mind, had its home, not in Athens, the city of culture; not in Rome, the city of empire; but in Alexandria, a city whose kings were merchants, and whose merchants were kings." The same held true through history. Florence and Venice, the cities of merchants, had done the most to transmit ancient learning to the modern world. Hence it was "normal" that "here in Manchester, amid factories and warehouses, within reach of the Exchange and the Town Hall," the "home of one of the greatest collections of art and literary treasures should be built."[26]

Fairbairn's was celebratory rhetoric, and in this sort of performance piety matters more than documentation. True, Rylands had been a remarkable man: a liberal in politics, Congregationalist in religion, a quiet and munificent philanthropist. But Fairbairn's address raised the individual to a type; it aptly mirrors the self-description of Manchester bourgeois during the Victorian decades. They saw themselves the heirs and custodians of a culture acquired, cherished, perpetuated with largely perfunctory assistance from the provincial gentry and the crown. Local government, to be sure, had its say in managing or sponsoring several of the city's cultural institutions. But that government was, after all, simply its most influential citizens wearing formal attire.

It was characteristic of this style that when, late in the nineteenth century, Manchester's performers and musical amateurs felt the need for a conservatory, they launched it on their own initiative; Sir Charles Hallé—of course!—had already taken preliminary steps. Confident that Manchester could support such an institution, he prevailed upon the directors of the Gentlemen's Concerts to convene a public meeting at the town hall in December 1891. The assemblage formed a committee that devised a constitution and raised pledges of more than £11,000. By early 1893, it was ready to ask the lord mayor to convene a town meeting concerning a college of music and, to no one's surprise, got the votes to proceed. The cost for a building was met by an anonymous gift from Charles Lees, a cotton magnate from neighboring Oldham, and in October 1893 the college opened its doors, another triumph of private enterprise and patriotism.

In 1895, writing in the last year of his life about this beloved child of his old age, Hallé observed that the "Committee were honoured by information from the Home Office that Her Majesty the Queen had been graciously pleased to confer upon the College the title of *Royal*."[27] The respectful tone conceals that such sponsorship, though honorable, even flattering, was inessential, just as it was to Manchester's university. To be sure, being only human, Manchester merchants crusading for culture valued the company of gentry, if possible of a lord; they were only too pleased to have lustrous names chair their meetings and head their committees. But even without the royal blessing the Manchester conservatory would have prospered.*

---

* To take two telling instances: when in 1852 the Free Library was inaugurated, the organizers formally invited His Royal Highness Prince Albert to the proceedings. Unable to attend, he sent a cordial letter and a collection of books, a display of "condescension and good feeling" much appreciated in the hall. Manchester Free Library, *Report of the Proceedings at the Public Meetings Held in the Library, Camp Field, Manchester, on Thursday, September 2nd, 1852, to Celebrate the Opening of the Free Library* (1902, slightly abridged from 1852), 9. In late January 1858, the Princess Royal married the Prussian crown prince, Friedrich (to become Germany's pathetic emperor who ruled just ninety-nine days, dying as he was of throat cancer; their son, of course, was the fateful

In one domain of culture, art, Manchester proved for long years as disappointing as it was well intentioned. Growing numbers of merchants showed a lively interest in prints and, if they could afford it, in original paintings. The best-qualified experts recognized many of the "old masters" that Manchester's early collectors had snapped up from unscrupulous art dealers—"Picture Jockeys," they were called—as daubs that only a rank novice could imagine to be a Rubens or a Rembrandt.[28] Recalling the 1870s, Richard Whiteing, the suave and patronizing art critic of the *Manchester Guardian,* likened the way Mancunians bought paintings to their behavior on the stock exchange: just as they bet on shares to rise, they spent good money on promising artists. "You bought at a stiff price to stimulate the sense of luck in the purchase, and four figures was the almost inevitable rule. The idea was that you had better make haste about it, or they would soon be five."*

Perhaps, but Manchester also boasted collectors who let themselves be guided by responsible dealers or reined in their passion for pictures with as much cool rationality as they mustered in their office. The age of the aristocratic collector was not yet over, but that of bourgeois collectors was on the horizon, and their best insurance against being defrauded was to acquire knowledge or, recognizing their ignorance, profit from borrowed erudition. "The dealers," wrote the English artist Thomas Uwins in 1858, "can no longer get a market for their Raphaels, Correggios and stuff, manufactured in their back shops, and smoked into the appearance of antiquity. The old nobility and landed proprietors are gone out. Their place is supplied by railroad speculators, iron mine men, and grinders from Sheffield, etc., Liverpool and Manchester merchants and traders."[29] Not all bourgeois were easy butts. More and more of them, whether from real liking or sly prudence, shifted their collections from sixteenth- and seventeenth-century paintings to contemporary English pictures. The domestic product was cheaper and more reliable.

What is more, as early as 1823, 140 Mancunians, subscribing £50 each, founded the Manchester Institution for the Promotion of Literature, Science,

---

Wilhelm II. The *Manchester Guardian* covered the festivities at extraordinary length, for four days, leaving no detail, not even the mood in Berlin, unmentioned. On January 25, it offered the moving spectacle of the ceremony just ended, "the bride, giving vent to her evidently long pent-up feelings, turned and flung herself upon her mother's bosom with a suddenness and depth that thrilled every heart" (p. 2).

* Whiteing, *My Harvest* (1915), 131. Recalling his Manchester days, Whiteing underscored the collectors' innocence: "The authority of our picture dealer over his customer was one of the strangest things. It was quite spiritual in its nature. The very shopman who could hold his best on 'Change became as a child when he passed into the show-rooms. He took charge of him, led him round the gallery and told him what he really wanted to buy." Ibid., 133.

and the Arts. It was their way of showing their desire to raise their eyes above the countinghouse. The institution would open "a channel through which the works of meritorious artists may be brought before the public."[30] This meant lectures, exhibitions complete with awards, purchases of art to be auctioned off to members, and purposeful sociability. Thus with art, as with music, Manchester tried to make aesthetic education entertaining.

Despite all these efforts, the Mancunians who set about founding a museum suffered from a crippling uncertainty of touch in collecting objects and misguided ambitions for grandiose facilities. It was not until 1889 that Manchester's principal art museum was established by local worthies to commemorate one of their own. Sir Joseph Whitworth had made a great deal of money with ingenious inventions improving cotton machinery. When he died in 1887, he left most of his money to support high culture, and his principal legatees organized a committee to establish appropriate memorials to their departed friend. Committees are a supreme instrument of self-government and they were characteristic for Manchester, but obviously no committee can rise above its membership, and Whitworth's legatees knew too little and asked too few questions. One of its accomplishments was the Whitworth Art Gallery, designed as "a source of perpetual gratification to the people of Manchester, and at the same time a permanent influence of the highest character in the direction of technical education."[31] As we have seen before, in the minds of its sponsors, edification and the recruitment of trained personnel for industry or commerce, high culture and high profits, did not clash.

At the outset, the Whitworth museum's holdings, scattered and rather pathetic, reflected the donors' amateurish eclecticism; they ran from textiles to a few commonplace Victorian paintings. It took a civilized benefactor to provide a partial remedy: in 1892, John Edward Taylor, editor of the *Manchester Guardian,* presented the Whitworth with a splendid collection of 140 early English watercolors, a genre in which the museum would retain a major interest. Governance, though, remained casual and dilettantish; those in charge spent far too much on embellishing the building and the gardens, far too little on endowment. But the mistakes the donors and administrators made were all their own.

2. Majestic Dispensations

In Munich, middle-class culture was far different, far more conflict-ridden, than in Manchester. Although it could boast a rather exclusive stratum of educated citizens—the *Bildungsbürgertum*—it was indelibly stamped by the taste of its ruling house, willful and attentive, magnificent in its lavishness, at times downright utopian in its aspirations. While the political and the cultural elites of Manchester were in essence identical, Munich's society experienced strains between those who ran the country and those who just made money in it. To confound matters further, the royal administration and the *Bürgertum* were alike rent by internal tensions. The groveling vocabulary that Munich's burghers employed to address royalty disclosed the melting respect most commoners thought they owed titled mortals, but others, more self-reliant, were hardly so servile. Unlike Manchester's middle classes, then, Munich's *Bürger,* a nest of contentions and contradictions, defy ready diagnosis.

The capital of what had been the kingdom of Bavaria since 1806 and the principal residence of the Wittelsbach dynasty, Munich showed the royal hand most manifestly. Provincial towns like Erlangen or Würzburg profited from their monarchs' persistent interventions in behalf of their universities; in the mid-1870s, a once insignificant hamlet, Bayreuth, was turned into a world-renowned mecca for musical pilgrims largely through the lavish, if fitfully mobilized, resources put at Richard Wagner's disposal by King Ludwig II. Yet it was Munich, above all, that its monarchs changed almost literally out of all recognition. By mid-century its favorite self-description of Athens on the Isar, "Isar-Athen," seemed only marginally boastful.

Like Manchester, Munich looked back on a long pedigree, but also like Manchester, it began to grow exponentially early in the nineteenth century. In 1800, its population stood at about 40,000, which swelled by 1850 to 109,000 and reached 350,000 in 1890—a ninefold increase in ninety years, which out-stripped even burgeoning Manchester. Some of the medieval gates had escaped the wreckers' ball during an orgy of construction in the first half of the century. The massive brick cathedral, the Frauenkirche, a late-perpendicular Gothic structure that towered over the city and dated largely from the fifteenth century, was a reminder of Munich's venerable past. But it was mainly in the reign, and through the efforts, of that fanatical builder Ludwig I that the high-flying plans he had harbored before he ascended the throne in 1825 were realized. In 1818, when he was still crown prince, a group of German artists in Rome, whom he was visiting, toasted him as *"the greatest protector of the arts."* As king, he strove to deserve the accolade, and set about to make his capital into an "estimable vessel" for the arts and sciences, a "city with a European reputation."[1]

He succeeded. The opera house, also serving as a concert hall, had been built and rebuilt by his predecessor. But virtually all other representative features of the capital carved out of the old town—wide avenues, grand parks, elegant squares—were conceived and constructed under Ludwig I. He had churches built, as well as accommodations for the university, which he moved from

Langhut to Munich in 1826; the Glyptothek, a tribute to classical sculpture, was opened to the public in 1834, and the Alte Pinakothek, home to a splendid collection of old masters, was inaugurated two years later. Then, in 1845, came a neoclassical exhibition hall for artistic and industrial products, the Kunst und Industrieausstellungsgebäude.

This building epidemic was unmatched in any other German city or, until Baron Haussmann began to remake Paris in the 1850s, all across Europe. Ludwig's final project was the Neue Pinakothek, for which ground was broken in 1846. Designed to accommodate the king's magnificent acquisitions of contemporary German art—Ludwig I's taste ran not to old masters but to living painters—it was a preemptive strike that would secure strategic advantages over other collectors and other cities. All together, these massive shrines to culture were abundantly endowed and luxuriously decorated. They created a run on muralists.

The unexampled outlay of royal energy and funds acted as bait for the taste of Munich's middle class, as an invitation to endorse authoritative choices handed down from above. The majestic Wittelsbach bounty only added to the city's prestige for being the result of a centuries-long buildup: for generations, the ruling house had owned the bulk of the paintings on view in the Alte Pinakothek. Some had been acquired by its electoral princes in the sixteenth and seventeenth centuries, others added by ducal collectors in the eighteenth, and the whole rounded out early in the nineteenth by acquisitions from secularized monasteries. In every case, whether showing their artistic property in the museums or commissioning ceiling decorations for the Glyptothek, the royal touch was overpowering.

This did not mean that Bavarian bourgeois were irreparably passive. In 1848, the year Hermann Leo invited Charles Hallé to Manchester, Munich's burghers gave evidence that they had a will of their own, prompted to unwonted action by a scandal ripe for the operetta stage. There had been an active middle-class cultural life even before this tragicomic episode, though the royal shadow, made more oppressive by omnipresent agents, loomed over it all. In his reminiscences, the art critic and historian Friedrich Pecht recalled the joyless atmosphere prevailing in the early 1830s: "Everywhere, in the academy, in the museums, in the street, one got the feeling that these institutions were not at all for the *Bürger* who paid for them, but that he was merely being permitted to use them as much as the gracious favor of the ruler, and above all the convenience of the *Herren* bureaucrats, would admit."[2]

In Bavaria as elsewhere, private associations had begun to meet the bourgeoisie's desire for companionship, educational opportunities, exchange of information, eventually for lobbying the government. But these *Vereine* required the royal imprimatur, and that was not lightly given; the anxiety over subversive societies hanging over from the French Revolution did not abate for decades. The Royal Academy, founded in 1808, was not called Royal (*Königlich*) for nothing; slavishly following the dynasty's neoclassical tastes, it trained aspiring artists to respect the traditional hierarchies in painting and to meddle with landscapes or genre scenes as little as possible.

This quasi-governmental *Akademie* left room for a society of artists and art lovers, the Kunstverein, instituted in 1823. It, too, had to secure the king's assent and was compelled to live within the narrow framework that the royal authority assigned to it. While the precise history of its founding remains obscured by competing claims, clearly the most important among the founders were four middle-class artists. Their relatively modest specialties say much about the character of their *Verein:* one was an architect and the three others were painters, one doing landscapes, another genre scenes, a third portraits. In short, none of the instigators could be expected to steer the *Verein* toward the neoclassical summit of their craft—historical or religious paintings—on which the Royal Academy so forcefully insisted. What is more, aristocrats held strategic and uncontested positions in the Kunstverein.

The *Verein* saw as its mission to create a forum for members to meet informally, discuss their love of art, show paintings and graphics for those who could afford them, and hold regular auctions of pictures it had purchased. Both socially and economically it was a fairly exclusive club; while in the Munich around the time of Ludwig I's accession only 5 percent of its inhabitants were *Bürger* entrusted with the vote, officers of the *Verein* refused entrance even to full-fledged citizens if they worked in menial occupations. What is more, the annual dues of 12 florins automatically excluded the impecunious. While Jacob Bauer, the mayor of Munich in the 1830s, drew down a salary of 3,500 florins—he could pay his fee with a little more than a day's work—it was estimated that the lowliest of the city's inhabitants earned some 100 to 150 florins a year, and even many better off could hardly spare the sum needed to open the doors of the Kunstverein to them. Yet, despite all this insistence on rank, its impact on the royal direction of Munich's artistic culture was strictly limited; at best, it served as a conduit for small contemporary paintings that Ludwig I might wish to buy. No serious confrontations with the Wittelsbachs could be expected from so servile an organization.

When the challenge came in the revolutionary year 1848, it did so from political impulsions. Ludwig's eye for beauty was not confined to the elevated pleasures of contemplating a piece of Greek sculpture or an architect's model of a new museum. Much to the chagrin of his devoted queen, he was susceptible to lovely young women he happened to encounter—actresses or singers, daughters of bookkeepers or visiting English gentlewomen. He would fall in love with them all, flatter and embarrass them with poems and visits. And he had his court painter, Joseph Stieler, best known for his portrait of the aged Goethe, put the charming faces of many among them on the permanent record in a "Gallery of Beauties," the source of much malicious gossip. The king's eroticism was largely sublimated, but it spoke of a fateful fixation. In 1846, when his last pathetic adventure began, he was sixty. Autocratic, touchy, feeling himself aging and somehow less of a man, he became infatuated with a dancer of striking beauty, dubious antecedents, and avaricious appetites, who called herself Lola Montez.

He was sorely aware that her interference in state affairs was impudent and her greed unconscionable, but the refusal of his court and polite society to receive the woman he loved turned his attachment into a point of honor. An avalanche of jokes, lampoons, and gossip, compromising his reputation as man and ruler, left him unmoved. The gusto that had made him an unrivaled builder now compelled him to persevere. But his subjects, usually so indulgent with royal peccadilloes, found Lola Montez's ascendancy undignified and potentially expensive beyond bearing. Before it was over, Lola Montez briefly held the title and enjoyed the prerogatives of a countess; ministers, public officials, and professors had been dismissed; the University of Munich, scene of anti-Lola riots, was closed.

For a moment, the king postured as a liberal, but even if intimations of government under the rule of law could only please middle-class activists smarting under absolute rule, its origin was not reassuring and its continuance in doubt. Since the late 1820s, and even more after the revolutionary days of 1830, Ludwig I had abandoned all pretense at constitutional rule. After a few experiments, he had come to perceive the political opposition and the free press as nuisances, perhaps as tools of treason. Anyone harboring the notion that he would tolerate strong criticism or share power with his ministers, let alone his subjects, was quickly disillusioned. The Lola Montez affair, then, was more an occasion for middle-class self-assertion than its cause.

On February 10, 1848, more than a thousand of the city's "most respectable *Bürger*" marched to the royal residence to submit a respectful petition. The king's marginalia intimate both a nagging anxiety and a paternalistic pride. The great lover was getting old ("To yield would be weakness"), and the people were misbehaving (If the *Bürger* "do not behave quietly, they will force me to move my court headquarters elsewhere. They should be told this").[3] To a bourgeois of Manchester this tone, and the familial intimacy of royal father with insubordinate subject-children, would have been anachronistic; to the incensed *Bürger* of Munich, though goaded into action, it still seemed appropriate.

In early March, having rejected yielding, the king yielded; he decreed the reopening of the university and the banishment of Lola Montez. Encouraged by these successes and by the revolutionary stimulus spreading from France, middle-class malcontents, allied with bureaucrats and students, extracted proclamations that promised a responsible ministry, a free press, a tamed censorship, the introduction of trial by jury, an amelioration of the legal status of the country's Jews. All seemed well in the family once more. Yet a few days later, convinced that events had proclaimed his impotence, Ludwig I abdicated. He did not want to be an *Unterschreiber,* a monarch who merely signs what his ministers put on his desk.

Most of the reforms Ludwig promised were enacted, and retained, by Maximilian II. Though not so autocratic as his father and not so sensitive to harsh words in the press, he remained a formidable political and cultural force. His passion for sustaining the building boom was more moderate than his father's, but he did found three museums—two of them in Munich—devoted to modern subjects like the sciences and technology. One of his characteristic gestures, documenting once again the capaciousness of the royal purse, was his purchase for the Royal Library of the unmatched Quatremère collection of Arabic manuscripts and printed books, a daunting treasure of 40,000 items. And, while his father had been more bountiful, Maximilian did donate important recent canvases, including a Böcklin, to the Neue Pinakothek.

The king's heart, though, lay in enriching Munich's rather sparse cultural rations with imported outsiders to grace Bavarian universities, laboratories, literary circles, and, once a week, his table. This distinguished roster included Heinrich von Sybel, who, once there, founded the *Historische Zeitschrift,* the first and still the leading scholarly journal for Germany's historical profession, and taught at its university for five years; Wilhelm Heinrich Riehl, a facile, widely read sociologist and conservative cultural critic; Emanuel Geibel, a poet as uninventive as he was polished; Count Schack, the amateur scholar and patron of the arts we have met before; Paul Heyse, a short story writer and novelist who, many years later, when modernists dismissed his fiction as hopelessly old-fashioned, won the Nobel Prize in literature. To top it all, the king had Leopold Ranke deliver a series of private lectures on history.

All these "Northern lights," several of them holding positions of authority, put substantial pressure on Munich's cultural life. "For Munich's sociable circles these appointments were a great gain," wrote the Swiss jurist and political scientist Johann Caspar Bluntschli, who moved to Munich in 1848, in his memoirs. "Life grew more animated, more interesting, more intellectual. The gray of philistine existence was beautified by brighter tints."[4] In the Bavarian capital as in other major centers, a diverse population seemed an essential yeast to

generate aesthetic vitality. Interestingly, Theodor Fontane was sure that without
its Jews, added to its Huguenots and immigrants from the surrounding Mark
Brandenburg, Berlin would not have been half so interesting. Yet in Munich
the imports were not unanimously welcomed; they provided ideas and generated antagonism, and did not always stay very long. The local population
thought them condescending and incapable of appreciating the talents of
native Bavarians. In sharp contrast to Manchester's citizens, who had integrated their German middle-class newcomers, Munich's burghers had evidently
failed to acquire sufficient self-confidence by 1848 to escape a certain xeno-
phobia. Could not natives of the city, or at least of Bavaria, manage their own
poetry, music, theater, academic affairs?

Apparently not. Yet many Bavarians saw 1848 as a starting point. Looking
back, the drama critic Alfred von Mensi-Klarbach praised it as a glorious dawn:
"There was in those days a stimulating artistic life in the Bavarian capital,
which did not yet, as it does today, live off its artistic fame, but was about to
create it."[5] The post-1848 Bavarian bourgeoisie, struggling for psychological
enfranchisement, was, of course, not writing on an empty slate: well before the
year of revolution, it had organized societies to cultivate church music, display
works of art, search into local history, to say nothing of enjoying sociability
simple if not always pure. As we know, the Kunstverein, taking societies in
Nürnberg and Karlsruhe as its model, was by then a quarter of a century old.

Music, too, had assembled sizable audiences through informal channels. In
1835, as the *Allgemeine Musikzeitung* noted two years later, some adventurous
entrepreneurs launched "musical-declamatory evening entertainments," at
which professional musicians, usually members of the court orchestra, offered
strenuously frivolous cuisine: popular duets or trios, bravura pieces for solo
instruments, and recitations. Among the organizations offering such entertainments were the significantly titled Gesellschaft Frohsinn and the Privat-
Musikverein, advertising with their very names their commitment to
cheerfulness and individual initiative. "Experience teaches," the *Musikzeitung*
complained, "that the members of such societies prefer contenting themselves
with mediocre and even poor stuff to paying for something good, no matter
how low the price."[6]

This criticism had large cultural implications. The private clubs fostering art,
literature, and music in Munich could sporadically compete with state-sponsored events by offering truly popular fare. In concerts, competition for
uncommitted cash could be lively; in the mid-1830s, the evenings of the
Musikalische Akademie were sparsely attended, despite its royal charter. Here
was one way in which Munich's *Bürger* could convert their habitual passivity
into activity: they could stay away from the sober pleasures the royal house

deigned to provide for them and gratify their appetite for musical offerings in less exacting halls. And the painters showing in the Kunstverein could register mild protests against court-imposed rations by exhibiting the small canvases that were easy to enjoy and cheap to buy. Plainly, their policy met a need: starting out with some two hundred members, they numbered two decades later more than three thousand. At a price: the larger its membership, the greater the influence of upper-bourgeois "amateurs" at the expense of the artists. Since the association functioned as an efficient marketplace, there was an evident danger that painters working to sell would compromise their art. Founded to raise the taste of its supporters, the Kunstverein only too often served to lower the taste of its artists.

In Munich, then, appeals to middlebrow publics were not without effect, but in the long run they could not withstand the Wittelsbachs. Considering the kings' riches, this could mean a boon for high culture—provided they were expended in the cause of good taste. When private enterprise shouldered its way into prominence, it did so largely when the incompetence of bureaucrats made an opening. A striking instance of Manchesterdom invading Munich came in the early 1850s, when the Royal Academy invited local artists to share the labor of mounting major exhibitions. Though assigned to the academy by its charter, its management had repeatedly bungled this responsibility and was only too pleased to enlist those whom a salon would benefit most directly. This devolution led by majestic steps to the formation, in 1868, of Munich's Artists' Cooperative—Münchener Künstlergenossenschaft—when it was granted its royal charter, a formality that remained as mandatory as it had ever been.

These private bourgeois activities, though eventually palpable, added up to a litany of missed opportunities. From 1869 on, the cooperative held annual salons of local artists and until 1892, when the Secession broke up their consensus, four ambitious international exhibitions.* And these brought to Munich an iconoclast like Courbet, who gave encouragement to the naturalist Wilhelm Leibl and became his friend. Posterity has recognized Leibl as the most talented artist working in Munich, but his paintings, which might have pointed the way out of the city's partiality for historical machines or for genre, found little resonance and only one important patron—and he was from Cologne. The experience of Liebermann, who settled in Munich for several years in the late 1870s, was almost as disheartening. His *Jesus in the Temple*, a realistic rendering of Christ as a Jewish boy in earnest colloquy with rabbis, scandalized viewers at the salon of 1879 and precipitated a stormy debate in the Bavarian legisla-

---

* As we shall see, Secessions were never stable, and broken up by later Secessions.

ture. Evidently the conventional tastes of royal patrons, the academy, and the bulk of the art-buying public were impossible to dislodge. Before 1900, Isar-Athen had been overtaken as a seedbed for consequential aesthetic experiments by Berlin: "Spree-Athen."

In both of these self-proclaimed heirs to Athens, august fiat could impose decisions that no indignant artist or collector could overturn. In 1889, the year after his accession, Germany's emperor, Wilhelm II, set a competition for an imposing monument to his adored grandfather, Wilhelm I, to be erected in Berlin. The selection committee awarded first prize to a design by Adolf Hildebrand, the most imaginative among German sculptors, but the emperor arbitrarily ordered the commission handed to the commonplace sculptor Reinhold Begas, whose empty monumentality suited Wilhelm to perfection. Furious, Hildebrand exploded to a friend, "I have once again found that artistically Germany is hopeless. The artist exists only to realize the ideas of so-called authoritative personalities, and these authoritative personalities are entirely the emperor's puppets when official matters, like a monument, are involved." Unfortunately young Wilhelm "is a know-it-all and sets the tone"; hence "the servility on one side and the emperor's tactless interventions are a power against which you can't get anywhere." It is worth noting that Wilhelm II's musical taste ran mainly to marches.[7]

The story ends with an instructive twist: in 1891, Luitpold, Bavaria's prince regent, who had succeeded Ludwig II after his death five years before, invited submissions for a Wittelsbach fountain in Munich, a highly desirable assignment. Hildebrand, member of the prize committee and dissatisfied with the sketches he was judging, offered one of his own, and, disregarding objections to giving the fountain to an outsider, the prince regent personally selected Hildebrand's design. Having earlier denounced the "age of democracy and omniscience," Hildebrand, overjoyed, discovered that absolutism could be beneficent after all.[8]

Munich's music further documents the weight of imperious dictates on a public more receptive than rebellious. "Is Munich a musical city?" the experienced critic Theodor Goering asked provocatively in 1888 and gave an equivocal answer. He acknowledged the city's fine orchestras, choirs, soloists, and singers, and expressed his admiration for its internationally renowned chief conductor Hermann Levi. But, Goering thought, though times were beginning to change, Munich was still essentially dominated by "princely hobbies" rather than by musical tastes freely developed by the educated middle classes. The whole struck him as a spectacle of "artificial breeding."[9] Munich could have benefited from a solid dose of Manchester.

Levi, who from 1872 to 1896 presided over Munich's orchestral and operatic life as the civil servant in charge—he had the resounding title of *General-musikdirektor*—had proved a felicitous choice. He was the Hallé of Munich. Sensitive and scholarly, Levi pioneered in rescuing the libretti and scores of Mozart's major operas from the "improvements" inflicted on them by decades of performance, and in rehabilitating the sadly neglected *Così fan tutte;* a champion of Brahms *and* Bruckner, Berlioz *and* Chabrier—he was nothing if not catholic—he impartially enlarged the horizons of Munich's music lovers, all the while trying to keep his absorbing passion for Wagner in check.

Not very successfully, and his fixation, which exposed him to gratuitous insults from his tactless anti-Semitic demigod, made him the ideal instrument for Ludwig II, a monarch who remains memorable largely for his infatuation with Wagner. Ludwig's performance as the most spectacular and most outlandish patron in the Wittelsbach dynasty impinged on Munich's middle classes in dramatic though largely indirect ways. The king initiated no dialogue between royal and bourgeois tastes: the middling orders watched on the sidelines a distant encounter, half love affair and half duel, brought nearer by gossip inundating what was, among its leading circles, still a small town.

Whatever good *Bürger* might murmur in private, for skilled craftsmen—architects, masons, carpenters, painters, landscape gardeners—it was a time of prosperity not seen since the headiest days of Ludwig I; all of them were kept busy for years on the king's ruinously expensive fairy tale castles. The most spectacular and best known of these childish fantasies realized was Neuschwanstein, built into hilly terrain with fine views. Largely neo-Romanesque on the exterior with neo-Gothic prevailing in the interior and some Moorish touches, it boasted a throne room that was never to be used, the most elaborately carved furnishings and murals illustrating the medieval German myths which Wagner had pillaged for his music dramas. What mattered more to bourgeois as consumers of high culture, though, was the prodigious outpouring of Wagner's creations. Several of them had their world premiere in Munich: *Tristan und Isolde* in 1865, *Das Rheingold* in 1869, *Die Walküre* in 1870, interspersed with dazzling performances of *Der fliegende Holländer* or *Lohengrin*. It was hearing this last-named opera that had provided Crown Prince Ludwig with his Wagner epiphany, the moment that gave his life whatever purpose it would have.

Ludwig II ascended the throne in 1864 and would rule—if that is the right word—until his mysterious drowning, probably a suicide, in 1886. At his accession he was eighteen, intent on exercising the privileges of command though really unequipped to govern. He was majestic in stature; women thought him handsome, an accolade that did not alleviate his indifference to them. Ill-educated, interested in very little, he was easily bored; even Wagner's music, which he professed to adore, really left him cold. What he craved was spectacle, with himself in the leading role. He wanted to be the Louis XIV of Bavaria.

His discovery of *Lohengrin*, nectar for Ludwig's famished soul, seduced him to adopt Wagner's call for the Artwork of the Future as his own sacred task. As soon as he was king, he had the composer brought to Bavaria so that the two might plot how to realize this fantasy. Their tête-à-têtes centered on a theater worthy enough, and on the *Ring of the Nibelung*, next on Wagner's docket. Much was at stake, they believed, nothing less than the spiritual redemption of Germany; yielding to the illusion of a lordly didacticism, the pair agreed that Wagner's music dramas were to raise the people's level of appreciation for the great and the noble.* This was the spirit, so congenial to middle-class idealizing of higher horizons, that had Munich's opera management put Wagner on the program at reduced prices—occasionally.

Contemporary memoirs attest that for Munich's bourgeois, manifestations of Wagner's vision were the source of deep pleasure but also of spirited, at times highly skeptical, debate. Numbers of discriminating listeners who had relished *Der fliegende Holländer* or *Tannhäuser* found *Tristan* overlong and the *Ring* incomprehensible. The heavily perfumed, quasi-religious air emanating from the Wagnerians was as likely to arouse resistance as the yearning to become one of them. In her reminiscences, Rosalie Braun-Artaria (we met her before as Lenbach's friend) finely captured the mood of those untouched by this magic: "The whole Wagner congregation of that time had all the marks of a sect, and it was not tempting to join it. And so I remained true to my old gods Mozart, Beethoven, Schubert."[10] Others, though, gratefully added a new god to their pantheon, sent their way courtesy of the royal purse.

The honeymoon between worshipful king and manipulative composer was disrupted in late 1865, after Ludwig had installed Wagner in a princely Munich mansion. It all painfully reminded local *Bürger* of the king's grandfather and his last fling. The farce of the late 1840s was threatening to repeat itself in the mid-1860s; "Lolotte" Wagner, a worthy successor to Lola Montez. King and composer were friends and more than friends; Ludwig's missives, alternating between lyricism and ecstasy and strewn with exclamation points, read like an adolescent's outpourings to a matinee idol. Wagner's responses, deftly calculat-

---

* In November 1864, Ludwig II wrote to Wagner, "It is my intention to bring the Munich public into a loftier, more reflective frame of mind through performances of serious, significant works like those of Shakespeare, Calderón, Goethe, Schiller, Beethoven, Mozart, Gluck, Weber, thus helping it gradually to shed its taste for cheap, frivolous entertainments and so to prepare it for the marvels of your works, and to ease its understanding of them by first of all presenting to them the works of other significant men; for everything must be filled by the seriousness of art." *Ludwig II von Bayern in Augenzeugenberichten*, ed. Rupert Hacker (1972), 73.

ed displays of spontaneity, strove for the same temperature; little masterpieces of flattery, they were larded with demands for money—much money.

This is where the more articulate elements in Munich's middle class drew the line, supported behind the scenes by the king's parents, the cabinet, and the clergy. Reports of Wagner's sybaritic manner of living were circulating in the city; people talked about precious wallpaper, finely crafted furniture, exquisite perfumes for Wagner's bath, and no less exquisite silks for his dressing gowns. The rumors, including most of the fanciful ones, were true, as were those retailing news of vast sums granted Wagner for his living expenses and plans for a theater to cost the staggering sum of five million gulden. Many years later Braun-Artaria recalled "the embittered war of opinions" that dominated "Munich during the short year Richard Wagner spent in the bright sunlight of the royal favor. Hatred and enthusiasm, contempt and adoration found their spokesmen—it was a time of continual excitement."[11] Driven to action by the anti-Wagner alliance, whose cause Wagner's machinations inadvertently strengthened, the king reluctantly asked him to leave Munich.

It was the end of a Wagner theater in Munich, but not of Wagner. He never returned for more than a few days to the city that had scorned him, and in the years that remained—he died in March 1883, a year after the premiere of *Parsifal*—relations with his dream king fluctuated. Yet what he most wanted, a *Festspielhaus* in Bayreuth for an annual season devoted solely to his work, he got, in large part through Ludwig's largesse. Not without turmoil: the king was showing escalating signs of mental instability as he retreated from his capital to superintend the building of his castles, and from public appearances to have plays and operas performed for him in solitude.

But Ludwig II retained a measure of sanity. At least with Wagner, he hedged his expenditures, imposing shrewd conditions on his loans. Nor was the superstition of anti-Semitism one of his symptoms. When Wagner protested against Levi's conducting his Christian drama, *Parsifal,* unless he had himself baptized, the king would not hear of it. And Wagner, who needed the Munich orchestra and who, for all his bigotry, valued Levi's talents, felt compelled to accept what he could not do without. Thus, in 1882, in a final ironic confrontation, a royal dreamer, without consulting Munich's burghers, forced a headstrong genius to bow to sober realities. If Munich's bourgeoisie did not play a leading role in this melodrama, it was at least a chorus on stage.

And the future? Reflecting on Munich, Alfred Lichtwark, the director of the Hamburg Kunsthalle whom we shall meet again, wrote around 1890, "We may count as a matter of course on the prince to foster all culture in line with the great tradition of the house of Wittelsbach." But this patronage gravely burdened Munich's middle class: "Now it becomes necessary to awaken in affluent *Bürger* an awareness that they have a duty and obligation to champion local art in accord with their capacities and resources."[12] He was too courteous to say so outright, but plainly Lichtwark doubted that Bavaria's bourgeoisie would rise to the occasion.

The two ways for bourgeois to secure high culture, and the two self-perceptions just delineated, are not abstractions, but they are extreme types. There were self-propelling and self-respecting *Bürger* in Munich as there were inactive, dependent bourgeois in Manchester, to say nothing of ambivalent middle-class citizens who harbored elements of each. Bourgeois styles, as the chapters to follow will show, were uniquely mixed and slowly evolving. The dominance of taste almost never rose wholly from below and rarely cascaded wholly from above. What is more, the bourgeoisie of the 1890s was no longer the bourgeoisie of the 1830s: its growing influence at the polling place, the emergence of a vast subclass of clerks, and the explosion of modernist styles in the 1880s, made the later generation see the world of its grandfathers as downright quaint. In short, definitions of bourgeois culture, complex every time, must start from scratch city by city, almost decade by decade.

Paris offers a good instance. "Centralization is the ruling principle of France," lamented the art critic Théophile Thoré in reviewing the Salon of 1864, after the state had forcibly reorganized the Ecole des Beaux-Arts. He feared, not without justice, that "governmental logic," a legacy from Napoleonic days when cultural activities including publishing and the stage had been under rigid supervision, would give the state control over the arts as it had over so much else. It was the central administration that had long regularly farmed out paintings to the few provincial museums that then existed, museums that had to wait until the 1880s until they exercised a measure of weight in these choices.

In 1860, reviewing Dutch museums, Thoré had declared his admiration for the way that "in rich and free Holland, as in rich and free England, almost everything is done through associations," with voluntary contributions. In those countries "a dozen amateurs," he observed enviously, band together to found a museum with an ambitious program—and they will succeed.[13] Indeed, when Thoré wrote, the French School of Fine Arts, the salons, the imperial awards and commissions showed the nephew imitating the uncle only too closely. This certainly held true for painting and sculpture, though a subterranean, increasingly aggressive subculture sniped at official art. Yet at least during the empire the conflicts between artistic agitators and the establishment were by no means clear-cut: the Salon des Refusés of 1863, ordered by Napoleon III to house paintings rejected for the Salon, had given unconventional painting the imperial imprimatur; it was a rebellion on imperial command. Other domains of French high culture, too, in music and the theater, were a mixture of private enterprise and government sponsorship.

The intermingling of state patronage and bourgeois initiative could grow so intricate as to bewilder even well-informed contemporaries. In 1869, in his informative and affectionate history of musical life in Vienna, Eduard Hanslick, the most feared critic in Vienna, hailed the celebrated Society of Austrian Friends of Music—Gesellschaft der österreichischen Musikfreunde—with its concerts and its conservatory as splendid middle-class achievements. He made a point of noting that it had been "an association of private individuals" who had in 1813 founded, and continued to support, these valuable institutions. To be sure, Hanslick reports, the statutes of the *Gesellschaft* had to be submitted to Emperor Francis I, who graciously confirmed them in 1814. But what mattered to him was that "one cannot say that the Austrian nobility, which otherwise had played such a praiseworthy role in the history of our country's music, supported the Vienna conservatory at all actively." The Friends of Music and its conservatory had been "purely bourgeois—*rein bürgerliche*—creations," its source "the active enthusiasm of the music-loving middle class."[14]

This passage is a tribute more to Hanslick's pride as a self-respecting *Bürger* than to the facts. Aristocratic patronage of music, long familiar in Austria, did not quickly wane in the nineteenth century. And while the moving spirit behind the society was Josef Sonnleithner, a commoner though a high government official, the public appeal for its founding was signed by a prince, a count, a countess, and a baroness, and the invitation to join the venture was signed by the Society of Noble Ladies for the Furthering of the Good and the Useful. Significantly, the "protectors" heading the Friends of Music in its early days, delegated as liaison to the imperial court, were two archdukes in succession. Even after this post lapsed in 1835, for three more decades a prince or a count headed the Austrian Friends of Music.

This patronage was more than cosmetic; the society's membership greeted news of exalted favor with unfeigned joy. It had good reasons: the conservatory, the breeding ground of professional musicians, kept losing money year after year, and it was imperial subsidies and imperial prodding of less exalted patrons, that kept the expensive institution alive. In 1832, the emperor donated 1,000 gulden, promptly followed by the empress, the crown prince, and four archdukes offering smaller, but equally welcome, sums. It literally paid to have friends in high places.[15]

Although distinguished commoners like the playwright Franz Grillparzer and upper-middle-class public servants on their way to a title played highly visible roles in the Friends of Music, its governing boards fairly begged to be robbed of their onerous independence. In 1837, when the specter of deficit loomed more threatening than ever, its officers came up with a seven-point program that included practical measures like a call for new subscriptions, adding seats to the concert halls, and (most prominently) appeals to the emperor for a continuing subvention of 3,000 gulden and, once again, to the Noble Ladies. Failing all this, the private society would have to turn the conservatory over to the imperial government or the regional estates. For all its notions about raising money from the general public or from its members, its first and second thoughts were to have the crown, the nobility, and the state come to the rescue. While in Amsterdam or Rotterdam enterprising burghers were beginning to raise funds for impressive museums and equally impressive orchestras, in Vienna what Hanslick called "the music-loving middle class" wanted above all to be taken care of by its betters.[16] This was not true of Zurich, only half true of Berlin, with other configurations taking their lead from the political style of the country.

For all this variety, the extreme types that have taken up this chapter did exist. As early as 1823, Thomas Dodd, a print dealer, auctioneer, and art collector in Manchester, had taken a confident line in a circular. "An alliance between commerce and the Liberal Arts is at once natural and salutary," he wrote. "The wishes of mankind increase with the means of gratifying them, and the superficial wealth, which is the fruit of extensive and flourishing trade, finds an object in those elegant productions of human genius and skill, which minister to the luxury of the imagination." Some twenty years after, in 1844, the *Times* of London proudly noted that the opera in London was the only house in Europe taking no subventions from the government. "The public here have the remarkable satisfaction of saying, 'It is we that have made it.' "[17]

That was one side. Munich showed the other. When in 1826 the cornerstone was laid for the Alte Pinakothek in Munich, the ground plan of the museum was etched into it, and a nearby copper plaque listed the principal collections to be housed in this temple to culture, complete with a dedication both obsequious and accurate: "Bavaria owes the building and its art treasures to the noble disposition of its rulers, the house of Wittelsbach." Some six decades later, in 1885, the founders of the Birmingham Art Gallery formulated the Manchester way to culture very differently: "By the gains of Industry," reads their plaque, "we promote Art."[18]

➤ THREE ❧

Acknowledged Legislators

Victorian middle-class tastes are easier to observe than to explain. There were concertgoing or art-buying bourgeois who developed predilections on their own, educating themselves in museums and concert halls. But others bore the stigmata of what might be called conformist individualism: an anxious surrender to ruling fashions in the deceptive guise of private judgment. In certain exclusive upper-bourgeois households, taste followed status. Toward the end of the century, the American novelist Henry B. Fuller invented a Mrs. Bates—or, rather, quite unfairly patterned her after a splendid Chicago patron, Mrs. Potter Palmer. Showing a young woman around her house, she calls attention to a Corot, "at least we think so." Although her husband had bought it "on his own responsibility," she tells her guest, "I let him go ahead, for, after all, people of our position would naturally be expected to have a Corot."[1]

Facing the bewildering variety of temptations, affluent men and women of taste saw nothing discreditable in entrusting themselves to self-appointed pedagogues: an astute dealer, a scholarly expert, a social arbiter. The sway of a persuasive enthusiast over monied collectors could be consequential; Mary Cassatt, among the richest of American expatriates settled in Paris and a considerable painter in her own right, advised visiting art lovers just what pictures to buy and was responsible for enriching American collections—which is to say, in later years, American museums—with fine Impressionists.* Not without

---

* And not Impressionists alone: Mary Cassatt discovered El Greco's magnificent *Assumption*, one of the parade pieces in the Chicago Art Institute since 1906, in Spain and persuaded the local magnate Martin Ryerson, the institute's most munificent patron, that this masterpiece by this then much neglected painter was worth the enormous sum of $40,000.

reason, the great American collector Louisine Havemeyer, who much admired her, called Cassatt a "godmother."[2] Aesthetic decisions could result, too, from chance encounters: a delighted revival of fond, long lost memories in an opera house or a theater or at an auction that awakened a slumbering passion. Some such delightful fancies to spend time and money on high culture made part of many an art lover's life history. But one opinion-forming institution rose to unprecedented prominence in the Victorian century: the critic.

I. Guides to Pleasure

The significance of the critic's ascent is ambiguous. It may seem to support the contention that Victorian individualism was indeed conformist or, on the contrary, that it was not. On the one hand, critics came to sound as though docile followers eager for trustworthy experts were prodding them to behave like legislators. As early as 1814, William Hazlitt, himself a formidable critic, observed that "the reputation ultimately, and often slowly affixed to works of genius, is stamped upon them by authority, not by popular consent or the common sense of the world. We imagine that the admiration of the works of celebrated men has become common, because the admiration of their names has become so. But does not every ignorant connoisseur pretend the same veneration, and talk with the same vapid assurance, of Michael Angelo, though he has never seen even a copy of any of his pictures, as if he had studied them accurately,—merely because Sir Joshua Reynolds has praised him?" This image of passive, easily led lovers of culture persisted through the century. "There is a certain portion of the reading public," brooded the *Musical Times* in 1889, "whose minds are of so invertebrate an order that they are either unwilling or unable to form an opinion for themselves. To them any statement proceeding from an authoritative source appeals with convincing force."[1] This critique of mid-level taste formation became a staple in the antibourgeois cause.

On the other hand, the critic, almost by definition a writer with marked personal views, could serve as a model for a class that professed to value private judgments. His tone was intimate, often confessional, and the first-person singular loomed large. Here is Théophile Gautier writing on François Villon but thinking of himself: "In the poets of the second rank you will find everything the aristocrats of art have disdained to work on: the grotesque, the fantastic, the trivial, the ignoble," and all the rest. "It is mainly on the dunghill that we find pearls." I, for one, he added, prefer that second rank, minor Roman poets even to Vergil. And here is Theodor Fontane sharing his impressions after reading Viktor von Scheffel's *Ekkehart;* this once famous historical novel "counts among the best books I have read."[2] Throwing such bridges between critic and reader eased the commerce between them.

So did the vastly enlarged market for opinions on the arts in print. But not without costs: the partial democratization of high culture produced something like a crisis in authority. One can understand why the respectable resisted reviewers touting new colors, new sounds, new topics, as though the old landmarks were no longer interesting or even valid. As always with change, anxiety followed. At the same time, the cacophony of critics' voices generated unexpected dividends for middle-class publics: clashing pronouncements did their part for the aesthetic liberation of the Victorian bourgeoisie. Even if laymen felt obliged to defer to a professed expert, conflicting judgments from critics could inspire their readers to go their own way. In the Victorian century nothing went uncontested—not religion, not politics, and certainly not criticism.

Thus Beethoven's *Eroica* elicited a mixed response; one early reviewer divided listeners to the towering Third Symphony into three parties: the enthusiasts who blamed the audience's musical illiteracy for its quizzical reception, the detractors who thought the music an unvarnished display of eccentricity, and a small minority of judicious music lovers who enjoyed the *Eroica's* many beauties but could not easily absorb its length and difficulty. Again, John Constable's *Salisbury Cathedral from the Meadows,* now one of his most highly regarded canvases, aroused contradictory reactions, ranging from excited approval to the harshest condemnation: some viewers hailed it as a masterpiece, while the *Morning Chronicle* denounced Constable's "coarse, vulgar imitation of Mr. Turner's freaks and follies."[3] All this rampant subjectivity, Victorian readers were to find, far from discrediting, only widened the critics' scope.

Bourgeois consumers, then, lived amid a chaos of desires; the fissures dividing aesthetic conservatives from their radical competitors ran not between the middle class and antibourgeois bohemians but between incompatible definitions of what is beautiful, or stirring, or elevating. Far more than anxiety about status, divergent, often quite unstable perceptions of pleasure governed the dissensions that plagued Victorian middle-class culture. This discord gave the critics their opportunity. Most of their readers would have agreed that reviewers were performing a public service. Many bourgeois did not know what they liked or, worse, what they ought to like. The critic, then, offered himself as the appointed guide to aesthetic pleasures. He pointed out their beauties, he explained their deeper meanings, he supported his preferences with reasons that mere consumers could parrot as their own. It was all so complicated!

Today, after Freud, we can complicate these complications further. We have learned that an act of choice in art, literature, or music is virtually never wholly free and seldom based wholly on artistic grounds. Political pressures and religious beliefs, family demands, reigning customs, and inner resistances constrict options in more or less elusive ways. Urges are triggered, too, by the stages of life in which they develop; with the passage of years, youthful ardor may ripen into more measured enjoyments, and parents with grown children are likely to have more time and money for the arts than the same couple had at its disposal two decades earlier. Rather more elusively, almost invisibly, buried memories may play as great a part in aesthetic choice as conscious decisions. A Victorian selecting an architect for his private house may have thought he was simply following his own bent, but when we see certain nineteenth-century tastes in houses remaining static through generations, we recognize the unconscious at work. A man's home was often his parents' castle.

These reflections confirm what we already suspect: commanding though the sway of financial resources over what one might have, they could not dictate what one might want. And the intriguing nonrational springs of action, the submerged psychological contests that have little to do with taste directly, are always at work. One bourgeois bought rugs, sculptures, sheet music because his parents had liked them; another did so because his parents had *not* liked them. Much that made for aesthetic pleasure was kept away from awareness because it could not have measured up to the respectability so close to Victorian bourgeois hearts. Much of it, in a word, was sheer unfocused sensual gratification. Commenting in 1840, the *Musical World* sternly charged that operagoers heard a singer without inquiring whether their delight is the performer's doing or not. "In the broadest meaning of the term, they are Sensualists:—gratify but their eyes and ears."[4] Such a judgment points once again to the depths of emotion on which human longing can draw. Only the most perceptive of critics could glimpse these hidden causes.*

Even national styles in taste, for which the Victorians liked to make a case and which critics often made their touchstone, proved of limited reliability. Although certain styles did not export well, many subjects and attitudes knew no frontiers: untold thousands of bourgeois in many countries wanted little more from high culture than moral improvement, access to elevated ideas, or a bit of amusement. Hence engravings of work-worn peasants praying, illicit lovers smitten with pangs of conscience, alcoholics and adulterers suitably punished, remained favorites among nineteenth-century consumers across Europe and the United States as reproaches to complacency and barriers against temptation. Generally, in the teeth of intensifying nationalism, the passage of years and the easing of travel did much to homogenize cultivated taste across Europe and the United States, so that national distinctions grew ever subtler.

---

* For Henry James, who could, the most valuable artist revealed most about life.

Nineteenth-century wars over matters of taste, then, were often fought out not just among rival schools and collectors but within individual bourgeois. A sophisticated Victorian music lover could intently respond to a late Beethoven quartet yet dissolve in tears at a cheap ballad from some operetta. An art collector could prize, without feeling at all torn, William Etty's seductive beauties and Constable's chaste cloud studies. An ardent theatergoer could delight in one of Dion Boucicault's dramas in which improbable uncomplicated heroes confronted improbable uncomplicated villains, yet hail Henrik Ibsen's astringent problem plays as a gift to civilization. Pleasures, in short, arise from distinct levels of the mind, ranging from the coarsest erotic relief to the most refined appreciation of subtleties in form and execution.

The apparent inconsistencies in Victorian taste, which no critic could resolve and which later generations derided as incomprehensible or as symptoms typical for bourgeois shallowness, begin to make sense once we appreciate the decisive vote of emotions in the making of aesthetic choices. Victorian theorists contemplating art, literature, music, or the theater seem to have taken for granted that pleasure has several sources and may undergo marked vicissitudes in the course of life. Antoine Quatremère de Quincy, a French archaeologist, sculptor, and widely read writer on the arts, spoke for much of the century in a major treatise as early as 1823. He contended that the purpose of imitation in the arts is to give pleasure, not merely physical gratification for eye, ear, or touch but moral satisfaction. Some eighty years later, Freud amended this position without abandoning it: aesthetic pleasure reaches down to the foundations of human development, to the drives, especially the sexual drives, whose raw demands the artist sublimates into objects of beauty through a happy junction of imagination and craftsmanship.

Late in the Victorian era, these insights were trickling down from savants to the educated public, often in banal form, even if at times the debt that high culture owes to sexuality dimly emerged. Even before, though, knowing Victorians had not been naive innocents: a few artists and critics identified sexual appetite as a subterranean, seldom publicly acknowledged ground for aesthetic pleasure. Officially, nudes were painted and sculpted with the purest intentions. So carnal an artist as Etty, who specialized in buxom nudes with firm, rounded breasts and seductive buttocks, rejected all allegations of harboring lewd notions. He was only saluting Beauty by celebrating Woman, "God's most glorious work." All innocence, he protested in the late 1840s, "People may think me lascivious, but I have never painted with a lascivious motive." His viewers knew better, and said so; when in 1844 Thackeray complained that the canvases Etty was exhibiting were "a classical and pictorial *orgy*," he was echoing the strictures of others.[5]

In sculpture and painting, then, Victorians detected an erotic subtext however earnestly artists might declare that sensuality had never entered their minds.* But at least one painter, William Mulready, let the cat out of the bag, though not very far. He judiciously chose the privacy of his sketchbook for the observation that "female beauty and innocence will be much talked about, and sell well. Let it be *covertly* exciting." A painting approaching "a more sensual existence," he added, will be "talked more about and sell much better." Yet a certain defensive adroitness was necessary; once "excitement appears to be the object," he warned, the "hypocrites will shout and scream and scare away the sensualists."[6] Nor was Mulready the only Victorian to understand that civilization, no matter how open-minded, exacts some necessary lies.

More generally, though, Victorians explained pleasure in a less erotic vein. In 1888, the city of Hamburg unveiled a bust of the merchant Gustav Christian Schwabe in gratitude for his generous gift of paintings to his native city. Responding with enthusiasm, a local patrician observed as he praised the donor's selflessness for his "magnificent" donation, "The affection and love for the place in which our cradle stood, which has already produced so much that is great and beautiful in the world and is celebrated by poets of all tongues, is deeply anchored in human nature."[7] The writer recognized in his homely way that aesthetic pleasure starts, and in important respects remains, at home.

That is why mature taste is almost sure to draw on its earliest manifestations. Even at puberty a young man or woman is already a sophisticate, for the keenest appreciation of color and composition, rhythm and melody, suspense and resolution has its primitive beginnings in childhood events—a mother singing to her child, a father pushing it in a swing, a grandparent reading it a story or pointing out the beauties of nature on a walk. Wordsworth's overworked "the Child is father of the Man" ratified for the nineteenth century a truth that Jesuits and other teachers had long known and that Freud would conscript for a general theory of psychological development. There was no better teacher across the gulf of years, it seems, than the resurrection of the past or, at the least, of inchoate feelings about affectionate others being in close touch—literally. Proust's Marcel, recapturing a world of gratification he thought forever lost, was not alone. Many Victorians had their madeleines.

All this is to say that without exposure to attractive new stimuli, patient absorption of unfamiliar shapes, colors, and melodies, and hard-won inner freedom, a vote for beauty was likely to be conservative. We shall see that even collectors adaptable enough to revise their first infatuations normally moved into

---

* It will emerge, to no one's surprise, that Victorians enjoyed the sight of lovely bodies, especially female bodies, as much as their grandparents and grandchildren, as long as the artist's motives were "pure."

unconventionality step by cautious step. Even in a century like the nineteenth, committed to change and professing enjoyment in innovation, aesthetic pleasure was often literally regressive. It is worth reiterating that the rule of habit in taste is psychologically easier to account for than originality, which always requires, for consumers as much as for creators, a mental effort.*

This explains why nineteenth-century agitators against accepted canons, often outsiders less by choice than from neurosis, aroused such furious opposition to their unaccustomed ways of seeing and hearing. It explains, too, why those made uncomfortable by the new in the arts liked to accuse the avant-garde of a passion for ugliness; to depart from safe, long-honored artistic sentiments was to step from the circle of beauty in which everyone could, or should, dwell content, into a whirlwind of anarchy where no standards were secure. The new threatened to uproot comfortable boundaries. This was the atmosphere in which nineteenth-century critics quarreled—and flourished.

Well before Queen Victoria's accession, critics had begun to make great claims for their profession. Around 1800, Friedrich Schlegel, the source of much thinking about criticism through the century, held that although sentiments on literature and the arts are subjective in origin, they need not be capricious. Such a view, adopted by other German romantics, could only reassure anxious readers that expressive criticism would not surrender to an arbitrary relativism that invited sheer chaos. In fact, no romantic critic ever believed that one opinion is as good as another. We cannot prove aesthetic judgments to be true, Schlegel wrote, "but we must have the knowledge without which aesthetic judgment would be impossible."[8] Criticism was a responsible calling.

In laying down essentials, Friedrich Schlegel tried to secure a bedrock for "the high science of authentic criticism." Eighteenth-century practical criticism had been largely limited to discovering the rules governing the work under review and then to classify it, justifying admiration or detestation on largely technical grounds. Schlegel bid up the stakes: had the critic's share in the creative process not been underrated? To make this implicit self-idealization a reality, Schlegel prescribed a demanding education for the critic. He must study aesthetic objects, their place in the author's work and character, and their literary heritage, which, it went almost without saying, included the classics.

Hence, as students of his theories have duly noted, for Schlegel literary criticism and cultural history virtually merged. His model critic is a close reader, an adept philologist, a penetrating analyst of minds, an alert historian, "a reader who chews his cud. That is, he should have more than one stomach."[9] The

---

* That is why children are the true conservatives.

ungainly image makes its point. Nor were sensitivity, knowledge, and patience enough for Schlegel's complete critic. He must be a poet no less than a detached observer. But detachment is indispensable; this is what Schlegel meant by romantic irony—a distance from cherished predilections. It seemed the only hope for escaping the prison house of unbreakable rules that neoclassical critics had built.

These were not just theoretical reflections on expressive freedom and on guidelines long taken for granted. Traditionalists, clinging to the certainties that had served them so well, felt under attack and deployed the defensive maneuvers to which hard-pressed authorities usually resort. Confronting change, they chose continuity. As late as 1828, when two well-known English painters, Etty and Constable, were competing for a vacant place in the Royal Academy, academicians like the portraitist Thomas Lawrence declared their unwavering support for Etty. After all, Etty was working in the classical vein, taking inspiration from mythology and other sources of dignified subjects, while Constable was only a landscapist. That Constable's canvases were distinctly more important than Etty's lush nudes, counted for less than the time-honored hierarchy governing the art of painting.

Whatever their self-definitions, the principal Victorian critics were bourgeois busy refining the palate of other bourgeois. Their proliferation was the necessary consequence of dramatic shifts in consuming publics. Concerts mainly attended by middle-class listeners were overtaking aristocratic soirees accessible by invitation only; newly founded museums, steadily soliciting gifts to improve their permanent collections and open to all at stated hours, were invading the once privileged domain of hoards shown whenever their owner, usually an aristocratic amateur, felt so disposed; the novel, which had grown into a quintessentially bourgeois phenomenon, was securing a readership and occasioning scrutinies hard to imagine a century earlier.

These servants of modern leisure spawned new professions, bourgeois in inspiration, management, and clientele: managers of virtuosi, booksellers, publishers with sizable lists, manufacturers of reasonably priced musical instruments. Periodicals specializing in well-defined domains of the arts grew into familiar presences on the cultural scene. And we recall mushrooming across Western civilization voluntary organizations intent on cultivating their members; they were composed of, and dominated by, lawyers, physicians, professors, architects, bankers, businessmen, and rentiers.[10] These were the readers, viewers, and listeners for whom the Victorian guardians of culture wrote their reviews.

The didacticism of the critics, as they settled into evolving middle-class culture, was perfectly unabashed. In 1862, in a collection of essays on modern French painters, Ernest Chesneau, an intelligent, well-connected critic and art historian, declared that he wanted his book to be a work of "free and sincere teaching" that disdained "pedantry and tediousness."[11] Three decades later George Bernard Shaw, far less polite, stated the same case in the most superior tones. "That great booby, the public," whose preceptor he had been chosen to be, was helpless without guidance—*his* guidance—and the representative booby was, of course, "the British bourgeoisie."[12]

The most self-assured critics, then, arrogated to themselves the role of mentor to a middle class badly in need of being scolded into good taste, weaned away from philistinism. Shaw's combative tone was fairly typical for these patronizing pedagogues. What good bourgeois seemed to lack most, critics would tell them, was the will for the difficult; they must learn that the response to great art or music is only partly enjoyment and largely hard work. "What kills art in France," Camille Pissarro wrote to his son Lucien in 1886, "is that people appreciate only works that sell easily." The following year, attending an exhibition he disliked, he complained that it "reeks powerfully of bourgeois." There was the enemy! To pessimists like Pissarro, the craving to reduce the higher goods of civilization to mere amusement seemed long-lived, perhaps immortal.[13]

The sheer staying power of vulgarity led some critics to doubt whether the middle class really wanted their services. Shaw for one demurred. "Your average Londoner," he wrote in early October 1893, "is, no doubt, as void of feeling for the fine arts as a man can be without collapsing bodily; but then he is not at all ashamed of his condition. On the contrary, he is rather proud of it, and never feels obliged to pretend that he is an artist to the tips of his fingers." Bluntly, "The Philistine is not indifferent to fine art: he *hates* it."[14] Trying to teach so obstinate a readership day after day, week after week, Shaw mobilized all his endurance, all his sardonic wit.*

Hence it was hardly surprising that at times nineteenth-century critics, though posturing as leading players in the drama of high culture, wallowed in bouts of gloom, convinced that their educational impact was negligible. In the

---

* When Shaw was appointed musical critic of the *World,* he described himself in the *Pall Mall Gazette,* January 17, 1891, as "a bachelor, an Irishman, a vegetarian, an atheist, a teetotaler, a fanatic, a humorist, a fluent liar, a Social Democrat, a lecturer and debater, a lover of music, a fierce opponent of the present status of women, and an insister on the seriousness of art." A writer to the editor of the *Musical Times* of June 1, 1891, calling himself "PHILOMEL," sarcastically granted that Shaw had listed at least one of his qualities he had not exaggerated—presumably his lying. See "Amenities of Musical Criticism" (p. 366.) Clearly Shaw paraded these qualities to establish his innocence and incorruptibility.

early 1890s, Eduard Hanslick, after thirty years still the czar of music criticism in Vienna, lamented the "epidemic of concerts" he had been compelled to attend, and to review, for the *Neue Freie Presse,* the favorite daily of the city's liberal bourgeoisie. His slave labor, he feared, had added up to very little, as importunate impresarios and performers soliciting an opinion—needless to say, a favorable opinion—had had a disastrous effect on apathetic audiences, unemployed soloists, and exhausted critics alike. Apparently, at best, serious criticism changes the minds only of constant and civilized readers. For the rest, the enthusiastic, tasteless popularity among operagoers and concertgoers for third-rate compositions made these into staples even though reviewers had unanimously damned them. The belief that critics leave their impress on composers, conductors, or soloists, let alone the public, is little better than a fond illusion.[15]

Taking the same tack in a moment of discouragement, Théophile Gautier, who drudged for decades pouring out criticism of art, drama, and dance to feed his family, was painfully aware that his reviewing left no permanent mark on anyone. "The newspaper article is a shrub that loses its leaves every evening and never bears any fruit." Theodor Fontane, who as both author and reviewer knew what he was talking about, was almost as gloomy. "Books must conquer on the quiet, from house to house," he wrote his editor in 1870. "What the newspapers do is fleeting."[16]

Such despair was no less excessive than its pendant, the sanguine assertion that critics were setting the signposts for nineteenth-century culture. These fluctuations in reviewers' self-appraisals were symptoms for an age of vertiginous movement and inconsistent signals. But none of their failures, real or imagined, could validate the critics' confessions of impotence. It is striking testimony to the anxiety of creative spirits in the presence of critics, after all, that beginning in the 1880s, Monet subscribed to two clipping services.[17] Two decades before, in the summer of 1865, a Daumier lithograph, *The Promenade of the Influential Critic,* illustrated a fashionable belief in the critic's authority: a superb, self-absorbed reviewer, catalog in hand, strides through a salon while artists, desperate to have him notice them, fawn on him. And Bruckner's oft-reiterated terror before Hanslick's hostile attentions is notorious, contributing further evidence that Victorian critics might make some difference after all.

Of course, the Victorians knew that they were not the first to produce judges and theorists of literature and art. They could appeal to Greece and Rome: to Aristotle, Horace, or Longinus. Closer to home, they could draw on the age of the Enlightenment, on practical critics like Denis Diderot and theorists like Edmund Burke, or on ambidextrous talents so familiar to the era. Voltaire, not content with writing acclaimed tragedies, had done extensive duty as a drama critic; Sir Joshua Reynolds had alternated painting the rich and eminent with authoritative lectures on art. Both had foreshadowed a contingent of nine-teenth-century architect-critics, painter-critics, composer-critics, and the rest of the doubly gifted: novelists like Henry James and Emile Zola, poets like Théophile Gautier and Stéphane Mallarmé, composers like Hector Berlioz and Richard Wagner all wrote provocatively about their craft. The Victorian age was, then, quite literally an age of criticism, swamped by the mass of opinion in newspapers and periodicals committed to informing its subscribers about the latest novel, play, symphony, or exhibition, to say nothing of occasional learned musings on the cultural scene. By the 1850s, a veritable tribe of critics was clamoring to be consulted.

Was it worth consulting? There were those, early in the century and late, who had their doubts. A critic's prestige or self-assurance did not guarantee insight, let alone profundity. As early as the mid-1830s, then still a fairly young critic, Charles Augustin Sainte-Beuve, complained that literary criticism was almost nonexistent, that poets and novelists wanted only servility and all too often got what they asked for. After the volume of criticism available to the reading public reached alarming proportions, more and more critics were ready to turn on their own craft. Théophile Thoré, reviewing the Paris Salon of 1864, noted that "the system—we dare not say, the aesthetic—of French critics seems to us narrow, quite incomplete."[18] Cultural aristocrats blamed the democratiza-tion of access to high culture for infecting the judges as much as those whose work they were judging. The slick and the second-rate were abundantly rep-resented in the press.* If the emancipation from entrenched prejudices is a principal goal of education, many Victorian critics were not educators at all but panderers.

This lament became a litany: producing an avalanche of mediocre and venal reviews, discontented literati charged, writers on the arts and literature were failing their noble calling. Criticism, ideally the cure for the aesthetic malaise of the age, had become one of its symptoms. Far from acting as retaining walls against the muddy flood (to resort to a metaphor favored by the critics of crit-ics), too many of them were easing its entry. The image of waters drowning high culture, or one of its variants, became almost obligatory. "In our time, when readers are deluged with newspapers, periodicals, books, and by the pro-fusion of advertisements," wrote Leo Tolstoy in praise of Matthew Arnold's frowning surveys of contemporary culture, "not only does such criticism seem to me essential, but the whole future culture of our educated world depends

---

* The greatest danger to culture seemed to be what we now call the "middlebrow."

on whether such criticism appears and acquires authority." It did appear, but its authority seemed unstable. In 1885, Alphonse Daudet told Henry James, "We are perishing from books, they swell over the banks, they stifle us, they are killing us."[19]

Henry James, distressed, agreed. Himself a major critic, he respected the occupation and detested its stupid or corrupt practitioners. There was much convincing evidence on his side. All too many editors had concerts, exhibitions, or novels covered by flickering literary lights who were genial and cheap, or who had well-connected sponsors. It had long been a common complaint that these editors, mostly unreconstructed philistines, had no way of recognizing, and no interest in employing, knowledgeable critics.

This held true, James believed, as much in painting as in fiction. The "profession of art-critic," he wrote, might cut paths through the jungle of contemporary styles, but he sadly determined that it was in short supply. In 1888, in a long novella, *The Reverberator,* he had already introduced an insensitive, sensation-mongering journalist who exemplified that modern vice—"reporterism." Three years later, in a short essay titled "Criticism," he turned to reviews of fiction, his own specialty, to draw even more disheartened conclusions about the journalism of his time. "Criticism" brilliantly sums up the grievances of avant-gardes against middle-class philistines. Literary criticism, James wrote, was flourishing all too widely, flowing "through the periodical press like a river that has burst its dykes." Seeking to define this outpouring, James adopted the rhetoric of the marketplace—the vocabulary of the enemy. Modern criticism had become a commodity and, with demand outrunning supply, an industry.[20]

Its true name, James asserted, was " 'reviewing,' " a word he put with tight-lipped distaste into quotation marks. The trade of reviewing and the art of criticism, he asserted, have nothing in common. Visualizing its principal consumer, the periodical press, with a calculatedly repellent image as "a huge open mouth which has to be fed," James anatomized it as starved for material. A little unfeelingly, he waxed sarcastic against the denizens of Grub Street who "may turn an honest penny" judging what they do not understand; the sheer quantity of reviews was crowding out high-quality criticism. The price for the "diffusion of penmanship and opportunity" was tremendous: vulgarity, crudeness, stupidity, and irrelevance. The whole was nothing less than a "catastrophe," adding up to "the failure of distinction, the failure of style, the failure of knowledge, the failure of thought."[21]

With their highly developed literary sense, and most telling for James, their wealth of lively experience, true critics are immensely useful to literature. In an emotional peroration, he abandoned the mercantile world for that of chivalry: the life of the critic is "heroic"; he must "understand for others" and remain perpetually under arms.[22] Only the knight battling for civilization can teach his audiences the necessary discriminations.

James's severity seems rather excessive. A century that boasted critics like William Hazlitt and Charles Baudelaire, Georg Brandes and Theodor Fontane, Sainte-Beuve and, toward its end, George Saintsbury, and, for that matter, Henry James himself, was scarcely a desert of taste.* But, as we have seen, much reviewing really was in a parlous state. For every expertly trained Hanslick there were ten dabblers, self-educated and ill-equipped.

In rare instances, the dilettante could be as strong a voice as George Bernard Shaw. He had largely picked up his erudition and passion for music in his youth, in a troubled household where it was a substitute religion. Endowed with an accurate ear, strong memory, technical competence, and a copious stock of musical examples, Shaw was a layman competently filling the role of professional pundit. He shared his colleagues' view that to be a trustworthy critic was not only a calling but also a burden, but for some years Shaw was willing to shoulder it. The readers of his music criticism in the London of the late 1880s and early 1890s were fortunate in this exuberant, opinionated—and knowledgeable—stylist.

French readers of reviews had their impressive cicerones as well. But the lower reaches of French criticism were a slum. We may doubt the ubiquity of ignorance, dishonesty, and recklessness among Parisian book reviewers that Balzac caricatures in *Les Illusions perdues.* Lucien de Rubempré, the dubious hero of that trilogy, an improbably handsome, ambitious provincial, and his Parisian companions are thrown into the poisonous maelstrom of literary life, where reviewers praise up or tear apart a novel on command from their superiors. They disregard its true qualities for the sake of repaying a slight, assuage their envy or puff an unworthy title for money. Much of this reads like Balzac's revenge on the publishing industry, which had given him some bitter experiences. Unscrupulousness and cynicism, however extensive, were not quite so unmitigated in real life.

But not all of Balzac's literary Paris was fiction. French music critics in particular were ill informed and incurably partisan, open to bribes from performers and pressure from editors. They wrote like worshipers or executioners, dealing out extravagant praise or extravagant censure. Not only were few edi-

---

* When James published "Criticism," he was going through a bad patch in his career. Two novels of the late 1880s, *The Princess Casamassima* and *The Bostonians,* for which he had had great expectations, had been commercial and critical failures and greatly reduced the demand for his work. Moreover, he was embarking on what would turn out to be a calamitous detour from his real strengths as a writer: he was trying to conquer the London stage. But a purely biographical reading of James's cry of pain would slight the true dimensions of the crisis.

tors willing to spend money on a trained music critic; most of them expected their own political ideology to infiltrate even the reviews of concerts. In 1862, near the end of his illustrious career, François Joseph Fétis, composer, virtuoso, biographer, editor, dean of music critics in the French-speaking world, likened reviewers to the primitive listener who says, "*I like this music,* or *It doesn't please me.*"[23] Bourgeois relying on this lot could hardly expect to have their tastes polished.

Even though scores of reviewers sold their opinions to earn a few francs or shillings, this did not keep serious critics from making the expansive claims for their cultural importance that we have quoted. Early in the century Shelley had called poets the unacknowledged legislators of the world; as the visibility of critics rose with the passing decades, their elite came to see themselves as the acknowledged legislators of taste. In an essay of 1861, Matthew Arnold famously observed, "Of the literature of France and Germany, as of the intellect of Europe in general, the main effort, for now many years, has been a critical effort."[24] Large segments of the educated public could endorse this claim and, unless their own taste was pummeled too severely, think it a good thing. There was something soothing about having one's choices directed by guides fit to point the way.

At the same time, critics still looked up to the "creative" artist, who, as that adjective broadly hints, was breathing an air purer than theirs. He reached for the laurels of genius; critics were at their best competent craftsmen. Even Matthew Arnold, warding off the charge that he had ranked the critical enterprise too high, partially capitulated in 1865; everybody, he wrote, "would be willing to admit, as a general proposition, that the critical faculty is lower than the inventive."[25] But this concession, he urged with characteristic energy, did not amount to a denigration of the critical enterprise.

For all their lofty air as teachers of society, then, nearly all Victorian critics retained a fig leaf of reticence. Even when they fancied themselves but one small step behind, they stood ready to take second place to the great composer or the great architect. Surely there *was* something creative about criticism—had Schlegel not called the critic a poet? That many distinguished novelists, playwrights, painters, and composers also followed the trade of reviewing only lent credibility to this posture. Baudelaire spoke for the fraternity in an essay on Wagner's *Tannhäuser:* "It would be an entirely novel event in the history of the arts to have a critic making himself into a poet," but "all great poets become naturally, fatally, critics. I pity the poets guided by instinct alone."[26] Thus professional critics could turn aside as spurious Oscar Wilde's quip, exceptionally feeble for this wit, that those who cannot create criticize those who can.

Indeed, as we shall see, Wilde himself, undeterred by inconsistency, undercut it by trying to erase whatever gap remained between creator and critic as he assigned the latter pride of place.*

Virtually no other critic dared to take so daring a leap. But whatever positions they might take in particular instances—and they occupied, we know, virtually every point on the cultural landscape—they believed their status worth struggling for, worth acquiring, and, later, worth keeping. Hence they publicly expected to be thrown into ambushes, into battles, into war to the end—Victorian critics, and not just the hacks who had no other note to strike, overworked these military metaphors. Quite incidentally their bellicose style proved a help in sustaining their claims to prestige and influence: warring critics could claim that they mattered because they were defending the heights of culture, rising above gross utility against barbarians on the march. The learned and clearheaded Hanslick was only one reviewer to find emphatic language at once necessary and enjoyable when dealing with Wagner. Though he was proud of having done his utmost to foster young, unknown, talented composers and performers, he relished the pugilistic side of his work. The issues, Hanslick told his readers, were important and forbade bland responses. To be silent in the presence of Bayreuth, or polite, would be a betrayal of the critic's vocation.

The combats over Wagner offer exhilarating moments of critics at arms. In 1894, in his reminiscences, Hanslick suggested in all seriousness that a ten-year moratorium on books about Wagner could only benefit the composer. Obviously he did not mean to silence himself or sensible musicians like Hans von Bülow who had recovered from their infatuation with the Music of the Future; his own preoccupation with Wagner, he insisted, had been imposed on him by the man's megalomaniacal posturing supported by his acolytes. It was essential to expose Wagner—the incense-laden atmosphere at the annual Bayreuth festivals, the rape of music by the word, the pseudo-religious Wagnerian program. What of the blasphemous Wagner Museum in Vienna, complete with relics? the nauseating effusions of performers who swooned over the privilege of serving him? the scholastic and adoring interpretations of leitmotifs? Nor could one overlook Wagner's anti-Semitism, one of the "ten commandments of his adherents."[27]

Hanslick was of course aware that Wagner had cruelly lampooned him as Beckmesser in *Die Meistersinger;* Wagner had actually considered calling that absurd pedant "Hans Lick." And his vehemence against Wagner had an even more intimate dimension—his mother was Jewish. But in the main it reflect-

* See below, pp. 131–36.

ed Hanslick's partisanship in the music wars of the age. Brahms, his good friend, was also Hanslick's favorite living composer, and this commitment entailed the repudiation of Wagner's musical pipe dreams. And so, Hanslick joined untold numbers of commentators on Wagner, an outsize figure who invited, and got, strong responses, not all of them the responses he wanted. Caressing, never questioning, a full-blown sense of his historic importance, utterly humorless as he asked the world to bow down before his crusade, Wagner was not a figure calculated to evoke moderate reviews.

In 1876, the year that Bayreuth opened, the devout Wagnerian Wilhelm Tappert, music teacher, historian, and editor, gathered the first harvest in a substantial dictionary of the hostile comments thrown at the Master. And since the flood of invectives never receded, Tappert could bring out an enlarged edition in 1903. It is a reference work filled with examples of animosity, vulgarity, blind ignorance, as well as a number of fairly pointed entries. Wagner's music, said one critic, is "the adroit ape of reality." *Die Meistersinger,* said another, is "a mountain of silliness and banality." Before 1848, said a third, Wagner had been a gifted dramatic composer who, after 1848, became a "vain, insane zealot." Trying to blend recitatives and arias, said a fourth, Wagner had produced "a freak—neither fish nor fowl."[28] To be sure, Tappert never intended to amuse anyone; he only wanted to show the world how scribblers masquerading as critics had misled innocent music lovers. But whether one cheered him on in his enterprise of defending the Master, or cheered him on because he had amassed so many good reasons to despise Wagner, was a matter of taste. Whatever the claims of criticism, not even the most infatuated ever called it a science.

2. Master Craftsmen

The incessant warfare among critics generated extreme views of the critical enterprise itself. An important assertion of the critic's place, far more reasonable than Wilde's, dates from 1857: Sainte-Beuve's review of *Madame Bovary.* Since the previous October, this masterpiece had appeared serially in the *Revue de Paris,* but, much to Flaubert's voluble disgust, Maxime Du Camp, the editor and his friend, dropped the passage about Emma's ride through Rouen in a hackney cab with Léon. Du Camp had sound reasons for self-censorship: the police were likely to confiscate the issue and threatening to close down his liberal *Revue* altogether. In January 1857, even without this brilliant carnal scene in which nothing scandalous is explicit, the government haled Flaubert into court for obscenity. He was acquitted, and in April *Madame Bovary* appeared in book form, including the offending pages, and proved an instant success among readers, if not all the critics. In May, Sainte-Beuve, an acknowledged authority on French literature, applauded *Madame Bovary* with only minor cavils. Flaubert represented a new generation, and Sainte-Beuve welcomed him: "Son and brother of eminent surgeons, Monsieur Flaubert handles the pen as others do the scalpel. Anatomists and physiologists, I find you on every hand!"[1]

That was speaking literature, but Sainte-Beuve did not intend to ignore politics. He informed his readers that the unliterary attention recently paid *Madame Bovary* was much on his mind, and he praised the judges' wisdom in finding Flaubert innocent. "From now on," he added firmly, as it were addressing the authorities, "the work belongs to art, only to art; it is accountable to criticism alone, and critics can deal with it in complete independence." When an "authentic and living work swims into our ken, full canvas flying and banner floating in the breeze as though to taunt us with the question *What do you think of us?*," the "true critic," smarting with frustration at having been silent, will want "to speak up, to greet and salute the work as it passes by."[2] The ship the author has designed must remain the focus of attention, and to welcome it is a worthy task, making freedom indispensable to the critic. A sturdy assertion of stature animates this review from start to finish.

Among the most interesting of Victorian critics, Sainte-Beuve deserves a prominent place in this history. Around mid-century, almost fifty, he voiced his desire to "renew Art and liberate it from certain conventional rules." Long after he had fought down the romantic ideology he had adopted in his apprentice years in the wake of Victor Hugo, he continued to bear witness to the "religion of literature."[3] It was a creed that engrossed him all the more as he gradually shed his literary and religious allegiances. Born in 1804 at Boulogne-sur-mer in modest circumstances, he refused to apologize for his origins and remained a principled, though hardly activist, liberal all his life. Goaded by his lust for literature, he halfheartedly pursued the study of medicine much the way that Flaubert would study law: eager to fail. He wanted to be a poet. From 1824, the year of its founding, he contributed reviews to the *Globe*, a well-edited liberal paper that assembled the French romantics to whom Sainte-Beuve was professionally and socially close in those years.

He began with intimate, largely confessional verse, but around 1830 he experimented with portraits of writers and found his calling: the judicious literary-biographical-historical essay, which became his signature. In 1834, he published a self-referential novel, *Volupté,* and soon after undertook a massive project, *Port-Royal,* a scholarly history of Pascal and the early-seventeenth-century founders of Jansenism. But his wider reputation rested on the famous *Causeries du lundi,* weekly articles carefully pondered and carefully written, which appeared every Monday from 1849 to 1869, the year of his death. "I have

only one pleasure left," he wrote in 1846, "I analyze, I botanize, I am a naturalist of minds—what I want to create is *literary natural history.*"[4] He would be
a scientific critic, scientific and historical.

Like Friedrich Schlegel, then, Sainte-Beuve was persuaded that the critic
must embed a work of literature in its author and the author in his world;
without that, a full interpretation must elude the most intelligent reader. What
he called "historical explanation" was essential not simply to secure just due to
the great French tradition that reader and critic shared but also to gauge what
place modern work should occupy in the pantheon of culture. To know the
present required knowing the past.

To prepare himself for his natural history much along Friedrich Schlegel's
lines, Sainte-Beuve accumulated a formidable store of erudition. No wonder
he frequently returned to Goethe, "the king of critics," another indefatigable
collector of nuggets, whose appetite for experience Sainte-Beuve enthusiastically endorsed.[5] In his maturity, he liked to quote Goethe's comment to Eckermann that the classical is healthy and the romantic sick. This aphorism was tired
by then, but it led Sainte-Beuve back to his principles: the critic must base his
verdicts on solid information rather than dreamy free associations, on facts
rather than a yearning for an imagined past or imagined future. Typically he
valued precision of language in creators and critics alike, and inveighed against
riots of imagination left unchecked. He established his credentials by specializing in French literature and French history, underscoring his conviction that
before a critic can tell others what to think, he must know what *he* thinks, and
give good reasons.

In an article on the French aphorist Joseph Joubert, born exactly half a century before him, Sainte-Beuve drew a wishful self-portrait. This was the critic
he wanted to be: spectator, listener free of envy and ambition, inquisitive, attentive, at once disinterested and yet interested in everything, a true lover of beauty. In his long and prolific career, he often pondered his vocation: to rebuild the
temple of taste by enlarging it, and to endow literature with a certain charm,
realism, poetry, and a bit of physiology. He made himself into the self-appointed custodian of literary quality, which, to his mind, has always been in danger,
never more so than in his age.[6] Half a century before Henry James, the condition of criticism depressed him. To share enthusiasms and teach appreciation
was not enough. The critic must confront his texts with as open a mind as
human frailty will allow and must forget, if possible, that he has read them
before and knows them well. No parti pris!

The sincere and candid judge of literature, Sainte-Beuve reassured his readers, need have no fear: the things worth admiring will continue to seem
admirable. His career demonstrated, though, that what such a critic had every

right to fear, and a solemn obligation to disregard, was the growing list of enemies. In the 1890s, Lord Acton would muse that an honest historian is unlikely to have any friends; Sainte-Beuve might have said as much about an honest
critic. From his first essays on, he had trumpeted his duty to remain unbought.
This made it essential to resist importunate acquaintances avid for helpful
notices. Early on, in 1834, he observed that whenever he counted on his fingers the friendships ruined by articles he had refused to write or by praise he
had lavished imprudently, he would muse on how unreal these friendships had
been. He grew frightened at "the wretched occupation of critic," which dissolved relationships he might have saved.[7] The thirty-five years that remained
to him gave him frequent occasions to watch his forthright essays wreak further havoc in his life. He took it stoically; a professional superego kept him
from betraying his highest priority: to tell the truth about literature past and—
more risky—literature present.

For all his sympathy with new writers, Sainte-Beuve was more a guardian
of standards than a discoverer of talents.[8] And since these standards governed
his own work, he could not permit himself simplistic judgments. He valued
Stendhal as an intelligent scourge of sentimentality and stuffiness, but he could
not warm up to Stendhal's novels, in fact found them detestable. He stood
astonished before Victor Hugo's energy, his dramatic and poetic powers, but
objected to his grandiloquence, hyperbole, and lack of taste. Deploying his
exceptional gift for subtle readings, he anatomized the way Chateaubriand had
spoiled his autobiography with unscrupulous revisions that had transformed
Mémoires d'outre tombe into an embarrassing display of vanity and claims to
omniscience.[9]

These shrewd readings and his tireless researches did not appease Sainte-
Beuve's detractors, who charged him with excessive rationalism.* Granted, the
temperature of Sainte-Beuve's essays, with their analytical finesse, was rather
cool. He did his work, he admitted, under the sign of the "eternal and sacred
laws of reason."[10] Still, he believed that his work was anything but unemotion-
al. And, to judge from the reception of his reviews, most of his bourgeois readers accepted Sainte-Beuve's methods as familiar and his opinions as sensible.
Forging a congenial accord with their favorite critic, they did not protest that
poems or novels are too fragile to bear the weight that biography and history
impose on it.

* Most famously Marcel Proust severely lectured Sainte-Beuve in a posthumously published
essay for relying on reason at the expense of intuition. No wonder he should have failed to give
Stendhal, Gérard de Nerval, Baudelaire, and Balzac their due! But Proust's critique of Sainte-
Beuve was, if at times telling, quite unjust; it is a reminder of the judgments we have come to
expect from a modernist, no matter how perceptive and intelligent, face to face with a Victorian.

Plainly Sainte-Beuve, much though he might have balked at the identification, was a good bourgeois in his own way. Lavishing high praise on the marquis d'Argenson, an influential official in the regime of Louis XV known for his talent, probity, and public spirit, Sainte-Beuve hailed him for his middle-class virtues, his "bourgeois simplicity and incorruptible even temper."[11] In a long, typically fair-minded essay on de Maistre, that uncompromising reactionary political thinker, Sainte-Beuve criticized him for ignoring that historic phenomenon—the modern middle class. "No spirit, however elevated he considers himself to be," he asserted, "has the right to show himself insolent with other spirits, however bourgeois they may seem to be."[12] The middle class, to Sainte-Beuve's mind, had the supreme virtue of common sense, a virtue he hoped was also his own. Just as middle-class, one might add, was the virtue of hard work, and in this, too, he was at one with the bourgeoisie: no one labored harder than Sainte-Beuve in producing a lucid and beautifully informed essay every week.

Though a far less prominent figure in histories of Victorian culture than Sainte-Beuve, Théophile Thoré was a compelling commentator who changed people's minds, if slowly.[13] Surely an art critic who put the virtually unknown Vermeer on the map belongs in this history. Impassioned about his vocation from his youth—he was born in 1807—Thoré trained himself to become a preeminent specialist in seventeenth-century Dutch painting and a learned, incisive, independent-minded reviewer of the Paris salons. In December 1835, fired up by his calling, he reassured his mother, who worried about his defection from Christian piety, that he too was devout. But not in her way: he was a votary in the religion of art, though not an unthinking enthusiast. In Thoré's book spontaneity was never a sufficient resource for the critic.

Why should he turn himself into a grocer—an *épicier*—or a lawyer? he asked rhetorically. He pointedly called himself a "priest" who, mediating between thought and the masses, "interrogates God in order to pass along his oracles to human beings." Republican and atheist, Thoré took so reverent a tone only to his mother, but his stormy career attests to his high seriousness, his private secular faith. "I have acquired proficiency, and am on the way to placing myself in the first rank of criticism." Typically he preferred the language of warfare to that of theology. As "a journalist and an artist," he saw himself as a soldier fighting for the good cause. His life, he wrote, was—of course!—a continuous battle.[14]

Thoré had much in common with Sainte-Beuve, but what divided them is more intriguing. Both were on the left in politics, Thoré far more earnestly than Sainte-Beuve, who was more attached to the theory of republicanism than to its practice. A democratic activist with socialist leanings, launching opposition periodicals and scattering militant pamphlets in the July Monarchy and after, Thoré paid for his beliefs with time in prison and, for more than a decade, with exile. Neither was born amid ease, but while Sainte-Beuve soon made a good living from his publications, Thoré, embroiled in unprofitable ventures, long lived in poverty. Until his return to France in 1859, in his early forties, he importuned his mother for subsidies. But there was always art. It took him decades before he would curb his relish for mounting barricades, but even in his most militant years he had haunted museums. Until he died—like Sainte-Beuve in 1869—he clung to progressive yardsticks as he judged art, but never deserted aesthetic criteria.

It is fascinating to watch Thoré trying to integrate his two great passions, politics and art, not without strains. In late March 1848, a month after the February Revolution had chased the Orléanist dynasty from the French throne, he published a skimpy article on the Salon in striking contrast to his substantial coverage of previous years. In these heady days he would not keep his readers focused on paintings. "Politics has more interesting spectacles in store for us. Today we are making better things than art and poetry: we are making living history." As a democrat, he pleaded for an art that would not exclude so-called ordinary mortals. "Formerly they made art for gods and for princes," he wrote in the late 1850s. "Perhaps the time has come to make 'ART FOR MAN.' " As a cosmopolitan, he wanted art to nurture all humanity: "There are no more foreigners." The true link among people is the compatibility of their ideals. "Do you love what is true, what is beautiful? That is enough. We are fellow citizens in the great city of the future."[15]

The supreme artistic style for Thoré was, as it almost had to be, realism; art must render nature animate or inanimate and concentrate on contemporary themes rather borrowing from antiquity or mythology. In 1867, Thoré assailed the Austrian painter Hans Makart, then much in vogue among the chic, for having "invented an *Ideal Landscape*." Why not paint a real landscape? he asked rhetorically. "To falsify nature is to falsify humanity! The false everywhere, when the truth is so attractive."[16] This taste, underwritten by his left-wing views, fed Thoré's hostility to the medal-winning art of the Paris salons. He granted that academic stars—Gérôme and the rest—had some talent. But they deserved neither their prizes nor their prices. With supreme hubris, Thoré predicted that the day would come when their canvases would fetch sixty francs apiece, and promised that he would not be among the buyers of these bargains. For once his prophecy was off the mark.

Thoré's democratic perspective made its most momentous contribution to the history of taste in alerting him to the mundane, often humble, subject matter favored by the Dutch masters. To his dismay, connoisseurs still ranked the art of Rembrandt, Hals, Terborch far below that of the Italians. The Venetians, the Florentines, the Sienese had been studied and appreciated only too thoroughly, while the Dutch with their "little masters" were being discovered far too slowly. No critic would do more to repair this oversight than Thoré. Still, he never lapsed into the vulgarity of judging a work of art entirely by its subject. "Doubtless art is in no way directly a professor of philosophy or a social reformer. Preachers' paintings are ridiculous. Art has beauty for its subject matter, not ideas." Yet he could not forbear adding, "Through beauty one should make people love what is true, what is just, what is fruitful for human development. A portrait, a landscape, a familiar scene, any subject whatever can have this result, as much as a heroic or allegorical subject." Only in this sense "can we say the subject hardly matters." It must "harbor something significant and admirable."[17]

In these professions of faith the radical and the aesthete were struggling for supremacy. Fortunately Thoré's definitions of what serves or harms humanity were imprecise enough to give his taste and intuitions generous room for play. His most cherished artist, Rembrandt, who "dominates all his compatriots beyond measure," was a "political" painter only in the oblique sense of choosing his subjects from all ranks. Yet Thoré devoted page after excited page to his praise and worked toward a biography all his mature years, a book he never completed.[18]

His discovery of Vermeer offers even more dramatic evidence for a critic who has freed himself from ideology, a critic of refined taste fertilized by scholarship. Thoré first came upon that painter in 1842, struck by Vermeer's luminous view of Delft. At the time, almost nothing was known about its maker; even the spelling of his name was uncertain, and his paintings were attributed to other Dutch masters, to Pieter de Hooch or Gabriel Metsu or Nicolaes Maes, to bring better prices. He had happened upon a Sphinx, wrote Thoré, and to solve her riddle became his obsession.[19] He pursued Vermeer through museums and private collections across western Europe to identify his paintings by noting his inimitable color—those tender blues and yellows—and his superb draftsmanship. No one painted arms and hands like Vermeer!

Yet Thoré's mission to secure Vermeer his rightful place at the summit of European art yielded results sluggishly. Down to 1888, when Vermeer's *Woman with the Pewter Ewer* was auctioned off for around $8,000, his paintings brought anywhere from $200 to $2,500.[20] In 1876, in his popular *The Masters of Past Times,* a report on his visits to Dutch and Flemish museums, Eugène Fromentin, himself a notable painter, spoke of Vermeer as being practically unknown in France. But, ignoring the splendid Vermeers he walked past, Fromentin himself did little to spread word of Thoré's epochal find. In matters of taste, it seemed, even the educated could be hard to educate.

Whom *did* the Victorian critics educate, and with what results? We know too little to offer assured conclusions, and some of what we do know is disheartening. Being only human, many bourgeois embraced a certain reviewer not to improve their tastes but to confirm their predilections. And with the venality we have noted before, much reviewing was the antagonist of cultivation rather than its agent. Yet there are scattered hints that reputable critics did not look or listen in vain.

Sainte-Beuve's prodigious output for one reached cultivated circles in influential periodicals like the *Revue des deux mondes* and no less influential newspapers like the semi-official *Moniteur universel* and, later, the *Constitutionnel,* both read across France by prosperous bourgeois. The audience for his essays, running into the hundreds, was large and faithful, and they did double duty gathered in widely circulated volumes: fifteen *Causeries du lundi,* thirteen *Nouveaux lundis,* three *Portraits contemporains,* and the rest. By the age of forty, he was entrenched enough in the establishment to be elected to the Académie Française. Flaubert did not care for Sainte-Beuve's style, his affluence, and the historical bent of his criticism, but more than once paid grudging tribute to his literary authority. The Goncourt brothers, whose vast diary is a sour commentary on their times and their fellow litterateurs, denounced him as a hopeless bourgeois—surely one ground for his popularity—but acknowledged Sainte-Beuve's gifts. Thus, despite opposition from principled radicals for making peace with the empire of Napoleon III, Sainte-Beuve came to be anointed as a minor national treasure. His fame spread: Matthew Arnold called him "the finest critical spirit of our time."[21]

According to the self-congratulatory memoirs of Louis Véron, the publisher who in 1829 secured Sainte-Beuve's pen for his new *Revue de Paris,* he recognized the young poet's expository gifts from the start. Introducing the first number of the *Revue,* Véron maintained that in an age of widely diffused knowledge, "criticism, that wholly new science," was best entrusted to a learned, elegant polemicist like Sainte-Beuve, who was bound to arouse a good deal of controversy.[22] In 1849, now publishing the *Constitutionnel,* Véron persuaded Sainte-Beuve to do a weekly column. The famous *Lundis* were born.

Thoré, too, wrote for Véron's *Constitutionnel,* mainly doing salons. But its remarkable rise in circulation owed virtually nothing to these eminent judges of literature and art. Before the revolution of 1830, it had been a leading paper boasting more than 16,000 subscribers, a respectable circulation for those days. In the excited times after the July Revolution, it rose to over 23,000. Then it drooped; in 1844, when Véron came to the rescue, it was practically moribund with a mere 3,600 subscribers. But the next year it rebounded to its former peak.[23] The secret? Véron had offered Eugène Sue, guaranteed a large following after the triumph of his sensation novel *The Mysteries of Paris,* 100,000 francs for its successor, *The Wandering Jew.* More than political scandals, more even than sex murders, serial novels by the right authors—Sue, Alexandre Dumas and a handful of scribblers with the right touch—were the royal road to a gusher of subscribers. Whether all, or any, of these new readers bothered to absorb the critics appearing in the same issue must remain an open question.

Still, critics could count on a following, often substantial. Baudelaire, whose art criticism was well known, published his salons as pamphlets and placed other critical writings in a variety of readily accessible journals. And for two decades, from 1870 to 1890, Theodor Fontane, by then something of a German celebrity as a travel writer and poet, did drama criticism in Berlin's *Vossische Zeitung* and was often drafted to review books and exhibitions. The city's oldest daily, "*Tante Voss*—Aunt Voss," as it was called with smiling and affectionate mockery, was old-fashioned in makeup and reportage compared with its livelier rivals. But its liberalism and imposing staff made it a house organ among Berlin's consequential *Bürger.* After doing duty for a decade, Fontane told his editor Hermann Kletke that *Tante Voss* is "very agreeable for its staff members, because it is never carping and petty and last not least has a circle of readers just right for my work, as far as materials, opinions, and treatment are concerned. Every one of my readers, including those of middling intelligence and those merely half-educated, understand me." This, he wrote, is "an enormous advantage."[24]

Other critics, too, had their supportive audiences among the educated and the merely half-educated. The authority of Matthew Arnold as a maker of opinions on matters of politics and literature was demonstrable in his lifetime and reached beyond it. The ubiquitous Danish essayist, lecturer, literary journalist and biographer Georg Brandes was around the turn of the century Europe's best-known commentator.* Gustave Lanson imposed his points of view of the history of French literature on untold numbers of students and general readers from his pulpit at the Sorbonne and with his popular textbooks and brilliantly written monographs—his little book of 1912 on Rousseau decisively revised common perceptions.

Then there was the long-lived, prolific George Saintsbury. He was born in 1845 and died in 1933 and, as an author of at least three dozen books and uncounted reviews, compiled the most meticulous and detailed atlas—it is his metaphor—of English and French literature. No writer was too insignificant

---

* Freud, who heard him lecture in Vienna in 1900, called him a great man.

for him; he read everything and everyone. This erudition made him a valued
contributor to the classic eleventh edition of the *Encyclopaedia Britannica* of
1910–11, for which he wrote more than thirty articles, all on French authors
from the late Middle Ages to Balzac and Gautier. No question: in a widening
lake of mediocrity fed by the polluted springs of greed and partisanship, there
were islets of critical talents neither unnoticed nor unappreciated. Bourgeois
who wanted to improve their tastes could find the instructors they needed.

3. From Zola to Wilde

The envenomed controversies over the academic lions of French painting
dramatize the tumult in criticism and the possibilities for taste. Art critics alert
to Impressionism accused Cabanel and Bouguereau of working to formula.
Cynically catering to the rich and powerful, ran the charge, they contrived
technically flawless displays of virtuosity—in a word, dead art. The modernists
before modernism called such painters obscene. They greeted Manet's provocative masterpiece *Olympia,* painted in 1863 and shown at the Salon two years
later, as an antidote to widely admired academic nudes, especially Cabanel's
creamy Venus lolling on the foam, his equally creamy nymph being abducted
by a satyr bent on rape. The reception of these luscious tidbits, one might add,
was a reflection not of bourgeois but of imperial taste: Emperor Napoleon III
bought them both.

Looking at Cabanel's *Birth of Venus,* anti-academic critics were particularly
offended by its sheer lack of naturalness. "This goddess, bathed in a flood of
milk," judged Emile Zola, "has the air of a delicious woman of easy virtue, not
in flesh and bones—that would have been indecent—but in a kind of white
and pink almond paste." In 1879, Joris K. Huysmans returned to this *Venus* and
captured the same quality: "a naked woman on a shell," that was all, with "no
muscles, no nerves, no blood," altogether a picture of "unspeakably poor quality." Cabanel's friends were just as bad. Gérôme worked, said Zola derisively in
1867, "for every taste," especially, exploiting his "piquant" subjects, for the men.
"To conceal his complete lack of imagination, he has thrown himself into
worthless old junk."[1] No doubt, the Impressionists had the wind of the future
in their sails, and it was critics who helped to prepare the shift of taste—but
they worked against stiff resistance.

The catalog of controversy could be extended without end. Exposed to the
glaring light of public judgment, piano concertos and railroad stations, landscapes and statues, poems and novels were crowned with laurels and covered
with mud. The incoherence was compounded by the fact that some of the

opinion makers who stand as giants among the Victorians made choices that now seem disappointing, almost perverse. Not that historians ought to judge the taste of the nineteenth century by their own, but it remains striking that Baudelaire, that astute reader of contemporary trends, held up the relatively minor illustrator Constantin Guys as the archetypal painter of heroic modern life—a role, one might think, that Baudelaire's friend Manet would have filled far more satisfactorily. And what are we to say about Shaw dismissing Schubert as charming but brainless, and Brahms as "a sentimental voluptuary with a wonderful ear," good at trifles but not to be taken seriously as a composer.[2]

The taste of Henry James, that master of fine discriminations, seems almost as remote. He vibrated to art as a cardinal experience for civilized men and women, chose painters as protagonists of important tales, made encounters in museums critical moments in his novels. He lived through half a century of drastic turns in artistic fashions—the fading of the French Salon, the rise of international styles like Impressionism, Postimpressionism, the Nabis, the Fauves, the Expressionists, and the Cubists. But his choice of pictures shows him unadventurous; James's copious correspondence and travel reports are virtually silent on Manet, Renoir, and Monet, Cézanne, van Gogh, and Gauguin, not to mention Bonnard, Picasso, and Mondrian. His favorite contemporary painter was John Singer Sargent, "that great man," who would do a celebrated portrait of him not long before James's death—and he had some reservations even about Sargent's "impressionism."[3] He shared the misgivings of his admired Sainte-Beuve about Stendhal's *Le Rouge et le noir,* a novel he judged to be "absolutely unreadable."[4] At times, Victorian critics even disagreed with themselves. In his early twenties Flaubert, reading *Le Rouge et le noir,* praised Stendhal as a stylist; seven years later, he declared the novel badly written, its characters puzzling, and Balzac's relish in Stendhal beyond comprehension.[5]

Manet's *Olympia* did not escape the kind of instructive disputes that like so many others stimulated reflective viewers to formulate an independent judgment. That in this uninhibited nude Manet was quoting, perhaps wickedly lampooning, classic Venuses by Giorgione and Titian—he had copied Titian's *Venus of Urbino* as an apprentice artist—only made it all the more shocking. Manet had openly affronted the accepted doctrine of distance that in Victorian days permitted respectable bourgeois to look at erotically charged naked bodies, mainly of women, without a twinge of embarrassment. The doctrine prescribed nudes in art to be "dressed" in titles like "Eve" or "Spring," or represent a desert princess or an allegory of electricity, a caryatid or a symbolic fountain.

The title was all, or almost all. A piece of sculpture or a canvas presumably recalling ancient and, rarely, recent history, mythology, or exotic climes could exhibit the most suggestive flesh without risking the charge of immorality once appropriate distance had been established. Hiram Powers's *Greek Slave,* a life-size beautiful nude young woman dressed only in manacles and a sad expression, was a triumph in London at the Crystal Palace in 1851; on tours through the United States, good bourgeois families paid to view the statue in almost religious awe. To visualize the plight of this virginal victim of Turkish conquerors was thought to banish all lewd thoughts.[6]

Manet's *Olympia* was aggressively different from earlier Venuses. With her square jaw, sensual body, and unveiled stare, she was overtly exciting; the canvas represented not an idealized, timeless beauty but a recognizable model at a suggestive moment—a mid-nineteenth-century Parisienne, Victorine Meurent, posed with her silk slippers, ribbon at her throat, and servant holding a bouquet. It must have been tempting for viewers to imagine the banker or industrialist keeping this enticing morsel.* Most professional reviewers, then, had no hesitation in calling the painting bad names, and cartoonists exploited it as a rewarding target. Surely, Manet's Venus was a courtesan, perhaps a prostitute, and the picture itself indecent, offensive, ugly, vulgar, ludicrous, repulsive, low, a spectacle worthy of hysterical laughter. Journalists reported that the picture drew large crowds, most of them anxious enough to jeer noisily. Aesthetically *Olympia* was pronounced a disaster; even Gautier, not on principle hostile to departures from respectability, described the model's flesh as literally dirty and the modeling of her body nonexistent.[†] Interestingly, some of the most perceptive critics, including Thoré, who can hardly be accused of timidity, pointedly refused to speak of the painting at all, or slid over it with a few vacuous comments.

Two dissenters from this consensus, Jean Ravenel and Emile Zola, merit special attention, since they touch on the central issue of this book: the highly ambiguous engagement of the bourgeoisie with the avant-garde. Ravenel, a political radical and Millet's close friend, writing under the pseudonym of Alfred Sensier, praised Manet's handling of light and shadows and the harmony of the composition. The disapproval of the majority amused him: *Olympia* was the painting that respectable viewers loved to hate, the "scapegoat of the Salon, the victim of Parisian lynch law." It was, Ravenel conceded, a piece of Spanish madness—Manet's debt to Goya, like that to Baudelaire, seemed only too palpable. Still, with all its oddity, *Olympia* was "worth a thousand times the platitude and inertia of so many canvases spread across the Exhibition," an "armed insurrection in the camp of the bourgeois: a glass of ice water that each

* In his *A Modern Olympia* of 1872–73, Cézanne made the implicit explicit: his naked Olympia has a sheet pulled away from her body by a black servant as her admirer, fully dressed, sits in front watching the scene.

† It was this stark quality that Courbet must have had in mind when he reportedly said that Olympia looked like the queen of spades in a deck of cards, fresh from her bath.

visitor gets in the face when he sees the BEAUTIFUL courtesan brightening up."[7] For Ravenel, *Olympia* was a splendid antibourgeois manifesto.

But was it? Manet was a pioneer, and aware of it. His paintings, as Thoré put it in the Salon of 1864, with their "splendid and bizarre coloration," were bound to "irritate the 'bourgeois' as much as an insult."[8] Thoré recognized that, like Baudelaire, Manet belonged to his time, gathering material for his art as a keen-eyed stroller in Haussmann's Paris. Yet he was, too, explicitly and emphatically, a quintessential bourgeois who craved nothing more than the ribbon of the *Légion d'honneur* in his lapel, the decoration his father had worn with pride. Despite his contempt for the favorites of the Salon, his friendships with other Impressionists, and his stylistic affinities with them, he would not join their exhibitions. His was the social style of a civilized revolutionary that the poet Théodore de Banville captured when he described Manet "with the air of a gentleman from head to toe—*de la nuque au talon, / Un bel air de gentilhomme.*"[9]

Zola jumped into the controversy over *Olympia* from a very different vantage point. He dismissed the question whether the painting was charming or obscene as simply irrelevant. Manet's nude was a purely formalist composition exhibited by an "analytical painter" far less concerned with bodily shapes than with "vivid contrasts and bold masses." Zola tried to persuade his readers that a good look at *Olympia,* surely Manet's masterpiece, would document his passion for color and design: "Look at the head of the young girl: the lips are two narrow pink lines, the eyes are reduced to a few black strokes." The bouquet proffered by the black servant was an equally abstract harmony of colors, a beautifully realized mass of pink, blue, and green.[10] In short, Zola invented a Manet virtually stumbling onto nonobjective art, a Mondrian half a century before his time.

This verdict was both satisfactory and unsatisfactory. Like Ravenel, Zola recognized Manet to be a bourgeois, if a rebellious one, intent on disturbing his fellow bourgeois not with immorality but with an artist's subversiveness. Hence Zola's rescue attempt was, though generous, beside the point. It could not explain why *Olympia* shocked so many viewers and delighted a handful. But in his bald, slashing manner, Zola underscored once again the difficulty of drawing a map of Victorian middle-class taste and its critics. If it managed to occupy so many distinct places on the map of culture, the reviewers who made theirs a century of criticism had much to do with this fruitful incoherence.

Bourgeois attitudes toward critics and criticism were far more benevolent than bourgeoisophobes allowed, but the experience of Oscar Wilde demonstrates that some aggressive gestures were too unpalatable to find many defenders even among advanced circles. In Wilde's dazzling and in the end tragic career as a critic of literature and society—the hero brought low by his fatal flaw—the two domains, usually distinct, blended into a fatal mix. In supreme acts of hubris, Wilde was so filled with anti-philistine animus, tried to undermine presumably unshakable truths with so much disdainful wit, that he aroused furious opposition. In a provocative late dialogue, "The Critic as Artist," he spelled out his subversion of accepted literary ideals. Any sharp distinction between the creative and the critical faculty, he asserted, is "entirely arbitrary." His suggestion makes psychological sense: all artists resort to their critical powers in the process of giving shape to beauty. Artists know, Wilde insisted, that "all fine imaginative work is self-conscious and deliberate." No poet, at least no great poet, "sings because he must sing." He "sings because he chooses to sing."[11]

In itself, this view of the creative process was not too disturbing; it had been intermittently reasserted from the romantics onward. But Wilde raised the ante, proclaiming an uncompromising aestheticism in which literature exists solely for literature's sake. For him, art has nothing to do with ethics or, for that matter, with truth, but everything to do with beauty. Wilde's remark that sunsets had grown more colorful once Turner had taught them to be glorious was but the most quoted, half-serious example of his attempt to reverse current hierarchies.

No wonder the gap between Wilde's extremism and the hesitations of more prudent critics proved too wide to be bridged, too drastic to be negotiated. In "The Critic as Artist," Gilbert, Wilde's spokesman, asserts that most modern critics are "far more cultured than the people whose work they are called upon to review." He finds this not surprising: "Criticism demands infinitely more cultivation than creation does." Anyone can write a three-volume novel: "it merely requires a complete ignorance of both life and literature." In contrast, the critic has serious work to do. "It is very much more difficult to talk about a thing than to do it."[12] These were the sorts of remarks one expected from Oscar Wilde, standing received wisdom on its head or stretching it beyond the breaking point. But contemporaries sensed pernicious social implications in them; they seemed to abandon the critic's mission to civilize the bourgeois and gave unwelcome space to immorality. What Wilde's denigrators would find "disgusting"—an adjective they liked—was not simply the sexual life he led and the disreputable company he kept but also the literary ideals he tried to propagate. They were impieties only the perverse could think up.

It is notorious that aestheticism was not Wilde's only "perversion." In early 1895, he stood at the summit of his fame, not without controversy. He had been lampooned for his effeminacy. He had been taken to task for the immoral drift of his stories and plays. He had been accused of setting, with his decadence, a bad example to susceptible young men. Yet Wilde refused to sniff danger and

J. Lemot, caricature of Flaubert dissecting Emma Bovary. In his famous review of *Madame Bovary,* Charles Augustin Sainte-Beuve had admired Flaubert for wielding the pen as other writers wield the scalpel. (From F. W. J. Hemmings, *Culture and Society in France, 1848–1898* [London: B. T. Batsford, 1971], 116.)

Musée des Beaux-Arts, Rouen, opened in 1880, the year of Flaubert's death. (Photograph by Daniel J. Sherman, in Sherman, *Worthy Monuments* [Cambridge: Harvard University Press, 1989], 182.)

Albert Auguste Fourié, *La Mort de Mme Bovary,* exhibited at the Exposition Universelle of 1889. A dramatic rendering of Emma Bovary's pathetic end, used for a 1905 edition of *Madame Bovary.*

Sir Charles Hallé, the man who made Manchester into a major musical power, not long before his death in 1895.

A program of the Hallé orchestra (this from its second year), exemplary in its ambitiousness, with Hallé conducting and at the piano.

FREE TRADE HALL, MANCHESTER.

MR. CHARLES HALLÉ'S

GRAND CONCERTS.

(THIRD SEASON.)

EIGHTH CONCERT, WEDNESDAY, JANUARY 4TH, 1860.

Vocalists.................................Miss BANKS and Madlle. MEREI.
Solo Pianoforte...........................Mr. CHARLES HALLÉ.

THE WHOLE OF THE MUSIC TO

"A MIDSUMMER NIGHT'S DREAM,"

BY MENDELSSOHN, WITH VOCAL SOLOS AND CHORUS.

Conductor - - - - - - - - - - - - - Mr. CHARLES HALLÉ.

ORCHESTRA OF SEVENTY INSTRUMENTALISTS, AND FULL CHORUS.

TO COMMENCE AT HALF-PAST SEVEN O'CLOCK.

Reserved Seats (cushioned), 3s.; Gallery, 1s 6d.; Body of the Hall, 1s.

Reserved Seats secured, and Tickets for the Gallery and Body of the Hall may now be had, at Messrs.
HIME & ADDISON'S, 19, St. Ann's-square, and at Messrs. FORSYTH BROTHERS', 4 and 6, St. Ann's-street.
Omnibuses will be in attendance at the close of the Concert.

Mr. HALLÉ begs respectfully to announce that on Wednesday, January 11th, will be performed, for the first time in
England, the whole of the Music of the celebrated Grand Opera,

"IPHIGENIA IN TAURIS,"

By GLUCK. The English Version by H. F. CHORLEY, Esq.

The following celebrated Artistes are already engaged for this performance:—Madame CATHERINE HAYES,
Mr. SANTLEY, Mr. THOMAS, and Mr. SIMS REEVES.

No efforts will be spared to produce this great work in a style worthy of its grandeur and beauty. Mr. HALLÉ begs to
announce at the same time that this will be the last Operatic Performance which can be arranged for this Season.

Prices of Admission:—Reserved Seats, 4s.; Gallery, 2s.; Body of the Hall, 1s.

[Price 1d.]

CAVE & SEVER, Printers by Steam Power, Palatine Buildings, Hunt's Bank, Manchester.

The "new" Free Trade Hall in Manchester, home of the Hallé orchestra; it was completed in 1856 at the impressive cost of £40,000, after lesser versions had been razed. (*Illustrated London News,* XXIX [October 11, 1856], 374.)

"Messrs. Watts's New Warehouse," according to the *Illustrated London News* of December 6, 1856 (XXIX, 571), a "superb pile, the largest warehouse in Manchester," some 300 feet long and 90 deep.

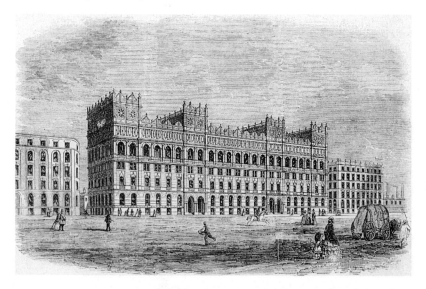

Mezzotint of Joseph Stieler's famous portrait of Goethe at seventy-eight. Court artist to Ludwig I, Stieler was kept busy portraying the several dozen beauties whom the Bavarian king found irresistible.

"Donna Lola Montez," Ludwig I's last love, as a dancer in London before she met the king. (*Pictorial Times,* I [1843], 285.)

Hermann Levi, the great musical director, equally versed in operatic and orchestral music, who (according to Wagner, whose slave he became) suffered from the defect of being a Jew.

Two major players on Munich's cultural scene.

Franz von Lenbach, saturnine portraitist to the great—he was a friend of Bismarck's—who built himself a Renaissance mansion in Munich.

Pierre Jean David d'Angers, Théophile Thoré (1847), bronze. Any independent-minded art critic (and political radical) and a leading expert in Dutch art, Thoré had the signal merit of rediscovering Vermeer.

Eduard Hanslick, Vienna's most influential and most feared music critic; he intensely disliked Richard Wagner, battled the Wagnerians, and was most enthusiastic about the music of his "dear friend" Johannes Brahms.

Three major critics.

Barthélemy Eugéne De-marquay, *Sainte-Beuve* (1870), painted by Sainte-Beuve's friend just after the death of this powerful critic, who brought the biographical method of criticism to unprecedented heights. In addition to the *lundis,* the famous weekly essay reviews, he wrote innu-merable literary studies and a brilliant, massive treatise on Pascal and other Jansenists, *Port-Royal.*

Edouard Manet, *Charles Baudelaire,* etching (1862). One great avant-garde artist immortalizing another. (Private collection.)

Henry Monnier, "Le Peintre et les bourgeois," vignette introducing his play. At bottom one reads, *"Bourgeois,* in artists' language 'philistine,' people who are strangers to the arts." (*Scènes populaires,* 2nd ser. [1879], 321.)

Peter Halm, *Emile Zola,* etching. The first authorized portrait of Zola in Germany. (Michael Georg Conrad, *Emile Zola* [1906], after p. 8).

offended pure souls with almost suicidal bravado. He had two hits running in London, *An Ideal Husband* and *The Importance of Being Earnest,* the latter hailed even by his detractors—and he had many—as a triumph of wit.

But the marquess of Queensberry, shocked into action by the suicide of a son apparently afraid of being exposed as a homosexual, determined to save another of his sons, Arthur Douglas, then engaged in a stormy affair with Wilde. Trying to provoke Douglas's lover, he left at the Albemarle Club a notoriously misspelled card addressed to "Oscar Wilde posing Somdomite." Wilde sued Queensberry for libel, lost, was prosecuted in turn for gross indecency, survived the first trial with a hung jury, was convicted in the second for consorting with teenage male prostitutes, and sentenced to two years in prison at hard labor. Had he been convicted of being a "Somdomite," he would have gotten ten years. During the tense weeks before his conviction, Wilde was deluged by some worried friends with appealing opportunities to flee the country. But, bravely, foolishly, or driven by a compulsion he could not master, he spurned them and served his time.

These are the bare facts. It appears as though Wilde, the principled nonconformist, had heroically faced down the howling bourgeois mob and paid a heavy price for it. Henry James, no friend of Wilde's but fascinated by the proceedings, spoke contemptuously of the "ghoulish public" that "hangs and gloats" over a "gulf of obscenity." Worldly admirers had warned Wilde that bigoted, self-appointed guardians of morality were only waiting for the right moment to destroy him. Were they not all vengeful hypocrites to the bone, whether they did their damage as journalists or as censors? Infuriated by the general pharisaism, the young music critic Ernest Newman excoriated the "bovine rage of the Philistine."[13] This reading has much to commend it, but it underestimates the varieties of responses to an ugly moment in late-Victorian moral history.

Wilde's life in prison was shadowed by degrading physical conditions and debilitating ill health; perhaps even harder to take, it plunged him into profound loneliness. He was allowed few visitors at distant, carefully regulated intervals and a single book, John Bunyan's *The Pilgrim's Progress,* hardly a copious intellectual diet. Several of his best friends, open to prosecution on the grounds that had landed him in prison, decided to wait out abroad England's attack of moralistic persecution mania. Robert ("Robbie") Ross, who had seduced Wilde nine years before, briefly returned from self-imposed exile but did not stay. Literary acquaintances like Shaw, though sympathetic to Wilde's plight, would not sign petitions for his early discharge from prison, because they feared, probably with justice, that their reputations as troublemakers could only hurt. And a few rejoiced in Wilde's humiliation; the elderly pre-

Raphaelite painter Holman Hunt took the self-righteous line that Wilde's punishment had been too lenient.

Most dailies joined the hunt. The gutter press had no hesitation: following the time-honored principle that its readers would enjoy seeing the great trampled in the dust, it was caustic and intrusive. Sometime in March 1895, near the beginning of the calamity, Max Beerbohm, then in the United States, reported to "Reggie" Turner, another of Wilde's homosexual intimates, that American headlines were "so short here and so relentless." They read, " 'Give Oscar what's for,' 'The Pretty Poet and the Mocking Marquis,' or 'Mrs. Wilde sticks to him.' "[14] Even if Beerbohm's impish wit led him to exaggerate, even invent, the American coverage, the English press was vivid enough. It further inflamed the indignation against Wilde the pervert that prosecutors and judges had fanned with their performances in court.

Even some of the more responsible newspapers played at being outraged. The *St. James Gazette,* drawing global conclusions, offered the maxim that modern tolerance was a virtue that had been degraded into a vice. Novelists were discussing crime and immorality without shame, everything was open to doubt, and the Wilde trials had proved the wicked effects of this "too-liberal" attitude. What England needed now was "a dash of wholesome bigotry in our art, our literature, our society, our view of things." Wilde's sentence might be heavy, but it was "well-deserved." With visible self-satisfaction, the newspaper recalled that five years earlier it had warned the public against Wilde's *The Picture of Dorian Gray,* a book "less worthy the attention of the critic than the policeman."[15] It was delightful to be so right in a cause so dear to the hearts of the *St. James Gazette*'s middle-class readers.

In linking Wilde's writings to the condition of England, the newspaper's comments were good instances of the wholesome bigotry it desired. Other papers instructively dragged aesthetics into their editorials on Wilde's fate in even more sweeping ways. For one, the *Westminster Gazette* singled out Wilde's literary theories as anything but innocuous poetic sentiments. The "salutary" sentence of two years at hard labor would "undoubtedly do much good," the paper judged, largely by "checking unwholesome tendencies in art and literature." Were these tendencies not embodied in Wilde's "attempt to separate 'art' from all relations to morality"? His doctrine was "at best a sophism, and at worst—what we have seen it in this case to be."[16] Bluntly: in the hands of this decadent, literature had corrupted life. The critic had turned into a criminal simply by being the critic he was.

Each daily handled the affair in its accustomed manner; the *Times* and the *Pall Mall Gazette,* known for their thorough coverage of sensational court cases, gave the Wilde trials ample space, with full summaries and long quotations from the attorneys' pleas, the judges' interventions, the defendant's testimony. They evidently preferred to let readers arrive at their own verdict. The *Manchester Guardian,* which normally disdained such coverage, printed the salient facts in terse notices and buried them among lesser stories, so that a reader practically had to look for them. And *Reynolds's News,* a popular newspaper that had never shaken off its radical mid-century origins, even showed compassion for the fallen poet; on May 20, just before the end of the second trial, it objected to the prosecutor's conduct and said editorially that it would not "gloat over the ruin of the unhappy man."[17] After all—*Reynolds's* seems to have been the only newspaper to make this point—the defendant had not seduced any of the blackmailing rogues who were as culpable as Wilde.

This is not automatically to group homosexual conduct, especially under the sordid circumstances to which Wilde was apparently addicted, among avant-garde acts. Yet some of his admirers, even when they did not invoke Socrates, saw his refusal to bolt as heroic—which is to say, with a distinctly anti-bourgeois ring to it. Wilde had made himself into an exemplary enemy of middle-class values, deploying the best weapons at his command. During the anxious discussions in his circle, his mother pleaded with him to leave the country, as did Frank Harris, the enterprising editor and, in later life, untrustworthy autobiographer. That Alfred Douglas, who hated his father, wanted Wilde to stand trial and thus embarrass the marquess of Queensberry, was no surprise, though it weighed in Wilde's decision not to flee abroad. But it was more significant that his friend William Butler Yeats strongly hoped that Wilde would stay and defy his cant-ridden culture.

Yeats came closer to grasping Wilde's mental state than did Lady Wilde or Frank Harris. Self-destructive urges were doubtless an ingredient in Wilde's decision, as was his pathetic, often severely tested infatuation with Alfred Douglas. But in its appearance, and its effect, standing up to the state and to public opinion seemed Wilde's path to fortitude. His recklessness had broken the accepted code of silence; making public what might be tolerated privately was to throw down the gauntlet to Victorians who might let a nonconformist live relatively undisturbed if he—or, for that matter, she—did not advertise it. But in his testimony Wilde dared to praise the passion that Arthur Douglas had called the love that dare not speak its name.

Worse, Wilde alienated much well-meaning support by remarks that most listeners and readers could only interpret as snobbery, arrogance, even impudence. "I have no knowledge of the views of ordinary individuals," he said during his first cross-examination. When the prosecutor read in court Wilde's observation, from *The Picture of Dorian Gray,* that there are no moral or immoral books, only well-written or badly written ones, Wilde did not yield an inch of his aestheticism. It was a point that few bourgeois, no matter how unconventional in their views, could take with equanimity. And by attempting to compare his casual coupling with adolescent professionals to the elevated model of David and Jonathan, or to the loves of Michelangelo or Shakespeare, he might get a round of applause in court and be deemed magnificent by Max Beerbohm, but this was too transparent an apologia to deceive the jury as to the facts in the case.[18]

And yet, Wilde did find supporters, not all of them avant-garde poets or painters; even, as we have seen, a few journalists spoke up for him. "Cultivated London," which had mocked his affectations, wrote Yeats, "was now full of his advocates," even though all were sure that he was guilty as charged. There were spectators at the first trial who cheered him. There were Ernest Leverson, a liberal businessman, and his wife, Ada, a clever writer whose conversation had impressed Wilde, a connoisseur in good talk. The Leversons, a cultivated, affluent, and it appears fearless couple, had recently become friendly with Wilde and now stood by him. When, as he was waiting out the time between trials, no hotel would admit him and he was miserably camping out at his brother's house, they made him welcome—in truth a grand gesture—visited him in jail, and helped to keep him comfortable after his release. And there was Adela Schuster, wife of a Frankfurt banker settled at Wimbledon, who put £1,000 at Wilde's disposal; "a very noble and cultured woman," Frank Harris called her, "a friend of both of us, Miss S——, a Jewess by race, tho' not by religion."[19]

It is striking how many of Wilde's most loyal supporters were Jews, as though outsiders could understand the needs of another outsider. But not all of them belonged to this group. The Liberal M. P. Richard B. (later Viscount) Haldane, who had met Wilde socially a few times and who, taking an interest in prison reform, worried that so tender a soul as Wilde might not survive his barbaric surroundings, visited Wilde and arranged to get him more books. Robert Sherard, a clumsy, well-meaning poet and boyish admirer of Wilde who later wrote his life, even challenged Queensberry to a duel.

And there was an anonymous humanitarian who fleetingly but unforgettably joined the cast of characters.[20] When Frank Harris, intent on getting Wilde away, asked a rich acquaintance if he could rent his yacht and indiscreetly told him why he needed it, the man offered his pleasure boat free of charge. It was well stocked with all the necessities and even luxuries, Harris observed, and ready to leave the country at a moment's notice. That yachtsman, too, whatever his name may have been, made himself a critic of the bourgeois consensus. Harris describes him as "a man of the widest culture, who had no sympathy with the vice attributed to Oscar." This Good Samaritan, who had never met Wilde, was a Jewish businessman.

❧ FOUR ❧

Hunters and Gatherers

I. A Map of Motives

"There is only one way of proving that you like a man's paintings when you have the material means to do it—buy them." Thus Alexandre Dumas fils in the mid-1880s. Though scarcely a pathbreaking insight, it was a sensible reminder to the affluent that taste has a practical dimension and that there is little reward for mere desire. In fact, in their recollections, bourgeois hunters and gatherers foraging in the rugged terrain of the arts liked to point to their loot with pride; saying little about the pains, they testified to the pleasures of yielding to what one of them called an "inborn and indestructible human trait."[1] As an American enthusiast wrote in 1898, speaking for the tribe; "Among the keenest pleasures of life in hope, in acquisition, memory, there is hardly one to surpass the Collector's joy. His field is the world; the objects of his desire range indifferently from blackened postage stamps to Greek vases and diamonds."[2] Collectors' conquests were heartfelt experiences that linked them to the exhilaration of their like across the centuries.

There was, then, nothing novel about nineteenth-century collectors—except their numbers, their opportunities, and their class. Princely cabinets of rarities and the walls of aristocrats' mansions decked with old masters or prized etchings no longer enjoyed their time-honored preeminence. And the catalog of things considered worth collecting was continually expanding: from paintings and sculptures to the autographs of celebrities, from unique, signed pieces of furniture to anonymous faience, from precious, hand-painted china to matchboxes. One did not need to be rich to become a collector, though many were. Jews collected Judaica: Edmond de Rothschild fancied rare medieval and Renaissance Haggadoth and illustrated prayer books. Composers collected scores, paying homage to the composers that meant most to them: Brahms prized his original manuscripts of Bach cantatas, Mozart's great G minor symphony, Schubert dances.[3] A few, with an active if perverse fantasy life, hunted up macabre relics like splinters from the scaffold of hanged convicts; others, more decorous, filled shelves with reminders of holidays or a vanished past. Some modern incarnations of Maecenas in search of social status even collected people.

It tells much about the Victorian middle classes, their sense of self and search for a place in the world, that this appetite should flourish among them. One way of reading the fact that the Victorians were a population of collectors is to see collecting as an emblem of individualism triumphant. No one tells a collector what to collect, how much time, money, or energy to allocate to his addiction. But motives for collecting occupied a wide spectrum of impulses, as they always have, and had their deepest roots in the unconscious. Not all of its presumed pleasures were unmixed, for too many collectors acted under the lash of an obsession they could neither explain nor shake off. Collecting, in addition to providing moments of intimate glory, also served to allay anxiety: collectors who had known desperate hunger might hoard food; Balzac's misers, squirreling away money, were not happy men. Hunters displaying moose heads on their walls certifying their manliness often failed to recognize that their exhibitionism might throw some doubt on precisely their virility. Whatever the dynamics, by the nineteenth century no class was more susceptible to the temptations of collecting than the bourgeoisie. In 1868, a writer in the *Musical Times* could allude to "the prevailing 'collecting' mania" without fear of contradiction.[4]

Musing over a canvas by Alexandre Decamps at the Paris Salon of 1846, Théophile Thoré, with his usual penetration, captured the symptoms of this imperious compulsion, an irresistible force meeting an unresisting object. Something of a technical innovator, Decamps was the best liked among the French orientalists who discovered, and colorfully rendered, the pictorial possibilities of the Near East. For all the relative indifference of official circles, he became a particular favorite among French collectors and garnered medals at the salons and at international exhibitions. "One could not start a collection without a Decamps," Thoré wrote, "and everyone who has a Decamps is lost: he starts to love painting; he must collect paintings and *voilà*, he's a collector."[5] *Il lui faut collectionner des tableaux*—the phrase lays bare the helplessness of the hoarder driven by covetousness.

In general, the origins of collecting are innocent enough. It normally starts in childhood, with objects like pebbles or insects or pieces of string that have meaning, and value, to the collector alone. Then the youthful appropriator will likely graduate to stamps or butterflies or books, a craving often carried over into adult life with greater sophistication, larger expenditures, and more tangled incentives. Childish hobbies become adult fixations. Whatever its shadow side, the psychological rewards of collecting can be immense. It gives control, which is to say, power over a selected domain. It summons up dim memories and fantasies. It serves to establish a close-knit fraternity among fellow specialists. It provides, at the other extreme, opportunities for boasting that one's accumulations are superior to those of one's competitors: more sizable, more complete, more exquisite, more select, more expensive.

Nor is this all. For those who magically convert their possessions into affectionate, uncomplaining companions, collecting may relieve the terrors of loneliness. It can be a token of, or an entrance ticket to, social respectability. And, though more obscurely, it can gratify sensual needs.* Only those who canvass the market in order to buy cheap and sell dear must be denied entry to the vast, motley club of collectors: lacking its members' impassioned engagement, they are only speculators.

There were those whom the collecting bacillus struck with a force little less startling than Saint Paul's shock on the road to Damascus. No Victorian conversion to art or to an artist was more spectacular than that of Charles L. Freer. Grown wealthy by establishing a virtual monopoly on the manufacture of railroad cars, he was a methodical, businesslike American bachelor—it is curious how many nineteenth-century collectors remained unmarried and made their collection their family. In the winter of 1887, not yet the multimillionaire he would become, Freer went to visit Howard Mansfield, noted for his portfolios of Whistler etchings. For some time he had been buying prints—cheaper and, he thought, requiring less knowledge than paintings—and had disparaged Whistler, already famous for his prints. But this evening made Freer reverse course from casual purchases to systematic acquisitions, from disdain for Whistler to near adoration. "I have no words," he said after looking over Mansfield's three hundred exemplars, "to express my admiration for the genius of this man."[6] And this genius he simply had, as it were, to bring into his power.

Acting on his sudden infatuation, Freer reexperienced the boyish yearning for completeness, for the delectable pleasure of exclusive possession. In 1890, he sought out Whistler in London, beginning a close friendship that would benefit both. He settled with Whistler that henceforth the artist would send

* The erotic side of collecting has been much neglected.

him a pristine impression of every new etching and lithograph. He bought up examples of Whistlers still missing from his holdings; more, he bought the Peacock Room, the dining room that Whistler had designed for his patron Frederick R. Leyland and installed in Leyland's house in Detroit. He even acquired—and here any daydream of completeness had to give way to reality—some of Whistler's paintings. While Freer made himself into a well-informed expert in Asian art and supported a handful of American painters, none of this compromised his love for Whistler. That evening at Howard Mansfield's house literally changed his life as a collector.

An account of hunters and gatherers, which makes for a substantial chapter in the Victorian bourgeois experience, is for the most part the history of an elite—or the elite within an elite: aristocrats of finance, industry, and commerce. This became particularly conspicuous after the 1880s, when, as we know, American millionaires invaded Paris and London, checkbooks poised. In Europe, dismayed collectors and museum directors, delighted art dealers and impecunious aristocrats anxious to sell masterpieces, marveled at "American prices," which transformed the market at its high end without appeal.

But not altogether—as we have briefly noted and shall amply confirm, cutting the paths that higher culture would take was not the undisputed monopoly of plutocrats with an unlimited budget. The anonymous student of Parisian nightlife who in the early 1840s coolly asserted, "Money is the guts of pleasure," was stating the obvious.[7] Plainly, the richest bourgeois had the means to shape their collections much as they pleased and wielded an influence over the market and over taste disproportionate to their numbers. But middling and even a few petty bourgeois living a world away from these magnates could accumulate respectable collections with their unpretentious investments. And some, like plantation owners in the South of the United States or affluent settlers in Australia, had enough money to commission family portraits and perhaps a landscape or two. Many of these collectors needed no tuition in taste, not even in avant-garde taste, from their better-placed contemporaries, and they spent what they could spare.

Freud's private museum of statuary, mainly antiques (and a few Renaissance pieces) from the Mediterranean basin—Rome, Greece, Palestine, Egypt—eloquently speaks to the wealth of motives and to the meaning of money in the collecting obsession. Analysands and colleagues visiting his apartment stood in awe of the brigade of statuettes he had gathered across the years. Toward the end of Freud's life, it added up to more than two thousand items, rounded out with a well-thumbed library on archaeology, which made him a knowledgeable collector victimized by only a few fakes. His massive display of silent witnesses to ancient civilizations crowded glassed-in cabinets and bookcases, invaded tabletops and his desk. His apartment at Berggasse 19 was truly a collector's haunt.

The first document showing Freud actually buying rather than merely longing for objects dates from December 1896. He was forty, settled, married, the father of six children, enjoying a moderately remunerative if still fluctuating practice. "I have now decorated my study with plaster casts of Florentine statues," he wrote to his confidant Wilhelm Fliess in Berlin after a visit to Italy. "It was a source of extraordinary refreshment—*Erquickung*—for me. I am thinking of getting rich so that I can repeat these trips."[8] His dream of riches was never fulfilled; his first purchases and even many of the later ones were fairly reasonably priced. Once he grew famous enough, assiduous friends or grateful analysands would give him valuable antiques, presents he did not reject.

At this point the footprints leading to Freud's passion fade. The great interpreter of motives left too few traces to permit a confident interpretation of what awakened his collecting impulse and kept it alive. Its roots ramified widely. Freud had lived with antiquity since he was a schoolboy, a brilliant pupil in a classical *Gymnasium*. A godless Jew, he never tired of searching for palpable connections with his remote ancestors. He envied Schliemann, the discoverer of Troy, more than anyone for realizing boyish wishes in his adult life. What is more, he was paying tribute to the great French neurologist Jean Martin Charcot, with whom he had worked in the winter of 1885, and in whose study in Paris he had seen cases laden with Chinese and Indian antiquities. He would make himself, he liked to say, into an archaeologist of the mind.

Nor was it insignificant for Freud's history as a collector that his lovable and somewhat pathetic father should have died in October 1896. It seems to have liberated Freud's desire to fulfill peremptory wishes that he had long denied himself. It also liberated his purse, since his father's death meant he no longer needed to support him. Money was at least some of the guts of Freud's pleasure. But not all. For apart from all the other springs of action at work in him, Freud found sublimated erotic satisfaction in his acquisitions, as he stared at them, handled them, stroked them, rearranged them. In one of his rare comments on the subject, he defined the collector as someone who "directs his surplus libido at something inanimate: love of things."[9] Collecting, for Freud as for others, was more than what Marx derisively called the fetishism of commodities, presumably so common in capitalist society. Beyond being an aide to self-approval, a ticket to social approval, and the rest, collecting was also a kind of love.

2. Collecting as Autobiography

A glance at the first collectors of Cézanne forcibly supports the lessons from Freud. For most of his life, art lovers dismissed and ridiculed Cézanne's work and made him the target of antimodernist clichés. Some called the man insane. As late as 1903, three years before his death, a reviewer lumped him with the "ultra-Impressionists"—whatever that meant—called him a producer of daubs, and ended in shoulder-shrugging resignation and incomprehension: "The love of physical and moral ugliness is a passion like any other."[1] Yet the few who, defying dominant opinion, bought Cézanne's pictures, had their discernment vindicated once he was catapulted to fame and the prices of his canvases, even his watercolors, climbed into the stratosphere.

In the 1880s and 1890s, enthusiasts for the new painting who were learning to take Monets and Renoirs in stride still balked at Cézanne's visible brushwork and unreliable perspective—he could not, his detractors observed, even draw a table correctly! In contrast to the rising demand for the Impressionists, prices for Cézannes advanced with agonizing sluggishness. A well-known incident of 1899 dramatizes this divergence: at an auction, when one of Cézanne's landscapes was knocked down for the substantial sum of 6,750 francs, the astonished audience wanted to know the name of the buyer, who stood up and identified himself: it was Claude Monet.[2] No commentary is needed. In 1903, at the auction of the ten Cézannes owned by Zola, who had died the year before, they averaged 1,500 francs apiece. Cézanne would not witness the frantic bidding for his work among collectors and museums that erupted after the eye-opening posthumous exhibition in 1907. Before that historic date, only a few sharp-eyed art lovers had been impressed by him.

This record makes the earliest collectors of Cézannes all the more interesting. Except for Gustave Caillebotte, an established painter in his own right, they are familiar names largely because they are indelibly linked with that isolated, moody genius whose revolutionary import they were the first to appreciate.* These bourgeois were a varied lot, but they had this in common: concentrating on Manets and Monets, Renoirs and Pissarros as more accessible artists, they also made room for at least one Cézanne.

Three of them—*père* Tanguy, Dr. Paul Gachet, and Victor Chocquet—occupy a privileged place among Cézanne's discoverers. Down to the 1880s, a good many more could have afforded one of his paintings; they were cheap enough.

---

* Caillebotte, as we shall see, was also the richest.

His large canvases sold for 100 francs and the small ones for 40—this was the tariff set by Julien François Tanguy, that hospitable, almost proverbially benevolent dealer in art supplies whom the Impressionists frequented in Paris. An average laborer, assuming he had any money for art, could have managed a small Cézanne for three, perhaps four weeks' work, but there is no record of any potential buyer from that class making his way to Tanguy's shop. And a large Cézanne would have cost a teacher about a month's performance in the classroom, but his like, too, stayed away. *Père* Tanguy was wiser than they; he took paintings in payment for the colors he sold to his impecunious customers. For years his unpretentious shop, crowded with artists who came to admire— at times to jeer—was the only Parisian gallery where Cézannes were on view.

Van Gogh more than once captured *père* Tanguy's benign, bearded face and stocky frame for posterity. Born in Brittany in 1825, an uncompromising political radical, Tanguy all his life skirted the edge of penury, working as a plasterer and, after he moved to Paris in 1860, as a color grinder. It was not until 1875 that he settled into his shop. Once there, he acted as a Good Samaritan to artists, mainly Impressionists and Postimpressionists, most of them even shabbier than their venerable father figure. He lent them money, shared his meals with them, showed their paintings with paternal pride. When he died in 1894, his grateful friends staged an auction to aid his destitute widow. And the six Cézannes in Tanguy's possession brought between 45 and 215 francs.[3]

Though a physician with a practice in Paris, Dr. Paul Gachet, probably the first to buy a Cézanne, was in his own way as much of an outsider as Tanguy, as radical in his political views and his readiness to treat the poor for nothing. He was an eccentric who championed homeopathy, phrenology, and (largely in theory, it seems) free love. Settled in the village of Auvers-sur-Oise, just north of Paris, where he built a house for himself and his consumptive wife, he frequented avant-garde artistic and literary soirees in the city, did etchings not without merit, and collected, among other new painters, Cézannes.

Cézanne's most zealous and consistent promoter, though, was Victor Chocquet, affectionately *père* Chocquet to Pissarro and to Renoir, who did a fine portrait of his wife, just as Cézanne did an equally fine portrait of him. At first glance, he seems a more commonplace figure than Tanguy or Gachet, but his missionary zeal set him apart from other bourgeois collectors, as he made himself something of a nuisance trying to talk painters, critics, and collectors into *seeing* Cézanne. Chocquet was a true hunter and gatherer: the fanatic who cares not what others say and who, to sate his lust, strains his means to their limits, at times beyond them.

As a chief clerk in the customhouse in Paris, Chocquet found his resources rather modest. When in his early twenties he took up a post in Paris after a brief stint at Dunkerque, he was earning 800 francs a year, a salary that rose with the years to a moderate 4,000 francs in 1877 when he retired, eked out with 2,000 francs of private income.[4] This meant that when he haunted auction houses for bargains he would drop out after bids rose above 300 francs. But he unerringly obeyed his discriminating impulse to amass an outstanding collection of modern French art. Delacroix was his first love, a taste he shared with Cézanne, followed by Monets, Pissarros, Renoirs. In 1899, at the auction of his holdings, there were no fewer than thirty-two Cézannes among them.

The upper-class bachelor Caillebotte, a formidable collector to whom we will return, seems miles from Chocquet. Yet, with his wildly unconventional taste for Cézanne, the millionaire joined hands with the small bureaucrat. In 1899, Caillebotte's Cézannes fetched on the average 1,600 francs apiece; clearly Chocquet had bought his Cézannes for a fraction of that sum. Whatever he paid for them—the facts of these transactions are lost to posterity—the clerk Chocquet, this archetypal bourgeois, sacrificed to his obsession all he had.

Only a few of these early collectors, like Georges de Bellio, a Romanian practicing medicine in Paris, had money. Far less prosperous and more typical were Théodore Duret, a peripatetic journalist and, as an art critic, one of the first to alert a wider public to the Impressionists; Eugène Murer, owner of a small pastry shop and unsuccessful novelist; Emmanuel Chabrier, impassioned Wagnerian, friend to Renoir and other Impressionists, composer of pleasing piano pieces and once widely performed lighthearted operas, and doomed to be mainly remembered as the composer of *España,* that irresistible rhapsody for orchestra. *

The presence of Chabrier in this exclusive fan club is a reminder that the Victorian century boasted a band of particularly knowledgeable collectors: artists—painters, sculptors, composers, and singers moving in artistic circles— who bought the work of artists or engaged in affectionate trades with each other. Monet once he was financially comfortable, Gauguin before he deserted his bourgeois existence, Cassatt always on the lookout for new talent, all bought fellow Impressionists. True, like Victorian collectors, these hunters and gatherers had distinguished ancestors. Perhaps the most arresting of these was Rubens, who amassed a substantial collection of major paintings. Catholic in his tastes, he specialized in contemporaries but spread his interests widely, buying German, Italian, Flemish, and Dutch artists—he owned Titians and Tintorettos, Jan van Eycks and Pieter Brueghels, Dürers and Holbeins, Elsheimers

---

* At the same auction, Chabrier also bought Manet's *Femme dans un jardin* for a mere 140 francs; his *Vase de fleurs* for 650 francs; his drawing *George Moore au café* for 110; and his *Skating* for 1,650 francs.

and Browers. But the prominence of a Chabrier in the art market makes the artist-collector characteristic of the nineteenth century.

In 1884, after Manet's death, Chabrier, never affluent and reputed to be more thrifty than he needed to be but buoyed by some money his wife had inherited, set his customary prudence aside. At the sale of paintings that Manet had left in his studio, Chabrier spent 5,000 francs on that much discussed late masterpiece *A Bar in the Folies-Bergère*. When Chabrier's collection was auctioned off in 1896, a year after *his* death, it emerged as a select hoard including a Cézanne, seven Manets, six Monets, three Renoirs, a pair of Sisleys.[5] Here again is proof: one did not need to be rich to be a respectable collector; all one had to do was to spend whatever one could scratch together, bet on the future, and be right.

Degas's collection of modern paintings was as notable as Chabrier's and far larger. With a financial cushion provided by a prosperous family and the income he could count on from about 1890 for his work, he indulged his mania to the full. His father had collected paintings before him, and he was surrounded by friends infected with the same incurable affliction. At the mercy of his obsession, he confessed, "I can't stop myself." Degas's inability to control his desires only drove up the prices of things he was determined to add to his treasures. "The trouble is that people are beginning to know about it, and are bidding against me; they know that when I want something, I absolutely must have it." In 1898, he implored his dealer Durand-Ruel to advance him some cash because he wanted to buy an Ingres. "I really *need* it."[6]

What he seems to have needed was 20 paintings and 88 drawings by Ingres, 13 paintings and 129 works on paper by Delacroix, sizable portfolios of Daumier and Gavarni lithographs, Corots and Cassatts. He even acquired a graphite study of a workman's head by Adolph Menzel, perhaps the first French collector to value this German master enough to invest in him. In 1896, he joined the slowly expanding group of artists who appreciated Cézanne, buying a fine still life, *Glass and Apples,* for 400 francs, and the equally fine portrait of Chocquet for a derisory 150 francs.

Menzel and Cézanne: two warrants for Degas's openness to the new. Ingres and Delacroix were his masters, each in his way, but he recognized that painting was moving away from nature in color and design alike. Hence he had no difficulty acting as a patron to Gauguin, praising him when approval of him was rare and badly wanted. It was in this spirit that he suggested to Durand-Ruel that he mount an exhibition of Gauguin's paintings when no other dealer would come near them, and that he supported Gauguin, destitute in the South Seas, by buying some of his Tahitian experiments.

Collecting is a kind of autobiography. Not unexpectedly, Victorian artist-collectors testified with their purchases to artists they admired most and whose work had shaped, and continued to shape, their own. The paintings that Max Liebermann bought are a case in point. He had spent five years in Paris in the mid-1870s and lightened his palette, but it was not until around 1885 that, settled in Berlin, he systematically began to study Pissarro, Morisot, and their fellows. Luckily his gregarious friends Carl and Felicie Bernstein, the first collectors of Impressionists anywhere in Germany, lived nearby and were lavish with invitations. At the time only a handful of Germans, including artists, had ever even seen a Monet, and German critics found it easy to malign Manet and his ally Zola as madmen and "pedants of filth and triviality."[7] The Bernsteins' Impressionists only intensified Liebermann's already lively anti-academic disposition.

His fortune enabled Liebermann to meet the ever-rising prices for Impressionists after 1900, as he began to collect their paintings and watercolors. In the midst of a desert of banal art, these artists were alive! He bought several Degas and Monets, a Pissarro and a Renoir, as well as two Cézannes. But Manet, with his economical brushwork, forceful finish, and precise effects, was his undisputed favorite: seventeen Manets, including the famous small still life of a bundle of asparagus, were his visible commitment to these French innovators.

Interestingly enough it was a singer, the baritone Jean Baptiste Faure, star at the Paris Opera, who assembled a more spectacular collection than Chabrier, Liebermann, or even Degas. His most stunning Manets, the *Gare St. Lazare* and *Le Déjeuner sur l'herbe, Mlle Victorine en costume d'espada* and the portrait of Faure in the role of Hamlet, eventually ended up as prized possessions in major museums. For the rest, Faure bought Pissarros, Sisleys, Degas, and Monets by the dozen, acting like a dealer anxious lest supplies dry up. He was wealthy enough to sustain his sprees: once established at home as a great singer—Verdi called him the only first-rate talent at the Paris Opera—he could earn more than 300,000 francs a year on his tours across France and the musical capitals of Europe, about fifteen times as much as Victor Hugo had grossed at his best. Faure's purchases were anything but indiscriminate; he acquired among other treasures Monet's glowing early cityscape of 1874, *Boulevard des Capucines, Paris,* and Degas's *Classe de danse* of the same year.[8] But, almost as capriciously as he bought, he sold; several times during his life he disposed of most of his collection, only to amass a new one. This habit raises serious questions about Faure's claim to the proud title of collector. There is no such question about the others.

An obsession more or less fierce, then, was the collector's identifying mark. But, though it was in essence a single urge steadily developing new modes of self-expression, it had diverse cultural consequences. Originality and competition alike benefited. Many collectors wanted only to set themselves apart from their fellows; others coveted what their rivals possessed or had in prospect. Both attitudes fed the market for art, literature, and theater, and gave it a zestful aura. Conflicts both familial and public loomed everywhere. Some domineering collectors grew so attached to their treasures that they tried to impose their tastes on future generations, forcing reluctant or indifferent offspring to keep intact what they had so laboriously stockpiled. At times exacerbating and at times resolving conflicts was reliable information, which acquired unprecedented value; forgers were so many warnings against ignorance and complacency. Hence by mid-century whole industries had emerged to serve collectors with technical information, trend spotting, investment counseling. Experts sold advice, as did dealers, impresarios, and, more cheaply, specialized periodicals.

With the same zest that they haunted auctions or dealers, collectors communicated their joys of discovery in memoirs, often privately printed, which gave them an opportunity to boast a little and to alert fellow addicts to the pitfalls of the marketplace. The self-satisfaction of such texts, usually slight in bulk and always lyrical in tone, is all too palpable. As we have noted, Victorian bourgeois had more than one reason for hoarding bronzes, first editions, or autographs of the eminent. The proliferation of books advising insecure householders on the most appropriate way of decorating the mantles over their fireplaces strongly suggests that some collectors at least wanted nothing more desperately than the approval of their social peers. Others hoped to perpetuate their names: to leave an important collection to one's birthplace was one road to immortality. And the socially ambitious among them, using their salon as a stage set to show off their latest acquisitions, could hope to ease access to cultivated, at times to politically or economically influential circles.

Bourgeoisophobes, observing middle-class collectors with the baleful eyes of travelers watching the antics of an exotic tribe, insisted that low-minded, utilitarian intentions always hid behind, and really explained, the display of splendid objects. At the turn of the century, in his sardonic *Theory of the Leisure Class,* Thorstein Veblen developed an anthropological theory to account for what he called conspicuous consumption: expensive paintings, like expensive women, were badges of prowess, pacific surrogates for honors once gathered in real combat. Literary satirists made the taste flaunted by the newly rich a staple butt of their disdain. Proust has his Verdurins with their pretentious musicales, hysterical exclamations over *Tristan,* and chatter about exquisite furniture. There certainly were Verdurins among Victorian parvenus, folk like the Verdurins' ancestors, the brilliantly named Veneerings in Dickens's *Our Mutual Friend*. At the Veneerings all things, including the owners, their baby—

and their pictures—were a trifle sticky from being "bran-new." Like the Verdurins, the Veneerings lacked nothing but authentic cultivation.

A classic passage epitomizing these onslaughts makes for a high point in a
comedy by Alexandre Dumas fils from the mid-1850s, *La Question d'argent*. Jean
Giraud, a pushy financier, invites one of the more polished characters to visit
him in his *palais* on the Champs-Elysées: "I'll show you my pictures and my
sculptures because I have been told that a man in my position should have a
taste for the arts. I don't understand anything about it; I have paid a lot for it
all, but I'm afraid it's not worth much. You'll tell me what you think of it, you'll
give me advice."

This was only one telling exemplar in a crowded catalog of imagined pre-
tenders to breeding. We recall Henry Fuller's novel *With the Procession,* and the
line he gives its well-heeled protagonist Mrs. Bates: "People of our position
would naturally be expected to have a Corot." But perhaps the most despica-
ble bourgeois art lover in nineteenth-century fiction—a savage travesty rather
than a searching portrait—is the corrupt publisher and speculator Walter in
Maupassant's *Bel-Ami* of 1885. At his glittering receptions, Walter likes to show
off his paintings. He owns a few Barbizon landscapes and is particularly proud
of some academic worthies like Bouguereau, whom he has grouped together
under the pretentious title "Major Painters." The pictures Walter prizes even
more for their presumed wit are anecdotes: a lubricious scene showing a pretty young woman climbing the steps of a tram, her face and legs being stared at
by men with just one thing in mind; or a soldier teaching a poodle how to play
a drum. Walter's greatest favorites, though, were by unknown artists whose pictures he had bought for virtually nothing in the hope that they would rise in
favor, and thus in price. That Maupassant makes Walter a social-climbing Jew
only underscores the contempt of bourgeoisophobes for such amateurs.[9]*

Bourgeois cherishing the right things for the wrong reasons were evidently
a rich lode to explore. In "The Madonna of the Future," Henry James introduced his own candidate: Mrs. Coventry. An American living in Florence, she
goes in for being "famously 'artistic' "—James's quotation marks are eloquent—
plays hostess in an apartment laden with Italian paintings and bibelots, and
prates with assumed expertise at "a high esthetic pitch." And in the early 1890s,
in one of his last novels, *Frau Jenny Treibel,* Theodor Fontane somewhat more
gently lampooned the book's eponymous heroine, who advertises her "heart for
poetry" while she broods on money and class. Profitably married, fond of
romantic talk about young love, she is at heart materialistic and patronizing,
"the very model," comments one of her oldest friends, "of a bourgeoise."[10]

---

* Jews were an easy target: "modern" = "rootless," or "showy" = "vulgar."

It would be humorless to consider these philistines posing as sensitive souls representative of the mentality rampant among the well-to-do. They are farcical typecasting, and fiction into the bargain. However deftly playwrights and novelists mocked the social pretensions of this type, they missed its grating anxieties in the need to find bearings in unfamiliar, often snobbish surroundings. Still, though we know that bourgeoisophobes were given to wild hyperbole, their lampoons had their origins in nature. Especially early in the century, frantic new captains of business and industry really did have little time and energy for the blessings of music and art. When Rembrandt Peale, the painter who established the Baltimore Museum and Gallery of Paintings in 1814, worried that "liberal views and the purposes of science" were being slighted in that city by "the sordid calculations of short-sighted commercial avarice," he was speaking from experience.[11]

We have in these chapters convicted bourgeoisophobes of malice and unmasked their diagnosis of middle-class tastes as tendentious. But there *were* ambitious bourgeois whose social or economic calculations dominated their aesthetic decisions; there *were* collectors who only wanted to fill their bare walls and smugly displayed mindless accumulations; there *were* those who, having arrived, felt obligated to pay tributes to taste in their palatial dwellings.

Instances come readily to hand. When in 1901 Andrew Carnegie built his mansion in New York on Fifth Avenue and Ninety-first Street, it contained as a matter of course a gallery in which paintings, large and small, none of them with any claim to serious artistic merit, crowded together in every available space. Carnegie was a firm believer in the moral force and moral obligations of art— he rejected Rubens as a mere "painter of fat, vulgar women"—but his aesthetic sense largely stopped there.[12] Again, the Vanderbilts, in New York and in Newport alike, commissioned opulent palaces costing millions to build and decorate, palaces that virtually screamed wealth with their chandeliers, their murals, their gilt furniture, their haphazard collections of objects. What John Kenneth Galbraith has called "competitive ostentation" was real enough; at times showy competitive collecting and building a worthy home for these collections were really domestic battles that set one branch of a family against another.[13]

Nor were American millionaires, whom patronizing Europeans snubbed as upstarts, the only collectors of this stripe. In 1873, after four years troubled by delays and tensions between the owner and his architects, Alfred Krupp, Germany's steel magnate and leading munitions maker, moved into an enormous pile in Essen, built on the grounds of his factory. He called it a villa, Villa Hügel; Emperor Wilhelm I, who visited it in 1877, called it a "castle"—not without reason. In its several incarnations it became what every modernist could only damn as a museum of bad taste.

Alfred Krupp, with little interest in art, focused on the materials, for both the exterior and the interior of his castle, and selected the choicest that money could buy. Then, upon his death in 1887, his son Friedrich Alfred Krupp filled Villa Hügel with treasures he would bring home from extensive travels to Spain, Morocco, Egypt, Turkey: "textiles, knotted and woven carpets, blankets and saddles, scarves and pillows," to say nothing of "daggers and lances, shields, pistols, hanging lamps, little tables, desks, glazed tiles, and much else," most of them, like the lances, artistically arranged. The "much else" included a stuffed horse greeting the visitor at the foot of a central staircase. Some, to be sure, admired this hodgepodge: "It was only with Friedrich Alfred Krupp," recalled E. Haux, who had worked for the Krupps as a financial adviser for almost half a century, "that art, too, a sense for the beautiful, moved into Villa Hügel." Thus "the walls were richly ornamented with paintings, mainly portraits of recent vintage." He neglected to point out that most of these portraits were of royalty and, massively, of the Krupp family. "Much admired in those days and also receiving many a condescending smile," we hear, "was a large painting that hung in the lower hall over the billiard table and showed a beautifully painted family of pigs."[14] This was art as souvenir.

We must question the dogmatic rejection of Victorian middle-class taste by avant-garde zealots. To regard cultural squalor as an essential bourgeois trait was rhetorical overkill. But it remains true of nouveaux riches, social climbers, parvenus—whatever name one applied to bourgeois rising with the tides of prosperity—that, faced with an uncanonical symphony or an unorthodox landscape, many of them were at sea without a compass. Even so, the bourgeoisophobes' case was distorted, one-dimensional. For, as the century went on and generation of bourgeois followed generation, less nakedly partisan students of middle-class culture could find enough evidence to reach for finer discriminations. All they needed to do was look around them to see heartening exceptions to the indictments leveled by Flaubert and his like.

What the antibourgeois caricature willfully forgot was the sheer craving that Goethe, himself a notable squirrel, called the "greediness for an object—*Begierde nach einem Gegenstand*," indeed for many objects.[15] Nor was there any incompatibility between the dividends from exhibiting a newly bagged trophy to select guests and those from contemplating it alone. At the same time, to write off as propaganda avant-garde strictures against bourgeois pretensions to high culture is to neglect a palpable Victorian reality.

In short, in the domain of collecting, simplicity is nearly always oversimplification. Patrons even earned the gratitude of creative spirits who were making a good deal of money on their own. Thus in the late 1820s, Gioacchino Rossini, who had written one acclaimed opera after another, became friendly with a prodigiously rich banker, the Spaniard Alexandro María Aguado—he left around 60,000,000 francs on his death—who lived in Paris and had taken French citizenship. In 1827, he made his first approach to Rossini, commissioning a cantata to be performed at the christening of his son, and remunerated him with a princely gift. He repeatedly had Rossini stay at his country villa or his Paris mansion to provide him with leisure and privacy. He introduced Rossini to friends who were, like Aguado himself, only too pleased to commission compositions from him. He loyally tried to help Rossini over the depressions he suffered in his middle years. He lent Rossini large sums of money, altogether some 50,000 francs. All of Rossini's biographers call Aguado Rossini's friend, justly so.

And who can disentangle the private motives that threw affluent late-nineteenth-century German Jews into collecting? Theodor Fontane, an astute commentator on his times, acknowledged that they were doing so to a degree far exceeding all other segments in the German *Bürgertum:* "All freedom and refined culture, at least here in Berlin," he wrote in 1890, "is made possible chiefly by its rich Jewry."[16] Certainly they reveled in finally having a toehold in a wider culture. To recall the old saying, they were behaving like others, only more so. A presentable collection could be not just an emblem of assimilation but a means to it: disinterested aesthetic delight and social anxiety combined in varied mixtures. But we know enough about them to say that pining for social acceptability or ascent was rarely their dominant incentive: calculations of this kind were dwarfed by the lust after objects for their own sake, a fixation on art that more than matched the hunt for status.

Among the elite of Jewish collectors in imperial Berlin, two stand out: James Simon and Eduard Arnhold. Neither took the convenient road to assimilation: baptism; both were active in Jewish charities. But the two, among the richest of Germans in commerce, industry, and banking, highly visible as philanthropists and benefactors, did not need to exploit their art as a passport to exclusive circles. They were what has been derisively called *Kaiserjuden,* Jews on good terms with Wilhelm II, who shared (or aroused) the emperor's interests in archaeological digs in the Near East or in societies fostering the natural sciences. Simon and Arnhold were both monarchists, patriots, conservatives who, except among principled anti-Semites, fitted seamlessly into Berlin's bourgeois elite. Whatever cachet their spectacular collections or their grandiose donations to museums might add to their reputation, they bought art because they loved art.

Until the ravages of the First World War ruined his firm, James Simon, born in 1851, was among the biggest taxpayers in the country. His business was textiles—cotton and wool. But his heart was in high culture: he was a proficient Latin scholar, a competent amateur pianist and violinist, a cultivated host in his art-filled mansion to artists, writers, museum officials. And his enthusiasm for paintings and sculptures secured him the friendship of Wilhelm von Bode, then on his way to becoming the powerful general director of Prussia's museums, a connoisseur whose expert advice he sought and public collections he enriched. In 1885, in a typical instance, Arnhold asked Bode to look at a Van Dyck and to let him know "1. whether the painting is an unquestioned Van Dyck; 2. whether it is well preserved, generally of good quality; 3. whether the price of 12,000 marks is appropriate, respectively whether it is likely one could get it cheaper." This last note, stressing that he was "short on cash," runs through Simon's correspondence. But it reads less as a repeated hint at financial distress than a defense against his own cravings. Thrift contended with appetite: in January 1887, Simon told Bode he had promised himself to buy no art that year, but in April he bid on a Ruysdael and a Weenix, though in self-protection he bid low.[17]

Although Simon's taste gravitated to the Italian Renaissance and Dutch paintings from the golden age—he owned a Hals and that rare treasure, a Vermeer—he occasionally ventured into other periods. When, in March 1885, Bode offered to look out for interesting items that Simon might want for his collection, Simon responded with the customary caution—he was low on funds right now—and then cheerfully gave Bode a free hand: "I don't tie myself closely to time, school, motif, because I don't want to be the collector of a specialty."[18] Then, in 1904, on the founding of the Kaiser-Friedrich Museum, Simon helped to celebrate its launching with a munificent gift of Renaissance art: coins, bronzes, Della Robbia terra-cottas, and paintings.

Among these jewels was a remarkable Mantegna, a half-length close-up depiction of the Virgin tenderly holding the sleeping Christ child, the whole in subdued light and dark browns. The connoisseur and art historian Max Friedländer, an aide to Bode, justly called it a "masterpiece."[19] Simon had seen it for the second time on February 23, 1897, and noted that the dealer had reduced the price to £3,000, which he still found "extremely expensive." Nor, he reported to Bode, was he in a buying mood. Yet he wrestled with himself: it would be hard to find so intimate a Mantegna again, and if it was really "*hors ligne*—outstanding," he would take the plunge, reluctantly. Four days later, Simon had resolved his struggle: "Well, I've got the Mantegna. It was a very difficult decision."[20] As usual with this collector, prudence ran a poor second to desire.

In such transactions, Simon's sheer pleasure in his purchases continually broke through. Early in 1896, he told Bode that he had hung a van de Velde he had just bought, "and naturally it looks even more beautiful; it brightens up the whole room." Eight years later, after acquiring a Metsu for 25,000 francs, he observed that this was "surely not cheap"—but, then, he had felt like having a Metsu. It was characteristic of him that he would spend time and energy on displaying his collection in carefully thought-out surroundings, and to involve his chief adviser in the process. "The Robbia has arrived in good shape," he wrote Bode in October 1891, "and gives me great pleasure. We must now put a small carpet behind it to show it off properly." A month later, still waiting for the carpet, he reminded Bode of his promise to supply the fitting decor. Late in life, in 1920, upon Bode's retirement, Simon reminded his old friend of their long collaboration, which, he wrote, "belongs to the most valuable things my life has brought me. It has always been a beneficial counterweight to my material activity."[21] Simon must have realized that he needed his material activity to let him indulge in his higher pleasures. Far from exploiting art for commerce, he exploited commerce for art.

This held quite as true of Eduard Arnhold. Born in Dessau in 1849, his father a physician and his mother a Berliner noted for her wit, he showed a precocious talent for business as he rose rapidly in one of Germany's largest coal companies; a partner at twenty-five, he was soon a multimillionaire. From his youth he spent as much money on art as he could afford. Widely traveled, he visited museums wherever he went, cultivating his taste by direct inspection and by socializing with artists. Like most collectors, he started conservatively, with undemanding modern German paintings, and, like others, as he outgrew them, disposed of them to make room for more daring purchases. Around the turn of the century, a printed catalog shows a wide range and strong preferences: among 114 items, 80 paintings were modern, 9 from an earlier period, and while he owned 5 sculptures from the Renaissance, 20 were of recent vintage.[22] As his friend Max Liebermann remembered him, Arnhold first collected contemporary Germans before he reached his true love: "In the beginning he bought Lenbach, Böcklin, Feuerbach, but it took only a few years before he found his way to the French Impressionists," which included five Manets, several Renoirs, Monets, Pissarros, Sisleys, and Cézannes.[23]

Arnhold was rich enough, and known well enough as a collector who liked to deal with artists face to face, that they did not hesitate to offer him paintings at exorbitant prices. Writing to him in 1913, Wilhelm Trübner, then at the height of his reputation, listed four of his paintings available at 20,000 to 40,000 marks.[24] One thinks of the 3,000 marks Max Liebermann had got some four decades earlier for his *Gänserupferinnen,* and notes the inflation largely caused by "American prices" for pictures. But as a magnate, Arnhold could keep up with the market. And in the manner of magnates, he had a gallery with skylights installed atop his mansion to display his gems. At the same time—and this goes to the heart of his collecting fever—he distributed his purchases through the house. As he told Liebermann, "Every morning, before I go to my office, I look at my pictures; then I have a cheerful impression all day long, and the disagreeable aspects of business have less power over me."[25] Unlike business, art was for Arnhold pure pleasure.

Such pure appetites supplied subjects for Honoré Daumier's finest work of the 1860s. In one of his lithographs, six admirers in a painter's studio crowd around a new picture and exuberantly exclaim, *"Fichtre! Epatant! Sapristi! Superbe! Ça parle!"* It is understandable that fellow artists like Delacroix and Courbet, van Gogh and Cézanne, should be fond enough of this print to buy it. And in an elegant drawing, *Le Connoisseur,* Daumier shows an elderly gentleman in a room filled with works of art, a portfolio by his side; he has made himself comfortable in an armchair, hands folded and legs crossed, and is staring at a tabletop reproduction of the Venus de Milo. He is alone with his thoughts as private as thoughts are, but his intent gaze speaks of unalloyed aesthetic excitement, of delight uncorrupted by base social or economic calculations.[26]

3. The Victorian Maecenas

For all the expanding number and rising influence of dealers as culture brokers, old-fashioned patronage had not outlived its usefulness in the Victorian decades, though it usually added, in that age of reverence for virtuosi and creative artists, certain egalitarian touches. Sir George Beaumont, the most generous protector of young English artists in the early nineteenth century, or Count Schack, who, we recall, half a century later patronized—in both meanings of the word—aspiring German painters, had bourgeois imitators. Many a local worthy who subsidized gifted youngsters to study music or art to develop their unformed talents was trying to reproduce in real life what had been a literary formula for centuries: the raw genius discovered and fostered by a beneficent sponsor.

Sometimes the results were spectacular: there was, for one, Carl Larsson, to become Sweden's favorite water colorist, whose precisely drawn, brightly lit, and imaginatively conceived domestic scenes stood as an effective criticism of the country's stultified academic artists. Returning in 1885 from a stay in France at the age of thirty-two with great plans and empty pockets, he found a generous patron in a financier and serious collector from Gothenburg, Pontus Fürstenberg, who commissioned paintings from Larsson and helped to launch him in his career. In the United States, Lyman Reed, who had accu-

mulated a small fortune in the wholesale grocery business after 1825, supported Thomas Cole, Asher B. Durand, and William S. Mount, all to become
prominent artists, by commissioning paintings from them. In 1835, Durand
praised Reed's disinterested patronage to a fellow painter: "He is determined
to make something of me, and if I ever attain to any excellence in painting it
will be more owing to him than any other cause." If few of these prodigies fulfilled the extravagant expectations of their well-meaning supporters, the
patron's conscious good intentions were unmistakable.[1]

Patrons could ease the careers of the impecunious or the lonely. Nadezhda
von Meck backed Tchaikovsky with timely loans and liberal subsidies: even
though the two never met, for thirteen years they exchanged the most intimate, at times pamphlet-length letters confessing almost all they had to con-
fess. Their peculiar friendship had many of the benefits and liabilities of
modern patronage, in which the respective roles of donor and recipient were
no longer so clear-cut as they had been in past centuries; the first indulging in
a whim that could change course without notice, the second in a false position
as a dependent who presumably prized independence above all. No wonder
that artists were often ambivalent about such alliances, glad to be free of them
yet eager for the security they promised. In one year, 1825, John Constable
could note both with satisfaction that he had got the public into his hands,
"and want not a patron" and with marked uneasiness that "the publick is hard,
cruel and unrelenting."[2] There were times when artists would wonder if the
callousness of the market was more bearable than the caprice of an exigent and
interfering backer.

Success or failure of the modern Maecenas-client liaison was mainly a matter of temperament on both sides, of the psychological demands each made on
the other. For years after the mid-1860s, the wealthy German aesthetician and
collector Conrad Fiedler supported the painter Hans von Marées, who had
impressed him with his native intelligence, vaulting ambition, and unremitting
devotion to his mission to the world. The help was substantial—Fiedler repeatedly exceeded the agreed-upon annual subvention of 5,200 marks, even reaching 7,900 marks in 1882.[3] In the modern manner, patron and painter were
friends, and Fiedler's subtle long essays on artistic creativity and aesthetic judgment, dating mainly from the 1870s and 1880s, were lent considerable authority through his stimulating associations with German painters and sculptors.
His life was a never-ceasing conversation about art, and he included Marées in
his circle.

An openhanded, disinterested, and patient benefactor, Fiedler was the
antithesis of Marées, exacting, quarrelsome, self-absorbed, beset by grievances
that approached paranoia.[4] As a painter mainly of the human body, he tor-

mented himself even more than his friends, continually reworking his canvases in search of a perfection obscure even to him. It was almost fated that, well before his early death in 1887, he should break with his patron, irrevocably. Three years earlier, as if anticipating the outcome, Fiedler wrote a little sadly to a friend that with Marées, as with all of life, "everything is simultaneously a tragedy and a comedy."[5] The romantic notion that a genius must be fondly indulged and forgiven much had stayed Fiedler's hand for years, but there were extremes beyond which Marées could not stretch even Fiedler's carefully cultivated forbearance.

These traumatic denouements were not foreordained. In 1873, William T. Walters, a Baltimore businessman who had greatly flourished in the liquor trade and investments in railroads, commissioned from the prolific French sculptor and painter Antoine Louis Barye a copy of each piece he had produced.* Born in Pennsylvania in 1819, Walters had been interested in art from his youth and been buying Baryes since 1861.† Barye was best known for his small-scale, meticulously worked bronzes depicting animals in Darwinian combat for survival: a jaguar devouring a hare, a python crushing a crocodile, a bear brought low by hounds. Those of his animals not caught in the act of killing were quite as vivid: his lions were leonine, his horses noble. Barye, who had been eminently successful in selling casts of his statuettes to avid collectors, found his arrangement with Walters psychologically rewarding. So did Walters. "To have been enabled to give this commission," he wrote in 1885, "was one of the most agreeable acts of my life in relation to my art experience," and "it was not the less so to the artist, who observed, 'My own country has not done this for me.' "[6] The commission recalls the search for completeness that animated Freer's appetite for all Whistlers.

Producing very similar results, the Berlin industrialist Bernhard Koehler was no less sensitive in his role of Maecenas: starting in 1910, he granted Franz Marc, then a penniless young artist, a modest monthly stipend of 200 marks to provide him with free time and took Marc's paintings in trade. This proved a bonanza for Koehler, since his protégé was productive and inventive, experimenting with unnatural colors—his celebrated canvas of blue horses dates from 1911—and pouring his nature mysticism into powerful semi-abstract compositions. In 1912, Marc, teaming up with Wassily Kandinsky, published a copiously illustrated almanac, *The Blue Rider,* and it was Koehler who financed this

* For more on Walters, see below, pp. 163–64.

† Looking back, he claimed that he had started his collection with the first five dollars he ever made, a history painting, *Bonaparte's Retreat from Moscow,* by a minor French contemporary, E. A. Odier. William R. Johnston, "William Thompson Walters," *The Taste of Maryland: Art Collecting in Maryland, 1800–1934,* ed. Johnston (1984), 50.

costly publication. Marc's death at the front in 1916 put a cruel end to this mutually profitable friendship, but in his short career as a patron, Koehler showed himself a rare human being.* He was, to be sure, not a typical bourgeois, but he was a bourgeois just the same.

However disinterested a middle-class patron's impulse to support artists might be, his power to dispose over their talents could not help bringing narcissistic dividends. At times, self-absorption was so conspicuous that it could not escape notice. As a young man in the early 1850s, Abraham Willet, the son of an eminent surgeon and active among art amateurs in Amsterdam, began to amass a collection of contemporary paintings. His marriage in 1861 to an heiress, Louisa Holthuysen, largely it seems for her money, provided him with the resources to expand the range of his purchases and to furnish an elegant mansion on the exclusive Heerengracht suitable, he thought, to a grand collector. The house became a little museum before it became, after his and his wife's death, a museum in law, laden with prints, drawings, precious silver and glass, fine furniture, and pictures—flower pieces, still lifes, fetching young peasant women by modern Dutch artists, and landscapes largely from the Barbizon ambiance. The whole was a construction intended to impress.

In fact, Willet turned out to be a minor exhibitionist who could not help calling attention to himself. He left little to chance; restless in Amsterdam, frequently on the road, he and his wife lived for part of the year in a villa near Paris, which they immortalized with canvases depicting its exterior and its flamboyantly decorated rooms. Back at the Heerengracht, visitors could not miss a glass bearing the Willet clan's coat of arms, or a solid, highly ornamented bench in the front hall that featured the same heraldic device, this time intertwined with that of the Holthuysen family. As if this was not sufficient self-display, portraits of the master were conspicuous: Willet as a young man; Willet in elegant company; most grandiose of all, Willet impersonating an officer in a seventeenth-century Dutch militia company costumed with ruff, sash, pike, dagger, boots, the ensemble shown off to advantage by Willet's heroic posture. He had even his dogs immortalized in two water colors.[7]

Still, when it came to preoccupation with self, Willet was an exemplar of modesty compared with Gustave Courbet's first sponsor, Alfred Bruyas. The underoccupied son of a banker in Montpellier, Bruyas exhibited himself as an ardent patron of painting with neurotic, that is to say abnormal, clarity. Blessed with more money than he could readily spend, he started out studying art and

---

* Marc, visiting him in 1912, voiced his pleasure at knowing him, "wholly different from all others with whom I have had financial or more or less businesslike dealings." Klaus Lankheit, "Wissenschaftlicher Anhang," *Der Blaue Reiter,* ed. Wassily Kandinsky and Franz Marc, newly ed. Lankheit (1965), 274–75, quotation at 275.

ended up buying it. In 1853, at thirty-two, he discovered Courbets at the Salon and, soon after, the painter himself and impulsively made himself Courbet's backer and friend. Courbet in his first letters to Bruyas affectionately treated him as a *cher ami*. Bruyas, exceedingly odd and self-willed, was given to pseudo-profound, barely comprehensible maxims that savored of confused political sentiments. And something of an egomaniac, he ended up with around thirty depictions of himself, mainly oils—one of them showing him as the suffering Christ crowned with thorns—and drawings, sketches, and medallions. Three of the portraits were by Courbet.[8]

That is how Bruyas launched his career as a patron: he commissioned a portrait from Courbet holding a book inscribed with the flattering text *Etudes sur l'Art moderne. Solution. A. Bruyas.* Flattering and telling: Courbet was as unacademic in painting as he was in politics and equally aggressive about both. A munificent and open-minded admirer was indeed an ideal solution to the vexing question just how an unconventional artist is to live. And not content with having Courbet paint him, Bruyas bought two of his entries to the Salon of 1853, the *Spinner Asleep,* a tender study rare in Courbet's work, and the *Bathers,* his early and controversial venture into doing nudes.

These purchases made the solution called Bruyas all the more plausible, especially since he assisted Courbet emotionally no less than financially. Courbet made a confidant of him, pouring out boastful and voluble confessional letters. Later, even after some of Courbet's indiscretions had cooled the temperature of their friendship, Bruyas bought more Courbets, lent them to exhibitions, and made himself available as a trustworthy listener. The alliance shows the modern Maecenas at work.

It was characteristically Victorian, with the patron a bourgeois rather than an aristocrat and the artist in the vanguard of self-appointed guides to a culture badly in need of superior spirits like themselves. In 1854, Courbet did a large-scale canvas at Bruyas's request, *The Meeting,* which has him striding along a country lane, sturdy walking stick in hand, as he encounters Bruyas accompanied by servant and dog. Courbet's vigor and Bruyas's somber rigidity are too palpable to be overlooked. The picture has been variously interpreted, but at the least Courbet stands as his patron's equal, possibly his superior: one revealing caricature, by the cartoonist Quillenbois, has Bruyas, servant, and dog on their knees to the painter.[9]

Despite all his arrogant disdain for the philistine, Courbet, who matched his patron in egocentrism and surpassed him in the arts of publicity, never ceased trying to place his work in the Salon. The erotic nudes he painted on commission from buyers who loved the sheen of female flesh in art as in life, suggests the same practical bent. His most notorious client was Khalil-Bey, the

Ottoman ambassador to France, for whom Courbet painted the large-size *Paresse et luxure,* two reclining female nudes in somnolent and sensual embrace, and the scandalous *L'Origine du monde,* a female torso from waist to thigh, genitals open to view. The shocking could be profitable. This truth, too, was not new, but the bourgeois age showed a particular aptitude for it.

There is more than one way of reading a naked body, especially when painted by a master. A nude is a Rorschach test: viewers take away what they give to it. Certainly Courbet's great champion in the United States, Louisine Havemeyer, had a perception of his nudes different from that of the Ottoman ambassador. Her first exposure to one of his paintings came in 1889: a landscape with deer. A dozen years before, still Louisine Elder, she had bought a Degas pastel in Paris under the guidance of her closest friend, the irresistible Mary Cassatt. From 1883, after her marriage to Henry O. Havemeyer, a quick-witted capitalist who amassed millions as the organizer of the American sugar trust (he almost went to jail for his enterprise), collecting became a joint venture. The Havemeyers looked at paintings together, earnestly discussed their impressions, and did their best to harmonize their desires. This meant on the wife's part firm though respectful persuasion; when it came to taking risks with nonconformist artists, Louisine Havemeyer regularly took the lead.

The result: in 1892, the Havemeyers bought their first Courbet nude, a three-quarter length *Torso d'une femme,* which, after the wife overcame her husband's strenuous resistance, became one of his favorites. A second nude entered their collection the following year, again on Louisine Havemeyer's urging. Far more provocative than its predecessor, *La Femme à la vague* depicts a buxom nude immersed to her waist in water, her arms raised to emphasize her firm opulent breasts. It cost them $5,000, about ten years' income for the average industrial worker in the United States.

But it was the Havemeyers' third Courbet nude, the suggestive *La Femme au perroquet,* which they bought in 1898 for $12,000, that best exhibited the couple's commitment to subversive art. The erotic implications of the painting were apparent to the sophisticated and the unlettered alike: a luscious naked woman stretched out on her back, her long red hair streaming behind her, on her left forefinger a parrot perched, its colorful wings spread. Durand-Ruel had shown this canvas in New York and, finding no buyer, was about to return it to France when Louisine Havemeyer intervened. As before, she was the one responsible for gently forcing the issue. As she recalled in the artless memoirs she wrote for her three children during the First World War, a decade after her husband's death, "I begged Mr. Havemeyer to buy the picture, not to hang it in our gallery lest the anti-nudists should declare a revolution and revise our Constitution, but just to keep it in America, just that such a work should not be lost to the future generations nor to the students who might with its help, and that of other pictures, some day give a national art to their own country." Fortunately, "Mr. Havemeyer at once consented," aware that his wife thought Courbet one in the supreme trio of painters, ranking with Velázquez and Rembrandt.[10]

A key word in this recollection opens a window to the limitations of broad-mindedness in late-Victorian manners. Louisine Havemeyer was a strong-minded person with firm views; from her youth she had actively advocated woman suffrage. No doubt, the husband respected her judgment and tried to please her, but he was the undisputed head of the family. When one of her enthusiasms made him uneasy, she "begged" him to see it her way, and she intimates that she would not contradict him when he continued to balk at a possible purchase or returned to the dealer a painting he had come to dislike. To bring his taste in line with hers, she played subtly on his fondness for her.* Significantly, prudery was not an issue between them. He did not flinch when she privately mocked the all-too-shockable disciples of Anthony Comstock and declared nudes, as long as they were well painted, an enjoyable part of life—and art. She saw herself in league with her husband working for the future by widening the aesthetic horizons of American society.

The history of the Havemeyer collection is an exemplar of upper-bourgeois education to modernism. In 1876, at twenty-nine, upon visiting the Centennial Exhibitions in Philadelphia, Harry Havemeyer bought a quantity of Japanese silks and brocades, lacquer boxes, and other paraphernalia, a predilection he continued to pursue in later years. After that, as if testing the waters, he acquired a few inoffensive and insignificant canvases; his first purchases that posterity might note came in 1882, with a Corot and a Millet. But after his marriage, his collecting took fire. He coveted Rembrandts, starting with etchings and late in the 1880s graduating to paintings—not all of which would survive their attribution. But gradually the moderns monopolized center stage; by the early 1890s, as the tempo of their collecting accelerated, the Havemeyers bought important Degas, Cassatts, Monets, Manets—a favorite—to say nothing of Cézanne still lifes and landscapes. By now, Harry Havemeyer had integrated Louisine Havemeyer's aesthetic adventurism. They built up their private gallery, lent masterpieces to exhibitions, and enriched the Metropolitan Muse-

---

* When Mrs. Havemeyer had a Courbet nude sent home for her husband's inspection, he strongly objected, and she returned it to Durand-Ruel. He was glad: "'I knew you wouldn't want it,' he said, quite pleased. 'But I want it,' I had to answer. 'I want it very much! It is one of the loveliest pictures I have ever seen, and if I had it I would keep it right there in my closet and not hang it in the gallery at all, but just to go there and look at it all alone by myself.'" The next day, Mr. Havemeyer bought the painting. Louisine W. Havemeyer, *Sixteen to Sixty: Memoirs of a Collector* (1930; ed. 1961), 192.

um. The finest of their purchases have a place in the history of modern art.*

In her memoirs, Louisine Havemeyer certified her husband's consuming appetite for art: "It was pleasant to listen to him as he spoke his enthusiasm, to see his soul revealed in his eyes. It was singular that a man without technical knowledge could be so convincing in his appreciations, but he had an exceptionally keen and sensitive perception of truth and beauty." Mary Cassatt thought him the quickest study she had ever seen: "There will never be another collector like him."[11] When the Havemeyers, usually accompanied by Cassatt and a local scout, went hunting for pictures in remote Tuscan hills or Spanish castles, he would display all the energy he had employed to engross the American sugar market. The conquering robber baron and the emotional lover of art coexisted in him, as in other capitalists, with ease.

What I have called an education to modernism was far from rare among bourgeois collectors. The French banker Isaac de Camondo, like many nineteenth-century French entrepreneur-collectors a Jew, launched his collection with "safe" Renaissance paintings and eighteenth-century furniture, moved on to Japanese woodcuts and, still more venturesome, to contemporary avant-garde painters: Manet, Sisley, van Gogh, Cézanne. Shifts of this sort could be relatively moderate. The first collection that the tenor Faure auctioned off, in 1873, before he discovered the Impressionists, had consisted of Barbizon painters like Rousseau, Millet, and Troyon.[12] But at times—we have seen it with Freer—such second thoughts had the force of a conversion. In 1843, Paul Perier, from a prominent political family that had grown rich in railroad construction, had a valuable collection of old masters auctioned off after he became enamored of the Barbizon school.[13]

Koehler, Franz Marc's patron, offers an even more heroic instance of openness to aesthetic experience. He had been casually collecting for years, mainly embroideries and porcelain as well as mediocre modern paintings. Then Koehler became acquainted with August Macke, a young painter who was courting his niece, and who would, like Marc, become a casualty of the First World War. Something happened. Risk taking conquered conventionality: already in his fifties when he grew infatuated with modernist art, "Uncle Bernhard" went to Paris with Macke in 1908 and came home with Manets and

* This is no exaggeration: the Havemeyers' collection included Manet's great *Gare St. Lazare* of 1872–73, which Faure had been the first to own. The Havemeyer Monets, too, are masterpieces: *La Grenouillère* of 1869, one of the first of his Impressionist paintings, and *Le Pont Charing Cross* (1899), one in a series of foggy London. Degas, too, was represented by extraordinary pictures: the accomplished early oil *Femme aux chrysanthème*, dating from 1865, and *Chez la modiste* (1882), a charming pastel capturing a young woman trying on a hat. And this is only a small sample.

Monets, Corots, Pissarros and Seurats, even Kandinskys and Delaunays. Marcs and Mackes followed.[14]

These trajectories obeyed none but the laws of desire. The German-Jewish merchant Ludwig Fischer and his wife, Rosy, are added proof. Settled in Frankfurt around the turn of the century, they were a very domestic couple occupied with their two sons, a few art-loving Jewish families much like themselves, and a dealer they could trust. Once Fischer retired from business, he and his wife began to buy pictures without much system at first but with admirable flexibility; minor paintings of the nineteenth-century realist school gave way to work by German semi-Impressionists like Liebermann, which they sold in turn to make way for the German Expressionists. Before 1920, the Fischers had one of the finest collections of Kirchners and Noldes in the country; the crowded walls of their living and dining rooms were a veritable manifesto in behalf of modernism.[15]

Unlike the majority of collectors buying modernist art, the Fischers specialized in fellow Germans, only exchanging one German school for another—twice. But many collectors undergoing this kind of education boldly crossed frontiers. Among the most spectacular exemplars of this aesthetic cosmopolitanism was a Russian merchant, Sergei Shchukin. He was one of six brothers, highly educated and Western-oriented sons of a thriving merchant and industrialist doing business in Moscow. Poets and painters were among their regular company, and except for Nikolai, who preferred keeping an opera singer, several of Sergei's brothers spent much time and much money on art. Piotr, for one, accumulated a notable though indiscriminate pile of lithographs, photographs, coins, antique carpets, domestic implements; according to an inventory of his holdings, they added up to 23,911 items, enough to fill the small museum he had built for the purpose. True, almost by accident, on impulse, he also bought some French Impressionists during a quick visit to Paris in 1898. But this hardly puts him into the league of a major collector.[16]

It was Sergei Shchukin, as able a businessman as his father and as assiduous a host, who became the undisputed prince of collectors in the family. Like many another hunter and gatherer, he started at home, buying Russian painters of recent vintage, "an art of the golden mean," in the words of a critic who knew him well, "remote from the great, wildly agitated path of modernism."[17] But this was just an opening phase, a novitiate in art, succeeded by a rash of haphazard purchases of paintings in Paris as the spirit moved him. Then, after the turn of the century, by now in his late forties, he outgrew his habit of throwing together now forgotten mediocrities and now acclaimed Monets. He had come to *see* the Impressionists and, after that, the Postimpressionists—Cézanne, van Gogh, Gauguin—and seeing meant buying.

Nor did Sergei Shchukin stop there. In 1906, he acquired his first Matisse. Within a few years, the Matisses in his collection were a commanding sample of the painter's work; all of them exotic, even incomprehensible, to most Russian eyes. He went further, commissioning two large canvases, *Dance* and *Music,* for his mansion and suggesting themes to Matisse he wanted in his collection. The customer had become a patron. By 1911, when Matisse came to stay with his Maecenas, Shchukin owned some twenty-five of his paintings. That same year, he told his favorite artist in a heartfelt letter, "Your paintings give me enormous pleasure. I look at them every day and love all of them."[18]

From the 1880s, collectors and consumers of high culture put academic Victorianism under pressure everywhere, in the drama, the novel, music, and architecture as much as in painting and sculpture. Disputes over styles enlivened the capitals of culture. Even in conservative Moscow, Shchukin found a handful of allies among local art lovers, and a competitor, Ivan Morosov, who bought fine Impressionists, Postimpressionists, and Cubists with equal avidity. Yet the prices that salon painters kept charging for their canvases attest that their vogue persisted. To judge from the art that most dealers had on offer and that most exhibitions prized all the way to 1914 and beyond, influential art lovers continued faithful to the palatable offerings of Meissonier, Cabanel, and their like. Popular series of artists' biographies addressed to a wide middle-class audience, quite distinct from avant-garde polemical squibs that excited a few partisans, usually chose painters safely dead, and dead long ago: Raphael, Rubens and Rembrandt, Dürer, Titian, Michelangelo, and Velázquez. When publishers ventured to add a living painter to the list, though guaranteed to be anything but subversive, they introduced him with apologetic self-praise for their daring.[19] It is telling that when in 1885 Louis Viardot published a volume in his *Merveilles de la peinture* that dealt among other schools with French art, he did not get beyond Delacroix.

In short, if the taste of collectors like the Havemeyers or the Shchukins was as spectacular as their buying power, these avant-garde gatherers did not have it all their own way. Witness William T. Walters, whom we have already met as a patron of the sculptor Barye. After his businesses provided him with ample disposable income, he started to collect contemporary American painters and sculptors. But in 1859, in a distinct change of direction, he bought Jean-Léon Gérôme's dramatic scene *Le Duel après le bal masqué,* a harlequin dying at the dawn of day, for $2,500—a solid but hardly extravagant investment. A long stay in Paris during the Civil War years strengthened his attachment to French academic art, and the rise in prices did not intimidate him. In 1886 he paid 71,000 francs for a Troyon showing cattle drinking; by that time, the Barbizon landscape painters had gone beyond being respectable to being fashionable. In the same year he acquired a favorite, Meissonier's *1814*—a grim-faced Napoleon mounted on a white charger—for a princely 128,000 francs. Before he died in 1894, he had rounded out his holdings with more Gérômes.

Walters left not a hint that he felt at all defensive about his choices. And Baltimore applauded; the collectors who made up his world almost wholly shared his tastes. His friend, adviser, and agent in Paris, George A. Lucas, an expatriate very much at home in French artistic circles and like Walters an assiduous collector of Baryes, amassed minor modern French artists almost exclusively. A few Corots and Théodore Rousseaus only added a little spice to a bland menu. When he had his portrait painted, Lucas chose Cabanel and Bonnat—nothing could have been more aesthetically correct. Back in Baltimore, Walters's fellow businessmen, who collected ancient Egyptian artifacts and medieval manuscripts as much as paintings, bought Bouguereaus and Gérômes, only throwing in an occasional Renoir—and even one Manet—for variety.[20]

Consumers who shopped in the artistic bazaars of the time, then, were of the most diverse persuasions, and many of them harbored complicated, even inconsistent, tastes. "We are all eclectics," wrote the *Gazette des beaux-arts* in 1897.[21] Few major collectors displayed the iron consistency of Mrs. Potter Palmer of Chicago, who decorated her family mansion with precious rugs and tapestries from several lands and several centuries, but who, when it came to paintings, craved French Impressionists alone. The majority of collectors traveled across broad fields of Beauty, sampling as they went. Mrs. Isabella Stewart Gardner, who opened her idiosyncratic, strongly held tastes to public inspection at her private museum in Boston, Fenway Court, acquired Titians but also Manets, Anthony Van Dyck but also Rosa Bonheur. The steel magnate Henry Clay Frick bought bronzes and porcelains and, with an eye to exceptional quality, Dutch, French, Flemish, English paintings.

These collectors had their advisers and their favorite dealers, but in the end their collection spoke most emphatically of their private delights. The relationship of collectors to the revolutions in late-nineteenth-century and early-twentiety-century taste proved to be quite unpredictable. It covered a large terrain, all the way from Walters's Meissoniers to Shchukin's Matisses. This much, though, seems certain: in their own way, bourgeois collectors acted as agents of cultural change. If, as the avant-garde charged, they all too often followed the fashion, there were times when they made it.

❧ FIVE ❧

Movers and Shakers

I. Founders

Victorian bourgeois celebrated the ideal of privacy, but not even they could insulate the personal from the public domain. When collectors decided to donate or bequeath their treasures to a local museum or to the state, they graduated from the status of hunters and gatherers to that of movers and shakers. The Havemeyers, who left to the Metropolitan Museum in New York whatever art they did not reserve for their children, are one striking instance. Alfred Bruyas, Courbet's patron, is another: in the early 1860s, after two decades of collecting, he formed the plan of leaving his modern French paintings to the local Musée Fabre in Montpellier. And just before his death in 1877, after keeping the curators and his fellow citizens in suspense, he finally made his donation official, to great civic delight.

The overlapping of roles among collectors keeping their trophies and collectors giving them away was naturally accompanied by overlapping rationales. But each founder and donor—a collector who, as it were, went public—had some particular private motive: a revenge on offspring lacking the collector's obsession; a memorial that celebrated the love for a dead spouse; a strategy for acquiring, and retaining, high social status; a patriotism local or national that enhanced the benefactor's reputation by enhancing that of the beneficiary; a desire to immortalize one's name in the most conspicuous manner possible. Critics of capitalism added yet another spring of action: a greedy, unscrupulous accumulator making restitution, whipped into munificence by a sense of guilt, conscious and unconscious alike.

As usual, such motives were mixed; pride and shame actuated benefactors in distinct personal amalgams. Among them a need to remove the stigma of brutal acquisitiveness, or at least to veil it with grandiose offerings, certainly had its place. Upton Sinclair, an American socialist whose political novels became best-sellers, said a century ago that he saw no point in being grateful to generous millionaires; a sensible political system would have prevented them from stealing the money they were now so self-righteously giving back, and allowed ordinary people to build museums and concert halls on their own.

Few who benefited from largesse saw it that way, or allowed themselves to say so publicly. But, whatever view one takes of Sinclair's sally, there is no doubt that more than one great Victorian philanthropist testified to being uneasy with pure avariciousness. "No idol is more debasing than the worship of money," Andrew Carnegie wrote in 1868 in a memorandum intended for his eyes alone, and he determined to give up its degrading pursuit before he ruined his moral health "beyond hope of permanent recovery." It was not until the early 1890s that he followed the advice he had addressed to himself; in 1891, launching the benefactions that bear his name, he noted that the rich justly chastised for their extravagant and selfish way of life might "find refuge from self-questioning in the thought of the much greater portion of their means which is being spent on others."[1] Plainly, he had undergone some self-questioning of his own.

Whatever the precise compound of motives in each case, donors disposing of their art collections joined other upper-middle-class philanthropists who founded orchestras and endowed university chairs. All of them participated, often quite explicitly, in the making of tastes and opinions. As they did so, they formed one corner of a triangle, with consumers of culture at another corner and men in charge—bureaucrats, conductors, university chancellors, museum directors—at the third. Each situation was shaped by its time and place, and by the temperament of the players. Each could become a source of friction, for many movers were almost literally shakers. Some, we have seen and shall see again, sought to protect traditions they feared imperiled by aesthetic anarchy; more of them promoted new ideas, new composers, new painters, further unsettling an atmosphere already electric with confusion and conflict.

In their programmatic statements—manifestos, speeches, interviews, testaments—they would describe their aim as the cultivation of a public larger than their own elite of knowledgeable and financially secure lovers of art and music. The cultural pedagogues of modern Manchester, the John Owens or John Rylands, were exemplars of these intentions, and they had articulate companions elsewhere. On November 5, 1895, at the opening festivities of the Carnegie Institute in Pittsburgh, a complex that included a concert hall, a library, a natural history museum, and an art gallery, Andrew Carnegie generalized from some autobiographical reflections to contemporary culture as a whole: "It is because of my own experience that I feel so deeply and see so clearly the great and good work that we shall accomplish if we succeed in bringing to the toiling thousands of Pittsburgh a little of the sweetness and light which flows from the knowledge of music, literature and art."[2] He spoke for the tribe. Often the education these generous and anxious philanthropists envisioned constituted an admission that in their city—perhaps even in their circle—high culture was thinner than they liked. That is what Hermann Leo told Charles Hallé in 1848 when he invited him to awaken "the dormant taste" of Mancunians for good music.

Such didactic purposes were often aggressively explicit, as the urge for self-education merged with self-defense against the ravages of the low-minded. In 1808, three prominent citizens of the German Free City of Frankfurt am Main, then ruled by Archbishop Carl von Dalberg under Napoleon's auspices, founded the Frankfurt Museum. It was, as the name suggests, a home for the muses, a private society designed to foster all the arts, mainly with lectures and concerts. Its principal initiator was Nikolaus Vogt, a gifted amateur musician, historian of neighboring Mainz, the city of his birth, and prominent political official whom Dalberg trusted; his two associates, Johann Friedrich Christian Hess and Clemens Wenzeslaus Coudray, were architects—each a representative specimen of the good *Bürger*. Hess was an influential neoclassicist whose buildings, like the historic Paulskirche, which he completed, did much to shape the urban profile of nineteenth-century Frankfurt. And Coudray would in later years achieve prominence as a high-level official architect in the grand duchy of Weimar, where he worked closely with Goethe.

Like other reformers nostalgic for the old days when, they fancied, high culture had been the possession of many, Vogt and his friends hoped to counteract what the statutes of the Museum denounced as the "poverty-stricken one-sidedness" of their times, which they proposed to overcome by "joining aesthetic cultivation with moral culture."[3] For decades, the chief executive officers of the Museum were leading citizens from the professional classes—lawyers, physicians, editors, Protestant ministers, high-level bureaucrats—all of them voices of the local patriciate.

In March 1808, sounding the theme of other bourgeois founders before and after him, Vogt greeted his audience at the inaugural ceremonies of the Museum with the prediction that precisely because the chief occupation of Frankfurt was trade, the newborn institution could anticipate a glorious future. In a rhetorical gesture, sounding much like self-congratulatory Mancunians later, he wondered if the great Greek and Italian cities, all of them commercial centers, had not been at the same time havens for art and literature. Far from ashamed of being in trade, bourgeois like Vogt took undisguised pride in it. They knew themselves to be anything but philistines. Around the same time, Justinus Kerner, poet and physician, evoked the self-confident atmosphere of Frankfurt's thriving bourgeoisie: "Wealth, cheerfulness, beautiful women, flowers and music, everything splendid."[4] The muses would be right at home.

Vogt could count on assistance from the prosperous Frankfurt society in which he traveled. Attempting to deserve its reputation as a model that joined cultivation with commerce, the city had a record of lavish contributions for public purposes. In 1815, seven years after the founding of the Museum, to mention only the best known, the merchant and banker Johann Friedrich Städel made a will leaving his house, his library, his collection of paintings and graphics, and his fortune to the city. The art institute he envisioned would establish a museum and, as soon as practicable, a school to train future artists.

Significantly he wanted it named after himself, a bourgeois among bourgeois. But in a fit of modesty, as though confessing his amateur standing, Städel asked his executors to dispose freely of his least interesting paintings—the best of them were Dutch and Flemish pictures from the golden seventeenth century—in order to improve the collection. As the name left no doubt, and the will made explicit, the "Städel" was a private affair, independent of other institutes and in no way beholden to the magistrates.[5] No burgher could have expressed civic self-respect and the pleasures of autonomy more emphatically than this.

It was in this atmosphere that the Frankfurt Museum flourished. At first exclusive in its membership, it imposed strict rules of conduct, and the prices of its tickets were steep, to say nothing of its dues.* Critics assailed the society for its snobbery and its traditionalism, charges that its defenders converted into grounds for satisfaction: they saw its true purpose to rescue high culture from the contamination of the merely popular, of dignified public demeanor from casual vulgarity. This overarching objective (and probably a shortage of funds) even wrestled down time-honored prejudices: in 1832, after solemn discussions, the Museum admitted "six gentlemen of the israelitic community" to membership.[6] But with Jewish members or without, decorum remained the standard and a persistent problem. The statutes of 1808 had enjoined silence during concerts, strongly expressed the society's partiality for quiet listening over noisy applause, deprecated outbursts of disapproval as unworthy of a member's discretion, and banished dogs. Yet, as late as the 1890s, the management felt com-

---

* Annual membership for those who were active in performances was 11 gulden; for those "amateurs of art" who were, as it were, passive members, the cost was double that. The best tickets cost 2 gulden; more modest seats could be had for 1 gulden 22 kreuzer. Andreas Hansert, *Geschichte des Städelschen Museums-Vereins Frankfurt am Main* (1994), 28; Franz Lerner, "Das Frankfurt des Fürst-Primas," ibid., 224.

pelled to implore members of the audience to remain seated until the end of
a number and to request that ladies leave their hats at home.

The Museum matched this insistence on good manners with resolute concentration on the classics: Beethoven above all, Haydn, and Mozart. In 1861,
when the institution, now undeniably prosperous, built adequate quarters to
devote itself exclusively to music, the inaugural concert featured two
Beethoven standbys, the Fourth Symphony and the violin concerto, and
Mendelssohn's *Fingal's Cave*. Three years later, when its orchestra ventured to
present Schumann's overture to *Genoveva* for the first time, a correspondent
noted, "Our audience, still tenaciously opposed to Schumann's orchestral
work," although it had already been made to endure some of his compositions,
"could not warm up to it." Clinging to safety, the Museum responded to the
needs and reflected the tastes of Frankfurt's upper bourgeoisie and made only
timid efforts to lead it away from conventional tastes. Its orchestra began to
make concessions only in the mid-1890s, the decade its directors were fussing
over ladies' hats, just as, lowering its ticket prices, it opened its doors to less
well-to-do listeners. Not all movers were shakers.

Whatever local tastes, many cultural institutions neither wanted nor got much,
if any, help from the public purse. In 1912, the author of a pocket-size survey
of the British National Gallery in London noted, visibly pleased, that the museum, "like most typically British institutions, owes its existence to private enterprise rather than to the initiative of the State." He pointedly denied the
persistent tale that King George IV had had anything to do with its founding.[7]
During the Victorian century this style of bourgeois self-help, which we have
explored in detail in Manchester, was no British monopoly. It set the tone in
some German, most Dutch, and virtually all American cities.[8] The choice
orchestras founded in the age, whether in Paris or Berlin or New York, resulted from the prodding of music-loving citizens.*

Although a shift from blue-blooded to middle-class benefactors was a conspicuous ingredient in the history of nineteenth-century culture, it was by no
means a uniform process. In countries like Germany it was slow to emerge: it
is striking to read in 1884, in *Die Nation*, a weekly favored by the educated liberal German middle class, that the Maecenas of earlier centuries was being
replaced by state legislatures—a development of which the author highly
approved. He found it gratifying to see the Prussian Landtag allocate literally
millions of marks for paintings and sculptures: "It is the task of the state to foster the cultivation of art." Yet only a year later, the *Gartenlaube,* in an article on

---

* As we saw in Manchester, a few could make a decisive difference.

the new Gewandhaus orchestra hall in Leipzig, pointed out that it had been largely paid for by a few rich local *Bürger,* who had donated the real estate and raised most of the 1,350,000 marks needed for construction: "It is certainly among Leipzig's most praiseworthy merits that it owes its most valuable buildings and institutions to the magnanimity of its citizens."[9] We see it over and over: although the history of Victorian bourgeois culture varied from place to place, resemblances were striking.

Generally, even where traditional sources of funds remained active through the Victorian era, the ascendancy of middle-class movers and shakers was undeniable. Even the Danes, who had since time out of mind trusted their ruling family to foster writers, painters, sculptors, or composers, saw a reigning dynasty of brewers, J. C. Jacobsen and his son Carl, rival the royal house with its public benefactions. The father supported the sciences and the son the arts; in 1888, Carl Jacobsen and his wife, Ottilia, founded a new museum, the Ny Carlsberg Glyptothek in Copenhagen, for years independent of the state. It held an eclectic assemblage of paintings and sculptures from antiquity to the present, and its collections of nineteenth-century French painting and, even more, of nineteenth-century French sculpture—it was said that the Ny Glyptothek possessed more Carpeaux and Rodins than any museum outside of Paris—owed their excellence to the Jacobsens' solid support.

Promoters of the finer things who, with munificent legacies, transformed local and at times national taste stemmed from the most diverse backgrounds. But virtually all of them were bourgeois, including prosperous artists like Liebermann, who donated some of his cherished artworks to museums in Berlin. This was the sort of public spirit that allowed an anonymous writer in the *Pictorial Times,* as early as 1843, to assert, "I am sure the people of England are likely to be better patrons of art than the English aristocracy ever were, and that the aristocracy had been tried and *didn't* patronise it." This harsh critique referred to the habit of the English nobility to concentrate on foreign old masters, whether Italian, Flemish, or Dutch. "No, no," the journalist kept up the assault; "*they* are not the friends of genius. Their day is over; its friends lie elsewhere; rude and uncultivated as yet, but hearty, generous, and eager." No question, he concluded, the pit is as knowledgeable about serious music as the boxes ever could be. Almost three decades later, in 1870, Lady Elizabeth Eastlake, a civilized student and tart critic of the contemporary English art scene, noted that "the patronage which had been almost exclusively the privilege of the nobility and higher gentry, was now shared (to be subsequently almost engrossed) by a wealthy and intelligent class, chiefly enriched by commerce and trade."[10] That much for centuries of aristocratic patronage.

What united these upper-middle-class patrons was not only that they had enough money to support artists and local culture but also that they had enough energy to battle obstructive bureaucrats or obtuse, miserly legislatures. Sir Henry Tate, the English sugar baron and an experienced humanitarian, was forced to squabble for two years and more with the Treasury and the trustees of the National Gallery, who made difficulties about accepting his splendid collection of contemporary English art. They treated Tate as though they were doing him a favor if they took his pictures. He had to donate £80,000 to finance a museum for his treasures, and even then the London Corporation tried to extract still more money from him. In 1898, a year after the museum was finally launched, a short guide to its treasures proudly trumpeted, "The 'National Gallery of British Art,' opened to the use and enjoyment of the public in the 'Diamond Jubilee' year of Queen Victoria, is characteristically national in this respect among others, that it owes little to the State and much to the munificence of private citizens."[11] Yet the conflict, resolved at last, had not been one between an individual and the state but a characteristic clash within the bourgeoisie: Tate the great entrepreneur at odds with the businessmen in control of London's government.

As sons of successful merchants, many merchants among the founders started out life with bounteous bank accounts. John Sheepshanks, collector and benefactor, was a magnate and the son of a magnate, a successful cloth manufacturer at Leeds. After working in his father's factory for some years, the son, never married, retired to devote himself to his art collection, and poured most of his wealth into paintings, drawings, and sketches. He had begun like many others with copies of old masters, but moved to contemporary British artists who satisfied his craving for sentimental anecdotes. Yet he also bought Wilkies, Boningtons, and Stanfields, and liked to socialize with artists at congenial dinners. In 1857, he gave his representative collection—236 paintings and about 300 drawings—to his country. He specialized in Mulreadys (he owned thirty of them), Leslies (twenty-four), and Landseers (sixteen), mirroring the conventional taste of his age.[12]

Not all benefactors enjoyed Sheepshanks's advantages. Although the collection of Robert Vernon, whose life spans the age of the French Revolution—he was born in 1774—closely resembles that of Sheepshanks, in all other respects the two men were opposites. Vernon, we are told, came from "humble origins."[13] Far from being a gentleman, he was a horse jobber grown rich supplying the English forces battling Napoleon's grasp for European hegemony. Unlike Sheepshanks, he never abandoned his taste for living English painters. Aware just how few artists could sell even their best work, and how little they got if they did sell it, Vernon sought their friendship and commissioned many now well-known canvases.

It was only gradually that the destination of his collection, housed in his Pall Mall mansion, became clear to him. His nephew Vernon Heath, Vernon's secretary and intimate, recalled that "one fixed purpose," a resolve he never abandoned, meant "weeding out and buying until that condition of perfection was reached" that he thought deserving of public attention. As a patron of modern English art, Heath insists, Vernon relied on his "good taste, discrimination, and sound judgment."[14] These qualities—and Heath boasted that Vernon was following his own intuitions—led him to buy some good Ettys (eleven), Landseers (seven), Stanfields and Wilkies (five of each), Turners and Mulreadys (four each), Constables, Eastlakes, and Wilkies. Then, in 1847, two years before his death, he deeded 159 paintings and sculptures to the National Gallery, graciously permitting its trustees to reject whatever they might find unworthy, greatly enlarging, in company with Sheepshanks, the nation's holdings in recent domestic art.

By this time, such dispositions were beginning to arouse great expectations, as though bourgeois collectors had somehow acquired a duty to be open-handed with their town or their country. But some of them held out hopes without in the end gratifying them. The Birmingham manufacturer Joseph Gillott grew rich in the 1830s producing nibs for steel pens. A man of highly developed tastes, he started to collect as soon as he could afford it and, spending well over £100,000, amassed 60 old masters as well as 305 paintings and drawings by modern British artists. He was as canny a collector as he was manufacturer, bargaining with dealers and selling off parts of his holdings to free up resources for pictures he craved more. At the same time he was a considerate patron, commissioning paintings from, and financially backing, needy artists and freely lending his pictures to exhibitions in several English cities, including his own. But, on his death in 1872, Gillott's paintings were auctioned off, and the princely sum of £165,000 that his works of art realized only underscored the magnitude of Birmingham's unrealized opportunity. The auction, the *Birmingham Daily Post* lamented, was a "grevious loss to all lovers of art."[15] This was the shadow side of the Victorians' respect for private property: could you not do what you wanted with your own?

Increasingly, though, well-to-do bourgeois proved more public-spirited. One great American symphony orchestra offers an extraordinary instance of individual initiative making a difference; to the degree that any important cultural event can ever be the work of a single person, Henry Lee Higginson's role in founding the Boston Symphony Orchestra earns that accolade. Higginson is proof that moneymaking was not inevitably the principal passion of Victorian moneymakers. And the unquestioning backing from his "old daddy" for his choice of career and benefactions underscores the fact that Henry Higginson was not alone, or an eccentric, in his class. In May 1857, his closest friend, Charles Russell Lowell, reported to a friend that Higginson was planning to spend three years in Europe to study music: "With immense good sense he sees that he will be far more of a man and no less of a merchant when he has duly cultivated the best gift nature gave him."[16] He was realizing a long-familiar commonplace particularly fashionable among Victorians: commerce and culture need not be enemies but can become partners, and enterprising, sensitive, and well-informed bourgeois can make money serve civilization.

In the same year, in a long confessional letter to his father from Vienna, where he was training his voice and practicing the piano, Higginson reiterated his priorities, without apologies. "Music is almost my inner world; without it, I miss much, and with it I am happier and better." The "almost" reads like a last concession to prudence. Business had proved unrewarding. "Trade was not satisfying to the inner man as a life-occupation." What if a career in music was a failure? "I have a resource to which I can always turn with delight, however the world will go with me. I am so much the stronger, the wider, the wiser, the better for my duties in life. I can then go with satisfaction to my business, knowing my resource at the end of the day."[17]

Reviewing his options, Higginson noted that he might end up teaching music. In language that has come to sound stilted and self-conscious but which in his time was both sincere and weighty, he called *"Education"* the "object of man" and "the duty of us all to help in it, each according to his means and in his sphere." He never doubted that his father fully subscribed to his ideal: "It is only carrying out your own darling idea of making an imperishable capital in education." What mattered most to him was his bracing sense of autonomy. "The pleasure, pure and free from all disagreeable consequences or afterthoughts, of playing and still more of singing myself, is indescribable." And he laid down his credo, a testimonial to bourgeois individualism in which desire becomes a solemn duty to oneself: *"I am studying for my own good and pleasure."*[20] He would not be captured in what the German sociologist Max Weber would famously call half a century later, with somber eloquence, the iron cage of capitalist obsessions.

Higginson's prospects of a musical career were frustrated by injuries sustained from excessive practicing and stupid medical treatments. Yet his devotion to the muse never wavered; if he could not make music himself, he would enable others to do so. There was an interlude when other concerns dominated his life: he came home on the eve of the Civil War, in which he served, got married, and went into banking. By 1880, he could retire and devote himself to his life's project: to finance music deserving of Boston.

The soil had been well prepared. Self-aware, often haughty about being guardians of high culture, the Brahmins of Boston created institutions—libraries, clubs of literary men, forums for public lectures—to secure and if possible improve it. Their poets and politicians loomed large on the American scene. In his *American Notes* of 1843, a highly subjective report on his travels in the United States, Charles Dickens paid the city a somewhat left-handed tribute: "The golden calf they worship at Boston is a pigmy compared with the giant effigies set up in other parts of that vast countinghouse which lies beyond the Atlantic, and the almighty dollar sinks into something comparatively insignificant amidst a whole Pantheon of better gods."[19] However grudging, this accolade captured one cardinal point: Boston culture was an expensive necessity for enough prosperous local citizens who recognized their obligations by freely serving on committees and donating cash, rare books, or valuable real estate to preserve their reputation for being leaders in American civilization.

Dickens waxed enthusiastic about Boston's charitable institutions, notably the Perkins School for the Blind, but had no words for the city's cultural facilities. He missed much exemplary activity. When he visited Boston for the first time, the Athenaeum, by then thirty-six years old, had become the gathering place for the city's gentry. In a circular of 1807 sent to prospective subscribers, the newborn institution, aiming at a wide audience, had undertaken to gather a worthy collection of books, periodicals, and works of art. It appealed to the "man of business" desiring "intellectual activity and enjoyment, without any injurious interruption of his ordinary pursuits"; to the "inquisitive merchant" eager to profit from consulting relevant materials; to "gentlemen of each of the learned professions" who would find "important assistance, in their respective pursuits"; to "men of letters, and studious inquirers in general" who could use "facilities in study, hitherto not enjoyed, but highly desirable and even necessary." The ladies, too, would benefit, if indirectly: "Whatever raises the character of men has a favorable influence upon that of the other sex."[20] In 1851, Josiah Quincy, long its president, observed in his history of the Athenaeum that it had taken a "strong hold" on "the affections of the intelligent and prosperous."[21] His tone was pious and self-flattering, but undeniably the institution had carried through its program.

Music had prospered rather more modestly. Between 1835 and 1843, no fewer than a dozen musical journals made their appearance in Boston. Few of them were long-lived, but the very number is a gauge of interest.[22] Once the virtual monopoly of religious music had been broken in the late 1830s, Bostonians had been well supplied with concerts by performers local and imported. A few were memorable: in mid-February 1841, the Boston Academy of Music introduced a Beethoven symphony—the First—to the city and six weeks later played the Fifth. In 1870, three decades after these historic evenings, John Sullivan Dwight, Harvard man, editor, historian, and authoritative spokesman for music in his city, could still recall their overwhelming impact. But, though promising, these occasions did not satisfy Boston's most urbane citizens. Many of them had been treated to far superior performances abroad, and the occasional visits of Theodore Thomas's orchestra, first-rate and well-rehearsed, led by a conductor with the severest classical standards, made the customary offerings look pale. More was needed, and Higginson was the man with the imagination and the capital to supply it.

In his enterprise, Higginson's worldly experience paid off handsomely; in a businesslike memorandum, he laid out his scheme for a permanent orchestra, specifying the number and kinds of players, complete with their respective salaries, the role of the conductor, the price of tickets, the need for rehearsals, and plans for a conservatory. In March 1881, Higginson hired a conductor, the young German-born baritone Georg Henschel, whose way with the baton had impressed him, and at the end of the month he was ready to go before the public with his agenda. Courteously acknowledging the exertions of existing musical societies, he announced the formation of "a full and permanent orchestra, offering the best music at low prices," at fifty and twenty-five cents an evening, "such as may be found in all the large European cities, or even in the smaller musical centres of Germany." He thought it important to avert any taint of provincialism.[23] The New York Philharmonic Orchestra, he knew, had anticipated his creation in Boston by some four decades—it was founded in 1842—but he was confident that he could build a superior orchestra at home.

The rest, as they say, is history. The Boston Symphony Orchestra went through the normal childhood ailments, as local newspapers, happy to have something fresh to write about, rivaled one another in lavishing praise or censure on the newcomer. Wilhelm Gericke, who succeeded Henschel in 1884 to lead the orchestra for the next five years, was hailed and damned for purging it of older players and his innovative taste for Berlioz, Wagner, and Brahms. When he introduced Bruckner's Seventh Symphony, the audience literally fled; at the end of the performance, he recalled with perhaps greater bitterness than accuracy, there were more people on the stage than in the audience. And Brahms continued to arouse resistance for his "difficulty," even though Bostonians were repeatedly exposed to his music. As late as 1900, a Boston newspaper columnist adapted an old joke when he reported that the fire escapes in the new Symphony Hall were marked "This way out in case of Brahms."*

---

* One local critic at least was on the side of the paying customers: Bruckner's symphony, he wrote, was "a prolonged moan and groan, varied now and then with a gloomy and soul-depress-

Still, subscriptions remained steady, the players coalesced into a disciplined ensemble, and audiences were, if not invariably content, at least interested in the orchestra's programming—precisely what Higginson the educator had hoped for. Better still, Higginson, who had financed the venture, met the substantial deficits year after year. By 1889, when he lured the brilliant and controversial German conductor Arthur Nikisch from Leipzig, his fantasy had become a Bostonian institution. We see Higginson in John Singer Sargent's portrait of 1903, when he was closing in on seventy, a sturdy, stocky, purposeful-looking gentleman leaning back, an arm draped over the back of his chair, the picture of a Bostonian who had known what he wanted and got it. The critics continued to quarrel over his orchestra, but it was the tempi the conductor chose, not the standard of the playing, that remained an issue.

None of this is to deny that Boston's satisfaction in its self-started high culture turned into self-satisfaction. In a well-known letter of 1903, Henry Adams, that quintessential Boston Brahmin, diagnosed his city as insular and lacking in imagination. "The painful truth is that all of my New England generation, counting the half century, 1820–1870, were in actual fact only one mind and nature," he wrote to Henry James. "The individual was a facet of Boston. We knew each other to the last nervous centre, and feared each other's knowledge." All were equally shallow. "We knew nothing—no! but really nothing! of the world." This meant that the Emersons and the Longfellows, the Motleys and Prescotts were all alike *"Type bourgeois-bostonien!"*[24] We may somewhat discount Adams, who, more dependable as a satirist than as an observer, would not exempt civilized Bostonians from his scornful cultural pessimism. But his verdict serves as a reminder that an official culture could deteriorate into little more than a habit. Yet the Boston Symphony Orchestra, with all its early ups and downs and the endemic grievances of critics, remains a bourgeois success story. It even passed the test of introducing new music both American and European.

In other cities, committees accomplished what Higginson had done singlehanded. The decades spanning the turn of the century saw the formation of major symphony orchestras in the United States, notably in Chicago, Cincinnati, Philadelphia, Minneapolis, and St. Louis, all brought into being by middleclass angels. The group of guarantors that the businessman Charles Norman Fay, an enthusiastic propagandist, enlisted in 1891 to establish a permanent Chicago Symphony Orchestra reads like a Who's Who of the city's mercantile and industrial aristocracy: Philip Armour, the meat packer; Cyrus McCormick, the inven-

---

ing bellow;—Wagner in a prolonged attack of sea-sickness; a huge barnacle-covered whale of a symphony but without any lubricating blubber." John H. Mueller, *The American Symphony Orchestra: A Social History of Musical Taste* (1951), 72; 73n.

tor and marketer of the reaper; Marshall Field, the department store magnate; George Pullman, the sleeping car baron. Although like their fellows elsewhere, these philanthropists chafed at the continuing deficits, they soon discovered that only exceptional conditions permitted a large orchestra to become self-sustaining. Thus onetime contributors became permanent sponsors, caught in the silken trap of the civic self-esteem they had so actively promoted.

The history of orchestra formation in other countries mirrored the American experience. In 1881, the year that Higginson presided over the launching of the Boston Symphony Orchestra, a consortium of six *burger* undertook to give Amsterdam what its serious music-loving citizens had long clamored for: a permanent orchestra in its own hall. Amateurs were moved to support the six all the more vigorously after the visit, in late 1885, of the highly trained Meiningen orchestra under the baton of the brilliant Hans von Bülow. Brahms, who had friends among the sponsors, made the issue even more pressing as he baldly applied to Amsterdam the ancient, still popular saying "Dear folks but bad musicians."[25] Something had to be done.

The founders who threw themselves into the good cause were typical of affluent local burghers. Two of them were lawyers, two stockbrokers, one a broker in cotton and metals, one a distiller and wine merchant. Assuming the burdensome, often contentious administrative duties incumbent on managers of so ambitious an enterprise, they struggled to find a suitable location, formed a company to finance a *concertgebouw,* took out mortgages, and trolled for funds. Shares were set at 1,000 florins, but one of the six, the lawyer J. A. Sillem, tried to set an example by subscribing to six shares; his investment of 6,000 florins in the future of music in Amsterdam amounted to twice the annual salary offered the first conductor, Willem Kes. After prolonged travail, the Concertgebouworkest gave a series of concerts in 1888.[26] Deficits accompanied the seasons, piling up with the years. In 1891, they had risen to 150,000 florins, and, as usual, the founders took a lead in meeting it; three of the original six contributed 25,000 florins each, cutting it in half. But on the musical front, brighter horizons beckoned, especially after Willem Mengelberg took over as conductor in 1895 and went on tour with the Concertgebouworkest to France, to Russia, to Norway, giving other countries a taste of what Dutch bourgeois were coming to idolize.

At times, the shakers were the performers themselves; it was orchestra musicians who established Berlin's Philharmonisches Orchester on their own initiative. They made a peaceful revolution. Among the capital's three leading if rather unsatisfactory bands, the Orchester des Liegnitzer Stadtmusikus' Benjamin Bilse was easily the most popular. In 1882, Bilse, who had been offering programs of "light" and occasionally of serious music for thirteen years, abruptly decided to share his financial risks with his players: in March he demanded that they sign new, noticeably inferior, contracts and do so overnight. Otherwise he would cancel the summer season in Warsaw and form a new orchestra. Far from intimidated, the musicians refused to knuckle under and, led by three of their own—an oboist, a french hornist, and a violinist— decided to leave Bilse and constitute an ensemble of their own.* It was to be self-governing, democratic, and musically first-rate.

But Berlin's Philharmoniker, like orchestras elsewhere, needed periodic injections of cash, and two rich, prominent Berlin families, the Mendelssohns and the Siemens, bailed it out. Though troubled by the usual birthpangs, the little democracy made imaginative decisions; it secured major composers— Tchaikovsky, Grieg, Brahms—to conduct their own works with them, and in 1887 engaged as its conductor Hans von Bülow, that splendid musician and disciplinarian, who in five years raised the Philharmoniker to international stature. But money remained an issue.

Money was an issue that never faded, anywhere. Late in the century, art and music lovers confronted a growing need for collective efforts to shore up faltering institutions. They tried to compete with foreign rivals—that is to say Americans—avid to import European treasures from paintings to conductors; they fattened acquisition budgets or funds for salaries which, however well endowed the museum or the orchestra, were never large enough. One of these salvage operations, the Vereeniging Rembrandt, dates from 1883, when several prominent Amsterdam citizens met to discuss the ominous fact that major Dutch paintings were disappearing into museums and private collections abroad. What particularly alarmed them was the threatened dispersal of the historical parade of Dutch art that a highly regarded Amsterdam collector, Jacob B. de Vos, had lovingly amassed over decades. Until his death in 1878, he had served for four decades as chairman of a society of artists and amateurs, Arti et Amicitiae, since its founding in 1839 under royal protection. Characteristically, the seven self-appointed members of the ad hoc committee to form the Vereeniging Rembrandt, all members of Arti et Amicitiae, included two philanthropists who just two years before had campaigned for a *concertgebouw* in Amsterdam. As one might expect, most of those who loved music also loved art.

Unhelpfully, the Dutch government cheered on the alarmed amateurs but regretted that it was in no position to make a financial contribution. This sent

---

* The London Symphony Orchestra, founded in 1904, had similar origins: musicians from Sir Henry Wood's orchestra, dissatisfied with the contract he offered them, seceded and started a respectable orchestra of their own.

the half dozen founders back to their own resources, a fate they had no doubt anticipated. They looked to form a board of forty members, hoping for "men of knowledge and taste in the domain of art, men of influence who respect the beautiful works of art left us by great geniuses of past centuries." And they were pleased but not surprised to gather quick support from local capitalists passionate about their country's art. "Happily," one of them wrote some months later, "such men still exist." Donations of 500 or 1,000 florins, one as large as 10,000 florins, flooded in, and at the auction of the de Vos collection, the Vereeniging Rembrandt bought paintings adding up to more than 45,000 florins—a major coup.

There were to be others: over the years the Vereeniging Rembrandt bought and turned over to Dutch museums two Vermeers, a Terborch, a Berckheyde, a Hobbema, a van Goyen, and others.[27] At mid-century, the French critic Théophile Thoré, who, we recollect, was the leading connoisseur of Dutch paintings of the golden age, had deplored the migration of that art abroad. The Vereeniging Rembrandt acted as if responding to his warning.

Other countries took note. In the mid-nineties, Wilhelm von Bode, who generously donated art to the institutions over which he presided and shrewdly educated donors richer than himself, founded the Kaiser-Friedrich-Museums-Verein in Berlin to lure private benefactors into making larger contributions of money or more artworks than ever.* In the course of years, the *Verein* secured important pictures for Prussia's museums, including *The Man in the Golden Helmet,* perhaps the most celebrated Rembrandt that Rembrandt (it now appears) never painted. Bode, said his friend Max Liebermann, was doing "practical art history: knowledge of art is to awaken love of art." Around the same time, Paris saw the founding of the Société des Amis du Louvre, designed to serve the same purpose.

The early history of Frankfurt's Städelsche Museums-Verein, founded in 1899, demonstrates a prominent—and obvious—feature that characterizes nearly all of these societies: their self-limitation to a financial aristocracy. In calling for gifts or bequests of valuable artworks and magnanimous financial contributions, to say nothing of levying an annual fee of 200 marks or 5,000 marks for a life membership, the society excluded not only the working-class majority in Frankfurt and the lower middle class as a matter of course, but also many well-situated bourgeois. We recall the public servant in Berlin whose annual salary totaled 5,450 marks in 1889: membership in the Städelsche Muse-

---

* In music, such societies were intended to withstand seductive offers from rival orchestras. Those with prominent conductors were particularly vulnerable to outside offers: it was grandiose invitations from American orchestras that pushed the salary of Willem Mengelberg at the Concertgebouw to unheard-of heights.

ums-Verein would have cost him half a month's work. No wonder that until the First World War, it could never attract more than 111 members.[28]

The membership of the *Verein* was not a faithful microcosm of the prosperous classes in Victorian Frankfurt, but mirrored its domestic history. Most were drawn from the city's patriciate, but they coexisted with rich amateurs and a sprinkling of new money generated by the stimulus of unification in 1871. Jews belonged in disproportionate numbers; though they constituted just over 7 percent of the city's population, they furnished over a third of the membership, perhaps some 40 percent. The first, for years the only one to buy a life membership was a Jew, Ferdinand Hirsch, who had made his fortune as a wholesale dealer in iron.[29] We have seen before that the political emancipation of the country's Jews, completed with the establishment of the empire in 1871, generated a powerful urge in the richest among them to be integrated among the movers and shakers. They were the very incarnation of the new money, another sign that in Victoria's days the bourgeoisie was in motion and that the population supporting the arts, too, was taking on unexpected contours. Yet it is worth noting once again that social climbing was only one among several motives for the collecting and founding passion. For many movers as for many hunters (to paraphrase a saying attributed to Freud), the love of art was just a love of art.

2. Buttresses for the Establishment

Indeed, not all movers were shakers. A number of them, summoning up as much energy as did the enthusiasts for artistic innovation, became public donors to sustain established styles. A look at three of them, a coal merchant from Amsterdam, a German wool dealer resident in London, and a banker in Berlin, will put flesh on the bones of this observation.

Born in 1801, Carel Joseph Fodor made millions in the coal trade. In his mid-thirties he began to collect on a grand scale at an almost feverish tempo, as if to atone for a youth wasted on business. A lifelong bachelor, he made his native city, Amsterdam, his sole heir in a testament dated early 1860, the year of his death, only setting aside funds for the relief of the local poor. The gesture gave Amsterdam a remarkable collection of some 900 drawings, more than 150 paintings, and three adjacent houses, of which one, he stipulated, was to be turned into an art gallery.[1]

Fodor's taste was consistently academic: it is only fitting that the parade piece among his paintings should be Ary Scheffer's *Christus consolator*, dating from 1837. Scheffer, a Dutch-born artist working in Paris, had gathered con-

Honoré Daumier, *The Connoisseur* (1860–1865), watercolor and gouache over black chalk. A masterly portrayal of the collector musing over one of his treasures. (The Metropolitan Museum of Art, the H. O. Havemeyer Collection, Bequest of Mrs. H. O. Havemeyer, 1929. [29.100.200]).

The immensely popular French sculptor Barye, who delighted American as well as European collectors. ([William Thompson Walters], *Antoine-Louis Barye: From the French of Various Critics* [1885], frontispiece.)

A youthful portrait of the eminent German surgeon, Viennese professor (and fine amateur pianist) Theodor Billroth, aged twenty-nine (1858). A model of a cultivated bourgeois, he had many of his intimate friend Brahms's compositions first performed in his house. (*Briefe von Theodor Billroth* [1895; 8th ed., 1910], after p. 32.)

The future novelist and critic with his father, Henry James, Sr. (Henry James, *A Small Boy and Others* [1913]. Frontispiece.)

Eduard Grützner, *Hochheimer.* A typical production by this German genre painter, who specialized in teasing smiles from his viewers with his tippling monks.

Jean François Millet, *The Angelus.* This reproduction (from a carbon print) is characteristic of the age, which showed massive and abiding interest in this painting and insisted on its religious significance. This exemplar is from Estelle M. Hurll, *Jean François Millet: A Collection of Fifteen Pictures* (1900), 39.

"Cham" (Amédée de Noë), *Manet, La Naissance du petit ébéniste* (1865), wood engraving. *Le Salon de 1865—Photographié* (1865). Manet's *Olympia,* exhibited at the Salon of 1865, caused head-scratching puzzlement and self-righteous moralizing. Even perceptive critics like Thoré were uneasy with it. Hence caricaturists like "Cham" were right at home.

"Cham," *Courbet,* wood engraving. *Le Salon de 1866* (1866). Courbet's provocative nude with a parrot perched on her finger was exhibited at the Salon of 1866 and ended up in the Havemeyer collection, now in the Metropolitan Museum of Art. It was as easy to caricature as it was in those days hard to defend as a moral work of art.

Jan Willem Pieneman, *Portrait of Carel Joseph Fodor.* The collection of this generous coal tycoon, though not confined to them, was particularly strong in drawings. Fodor-Collection-Amsterdams Historisch Museum.

André Mniszech, *Abraham Willet in the Costume of a Seventeenth-Century Militiaman* (1877). A tribute to the grandiose self of a Dutch collector and founder of a family museum. Amsterdamsch Historisch Museum.

John Singer Sargent, *Henry Lee Higginson,* photogravure after the oil painting. The bourgeois as founder—the sole begetter of the Boston Symphony Orchestra. (M. A. DeWolfe Howe, *The Boston Symphony Orchestra, 1881–1931* [1914; rev. ed., 1931], frontispiece.)

Ludwig and Rosy Fischer, photographs. Two German-Jewish collectors who moved beyond conventional German paintings to German semi-Impressionists like Max Liebermann and then showed their flexibility once again by concentrating on German Expressionists like Kirchner and Nolde. (*Expressionismus und Exil. Die Sammlung Ludwig und Rosy Fischer,* ed. Georg Heuberger [1990], 45.)

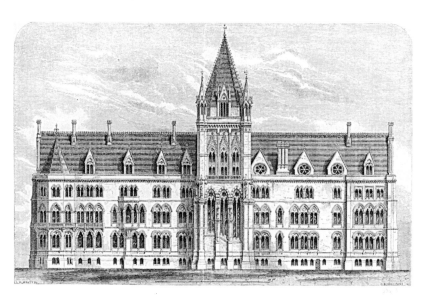

G. G. Scott, "Design for the Proposed New Foreign Office: Front next St. James Park, Mr. G. G. Scott, A.B.A. Architect," (*The Builder*, XVII [August 13, 1859], 537.) Scott at his most typical, as a proponent of nineteenth-century Gothic.

The British Foreign Office, London. Principal Designer, G. G. Scott. Since his Gothic design was rejected, Scott came up with this romantic classicist building—a triumph of craving a commission over holding to principle. (M. H. Port, *Imperial London: Civil Government Building in London, 1850–1915* [1995], 210. Courtesy of Yale University Press, London.)

"An Artist's Cottage Designed by C. F. A. Voysey," and accompanying floor plan. (*Studio,* IV [1894–95], 34.) The anonymous accompanying brief text notes that the cost of this "cottage" was estimated at from £700 to £800. The house was to have brick walls rough cast in cement, with solid and tarred timber. The roof was of boards, felt, and green slates. External woodwork was to be painted a bright green. Voysey strove for the "best materials . . . in a sound and durable manner, yet as cheaply as possible."

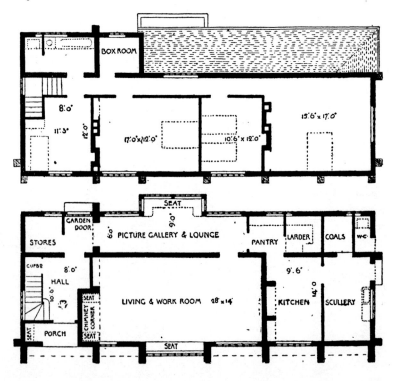

siderable renown in the ambiance of the salons and was suitably expensive. Fodor bought his smoothly painted, highly finished symbolic oil in 1853 for over 24,000 florins—roughly seventy-five years' wages for a Dutch factory worker. It illustrates two verses from Luke (4:18–19) quoting Jesus' sympathy for the victims of society. Dominating a crowded composition, he is backlit by what looks like dazzling, spreading sunlight and surrounded by suffering humanity: a mother crouching over her dead child, a naked black slave holding out his arms to the Consoler, a dying Pole whose chains Christ is loosening, three kneeling women facing the Savior in prayerful attitudes, while other figures, including a shipwrecked sailor and a suicide, hover in the background. The painting was politically progressive and aesthetically conservative.

Fodor's collection as a whole perfectly matched this commitment to the most pleasing, accomplished, and riskless art of his time. To judge by sheer numbers—fourteen paintings and twenty-eight drawings—his favorite painter was his compatriot Andreas Schelfhout, then much in vogue, who specialized in landscapes and seascapes. Charles van Beveren, another contemporary, who excelled in pastiches of Dutch old masters, ranked second, and the collection was rounded out with modern portraits and anecdotal genre scenes. Fodor's admiration for the highly regarded Barend Cornelis Koekkoek and his brother Hermanus, the first concentrating on landscapes and the second on sea pieces, is characteristic of these tastes. His choices of drawings and graphics were only marginally different. Unlike most other Dutch collectors, Fodor bought massive numbers of French works, but they, too, were picturesque, entertaining, beautifully done. There were Scheffers among them and Ingres, but no Daumiers. And the only Delacroix in his collection was the obscure French watercolorist Auguste Delacroix. The Fodor museum established after his death did nothing to move Dutch taste in new directions.

The same holds true of the collection that the German wool merchant Gustav Christian Schwabe donated to his native Hamburg. Born in 1813, he settled in London and, once he had made his fortune, invested much of it in more than 120 recent English paintings appraised at over a million and a half marks. At seventy, he bequeathed this collection to Hamburg's museum, and since the Kunsthalle was too small to accommodate his holdings, he added a gift of 120,000 marks to have the building reconstructed and enlarged. In gratitude, Hamburg made Schwabe an honorary citizen in 1886, an uncommon accolade he shared with Chancellor von Bismarck and Field Marshal von Moltke. In the same year, the transfer of the Schwabe collection began.

German reviewers boasted that with its concentrated focus, Schwabe's gift was a rare treasure. Modern English art, it seemed, traveled mainly to international exhibitions and was almost never sold abroad, so that with one stroke, the Kunsthalle had become the foremost owner of such art on the Continent. The collection, with its emphatic dose of what middlebrow viewers considered tasteful, was everything that avant-garde critics found regrettable: a gallery of pretty young women in fetching costumes, narrative canvases showing couples courting or peasants and sailors laboring on land or sea, wide-eyed winsome children in charming settings, tranquil landscapes and stormy seascapes, all meticulously finished. In his report to the mayor's office, the Hamburg painter Ascan Lutteroth, sent to Schwabe's English country seat to inspect the prospective legacy, called attention to the interesting fact that there was "not one undraped figure in the whole collection."[2] Schwabe had a sentimental Maclise, a minor Millet, two narrative canvases by Dyce, one dubious Bonington, and one equally dubious Turner—paintings meant to entertain rather than shock, none to trouble tranquility or strain the imagination.

In this trio of conventional benefactors, the Berlin banker Joachim Heinrich Wilhelm Wagener probably made the greatest impact in the formation— or, better, the confirmation—of reigning taste and best documents the intermingling of private and public spheres during the Victorian era. Born in Berlin in 1782, the eldest son of a well-to-do merchant and banker and a partner in his father's financial enterprises, Wagener began to collect paintings in 1815, the year of Napoleon's final defeat, restoration of Prussian power, and efflorescence of the country's economy. His father's sizable collection of minor old masters, described as dark and commonplace, seems to have stimulated his passion for buying pictures, but not what kind of pictures to buy.[3]

From a long retrospect, Wagener's first acquisitions appear singularly well chosen: between 1815 and 1818, he bought three ultra-romantic landscapes by the architect, stage designer, and painter Karl Friedrich Schinkel, then near the beginning of his spectacular career. They are expansive, beautifully painted fantasies, notably the *Gothic Church on a Rock by the Sea,* a backlit cathedral built on a rocky coastal promontory, framed by a vivid sky and a distant grand vista. A few years later, when more Schinkels that Wagener wanted were securely in the hands of others, he had them reproduced by the best copyists in the business. This was one of the principal functions of copying: to make the unavailable available.

Wagener's later choices were far less original, although he did buy two Caspar David Friedrichs in the 1820s, including *The Lonely Tree,* the symbolic portrait of a single tree surrounded by a flat landscape which has since become a showpiece in the Friedrich canon. Exceptional purchases of this sort stand out in Wagener's monotonous assortment of respectable competence. Systematically, he worked his way through the productions of academic painters in Munich, Düsseldorf, and Berlin, buying landscapes, small history paintings, genre pictures by German artists whom only specialists in the period would now recognize. Later, for comparative purposes, he added Belgian, French, Dutch, and English canvases by artists like Landseer or Vernet, well known but no less academic than his German choices.

While Wagener did business with more than one dealer, his decisions remained his own as he took a meticulous interest in his purchases. He painstakingly compared paintings on offer with competing canvases and returned, to dealers and artists alike, pictures that did not quite match his expectations. Typically, he gave his reasons in discerning, almost pedantic detail, finding fault with perspective, composition, or color. He was an autodidact with a trained eye and a demanding palate by his lights.

This inflexible seriousness emerged particularly in Wagener's way with commissions: he insisted on the program he had assigned the artist and would be satisfied with nothing else. In 1848, he asked the Düsseldorf painter Hermann Anton Stilke to do a "historical subject" for him and twice rejected the artist's sketches for straying beyond his brief. Not even a revised version, representing a scene from the medieval Tristan poem, met Wagener's demands. He wanted history. "Should it not be possible to combine history, romanticism, and the poetic?" he asked plaintively, wondering at Stilke's inability to come up with fitting subjects. "Surely history cannot be so poor in them." Always mindful that such transactions were also business deals, he offered the "rather brazen" comment that since the poet of *Tristan* was as little known as his tale— he was, of course, writing before Wagner's setting—he could scarcely be expected to pay a substantial sum.[4] In the end, Wagener got his wish, a large Stilke done in 1850, showing Richard III taking the two princes from his mother.

Wagener bore the stigmata of the true collector, possessed by an appetite as impatient as it was exacting. Prompting Karl Friedrich Lessing in 1842, he reminded the well-known landscape painter that he was aching for the picture he had commissioned. "You should not take this little letter as a thumb screw," he wrote, trying to contain himself, "but it should tell you that I am waiting like a child for the Christmas tree." Lessing promptly complied. Others were less obliging. In 1838, Wagener dunned Alfred Rethel, not for the first time, for a painting he had ordered. Rethel was a far more considerable artist and far more difficult man than other painters in Wagener's stable; apologetic, he promised to have the picture ready in a fortnight and only wanted to retain it to dry for a few weeks. The affair did not end happily: Wagener did not care for Rethel's painting and returned it.[5]

At first Wagener bought on an unpretentious scale, not exceeding 100 talers a year. This soon proved insufficient to slake his thirst; in 1851, he spent 8,800 talers, a magisterial sum.[6] Before long he yoked his purchases to an idea: he would build up a gallery of living German artists. That design was in place by 1828; in that year, already the proud owner of some seventy paintings, he issued the first printed catalog of his collection. There would be several others as his expenditures for art kept mounting.

In his correspondence with painters Wagener was the humble art lover engaged in a minuet of reciprocal fawning. He would profusely apologize for having disturbed artists at work with an unannounced visit; they would just as profusely declare their appreciation of being included in so "famous a collection." Thomas Ender, an Austrian painter, bubbled over with delight at having one of his landscapes, a chapel in the woods, placed in the hands of Wagener, known in Vienna and everywhere else as "such an outstanding connoisseur and friend of art." Phrases like "beautiful gallery" or *"votre magnifique galerie"* abound in the letters he received from painters. He wooed artists, and they flattered him.

At the other extreme, in his negotiations with dealers, he was the businessman eager to conserve his resources yet ready to spend—within limits. In 1841, responding to an offer of three paintings from Bolgiano, a Munich dealer with whom he had done business for years, he demurred: "I would be interested if you could possibly make low prices." Again, a year later, he complained to Bolgiano that some paintings by the German artist Max Emanuel Ainmüller, best known for his glass paintings, were simply too expensive. He had, he told Bolgiano, better Ainmüllers at home. Prices mattered. In 1852, he informed another dealer, G. de Vries in Amsterdam, that he was returning a painting —unidentified—because it did not quite meet his taste. Of course, if de Vries would accept 6,000 francs, he might bring himself to buy it. Prices, he moaned more than once, were so high as to make it "impossible for a private man to buy pictures."[7]

In 1859, this private man made a will, leaving a collection of 262 paintings to His Royal Highness, the Prince Regent of Prussia, soon to be anointed King Wilhelm. Wagener's stiff, self-abasing prose, which almost defies translation, reads like that of a plebeian subject who, for all his worldly success and bourgeois dignity, had not yet overcome his awe before majesty. "I dare to offer a collection that, if I may trust the judgment of many experts, has a not insignificant artistic value, one I have brought together with an expenditure of far more than 100,000 talers and brought along with steadily increasing joy and love." He wished to "beg humbly for its gracious acceptance in the name of art." His pictures, he hoped, would be kept together, but he left it to the "All-highest discretion whether this collection should be strengthened and developed further, thus to grow into a national gallery." After Wagener died in 1861,

His Majesty graciously accepted the gift and praised to his children their father's "warm love of country" and "high-minded patriotism."[8] In an age of nationalism, art was rarely untouched by politics.

The first exhibition of the Wagener collection was a temporary affair: in late March 1861, shown at the Akademie der Künste in Berlin, it significantly received the provisional title of the "Wagenersche und National-Galerie." Ground for the National-Galerie was not broken until 1866, and the building was ready for the hanging of pictures only ten years later. The founder's name had disappeared, in part to encourage others to donate modern German paintings. Though his collection remained as a point of reference rather than a guide to the directions that German art would follow in the decades after Wagener's death, its faithful coverage of conventional art gave it a historic role in the German collective memory. His holdings attest to the limits of taste more than to its range, but this, too, was part of the bourgeois experience—diligence rather than daring, comfort rather than experimentation.

3. The Perspiring Philistine on Trial

Two episodes from the late nineteenth century, one from Hamburg and the other from Paris, document the conflicts that movers and shakers could generate, arousing anxiety among bourgeois faced with the subversion of familiar pleasures, and the rage among avant-garde rebels at the obtuseness of what Robert Louis Stevenson once called the "Philistines perspiring after wealth."[1] And they document, too, the ambivalence of art lovers who could see a measure of justice in the rage of both antagonists.

In 1886, the year that Schwabe's bequest entered the Kunsthalle, Hamburg appointed Alfred Lichtwark as its new director. At the time he was too tactful and too new at his post to utter a skeptical word about Schwabe's taste. Once settled in his job, though, Lichtwark, who rarely evaded a controversy, would leave no doubt about his likes and dislikes. His imbroglios exhibit yet again incompatible bourgeois tastes; they also serve as a commentary on the role of new men in authority during the Victorian taste wars. Museum directors, whether they reported to a ministry or a self-perpetuating board of trustees, acted as important collectors in their own right—with other people's money.

The most instructive clash of Lichtwark's career came in the early 1890s over Max Liebermann's portrait of Carl Petersen, Hamburg's aged First Mayor. Lichtwark was one among a handful of resourceful spirits in charge of major museums across Europe and the United States. Fortunately, he could count on his German colleagues: professionals like Hugo von Tschudi in Berlin and Gustav Pauli in Bremen, both advocates of modern art, even French art. Pauli, a friend of Lichtwark's who would succeed him at Hamburg in 1914, was virulently abused as a "slave to foreigners" for buying a van Gogh. To be a museum director in Germany was to be on the front lines of culture. The same was true elsewhere.

Fastidious in habits and dress, refining his refinement and tolerating few intimates, Lichtwark presented something of an enigma to his contemporaries. Only his taste was transparent. When he died in 1914, at sixty-one, those who had known him dwelt a little helplessly on his devotion to his country's cultural renewal.[2] He was both aesthete and clamorous patriot, a cosmopolitan and a provincial fiercely attached to his native ground, a tenderhearted son and brother and a tough-minded fighter for causes he believed in. He started life in straitened circumstances but rose through sheer talent to hobnob with Hamburg's upper class on an equal footing. There was something of the outsider about him—artistic, social, perhaps sexual—that gave him a useful distance from the taste reigning in his country and his city. Still, his appointment as director of the Kunsthalle provided him with access not only to the local elite but to a national forum.[3]

Lichtwark's voluminous writings cover an impressive range—painting, sculpture, architecture, photography, furniture, interior design, popular education, the mission of the museum. But all aimed at a single target: the reform of German taste. To his mind, taste is an indispensable constituent and telltale sign of character. Hence collective good taste in the arts was, to him, almost literally a matter of national health. Thus aesthetics and ethics became virtually one; both were a kind of spiritual medicine. Having only recently overcome centuries of "shame"—he meant the splintering of his country into hundreds of domains—modern Germans after unification must take charge of their *Bildung* and recognize that they had "for too long lived for intelligence. It is time now for ethical-religious and artistic energies to develop fully."[4]

The distance between audience and artist, Lichtwark added, had stretched into a chasm; while painters feel isolated, "the public avenges itself through indifference, or it sees the artist who goes his lonely way as a subversive, as an exile, as a madman." Lichtwark made this characteristically hyperbolic charge in a two-volume monograph on portraitists in Hamburg, his only sustained text, written to raise his fellow citizens' awareness of neglected local talents and to smooth the way to a brighter artistic future. The book, he told Bode, with whom he was regularly in touch, "has nothing to do with art history. It is a work of propaganda for the portrait that is to come."[5] To serve his cause, Lichtwark did not hesitate to write propaganda.

Resorting to the manly rhetoric of sports and nationalism, Lichtwark contended that an elevated German taste would give his country a better chance in a race among the nations in which it had been scoring badly. This was the militant Lichtwark. He often sounded like a German Flaubert deaf to the tendentiousness of his sweeping indictments. Even though he lived among civilized *Bürger,* took his allies from them, and of course was one himself, he never hesitated to damn his class. The German *Bürgertum,* he lamented, had been replaced in the nineteenth century by a bourgeoisie that had erased all traces of the old culture. This meant—he was writing in 1898—that "whoever looks at the bourgeoisie from the standpoint of art and the artist will not be fond of it. A parvenu with all the disagreeable traits of the type, it is swelled-headed with its successes, opinionated, arrogant, the born and sworn enemy of all artistic independence, the patron and protector of all those who flatter his vanity and his narrow outlook. Fundamentally quite without artistic needs, the bourgeoisie as owner, client, and buyer has reduced architecture, the decorative arts, and painting to its level. It wants to contribute nothing and believes it may demand everything."[6] No French bourgeoisophobe could have put it more strongly.

This pronouncement, like much else in Lichtwark, sounds a note of despair, but his gloomy diagnosis of Germany's cultural malaise only stimulated his desire to cure it. That is why he lectured whenever and wherever he could, wrote introductions and postscripts to catalogs, and preserved his many words in small, handsomely designed volumes of essays. But his supreme servant in the campaign to heal the German spirit was of course the Kunsthalle. Its director at a time when one German city after another was founding or enlarging depositories of art and when the essential purpose of the museum was still being formulated, Lichtwark transmuted his bailiwick into a superb didactic instrument. He built up its collections of local painters medieval and modern. He introduced Hamburg to the much derided Impressionists by acquiring Renoirs and Monets. He committed himself to nineteenth-century German art in buying canvases by Philipp Otto Runge and Caspar David Friedrich, who had been almost forgotten in their own country.[7]

With such predilections, Lichtwark was bound to relish the art of Liebermann. By 1891, when he commissioned him to do a life-size, full-length portrait of Carl Petersen, Liebermann was a public figure, showered with prizes at exhibitions and execrated as a lover of the hideous. His homely subject matter, sunlit palette, and fluent draftsmanship gave him a reputation as Germany's foremost Impressionist; he was no Pissarro or even a Sisley, but the epithet kept Liebermann's notoriety intact.

Far from deterring Lichtwark, the controversies swirling around Liebermann only attracted him. In 1889, he had already bought his *Net Menders,* a large canvas showing women in an open field repairing fishing nets. Proud of his acquisition, he was aware that it was bound to offend conservative taste.* In fact, when Lichtwark proposed Liebermann for the mayor's portrait, the committee that had to approve purchases balked at first but was persuaded after Lichtwark found a private donor to underwrite the project. Greatly pleased, Liebermann promptly went to work. His canvas depicts a sturdy eighty-three-year-old patrician, slightly stooped, wearing his official garb complete with a white ruff that sets off his strong and handsome face.

Lichtwark exuded optimism. In July 1891, when the portrait was almost finished, he showed it provisionally in his museum and predicted "certain success." Even "L.'s open enemies have changed their mind." He was wrong. Petersen detested the portrait and called its hint at informality with its rapid brushwork unflattering, tasteless, a mere caricature, a failed experiment. His family, fellow *Bürger,* and art critics seconded him. In April 1892, Lichtwark reported to Bode that there was a "violent feud" in the city. He found it disagreeable to be dragged through the press by letters to the editor, but professed to be facing the future calmly: "Let the rage spend itself."⁸

This sounds like a strong public posture for a museum director, but Lichtwark had to compromise. The offending portrait was not opened to viewers in Hamburg until 1894, and then behind a curtain, a curious arrangement that was not abandoned until 1905, after years of Lichtwark's patient diplomacy. "You know that opposition pleases me," he had written to Liebermann in the middle of the affair, but even he had to tread warily.⁹ From today's perspective there is nothing very radical about the portrait, nothing in any way disrespectful. But in the skirmishes of the late nineteenth century, the narcissism of minor differences, a particularly intense hostility toward what deviates only slightly from one's own position, was much in evidence. With the sensibilities of the respectable rubbed raw by steady assaults on its taste and by artistic experimentation, any departure from academic norms could easily scandalize the solid conservative majority. Liebermann was the victim of an intrabourgeois conflict.

In February 1894, the year that Liebermann's portrait of Petersen was first shown, the painter Gustave Caillebotte died and left his substantial but select collection of Impressionists to the French state. Given the Impressionists' embattled reception, this private donation amounted to a cultural gesture that

---

* Having seen "our Liebermann" in Paris, where it was being exhibited, Lichtwark wrote home, "But whether the Hamburgers will find it fun is of course very much the question." Lichtwark to his mother and sister, [September 1889], *Briefe an seine Familie, 1875–1913,* ed. Carl Schellenberg (1972), 672.

inevitably aroused strong responses; it launched an epic struggle that pitted painters, museum directors, and the press against one another, and sometimes against their own kind. The episode offers yet more proof that bourgeois taste in the Victorian century, far from tending to mediocre unanimity, or any unanimity, was enlivened by clashing currents and countercurrents.

Caillebotte's name belongs on the long list of nineteenth-century bourgeois artists who enriched public institutions. After all, except for irreconcilable subversives like Gauguin, many Victorian artists played the part of collector or founder in solid, sober, genteel middle-class ways. Caillebotte was indeed in sizable company. There was Daniel Wadsworth of Hartford, Connecticut, son of a prosperous merchant, an accomplished amateur architect and sketcher, patron of later famous American artists like Thomas Cole and Frederic Church, diligent collector of recent paintings and sculpture. More than anyone else, he was the energetic organizer and angel of the Hartford Atheneum, which opened its doors in 1844, four years before Wadsworth's death. There was, too, J. M. W. Turner, bequeathing his works to the National Gallery, provided a room be built for them. With its complicated provisions, it may have been, to quote Lady Eastlake, "a very stupid will."[10] Her opinions are worth attending to: she traveled in high society and the world of artists as the wife of the painter, scholar, and art bureaucrat Sir Charles Eastlake. But after four years of litigation, most of Turner's vast bequest, including about 19,000 drawings and sketches, became accessible public property.

Caillebotte belonged to the party of Turner and, to place him into his own society, of Depeaux, the Rouennais cotton merchant who left his city an outstanding collection of French Impressionists.* Aesthetic patriotism did not necessarily make for aesthetic caution, but could single out uncanonical artists banished from the favors that the state chose to dispense. Born into a family grown rich in textiles and real estate, Caillebotte could devote his time to painting and his fortune to advancing the careers of his Impressionist friends. He showed with them in five of their exhibitions between 1876 and 1882, skillfully managed their prickly egos, and bought Impressionist canvases at prices he deliberately inflated to benefit his impecunious associates.

A painter of distinctive, long underrated talents, Caillebotte practiced, with the luminosity of his canvases and an idiosyncratic urban vision, what the sympathetic critic Théodore Duret had baptized "the New Painting." In his apparently realistic Parisian scenes of streets and bridges, he ventured into almost breathtaking perspectives. One critic rather oddly certified him to be an "inoffensive type of bourgeois": while he was indeed a bourgeois, there was noth-

* See above, pp. 28–29.

ing inoffensive about his work or that of his favorites. But in 1876, in a review
of the Impressionists' second exhibition, Zola endorsed the slander. Caillebotte's contributions to the show, he wrote, was "anti-artistic" and, with their
precise renderings, "bourgeois."[11] He seemed too decorous for most avant-
garde critics, not decorous enough for most defenders of academic hierarchies.

In short, what gave Caillebotte a name in the France of the 1890s was not
his painting but his will. Its central clause, first drawn up in 1876 and retained
in two later codicils, provided that his gift must not be shunted aside to some
attic or some provincial gallery, but go straight into the Luxembourg Museum,
which housed the work of living French artists, and eventually to the Louvre.
And he appointed Renoir as executor to safeguard his intentions.

These testamentary precautions proved Caillebotte's prescience. His legacy
was stunning and dangerous: eighteen Pissarros, sixteen Monets, nine Sisleys,
eight Renoirs, seven Degas, five Cézannes, four Manets.[12] But, far from overwhelmed with gratitude, administrators were quick to make difficulties, never
satisfactorily resolved for all of Renoir's exertions and all the legal maneuver-
ing on both sides. In the end, Henri Roujon, director of the Beaux-Arts, and
Léonce Bénédite, director of the Luxembourg, offered to accept thirty-eight of
the sixty-seven pictures put at their disposal. Bénédite was not hostile to the
New Painting: in 1897, after the contenders had reached this cheerless compromise, he even voiced his regrets over the Manets that had got away: "The
Luxembourg has seen disappear into foreign museums, which today fight over
his works, some of this frank and original painter's most finished and most
seductive pieces." And Caillebotte's friends could draw some consolation from
the fact that Bénédite had made his selections with the advice of Impressionists like Pissarro.[13] Finally, after long delay and undignified wrangling, the torso
of Caillebotte's collection was presented to the public in February 1897 in a
newly constructed annex to the Luxembourg.

Even this compromise, a most unenthusiastic commitment to the Impressionists, aroused furious opposition from the defensive art establishment; the
Luxembourg's less than gracious reception of its shocking acquisitions did not
appease the critics. After visiting the exhibition, Pissarro judged it badly lit,
miserably framed, and stupidly hung.[14] This did not stop Jean-Louis Gérôme,
full of years and honors; the "scandal" of Caillebotte's will propelled him into
action, writing articles and organizing protests filled with breathless barbs. He
professed not to know whether Caillebotte had done any painting himself and
denounced the Impressionists, literally, as madmen. He thought it a "moral dis-
grace" to have the state accept such "excrement"—he meant pictures by Manet
and Pissarro—and concluded, his panic out of control, "this is anarchy."[15]

Gérôme's anxious attacks found noisy echoes. Shortly after the will had become public, the *Journal des artistes* distributed a questionnaire and reported a consensus that the Caillebotte bequest was "a pile of excrement; to have it exhibited in a national museum publicly dishonors French art." Pissarro rather enjoyed this wrangle among the schools. "This idiot," he told his son Lucien, speaking of Gérôme, "has made himself ridiculous" and, with that, the whole artistic establishment.[16]

The sheer coarseness of Gérôme's invective and the enviable reputation of Impressionist art have long governed the modern perception of the Caillebotte affair. Until recently, when scholars have suitably complicated this episode, it was read as typical evidence for an ever-renewed duel between progress and reaction.[17] But the hesitations of the authorities were not all rooted in an ossified aesthetic ideology. French museum directors were public servants with diverse constituencies, and they knew that however they decided, agitated displeasure would come their way. Their guidelines were strict; it had long been the custom at the Luxembourg to hang no more than three or four paintings by a single artist. The apprehension that to take all of Caillebotte's gift would unbalance the museum's offerings was therefore not simply a pretext to evade innovation. Had the Luxembourg not recently shown its flexibility by accepting the gift of Manet's provocative *Olympia*?

More was in play, then, than a straightforward duel between the defenders of the past and the heralds of the future. Those offering the Caillebotte legacy and those designated to receive it had the same aim in view. Both were acting as educators, intent on including within the charmed circle of high culture people who could afford only to look rather than to buy. But the fundamental question of choice—whether to preserve the safe or make way for the risky—made for frictions that necessarily played themselves out in public disputes. And these disputes were, it seemed, growing less and less reparable. With the coming of modernism the breakup of a great if shaky bourgeois compromise was on the horizon, a compromise that had held culture together for decades.

⚹ SIX ⚹

Modernism

I. A Profusion of Alternatives

During the second half of Queen Victoria's reign, alternatives for gratifying the bourgeoisie's cultural appetites multiplied with exhilarating and alarming speed. It was around 1880 that rivulets of unconventional paintings, poems, and sculptures, buildings, compositions, and plays flowed together into a torrent of rebellion against dominant ways in the arts. Modernist styles were growing into a formidable force; even interior decorators started to scorn time-honored tastes. And just before the outbreak of the First World War, the novel, which had provided reliable entertainment for a century and a half, experimented with unprecedented, almost unpredictable forms. Already mired in controversy over candid renderings of sexual and sordid moments by Zola and his disciples, it now invaded the interior of its characters to map their stream of consciousness. For middle-class collectors, readers, and listeners, the question just what to do about modernist challenges became increasingly acute.

Modernism almost defies definition. There are certain landmarks, nearly all of them clustering after the turn of the century, that constituted its undisputed classics: Pablo Picasso's *Demoiselles d'Avignon,* finished in 1907; Stravinsky's ballet *The Rite of Spring,* choreographed by Vaslav Nijinsky; Marcel Duchamp's *Nude Descending a Staircase,* shown at the Armory Show in New York; and Walter Gropius's design for the Fagus Shoe factory, each dating from 1913. All but the Gropius provoked vocal, at times venomous resistance: the premiere of *The Rite of Spring* in Paris degenerated into a historic fracas. Disgruntled spectators began to laugh sarcastically, thus provoking the ballet's supporters to counter-demonstrations; the scene, Stravinsky recalled, "very quickly developing into a terrific uproar."[1] In a sense he was lucky: he caused but one famous riot. For his part, in his early years after abandoning conventional keys, Arnold Schoenberg was consistently hissed in Vienna's concert halls. Other exemplars produced somewhat subtler disharmonies: Picasso, we shall see later, did not care to show the *Demoiselles* publicly for years.

As early as 1860, Ralph Waldo Emerson had intuited such warfare in the making. "There are people, literalists," who still, "after hearing the music and poetry and rhetoric and wit of seventy or eighty years," lack humor and a sense of verbal play. These good folk are "past the help of surgeon or clergy. But even these can understand pitchforks and the cry of Fire! and I have noticed in some of this class a marked dislike of earthquakes."[2] Modernist earthquakes left many bourgeois indifferent or generated defensive maneuvers designed to minimize anxiety. Twenty years after Emerson's prescient diagnosis (to cull one example from a copious harvest) the English positivist writer Frederic Harrison, impatient with inherited ideas in everything but the arts, exhibited this apprehensive philistinism. He assailed the "discordant hubbub of modern Picture Exhibitions," which, he believed, seduced ambitious painters into sensationalism. The "root of decadence in art" was there for everyone to see, as modern artists encompassed the "divorce of art from the highest religious, social, intellectual movements of the age," and the "substitution of democratic license and personal caprice for grand traditions and loyal service in the larger forces of life."[3] The very freedom and individualism that was the avant-gardes' lifeblood was, for Harrison and his fellows, an invitation to cultural anarchy.

Emerson's plural—"earthquakes"—was apt: the age witnessed the most diverse tremors complete with telltale, quivering aftershocks. Although they differed from genre to genre, country to country, the unease about developments in high culture was almost unrelieved everywhere. Some of the endangered arts were located right over the geological fault of a fading tradition; insurrections abrupt and devastating made, in the words of the Austrian novelist Hermann Broch, for a "gay apocalypse." Others slid toward modernism circuitously, still further complicating, almost without knowing it, already complicated attempts at definition.

One of the most interesting modernists-in-spite-of-himself was the English architect C. F. Annesley Voysey, who opened his private practice in 1882. Much like William Morris, the great designer and champion of integrity in the arts to whom, like so many others, he owed decisive impulses, Voysey designed whatever came to hand: delightful, airy wallpapers and printed linens with gently stylized birds and animals, furniture and domestic objects, including

toast racks and teapots forthright enough to make their utility inviting.* Not
that Voysey was trying to anticipate Adolf Loos's much quoted slogan "Orna-
ment is crime," but he had early reached the conviction that designs do not
need to be ornate to speak for themselves.

In an interview of 1893, he distanced himself from what remained a reigning, though by now contested, mode of design: "The danger to-day lies in
over-decoration; we lack simplicity and have forgotten repose."[4] Voysey did not
mean to slight either of them. That a current highly critical of dominant tastes,
largely driven by the Arts and Crafts movement, supported his ideals stiffened
Voysey's backbone. The designers attached to Arts and Crafts abhorred geegaws
and vulgar eclecticism and, in Morris's wake, preached honesty in materials and
respect for craftsmanship. Let *Punch* mercilessly ridicule languid, effeminate
young men and poetic, worshipful young women as "aesthetic"; its targets
retorted, in the imaginative counterattack of the *Burlington* magazine just after
1880, by inventing "Mr Philistine Jones, who dubs all aesthetes idiots, while he
also adopts their ideas."[5]

In some fine country houses, Voysey put his principles into practice; they are
notable for intelligible lines and a clean look inside and out. Not surprisingly,
he became a favorite with the *Studio,* a copiously illustrated periodical
launched in 1893 to support new tendencies in furniture, tiles, tapestries, the
graphic arts. A year later, it published one of Voysey's first houses, "an artist's
cottage," and praised its "reticent simplicity." Plainly, Voysey was designing for
the upper bourgeoisie: this "cottage," for one, complete with a picture gallery
and four bedrooms on the second floor, was estimated to come in at £700 to
£800, the equivalent of anywhere from five to ten years' income of a clerk.[6]

Yet, though Voysey figured prominently in the parade of accomplished
designers whose work fed into the swelling stream of modernist architecture,
both his clients and Voysey himself regarded his houses as the application of a
sensible vernacular idiom, as anything but revolutionary. Some architectural
critics singled out their striking fenestration, transparent forms, and sparse
adornment as original departures, but late in life Voysey explicitly, emphatically disclaimed ever having striven for novelty. He had always believed in dignity and individualism, and detested departures from sound tradition for their
own sake. His roofs, as he put it a little smugly, had always been steep, never
flat—in short, they did not leak. This coexistence of prudence and daring was
fairly characteristic of many modernists; the army of innovators was swarming
with soldiers shanghaied to serve a cause in which they had not really believed.
Several key figures in Victorian culture—Corot in painting, Brahms in music—

---

* The clean designs of the Bauhaus in the early 1920s are Voysey's rightful heirs.

stood at the threshold of modernism without any conscious desire to invent a new dispensation. But history has its cunning; even when these great transitional figures looked to the past, they were paving the way to the future.

In the face of all these equivocal indications, it is safe to say that modernism was a call to authenticity. It detested formulas and prized originality. Whether a Realist, Symbolist, Expressionist, Vorticist, or proponent of any of the other isms crowding one another early in the twentieth century, each modernist liked to see himself defying stifling rules and deadening traditions, to stand as a nemesis to the tyranny of academicism. Modernism—at least that is what its votaries thought—was a crusade in behalf of sincerity, in behalf of an expressive freedom that no establishment could command or, in the long run, frustrate.

Much of that self-advertised sincerity recognized the deep roots of the arts in sexual and aggressive drives. Academic painters, poets, and playwrights had toyed with both, especially with erotic sensations, but generally in a sly, elbow-nudging way that covered up what it really was: socially acceptable pornography. Cabanel's sensual nudes, his luscious Venus and his lusty satyr, were only the most accomplished exemplars in a profitable genre, and they all struck modernists as prototypes of dishonesty: paintings that showed Ottoman merchants exhibiting beautiful naked European captives on the slave market; sculptures that professed to be imparting moral lessons when they only aroused libidinal fantasies; novels that made light of immorality by having the sinful heroine get married on the last page; well-made plays that evaded important social issues by providing cheap laughs over adultery. In sharp contrast, modernists explored their world and their senses—all of them—without apology.

There is a sentence in an essay by Liebermann on Manet that hints at the erotic energy shaping modernist art. Manet's paintings, even his woodcuts, he wrote in 1905, never lose the freshness of the sketch, an immeasurable asset to his art: "In the sketch the artist celebrates his wedding night with his work; with his first passion and the concentration of all his powers he pours into the sketch what had been in his mind, and in the intoxication of his enthusiasm he generates what no effort or labor could replace."[7] Surely Liebermann, a graceful stylist and by his own testimony a good bourgeois, did not intend to have readers take his extended sensual metaphor literally. But, knowingly or not, he was hinting at the vitality on which Impressionist painting, the model of early modernism, was drawing. Modernist art, he was suggesting, is praiseworthy, fertile copulation.

It was part of this quest for transparent honesty, as some modernists artlessly confessed, that they worked mainly in a trance-like passivity; they were only the recorders of inspirations whose origins they could not explain and whose grip they could not withstand. Schoenberg and Kandinsky reported that when

they were at work, they were simply putting down dictation that came from
within. Paradoxically this inward serfdom belonged to the modernists' quest for
absolute freedom. Shortly after 1900, Debussy spoke for them all in search of
that libertarian ideal by patronizing the academic composer for "listening
modestly to the voice of tradition which prevents him, it seems to me, from
hearing the voice that speaks within him."[8] Such deafness kept creative spirits
from listening to the only voice that mattered—their own.

The bourgeois share in the cause of modernism was in the main the business of an active minority engrossed in the drama of high culture. For the
majority, scratching a living with occasional time out for inexpensive recreation remained the principal business around 1900, as it had always been. The
perennial appeal of best-selling novels, light musical entertainments, sentimental or pious pictures leaves little doubt that a quarter century of pleasure wars
had left at best a modest imprint on the middlebrow public. Bourgeois, and not
the impecunious alone, continued to breed pigeons and organize Sunday pic-
nics, frequent music halls and read aloud from their favorite family weekly. One
can see them shaking their head as their daily paper reported the latest scandal
provoked by an exhibition of Symbolist canvases, a bellicose manifesto by a
Futurist poet, the premiere of a sexually explicit ballet. The best-publicized
avant-garde performances remained an alien country to them.

Not that embattled conservatives clinging to survivals of the past were helpless. Among their most effective defenses was co-option. Once extremist works
had lost the shock of novelty, they could be tamed into respectability by having their sting drawn. One could all too easily fail to see what one did not want
to see. Popular art was popular precisely because it was so undemanding, and
difficult pictures could be reduced to accessible levels by singling out their supposed charm, their supposed prettiness. Thus purchasers of brightly colored
reproductions misread Degas's sweating, awkwardly posed dancers as picturesque anecdotes suitable to serve as wall decorations for impressionable ado-
lescents; listeners to Brahms's First Symphony chose to ignore its enigmas by
recalling the comfortable cliché about its being Beethoven's Tenth. The copious
output of Winslow Homer, who overlooked none of the pathos in his emanci-
pated slaves laboring in the fields or the modest heroism of his Civil War soldiers, was vulgarized into calendar art; his brilliant evocations of the churning,
devastating sea were cheaply reproduced far more often than was good for
them. Thus reproductions even of modernist art could elicit a knowing or bit-
tersweet smile, a religious or chauvinistic thrill, a retrospective fantasy of innocent childhood or the little triumphs of being on the inside of a joke. Perhaps
most rewarding of all, consumers could bask in the delicious sense of having
been taught a moral lesson.

Even so, the inert or nervous mass of traditionalists could not dictate a uniform response to the cultural earthquakes that was modernism. We have seen
more than once that nineteenth-century bourgeois made up a deeply cleft
class; it is worth reiterating that the chasm separating traditionalists from subversives did not place a united bourgeoisie on one side and an aggressive antibourgeois phalanx on the other. And, perplexing as they were, these
confrontations became all the more perplexing as bourgeois who embraced
avant-garde causes often repudiated their class and joined the opposition, a
stratagem in cultural politics that allowed them to posture as bohemians or as
aristocratic aesthetes.

Bourgeois quite unintentionally performed their historic service to modernism almost as much by reviling as by endorsing it; they gave it the kind of
publicity the modernists would never have enjoyed without the shocked exclamations of insulted lovers of art, music, or dance. Still, for the most part it was
the commitment, or the conversion, of cultivated bourgeois to the unconventional that would make the principal difference in the rise and triumph of
modernism. Without widely diffused middle-class prosperity and middle-class
enthusiasm for departures from official culture, it would have been little more
than a spectacular meteor soon burned out.

By no means all bourgeois embraces of the modern were the work of new
money. Many a parvenu underscored his arrival in good society by displaying
the most understated conduct at auctions, the most orthodox of purchases.
Inconspicuous consumption could be the most conspicuous consumption of
all. But new money or old, the very class that derided modern poets as lunatics,
modern playwrights as pornographers, modern painters as apostles of the
repulsive also provided these seditionists with forums for their ventures into
unmapped domains, if not invariably with quick acceptance or a lavish
income.* In short, it was the middle classes that nourished their sworn enemies;
avant-gardes could not have made their way without massive bourgeois
patronage.

---

* Some contemporaries were, a little sardonically, aware of this situation. "For quite a while,"
wrote Ernst Wechsler, a German journalist, expressing widely shared views, "our time has not
believed in the fairy tale of the poet who, poor as a church mouse, starving and freezing, sits in
his little garret receiving the visit of the proud, royal muse." On the contrary, "the modern author
receives from the daily newspapers and family weeklies honorariums for his work that his brothers in Apollo would not have dreamt of a few generations ago." Wechsler, "Nikolaus Lenau. Eine
litterarische Studie," *Westermanns Monatshefte*, LXVIII (August 1890), 676. This was rather too sanguine a verdict if applied to the most alienated among the modernists—one thinks of Gauguin—
but it makes a useful point.

2. Modernists vs. Modernists

Fortunately for them, thousands of middle-class art lovers were never obliged
to make a stark choice between the extremes of an academic conformist like
William Bouguereau and a Cubist explorer like Georges Braque. Bourgeois
with time and money for culture discovered that one way of managing the
shocks of the new was to adopt one of several less drastic breaks with commonplace fare. There was always John Singer Sargent; there was always Jacques
Joseph Tissot, artists of and for the bourgeoisie—flawless craftsmen with just a
touch of unconventionality, easy to like.* Collectors might grow bored with
academic paintings, but, made uneasy by Monet's or Pissarro's light-handed
brushwork and intense luminosity, they would buy artists of the *juste milieu*
who for all their modernist pretensions remained safely within the accepted
canon. From the early 1870s on, the Paris salons graduated to fare remotely
comparable to that offered by the Impressionists; now little-known salon landscape painters like François Louis Français, Léon Pelouse, Antoine Chintreuil,
all of whom had canvases bought by the state, offered pleasing compromises.†
Or they might admire Impressionists but not Cézanne; they might go as far as
Cézanne but find the Fauves too unnatural; they might come to terms with
the Fauves but not with Kandinsky—or accept the Kandinsky of 1905 but not
the Kandinsky of 1910.

By the same token, music lovers might take to Debussy but spurn Stravinsky; relish Stravinsky but find Schoenberg incomprehensible. Theatergoers too
sophisticated for the well-made play might admire the problem plays of Ibsen
but abominate Strindberg for violating social taboos; they might appreciate
Strindberg but draw the line at *Ubu roi,* Alfred Jarry's scatological ambush of
time-honored stage conventions with its memorable first line: "*merdre.*" Such
decisions were not necessarily compromises but, rather, the point on the spectrum of current offerings that promised one consumer or another the great-

---

* In his admiring biography of Tissot, Christopher Wood, who considerably admires his subject, writes, "Tissot was an assiduous and highly competent painter, most of whose pictures are of
pretty, elegant women; his work is visually attractive, without being too demanding intellectually." That says it. *Tissot: The Life and Work of Jacques Joseph Tissot, 1836–1902* (1986), 9.

† In 1880, the one year that Monet tried to show at the Salon, he attempted a compromise of
his own, deliberately doing work "more judicious, more bourgeois." But, try as he might, his
Lavancourt, a village by a lake, the sunny scene lit up by blue and white touches, stood out uncomfortably against the others. See John House et al., *Impressions of France: Monet, Renoir, Pissarro, and
Their Rivals* (1995), 136–37.

est pleasure. Wherever collectors and audiences might settle, though, middle-class shoppers for cultural goods could scarcely ignore the motley modernist offerings.

Attending to the avant-garde did not mean to approve. Once again, generalizations suffer shipwreck on the rock of diversity. In countries like France, novelists could safely explore sexual entanglements that English or American readers would have considered indecent. Again, in some cities the forces of tradition were more securely entrenched and more militant than in others. In the Vienna of 1910, the chances of Schoenberg for academic preferment were slim, and he fled to Berlin. Two years later, offered a post in his native city, he turned it down, largely because he had not forgotten the demonstrations of concert audiences against him. "I am not yet reconciled," he wrote. Schoenberg was not one of those contrarian modernist rebels whom I described earlier as convinced that selling meant selling out. He was trying to make a living, craved an audience and well-informed musical criticism. "*I* do *not* want to become a martyr. All such posturing does not suit me."[1]

It did, though, suit others; the modernists had to contend with conflicting views about their proper stance toward society as much as their positive aims. Its troops did not make the establishment their only target but, as deeply divided as bourgeois, turned their weapons on one another with a will. In Vienna after the turn of the century, the city's two most impressive innovative architects, Josef Hoffmann and Adolf Loos, confronted each other with poorly concealed hostility. The first, a professional success, advocated a "total" architecture that comprehended every detail of a commission; the second, a witty outsider, became noted for his bare, unornamented façades—Vienna could barely accommodate them both. A few years later Richard Strauss, though he had magnanimously supported Schoenberg after his move to Berlin, came to think it politic to detach himself from this trying extremist: "Only a psychiatrist can help poor Schoenberg now," he said, and suggested that he "would do better to shovel snow instead of scribbling on music paper."[2]

At times, a modernist sniped at other modernists largely for failing to mirror his own development. Mondrian was disappointed in the Cubists' refusal to extirpate all traces of nature from their art: after arriving in Paris in late 1911, he felt "immediately drawn to the Cubists, especially to Picasso and Leger," but discovered "that Cubism did not accept the logical consequences of its own discoveries; it was not developing abstraction toward its ultimate goal, the expression of pure reality." Apparently it never occurred to him that the Cubists kept hold of their ties to the external world not from cowardice but from choice. Again, in February 1914, looking back, Edvard Munch called the Impressionists "façade people—*Fassadenmenschen.*" What mattered in the arts, he argued, was "what is behind the façade," a psychological penetration that to his mind the likes of Monet and Pissarro could never achieve.[3]

By this time, family feuds among modernists were no longer news. In the 1880s and 1890s, discontented artists seceded from established organizations to form progressive societies of their own only to find that soon some of their number thought *them* too closely tied to the timid establishment, and resigned, were expelled, or started a secession of their own. The Secessions of Berlin and Munich, of Vienna and Moscow, all suffered internal stresses, and lost their original verve as they failed to keep pace with even more uncompromising artists. Thus in Berlin, after years of relative harmony under the leadership of Liebermann and his semi-Impressionist allies, the Secession was riven when it failed to accommodate rebellious Expressionists and when the most unconventional of them, Emil Nolde, venomously attacked Liebermann. A new secession was the result. One generation's unconventionality was the next generation's conformism, and in the modernist earthquakes generations followed each other within a decade or less.

Modernism, then, was a moving frontier giving no hint just where the next revolutionary might strike. After all, the rebels' emotional styles varied almost as much as their technical innovations. A number of them, extremely prominent or at least extremely articulate, sounded a visionary note to prophesy the doom of Western civilization. Others reveled in fantasies of decadence, espoused utopian political or religious systems, or—a refreshing handful—caricatured pompousness and the arrogance of power—and, at times, their own—in feuilletons and little left-wing periodicals. The chansons they wrote and performed were exuberant and impartially disrespectful.

Their displays of aggressive wit went some way to counteract the gloom of modernists groaning under the self-imposed duty of cleaning the Augean stables of bourgeois corruption and bourgeois philistinism. In Montmartre from the mid-1870s, avant-garde performers, poets, playwrights, and a tribe of talented illustrators created a cabaret life that exposed in lighthearted badinage humorless and materialistic bourgeois as bullheaded adversaries of emotional, artistic, and political experimentation. In 1882, Rodolphe Salis, founder of the much frequented Parisian cabaret Le Chat noir and the periodical named after it, wrote a combative poem, "The Ballad of Joyous Bohemia," which identified the enemy without circumlocutions: bankers, kings of usury; stupid and conceited parvenus; censors and philistines; bourgeois with their "pure ears." Joyful bohemians, the poet promised, would put them all to flight by yawning at them, drawing caricatures of them, frightening them as they clinked glasses.[*]

---

* The poem was printed in *Le Chat noir* (January 14, 1882); it runs in part: "Porteur de lyre ou de crayons, / Pitre chatoyants de dorure / Qu'on nous excuse—nous baîllons / Chez les Ban-

Such reservoirs of irreverence and artistic license struck the most anxious among bourgeois as more dangerous even than portentous Cassandras. And this smiling climate of opinion papered over many of the dissensions dividing avant-gardes everywhere.

In fact, what looked to worried defenders of tradition like a sturdy alliance of insurrectionists was a loose coalition with inconstant, shifting memberships. Even the raucous bohemians, whether in Paris or in Munich, antibourgeois on principle, were far from at peace within their own circle. The most visible mark of unity among the modernists was, of course, their distaste for "official" art, music, and literature, for the dull, inoffensive—which is to say, offensive—pleasures that nineteenth-century bourgeois apparently favored over less regimented modern delights. But if the agitators could largely agree on their diagnosis of the adversary, their prescriptions occupied a wide spectrum of remedies. Nor were they at one in their attitude toward the bourgeoisie. Baudelaire had distanced himself from the bourgeoisophobes by lavishing praise on the art-loving French middle class and expected it to support real artists; in the same vein, that certified modernist Guillaume Apollinaire, looking back during the war, humbly appealed to the bourgeoisie to understand, and pity, searchers for "new fires and colors never before seen." There had long been a quarrel between "tradition and invention, Order and Adventure," he wrote in his long poem *La Jolie Rousse,* but the modernists' explorations of "vast and strange domains" were not signs of hostility: "We are not your enemies."[4]

The left-wing Belgian Symbolist poet Emile Verhaeren, a good friend of Pissarro's, captured this unstable atmosphere: "There is no longer any single school, there are scarcely any groups, and those few are constantly splitting," he wrote in 1891. "All these tendencies make me think of moving and kaleidoscopic geometric patterns, which clash at one moment only to unite at another, which now fuse and then separate and fly apart a little later, but which all nevertheless revolve within the same circle, that of the new art."[5] The new art could only benefit from this abundance, however splintered, precisely because it baffled and troubled good bourgeois.

With some notable dissenters, then, the modernists' prevailing rhetoric was antibourgeois—fierce and often unjust. Probably the best-known artist immune to this bourgeoisophobia was Edouard Manet, Parisian flaneur and faultless modern who, apart from his private agenda to paint "sincerely," lusted most after the *Légion d'honneur.* Even though he was tied to the Impressionists

quiers, rois de l'usure. / Nous faisons la caricature / De Turcaret bête et hautain, / Chacun de nous prete à sa hure, / Peintre, poète ou cabotin. . . . / Bourgeois, fuis, quand nous ripaillons / . . . . / Nos discours sur les cotillons / Effaroucheraient la Censure; / Et nous trinquons, mortelle injure / En disant 'BREN!' au Philistine."

by affinity and family—Berthe Morisot was his sister-in-law—he never exhibited with them, a momentous refusal. Camille Pissarro, the fatherly protector
of his Impressionist fellows, much as he admired Manet the artist, was stern
with Manet the bourgeois: "Manet, however great he was as a painter, had his
failings," he wrote to his son Lucien in 1883, shortly after Manet's death; "he
was madly eager to be recognized by the constituted authorities, he believed
in the establishment, he aspired to honors."[6]

Paul Gauguin, as programmatic an antibourgeois artist as the Victorian age
produced, approaches the widely accepted modernist model far more closely.
Others talked bourgeoisophobia; he lived it. A well-situated banker with a wife
and children—nothing could be more middle-class than that!—he deserted his
profession, his family, and his country to make painting, at first a mere hobby,
his exigent master. In Gauguin, fighting out an internal duel between impulse
and responsibility, the latter, that supreme bourgeois virtue, never had a chance.
Only Arthur Rimbaud could match Gauguin: a precocious symbolist poet,
political radical, and atheistic rebel, he was addicted to drugs and alcohol and
lived dangerously—his lover Paul Verlaine almost shot him to death—spending
the last years of his short life in mysterious business dealings in Ethiopia.
Beyond his poetry, his very existence stands as a consummate defiance of bourgeois civilization.

Few haters of the bourgeoisie made their point so emphatically as Gauguin
or Rimbaud, but even the more restrained among them were more numerous
and more boisterous than its apologists. In 1900, looking back on half a century of French musical taste, Camille Saint-Saëns, then in his mid-sixties, drew a
doleful portrait of middle-class superficiality. "The young musician of today
would find it difficult to imagine the state of music in France when Gounod
came on the scene." The real public, "that is the *bon bourgeois,* recognized no
music outside the opera and French comic opera." Hence "it was quite useless
to try and get a symphony, a trio, or a quartet performed except by the Société
des Concerts du Conservatoire or by one or two private chamber music societies." One would never guess from this mordant recollection that Paris supported other orchestras and half a dozen bodies devoted to chamber music.
Most of these concentrated on the classics—the Société des Derniers Quatuors
de Beethoven had been in existence since 1848—but the moderns, too, could
count on a hearing.

The reception of Debussy's string quartet, which he completed in February
1893, suggests that times were different now, and better. Performed by the Ysaÿe
Quartet in December, the opus 10 quickly established itself as a modern classic.[7] Yet Debussy cheerfully joined the pack of bourgeoisophobes; just after the
turn of the century, in a series of amusing and pointed articles, he denounced

the "deliberate indifference of the public" and the "mediocrity of the herd mind."[8] Hope for mass conversions to modernism was faint at best—on principle. Franz Marc was one of many modernists to agree with Debussy. "It is dreadfully hard," he wrote in 1912 in *The Blue Rider*, the famous almanac he had helped edit, "to give one's contemporaries spiritual presents."[9] Though exceptional pioneers like Schoenberg disagreed, to be misunderstood or, even better, despised by ordinary consumers of culture was for most of the others a virtual credential of authentic modernism.

The history of Liebermann's taste documents some of the tensions vexing avant-garde camps and some of the boundaries limiting adaptability. We recall that, denounced in the 1870s and later as a lover of ugliness, he made himself into the leading exemplar of German Impressionism. In 1892, when Edvard Munch's disturbing lithographs were first exhibited in Berlin to panic-stricken disapproval and the show was compelled to close, Liebermann came to their defense. Smart, forthright, independently wealthy, he was the natural spokesman for artistic outsiders and the predestined founder of the Berlin Secession in 1898. But, significantly, he was elected to the Berlin Academy of the Arts in the same year: Liebermann never completely cut his ties to the establishment. Yet during his presidency, the Secession sponsored exhibitions of anti-academic artists and invited foreigners to bring a breath of fresh air into the stuffy Wilhelminian atmosphere.

But Liebermann knew that he could never follow the modernist developments in painting during the first decade of the new century. Fauvism and Cubism, to say nothing of nonobjective art, only roused his derision. Nature remained his guide—a face, the human body, a garden, a horseback rider on a beach. To slight or, even worse, to abandon nature was to betray the mission of art. As he perceptively mused on the way that the iconoclasts of one generation become the conservatives of the next, he recognized that his repudiation of Kandinsky, Mondrian, or Picasso might disclose his blind spots. But, he said, "No one can leap over his shadow." He *had* leapt once, from academicism to Impressionism, but there he was determined to stop.[10]

One of the hurdles obstructing a stable definition of modernism was its ambivalence toward romanticism; the moderns were both its belated heirs and its stoutest critics. Like the romantics, they believed in individual genius; unlike them, they hunted in gangs. Like the romantics, they mutinied against all forms of external pressures; unlike them, they had little use for nostalgia. True, some of them made no mystery of their obligations to the past: Schoenberg went to school to Brahms, whom he hailed as an unrecognized modern; William Morris rediscovered the glories of medieval craftsmanship as he faced the muddle

of tasteless contemporary design; Picasso was influenced (to a still much debated degree) by primitive sculpture; Kandinsky found Russian folk art and
Stravinsky seventeenth-century church music highly stimulating. But the modernists' appeal to bygone artisans and once favored styles was rarely disinterested; far more often, it was a tendentious comparison useful to put what Morris
called "our wretched hypocrisies" to shame.[11]

Indeed, the long, vociferous career of William Morris testifies to the Victorian avant-gardes' sense of destiny. In 1878, in a public lecture on the true uses
of long-forgotten craftsmanship, he put the crux of the matter with his customary energy: "Let us study it wisely, be taught by it, kindled by it; all the
while determining not to imitate or repeat it; to have either no art at all, or an
art which we have made our own."[12] In other words, when modernists allowed
themselves to be guided by past masters, they appealed to the old largely to
make things new.

To make things new: it is striking how many of the modernists founded
movements and edited periodicals in which they promoted themselves as voices of the future. The New Woman joined the New Drama and periodicals like
the *New Age* which strove to focus public awareness on glaring blemishes in
design. And Art nouveau, that spirited if short-lived international style, reveling in swooping curved designs for subway entrances or desks or lamps, was an
explicit act of aggression on the dullness of conventional objects. In the Bel-
gium of the 1880s, avant-garde writers in Brussels and Antwerp called themselves La Jeune Belgique and published progressive reviews like *La Jeune Revue
Littéraire* and *Jong Vlaanderen*. Their influential German counterpart, *Jugend*,
gave its name to the Jugendstil, while Madrid saw a new journal in 1901, *Arte
Joven*, for which Picasso was to furnish the illustrations. This self-congratulatory epithet was largely justified; modernism displayed a vitality, an eagerness for
honest experience, that reverberates for the historian more than a century later.
Les XX of Brussels, symbolist painters, graphic artists, book and furniture
designers who blossomed for some two decades after 1880, were characteristic
of an overflowing talent and search for self-expression that marked such movements everywhere.

Meanwhile, quite as enthusiastic movements in Sweden and Austria—Unga
Sverige and Junges Österreich—usually May flies, emerged around the edges
of European avant-garde centers, while the German version topped the others
by claiming to be "youngest"—Jüngstdeutschland.[13] By then, these identifica-
tions with youth were no longer young; half a century before, self-conscious
would-be philosophical parricides had already formed circles with names like
Young Germany or the Young Hegelians. What differentiated the youth of the
1880s from the youth of the 1830s was their number, their persistence, and,

among the Italian, French, and Russian Futurists—a pregnant name—their deliberately cultivated frenzy. Who better to overthrow the crusted Old Regime than those least crippled by repressive habits and with long vistas ahead of them?

To take possession of the future meant rescuing what was forward-looking in the present. Testifying to their fresh, overflowing energies, modernists demanded, "One must be of one's time." Late in Victoria's reign, the saying had grown into something of a commonplace among advanced coteries. It was apparently coined by Daumier and became a favorite with Manet and with Félicien Rops: *"Il faut être de son temps avant tout."* In 1903, Voysey firmly restated it: he wanted to "live and work in the present."[14] Of course, modernists had not resigned themselves to the dominant tastes they intended to dethrone. On the contrary, they meant to convey that these tastes were an oppressive legacy to be discarded in favor of the dynamic forces that had arisen in recent decades, offering the century unexplored possibilities. Baudelaire was not alone in detecting splendid possibilities in modern life.

Most of the nineteenth-century aesthetic combats had prepared the way for the agreeable and bewildering chaos of its last decades. The tribe of modern bourgeoisophobes, whom I have traced back to the time of Goethe's *Werther* and whose rhetoric reached a climax in Flaubert's blasts at what he perversely denounced as the bourgeoisie, had already envisaged alternatives to middle-class aesthetic culture. Well before the 1880s these subversives recognized that the princes of philistines must be put in their place before the new art and literature could establish themselves. The gestation of modernism was a long-drawn-out affair, emerging from, and systematizing, the convictions of earlier avant-gardes. In the course of the century, Western civilization had witnessed revolutions in fashions as incompatible styles struggled for supremacy with revival following revival. It was an age given to historicism—a deliberate, at times downright slavish, reliance on older styles slightly brought up to date and all too often directly quoted. This recourse to historical models would encounter really serious opposition only late in the century.* Modernist uprisings had to wait until a critical mass of recruits filled the ranks, aching for action.

---

*In the Netherlands, the styles dominant between the mid-1830s and 1890s came to be called—later, of course—the Age of Ugliness. It was an age launched not by the bourgeoisie but by the royal family, which set the tone by commissioning extravagantly decorated furnishings. In royal castles and residences, untamed fantasies blossomed in wallpaper and chests of drawers, sofas and candelabras; in opulent rooms a mixture of styles flaunted an infatuation with incongruous survivals from past centuries. Bourgeois who could afford it followed their monarchs' lead, showing off pieces of furniture, silverware, paintings, carpets, curtains of gymnastic ornateness, adapting and further ornamenting an array of historical styles.

3. Causes and Effects

This historical sketch raises a pivotal question: why did modernist challenges proliferate just when they did? Loose cash was naturally a prominent ingredient in their making. A welter of economic statistics across Europe and the United States documents that from the end of the Napoleonic wars, the middle classes had been growing in size and affluence. Poverty, often extreme destitution, persisted among the working poor in town and country; financial anxiety remained the lot of petit bourgeois, as did uncertainty among the moderately prosperous. Even so, many of these middling and more of the upper ranges of the bourgeoisie were amassing unprecedented amounts of disposable income. Once their earnings covered necessities, expenditures on luxuries became a practicable option. Late in the century, substantial numbers of bourgeois regarded as necessities what had been luxuries for their parents' generation.

Take France. Between 1825 and 1914, in the face of drastic, repeated shifts in regimes, during decades of low inflation and modest population growth, per capita income almost tripled, from 325 to 876 francs a year. And this meteoric rise benefited mainly the middle class. If early in the century a physician might count on about 4,000 francs a year, toward its end he could earn twice as much and more. Other occupations recorded equally heartening figures.[1] This heady pattern of growth was of course distributed unevenly; sectors like government employees suffered in comparison with others, as their salaries failed to keep up with the expenditures their status imposed as appropriate. And the centuries-old hierarchy of middle-class income continued to be steep; a few bourgeois died as millionaires while many left their children little to inherit. Although many thousands of bourgeois bet on horses, only a handful bred them. Yet these necessary cautions do not alter the fact that sizable numbers of middling Frenchmen and Frenchwomen were better off than ever.

In this time span, from the 1820s to the years just before the First World War, French bourgeois further improved their comfortable existence by having fewer children. The birthrate dropped from 31.4 per thousand to a paltry 18.8.[2] Working-class families and peasants, too, used contraception, especially when they had some property to defend. But it was the bourgeoisie that profited most from restricting the number of its offspring; the notorious ideal of the two-child, or even one-child, family that so worried patriots after the defeat of 1870 was becoming standard for millions of middle-class couples, freeing up more spare cash for wall decorations, a small private library, or an occasional concert. Not that all thriving French bourgeois chose to attend serious plays or to read serious poetry. Consumers of choice spiritual refreshment remained a self-selected cultural elite. But in late-nineteenth-century France that elite was open to many a newcomer.

The same held true in other countries. As we have noted, though most bourgeois were not rich, adroit merchants of culture covered every step on the financial ladder of possible middle-class customers. This, we know, did not guarantee wide acceptance of avant-garde music or sculpture. Even after uphill campaigns by cultural entrepreneurs, most modernists never tasted what the English critic Philip Gilbert Hamerton once called "the insult of popularity." Near the end of the long nineteenth century, on May 20, 1914, Henry James, writing to his agent J. B. Pinker, grimly alluded to "that very minor and 'culti-vated' public to whom, alas, almost solely, my productions," the difficult late novels, "appear to address themselves." Nor were great collectors altogether immune to a certain aristocratic, and on occasion deserved, disdain on the part of museum directors privately talking to colleagues. "You know," wrote Alfred Lichtwark to Wilhelm von Bode, "how one has to treat donors."[3] But this was not the whole truth; substantial numbers of bourgeois broke out of habitual, conventional nineteenth-century molds and deserved more consideration.

Victorian demand for avant-garde works and their ready supply were insep-arable from the spectacular growth of cities. At their most numerous, the mid-dle classes remained a minority in their urban world, but a disproportionately influential force in politics, economics—and culture. The city awakened the anti-academics' creativity and provided their customers: it was inspiration and marketplace at once. To be sure, exceptions abounded—every blanket general-ization about modernist earthquakes can be subverted by contrary evidence. There was Worpswede, an artists' colony in the Bremen fen country formed around the turn of the century—its best-known denizens were the sophisti-cated naive painter Paula Modersohn-Becker and the poet Rainer Maria Rilke. There was the park Güell that Eugeni Güell, a Catalan textile tycoon and patron of the arts, commissioned Antoni Gaudí to design near Barcelona as a refuge from the city's bustle.* And a handful of artists preferred the stimu-lus of solitude to that of lights, noise, and never-ending traffic: Emil Nolde painted his Expressionist stormy seascapes, ecstatic savage rites, and biblical scenes in a remote Schleswig farmhouse. But most modernists were men and women of the city.

Even the Impressionists, to become famous for their haystacks, flowering trees, or rivers shimmering in the mist, celebrated the city with their panoram-ic street scenes, their steamy railroad stations, their London bridges, their

* By the way, this "modernist" venture was designed to foster a religious revival.

beflagged Paris on July 14. And not the Impressionists alone: Georges Seurat's masterpiece *Un Dimanche à la grande jatte,* with its promenading Parisians in a park, August Macke's charming *Hutladen,* showing a woman admiring the hats displayed in a store window, and Ernst Ludwig Kirchner's spiky strollers were so many testimonials to the rhythms, at times exuberant and at times menacing, inherent in the urban ambiance.

Expressionist poets and playwrights, too, lived off the city, responding to it as a devouring monster, a trigger for the wildest fantasies, an unsurpassed stage for love and loneliness. They anatomized the estrangement, the excitement and despair it aroused in so many of its denizens. In 1906, in a characteristic invocation, Richard Dehmel, a much admired German poet, playwright, and editor, addressed a "sermon" to city dwellers in which he makes their home into an overpowering giant.* Theaters, too, concert halls, and of course cabarets, were at home in large towns, as were museums, exhibitions, dealers, publishers, printers, and, we know, most of the consumers. Avant-garde painters or poets discovered that it was in Paris or Berlin, Vienna or London more than in bucolic conclaves that they could count on meeting the like-minded in favorite cafés, devise their slogans, work out their programs, and publish their journals. The individualism of artistic revolutionaries did not preclude collective expression.

This is to say that the modernists were people with a cause. They spread the good word with rousing exhibitions, staged commotions in front of museums, and issued calls to arms. Pissarro was not alone in calling for museums to be burnt; far more blatantly the Italian Futurists advocated the same escape from the dead hand of the past. Indeed the Futurists were cultural politicians, almost literally with a vengeance. Excessively verbal, uninhibited and assertive, in search of sensational confrontations, they were intoxicated with the heady sense of their originality and the thrills of modern motion. For Filippo Marinetti, their self-appointed spokesman, the new was good not when it was good but because it was new. He and his allies advertised their notions in a variety of theaters, broadcasting their manifestoes in newspapers and illustrating their commitment to sheer speed by exhibiting their "futurolatry"— Marinetti's word—with pictures of automobiles, fast trains, and airplanes. In 1910, in a supreme gesture, they blanketed the center of Venice by dropping thousands of leaflets—Marinetti, hardly reliable, said 800,000—from the Clock Tower on the Lido. If only a few responded to their propaganda, the Futurists saw to it that a large public at least knew of their existence, as they dramatized

---

* "Yes, the metropolis makes one small. / I look up with stifled longing / to the sun through a thousand human vapors; / and even my father, who among the giants / of his pine and oak forest / seems like a master magician / is among these boastful walls / only a countrified little old man." Richard Dehmel, "Predigt ans Grossstadtvolk," *Aber die Liebe,* 2nd ser. (1893; 1906), 171.

their craze for technological civilization and (to borrow their favorite noun) its dynamism.

Other modernists, only a little less impassioned than the Futurists, were just as firmly wedded to their dogmas and infused their sermons with brave attempts at offending middlebrow bourgeois as deeply as humanly possible. Their public venting of artistic loves and hates, reaching for virtually religious intensity, was an integral element in their bourgeoisophobic strategy. While devout and decorous Victorians attended traditional places of worship, leading avant-garde painters or poets toyed with, or firmly subscribed to, heterodox mystical creeds.

The late-nineteenth-century proliferation of esoteric faiths claiming to integrate religious and scientific world views in the service of a higher harmony was an arresting token of widespread perplexity and ambivalence. Christian Science (a stunning oxymoron, its detractors said), Mary Baker Eddy's invention, professed to combine the best of two incompatible ways of thinking. So did Theosophy, which Madame Blavatsky advertised as a happy synthesis of science, religion, and philosophy. Such modern superstitions claiming to be anything but superstitions look like last, desperate resorts of believers who needed to borrow prestige from triumphant physics or biology. In any event, what matters most is not that Eddy or Blavatsky promulgated these creeds, but that they enjoyed a considerable vogue and found notable recruits among modernists.

For modernist painters like Kandinsky or Mondrian or a poet like Yeats, Theosophy was a remedy destined to heal the disease called secularism. Deploring the disenchantment of the world and calling for its re-enchantment, Kandinsky sounded like a German or English romantic a century before him. In a manifesto on the spiritual element in art written in 1910, he asserted that after a period of seductive materialism apparently ending in the world's surrender to this "nightmare," the soul "was now shaking it off as a wicked temptation." Even unbelievers among the modernists who scoffed at such credos could credit Kandinsky's contention that the artist must obey *"the principle of inner necessity."*[4] If we take the Enlightenment's secularism to be its most distinctive modern quality, it was a pervasive irony of modernism that some of its most strenuous votaries, like Kandinsky or Yeats, were not moderns.

In politics, too, avant-gardes were more likely to cluster among extremists than in boring middle-class parties. Anything better than the middle of the road, bourgeoisdom incarnate! In 1908, in *The Man Who Was Thursday,* G. K. Chesterton, no revolutionary, has an unsympathetic modern artist exclaim, "An artist is identical with an anarchist." Indeed, "An artist disregards all governments, abolishes all conventions." Five years later, after the New York Armory

Show, that vast jumble, had closed, an editorial writer for the *New York Times* agreed: modern painters, he wrote, are "cousins to the anarchists in politics." Even Theodore Roosevelt, who detested the "dead hand of the reactionaries," worried, thinking of paintings like Duchamp's *Nude Descending a Staircase,* that "there is apt to be a lunatic fringe among votaries of any forward movement."[5] To be sure, there were modernists who, like good bourgeois, held mainstream conservative or mainstream liberal opinions, or took little interest in political controversies. But their very aversion to all established tastes—and with that, from established institutions—tempted many of them to become enamored of positions at either end of the political spectrum, allowing them to attack the bourgeoisie from the left or the right.*

With the rise of mass movements and of mass parties, modernist coteries found political entanglements hard to evade—particularly in France. Between 1789 and 1914, the country had undergone two empires, a monarchy, and three republics, two of these short-lived and the third for years on an unstable footing. Repeatedly, beginning with the Terror in the French Revolution and culminating in the horrifying spectacle of wholesale executions of "rebels" during the Paris Commune in May 1871, Frenchmen had killed Frenchmen in bloody clashes on the barricades or in government-sponsored mass shootings. No wonder that, shaken by repeated upheavals, French publicists and politicians indulged freely in political responses to artists, even when their work was at least overtly unpolitical. In 1905, the art critic Camille Mauclair, sturdy champion of the Impressionists and good republican, vehemently criticized "the detestable interference of political nationalism in the question of art."[6] In vain: France, the home of the doctrine of art for art's sake was also susceptible to art for politics's sake.

As though to confirm Mauclair's concern, in Paris, avant-garde concerts, plays, or ballets were welcome provocations: to some a source of vitality, to others a symptom of degeneration. Charles Maurras, editor of the widely read periodical *Action française* and undisputed leader of the royalist, xenophobic, and anti-Semitic movement that bore its name, was only one ideologue to link modernist art to a cultural rot they deplored and were busy combating. They wanted orderliness and tradition in painting as in politics. In sharp contrast, in those years at least, although a number of them returned to the Catholicism of their childhood, many avant-garde figures identified themselves with the left, sympathized with the victims of authority in state and society. To sturdy unbelievers, experimentation in art and revolutionary fervor in politics seemed to

---

* Ezra Pound's descent into Jew hatred and fascism, Knut Hamsun's affection for Nazism, and T. S. Eliot's "aristocratic" disdain for Jews, though a few traces of these show before the First World War, are beyond the chronological range of this study.

be natural allies. Among the painters, Camille Pissarro was only the best-known avant-garde artist to profess anarchist ideas; he was seconded by his son Lucien, by Signac, Seurat, and other neo-Impressionists.

But crises shattered old alliances: in the 1890s, the Dreyfus case estranged old friends, divided families, and even led one or two sensitive artists to question their national identity. It is characteristic of the friction besetting the late-Victorian art world that the Impressionists and their modernist allies in the sister arts took up positions on both sides of the question, often fiercely. Or, like Auguste Rodin, they stubbornly refused to commit themselves, angering their friends whether they supported Dreyfus or fancied him a traitor. Some internalized the affair deeply enough to drive themselves into incoherence. Renoir permitted himself gross anti-Semitic remarks that his young friend Julie Manet, daughter of Berthe Morisot and niece of Edouard Manet, faithfully noted down into her diary.[7] At the same time, Renoir, who refused to exhibit with "that Jew" Pissarro, because it meant revolution, kept friendly ties with Jewish collectors.

Degas was rather more consistent in his inconsistency. His early politics remain shadowy, but if he harbored anti-Semitic notions before the Dreyfus affair, they must have been purely conventional.[8] The old alibi that some of his best friends were Jews applied to him quite literally; he moved at ease among the Jews who bought his pictures, and he felt at home in the hospitable house of the librettist Ludovic Halévy, being particularly intimate with the son, Daniel, whom he met regularly for lunch. Again, Pissarro, Jew and anarchist, was his close associate for years. But the Dreyfus case propelled Degas into virulent Jew hatred as he allowed himself to be captured by anti-Semitic propaganda and came to the defense of what he defined as French honor and the good name of the French army. If Daniel Halévy, a pacific and large-minded cosmopolitan, had not taken care to keep a flicker of their intimacy alive, they would never have met again after 1897, when the case, simmering for three years, monopolized the news and became a cause célèbre.[9] Degas seems to have had a glimmer that his position was irrational. When he called Pissarro's work ignoble and was reminded that he had once appreciated his work, he snapped, "Yes, but that was before the Dreyfus affair.[10] Yet this was only a fleeting insight.

On the other side, Monet was the most enthusiastic among the Dreyfusard painters, cheering on Zola's courageous journalism. After January 13, 1898, when Zola published his historic indictment, *J' accuse,* in *L'Aurore,* then with a circulation of 300,000 copies, Monet warmly congratulated his friend for his heroism. This was one side of his response; self-isolation was the other: Monet took the case hard. It has been persuasively argued that it made a private artist out of him; having once thought to celebrate his French homeland with his paintings, he now retreated to his garden and his hidden personal world.[11] For some avant-garde artists, the best way to deal with the burdens of politics was to deny them.

To retire from the public arena did not imply abandoning the cultural politics of conviction. There was always the charge that materialistic, conventional bourgeois artists lacked principle as much as talent. Zealous propagandists against such artists had in fact some disreputable incidents to bolster their case. Starting in 1856, the prominent, eminently successful English architect Sir Gilbert Scott, known for his neo-Gothic structures, conducted a craven campaign to secure the commission for a new Foreign Office building in Whitehall. In the competition Scott, backed by well-connected friends, had drawn up a proposal consistent with the rest of his work. But, finding the prime minister, Lord Palmerston, adamantly asking for a neoclassical façade, Scott, though continuing to argue for his original design, redid it several times to come closer to Palmerston's preferences. For the sake of his family, he said, he bought books on the "Italian" style, studied them closely, and came up with the required neoclassical drawings. He won the commission.[12]

The making of Amsterdam's Rijksmuseum, inaugurated with colorful official ceremonies in 1885, restaged this minor English tragicomedy almost scene by scene. In a competition of 1864, the Dutch architect P. J. H. Cuypers submitted a Gothic design, his specialty. He was lucky: while he did not obtain the first prize, the committee chose no other proposal. Eleven years later, at a second competition, Cuypers secured the commission—with a Renaissance building.[13] Only an exceptionally businesslike modernist would have been so subservient to market forces, even for good money; to settle for half a loaf or less was not prominent in their moral vocabulary. The crusades of A. W. N. Pugin, the leading Catholic architect of early Victorian England, suggest that there had been aesthetic fanatics in the nineteenth century before the 1880s. But with the quickening diffusion of modernism, its outrageousness only intensified as doctrines hardened.

Thoughtful Victorian observers, then, visualized their culture as no longer the tightly woven fabric they believed it to have been before the French Revolution; to their eyes it had taken on the appearance of a tattered tapestry in which some disordered strands hung disconnected from the rest. A culture in commotion was pulling cultural elements apart until some had gained the dubious distinction of going their own way. Artists, the complaint went, were liberating themselves from moral, religious, to say nothing of aesthetic constraints, following their urges with not a glance at social obligations, good manners, or centuries-old artistic prescriptions. The very multiplicity of modernist styles was a demonstration, and agent, of this turbulence.

In short, the disarray caused by money, urbanization, ideology, and politics was intensified by the reality that underlay all the others: pervasive change that dominated the bourgeois experience of the age—the irresistible though arduously resisted pressures on respectable middling people to make political, social, economic, technological, intellectual, and, with them, emotional adjustments. We cannot emphasize enough that this turmoil produced elevated levels of gratification and anxiety. That is why modernism was so tempting to some and so frightening to many. Late-nineteenth-century bourgeois were flustered not just by an increasingly discontented, organized, and politically active working class but quite as much, perhaps even more, by private conflicts.*

In these ceaseless earthquakes, some edgy responses were realistic enough, while others were the anxious fantasies of bourgeois shaken in their long-held certainties.† The assaults on Christian civilization launched in the Enlightenment and trumped by the upheavals starting in 1789, had touched all of Western society for good or ill. The politicians of the Restoration, Metternich in the lead, had made frantic efforts to return Europe to legitimist rulers, clerical dominance, and respect for a historic rank order. Bourgeois who welcomed this reaction might have taken comfort in the realization that the revolution had not made everything new. Not all its program had been realized, or even tried. Napoleon himself, posing as the heir of '89, retreated from many of his views once in power, and his successors, the restored Bourbons, valiantly labored to drag France back to the Old Regime. Thus divorce, a legacy from the early 1790s, was outlawed in 1816, soon after Louis XVIII ascended the throne, and reestablished only in 1884 after a long, venomous campaign against it. But with feminists, socialists, atheists, distributors of contraceptive information—and modernists—clamoring for a place in the sun and even winning converts, it was only reasonable to respond with attacks of agitation.

This was the atmosphere in which modernists could flourish. Accusations against them of fraud, filth, mystification, and arrogance were common, but these overreactions attest at once to the attractiveness and the fragility of tried-and-true ways in all the arts. To freer spirits among bourgeois, ready to take risks, a more flexible response suggested itself. In their time in which nothing

---

* The conflicts were of course not new, but their definition as an ailment was.

† Not all anxiety is irrational. It is a signal of danger real or imagined. No Victorian shopkeeper feeling vulnerable to the competition of a gigantic department store opening nearby, no owner of a stagecoach upset by seeing trains along his route going double his speed, no investor worrying over his shares of stock as the market drops, needed to justify his anxiety: all were anchored in solid facts. The anxieties of interest here are those whose causes were not obvious or where reactions far outweighed the provocation: these are clues to traumas concealed behind traumas openly acknowledged.

seemed secure, a flight to the new might be realistic and even enjoyable. There were so many subversives offering the lure of uncharted terrain, so many fascinating surprises within each genre!

4. Against the Need for Probability

It would not be practical to map, even in outline, the rich history of modernism. Two very different crafts, painting and architecture, may represent its conquering march and suggest the chaos on the battleground, the temporary alliances among contending parties, the unpredictable cultural politics of bourgeois factions, and the inconclusiveness of the outcome. This much we may generalize: however irritated modernists might grow with one another, they justified the upheavals they caused in technique, form, and content in almost identical ways. They were all obeying a sacred duty to burst the shackles that, they thought, cant and conventionality had fastened on Victorian culture. The promise of freedom lurked in all their pronouncements. "External laws do not exist," the Russian composer Thomas von Hartmann, one of Kandinsky's closest friends, proclaimed in 1912. "Everything against which the inner voice does not balk is permitted."[1] He was tersely epitomizing the modernist program.

A little earlier, Gauguin had summed up the collective aspirations of modernist painters by putting their critique into a single phrase. The Impressionists, he said, had been "shackled by the need for probability." Liberation from rules regulating permissible deviations from resemblance to nature would finally give the artist's most personal voice its proper due. As Gauguin saw it, the Impressionists had stopped fatefully short of being true modernists. For all their plein air technique, they had been the slaves of surfaces. Monet had noted that with the time of day and changes in the weather, the look of a painterly subject—an allée of poplars, a bridge in fog-bound London, the façade of Rouen cathedral—changed so rapidly that an artist who prolonged his sittings would impair his truthfulness. In the seventies and early eighties, aficionados of academic art still criticized the first Impressionists for hasty, slipshod work. Yet from Gauguin's perspective, the Impressionists were still, so to speak, taking orders from outside. Their name alone testified to that. Gauguin and, later, the Expressionists, the Fauves, and the others worked from the inside out. This reversal was a decisive element in the self-definition of modernism.

Gauguin, for one, had no compunction painting a crucified Christ with startling yellow skin, exhibiting his internal distress by portraying himself as a devil, baring his soul in emblematic Tahitian canvases complete with esoteric inscriptions. "According to Gauguin," wrote the French critic Marius Ary Leblond in 1904, the year after the painter's death, "all that is European— deviant, shriveled, anemic, niggardly, calculated—is inferior to what is savage, to the spontaneous and unconscious manifestations of primitive instinct." Deploying a charged metaphor, Leblond added that, to Gauguin, "European art is only the domestication, poisoning, and castration of our most natural and primordial instincts." He was speaking of an artist who, shedding all the con- straints of middle-class domesticity, repaid his wife's brave willingness to coun- tenance his desertion by calling her a "filthy bourgeoise."[2]

His was no doubt an extreme case. But less vehement bourgeoisophobes also challenged reasonableness, self-control, respect for manners, qualities that the middle classes had cultivated through the centuries and inculcated in their children, on canvas and in the concert hall. This was war. The artist's "unfet- tered freedom," Kandinsky asserted, "must rest on the basis of inner necessity (which we call honesty). And this principle is not merely that of art but that of life. This principle is the largest sword of the true superman against philistin- ism."[3] The echoes of Nietzsche, the hidden father of so much antibourgeois ideology, are audible, even obtrusive.

Good bourgeois who wondered where it might all end, then, had every right to worry. "The artistic style that was the inalienable property of the old days, collapsed catastrophically in the middle of the nineteenth century," wrote Franz Marc in *The Blue Rider,* glimpsing daylight for the triumph of art for self- revelation's sake. "Since then, there is no style left; as though gripped by an epi- demic, it is perishing all over the world."[4] He was overstating his case; what was so taxing was not that there were no styles left but that there were so many. The Fauves—André Derain, Maurice Vlaminck, and the young Henri Matisse—had gone to school to Gauguin and van Gogh but drove the assault on nature beyond them in their urban scenes and Mediterranean seascapes, electric with slashes of unnatural colors. In 1905, reviewing the Fauves, the critic and painter Maurice Denis described their canvases as "painting beyond all contingency, painting in itself, the pure act of painting."[5] The viewer of a Derain or a Vlam- inck done around this time could still easily identify its subject matter, but the Fauves made their treatment of nature a vehicle for self-disclosure.

To call painting a pure act was not an unqualified endorsement, but the cru- sade against probability built up steam as the Postimpressionists and their fol- lowers trained—or, rather, retrained—the viewing habits of the more adventurous art-loving bourgeois. In early 1914, Edvard Munch, whose own work had been upsetting middlebrow art lovers for more than a decade, won- dered, "Why does the new always shock people so much?" He quickly mod-

erated his astonishment at philistine objections to originality by acknowledging that at least some consumers of art were displaying an astonishing ability to
learn. It struck him as strange that only a few years ago, his paintings "had still
seemed to be revolutionary; now they are tame."[6] This might hold true of
Munch's pitiless, melancholy woodcuts, since their meaning was relatively easy
to absorb. But it would take years more before Picasso or Stravinsky could find
anyone to ascribe docility to their work.

As receptivity to experimentation mounted, it eased Franz Marc's escape
from the derivative academic portraits he had painted at the turn of the century to the yellow tigers, green cows, and, most famous of all, blue horses he
painted a decade later. In 1911, keenly aware that he had reached a new, unmistakably personal style, he justified its rejection of probability, that discredited
master: "There are no 'subjects' and no 'colors' in art," he informed his wife,
"but expression alone!"[7] Marc was offering an objective correlative to an
arcane private faith, but religion was not a necessary precondition of modernist
improbability. His friend August Macke was influenced far more by modernists
like the Fauves and the Futurists, and he, too, played with color in his lively
portraits, still lifes, city scenes, and landscapes.

The choice of unnatural colors was one approach to the vexing question just
how to free oneself from nature. To distort familiar objects like faces or houses
was an equally effective method and in the years after 1900 a well-traveled path
to inner freedom. Cézanne had for decades pioneered with his impossible
pieces of furniture, willful perspectives, and strangely "incorrect" human forms.
And in his lifetime, other modernist painters, in Cézanne's shadow or not,
invented new worlds that made commonplace perceptions unwelcome.

In this search for the uncommon, Munch's *The Scream*, worked out in several versions during the 1890s, much admired, much maligned, and—a sign of
its vitality—much parodied, acquired the stature of a modernist icon. A tormented figure stands on a bridge, holds his—or her?—hands pressed to both
cheeks, its face a crudely outlined, skull-like form, its mouth an eloquent "O";
in the famous colored lithograph version of 1898, the background of land and
sky highlights this moment of panic with sweeping, intense bands. The whole
seems pure hysteria captured in art.* *The Scream* was an early manifestation of
a modernist confession, which owed little to the outside world and virtually
nothing to historical precursors.

It is fitting that Expressionism should have emerged at the turn of the cen-

---

* *The Scream* was autobiographical: six years later Munch recalled that one evening on a walk,
tired and ill, he had seen "the clouds turning blood-red. I sensed a scream passing through nature;
it seemed to me that I heard the scream. I painted this picture, painted the clouds as actual blood.
The colour shrieked." Munch, Saint-Cloud diary, 1889, in J. P. Hodin, *Edvard Munch* (1972), 48.

tury. The painters who gathered under this imprecise but suggestive rubric came close to matching the antibourgeois animus of Gauguin. They produced a handful of picturesque, even cheerful canvases, but their prevailing mood was tortured, frantic, in some hands apocalyptic. "Never was any period so shaken by such horror, by such dread," wrote Hermann Bahr, the Austrian drama critic, playwright, and novelist who never met a trend he did not like. "Never had the world been so deathly silent. Never had man felt so small. Never had he been so afraid. His misery cries out to heaven: man cries for his soul, the whole period becomes one long cry for help. Art cries out too, cries in the depth of darkness, cries out for help, cries out for the spirit: that is Expressionism."[8] This overheated description was itself an Expressionist document: frenetic, inflated, only remotely related to contemporary realities—certainly not to bourgeois realities. But with its extravagance it suited the Expressionists' temper.

The list of Expressionists is long; their alienated and alienating shouts of conquest and pain—mostly pain—found a home in many arts other than painting: poetry, music, the novel, the theater. And they spawned little avant-garde periodicals imbued with a sense of mission. The Expressionists were an international band, but German artists took the lead. That was only to be expected: for a century and more, Germany had fostered artists and writers given to existential anguish even in painting; now German Expressionists sought to convey deep-seated angst with subjects from the tropics or, in contrast, the modern city, rendered with emphatic distortions and broad expanses of raw colors. As these Expressionists saw it, nineteenth-century bourgeois had been makers of rules, champions of repression; German Expressionists defied the first and tried to undo the second.

Naturally enough, though not quite so inevitably as abstract painters later intimated, sooner or later artists' raids on probability ended in its total repudiation. Not long before the outbreak of war, Kandinsky, Mondrian, and Robert Delaunay broke through to abstraction. All three had started their artistic careers with accomplished realistic renderings of their world. But as they proceeded, traces of recognizable subject matter grew ever more sparse. Finally, in 1910, Kandinsky produced paintings, noncommittally called "Compositions," that bore no resemblance to natural or manmade objects. By 1912, the Cubist Delaunay was experimenting with abstract *disques simultanés,* while Mondrian's trajectory to pure patterns was rather more deliberate, moving stage by stage toward his celebrated rectangles. The puzzled art lovers patient enough to look at such mysteries tried to solve the riddles these paintings set them until they discovered that they were not to be read but to be experienced. Abstract art was an attempt to have the inner world of the artist speak to the inner world of the viewer—directly.

Then there was Picasso, a one-man modernist movement all in himself. When in the fall of 1906, at twenty-five, he started on *Les Demoiselles d'Avignon,* he had already traversed several experimental phases, including the well-known Blue and Pink periods. As a precocious art student, groping to realize his incomparable gifts, he had shown himself uncommonly susceptible to visual impressions. In the paintings he saw in Barcelona, Madrid, and Paris, he missed nothing and exploited everything he could appropriate.* From the beginning, in life as in art, Picasso was a bourgeoisophobe in full flower. Whether young and poor or old and rich, he lived his life as he pleased. In ménages regulated by his desires, he consistently violated middle-class maxims. He slept with his models, frequented bordellos, discarded his mistresses for new recruits, neglected his children even as he posed them in appealing attitudes. He was, in short, the incarnation of the modernist artist as apprehensive bourgeois imagined him.

Not all of his behavior was a social or political protest; Picasso was wrestling with an intimate enemy, his father, a painter mediocre in talents and traditional in tastes. Though recognizing his son's superior endowment, he detested Picasso's choices of artistic ancestors, depictions of prostitutes and naked lovers, and ventures into Expressionist deformations with his emaciated harlequins and long-fingered proletarians. His father was, Picasso once said, "bourgeois, bourgeois, bourgeois."[9] That Picasso joined a group of Catalan artists who took the provocative name of Modernisme hardly improved matters at home.

Picasso was engaged in a classic domestic battle, but, being Picasso, he lent that private contest wider implications. *"En el arte hay que mater al padre,"* he once told a friend—"In art one must kill one's father."[10] Obviously, these recovered unconscious wishes, exceptionally intense as painter-son faced painter-father, no more explain Picasso's genius than can the Oedipus complex serve as the single motive for the avant-gardes' bellicosity toward the Victorian bourgeoisie. But it supplies motives for the intransigence of their language and strident emphasis on their distance from bourgeois tastes. Certainly Picasso's epochal *Les Demoiselles d'Avignon* attests that the modernists' differences with academic culture were irreconcilable.

Guillaume Apollinaire, Picasso's close friend and a stalwart among modernist poets, defined the task of art as "the perpetual immoral subversion of the exist-

* In 1901—Picasso was then twenty—a French reviewer listed the influences he saw in Picasso's early canvases: Goya, Delacroix, Manet, Monet, van Gogh, Pissarro, Toulouse-Lautrec, Degas, Forain, Rops: "each one a passing phase, taking flight as soon as caught." The list is ample but incomplete; it misses such classics as El Greco, just then emerging from the shadows of disdain, and above all Gauguin. See Félicien Fagus (pseud. of Georges Faillet), *Revue blanche* (July 15, 1901), in John Richardson, *A Life of Picasso,* vol. I, *The Early Years, 1881–1906* (1991), 199.

ing order."[11] With its schematic nudes, elongated forms, mask-like. primitive
heads, and distorted perspective, *Les Demoiselles* flawlessly fits this definition. As
though he had read Gauguin, Apollinaire praised the canvas as a masterpiece
that would "free art from its shackles."[12] But, though this painting has been read
as a modernist manifesto, its circulation was long restricted; for a long time
Picasso kept it in his studio rolled up and brought it out only for a handful of
favored visitors. The stages of his astonishing career remain a matter of some
debate, but it is safe to say that, in concert mainly with Braque, Picasso was
launching himself on an even more daring, and far more public, foray into
improbability: Cubism.

For all this alienating art, it was middle-class collectors who rescued Picasso from indigence and saved his career. Still in his twenties, the undisputed
leader of his circle in Paris, Picasso had admirers who were unfortunately as
poor as he. Quite as disheartening, his paintings of these years, exhibiting his
disquiet and indecisiveness, suggest a still unmastered ambivalence about his
true place among the elite. It is illuminating that after 1900 he should have visited Paris three times only to flee back to Spain, until early in 1904 he ventured into the capital of modernism once more, this time to stay. And not long
after he had settled in Paris, he met Gertrude Stein and her brother Leo, comfortably situated patrons with an eye for the modern and a knack for making
quick purchases.

The Steins represent in interesting ways the emotional style typical for
influential upper-middle-class patrons of modernism. To be sure, these patrons
occupied any number of niches in the mansion of respectability: Louisine
Havemeyer was perfectly at ease in New York's high society; William T. Walters,
a mainstay in Baltimore's business community. But this brother-sister pair were
outsiders among collectors tuned to the wavelength of outsiders among artists.
Leo Stein was learned, didactic, neurotic, perpetually in search of a vocation or
just an interest to hold his attention for more than a year or two; but, though
vacillating in his tastes, he was often prophetic in his enthusiasms. His sister
Gertrude was an even more archetypal alien in her world: a woman, a lesbian,
an expatriate, a practitioner of linguistic experiments that a few hailed as literary breakthroughs and most ridiculed as gibberish.

In an early fragmentary novel, a penetrating study of conflicts over high culture, Gertrude Stein showed a fond attachment to her prosperous German-Jewish family and to the adventure that was the bourgeois United States. "I am
strong to declare even here in the heart of individualistic America that a material middle class with its straightened bond of family is the one thing always
healthy, human, vital and from which has always sprung the best the world can
know." She acknowledged that there was nothing "more attractive than a strain

of singularity," but it must keep "within the limits of conventional respectability; a singularity that is so to speak well dressed and well set up." In a heartfelt little speech, Adele, the protagonist patterned on the author, offers a blanket alibi for bourgeois cultivation intended to undercut all-too-familiar attitudinizing: "You have a foolish notion that to be middle-class is to be vulgar, that to cherish the ideals of respectability and decency is to be commonplace and that to be the mother of children is low." To hold that someone refined could not be middle-class, Adele-Gertrude argued, was a "perverted" idea.[13] She was speaking for bourgeois values that, for all her idiosyncrasies, she never recanted.

After studying with William James at Harvard and then medicine at Johns Hopkins, she settled in Paris with her difficult brother, and it was not until their ménage broke up that she came fully into her own. Early on, she had gone through an unsatisfying lesbian affair. Now, liberated by the broad-minded air of her adopted home, she established a lifelong partnership with Alice B. Toklas, another prosperous American who visited Paris and stayed. It was in its way an old-fashioned middle-class household, which exemplified the "straightened bond of family" with Gertrude Stein as the masculine head of the family and Alice Toklas as the recessive "housewife." In her autobiography, Stein observed that during her Saturday night salons, crowded with modern painters and poets, she would talk to the geniuses while Alice talked to their wives. Her life was a model of conventional unconventionality. Yet, if at heart she always remained a bourgeoise, she was a bourgeoise with a difference: she bought Picassos.

Leo Stein took care to claim that he had anticipated her when, in the fall of 1905, he brought home a Picasso, which (he conveniently recalled) made her sick. Not for long: on her first visit to Picasso's studio, accompanied by her brother, she agreed to spend 800 francs on his paintings and drawings. Quickly she assumed and faithfully carried through the twin roles of discriminating patron and devoted friend. Significantly, when brother and sister dissolved their joint household and divided their collection, she held on to practically all the Picassos. She had him do a portrait of her—it took him over eighty sessions and, with repainting, more than a year—and enjoyed his company in confidential chats. They talked art and gossip; she would listen sympathetically when he needed it, as he often did.

Gertrude Stein did more for Picasso than this: she introduced him to Dr. Claribel and Etta Cone, mutually devoted sisters whom she had known since her Baltimore days. Like her they were well-to-do, like her of German-Jewish descent, like her willful and eccentric. On their frequent trips to Paris, they bought unconventional art, with Matisse as their favorite and Picasso a close second. Their collection, which they bequeathed to the Baltimore Museum of

Art, discreetly stopped short of Cubism: of the forty-six Picassos they bought before the war, more than half of them drawings, virtually all had been done around 1905 and 1906.

The two enterprising Russian collectors we have met before, Sergei Shchukin and Ivan Morosov, both infected by modernism, had few such hesitations. Shchukin, repeatedly in Paris to attend exhibitions and visit dealers, met Picasso around 1906 and in 1908 bought his early Cubist *Woman with a Fan*. Other recent works followed. Though rounded out by representative canvases from the Blue Period, nearly all of Shchukin's eleven Picassos date from the years of Analytical Cubism. Morosov, who met the painter through his friendly rival, was rather more reserved: he bought only three Picassos. But, as art critics have noted, each was first-rate, one from the Blue Period, a second from the Pink Period, and the third, from 1910, a masterly Cubist portrait of Picasso's dealer Ambroise Vollard. The picture was simply irresistible.[14]

Picasso's work was then as controversial as ever, perhaps more so; in September 1911, the Parisian art critic Gabriel Mourey prophesied the demise of Cubism, that appalling display of "pretentious impotence and self-satisfied ignorance."[15] But by that time Picasso could afford to abandon the bohemian life, and it had been bourgeois collectors—the Steins and the Cones—who had freed him.

The ascendancy of modernist architecture came at a more deliberate pace than that of modernist painting and was even more circuitous in its progress. The vogue of historicism, the eclectic Victorian adaptations of Gothic or Renaissance styles, found its earliest critics before mid-century, but unconventional architects did not have enough clients until the 1890s and even later. The nineteenth-century passion for revivals was slow to leave the stage; daring proposals to explore new materials like cast iron generally met with bland indifference or agitated sabotage. But not all naysayers were bourgeois, not all modernists bourgeoisophobes.

Architecture is obviously the most public monument to current cultural values, their inner tensions as much as their dominance; in his widely read *The Seven Lamps of Architecture,* first published in 1849, John Ruskin called it a "distinctively political art."[16] Not counting a handful of exceptions like the Futurist Antonio Sant'Elia, who drew his utopian sketches for a modern city just before the First World War, designs left on the drawing board had little impact. Just as obviously, the architect needs clients before he can translate his sketches into the hard realities of brick, wood, steel, and glass. Modernist buildings required much money, ample time, and open-minded taste, whether those who commissioned them were industrialists or businessmen, bureaucrats, clerics, or private enthusiasts. To invest in an office building or a house that departed from reigning fashion was to make an audacious and principled commitment.

Like other purveyors of high culture, modernist architects were in a minority addressing a minority; surviving evidence leaves little doubt that most Victorian builders and their clients were perfectly satisfied to make conventional choices. Whether they lived in an apartment or a house, middling people wanted shelter as commodious as they could afford and as easy to keep up as possible. In 1864, summing up in a substantial treatise what an English gentleman would want in a house, Robert Kerr, a prolific and authoritative commentator on the architectural scene, listed three essential requirements: "Quiet comfort for his family and guests,—Thorough convenience for his domestics,—Elegance and importance without ostentation." None of these necessarily gave an opening to originality: Kerr has a baffled English client say that he wants "no style at all but the comfortable style, if there be one." This was a swipe at middling public taste; William Morris used the same language to lash out at the class into which he had been born: his parents had lived, he wrote in 1883 with marked disapproval, in "the ordinary bourgeois style of comfort."[17]

The requirements of most bourgeois, then, were simple apart from some vague notions about beauty, practical requirements like a well appointed kitchen, and the longing for a small garden. They struck modernists as singularly unaesthetic. Nineteenth-century critics of contemporary architectural taste were very severe—some thought, too severe—with the housing that average bourgeois seemed to find only too acceptable, houses thrown together by speculative builders that struck the sophisticated as dreary, monotonous, lacking all imagination. That the middle classes seemed to like them was all the more disheartening.

Some vexed connoisseurs spoke with the authority of the passionate, well-informed amateur. "The greatest writers on architecture," the notable progressive Glaswegian architect Charles Rennie Mackintosh said after 1890, "are not architects." But most of the unhappy modernists were practicing professionals, so that their criticism was in large part self-criticism. And, in a style typical for the Victorian bourgeois mentality, it was criticism soaked with sententious moralizing. Even Kerr, hardheaded as he was, preferred the Gothic to the Renaissance style because it was "truthful and sincere."[18]

Ruskin had anticipated him. Though not himself an architect, he was by far the most widely read and widely cited among Victorian commentators, even across the Channel. In *The Stones of Venice,* parts of which William Morris hailed as "one of very few necessary and inevitable utterances of the century," he denounced Renaissance construction as absurd and, worse, as dishonest: *"it is the moral nature of it which is corrupt. "* If he firmly came down on the side of the Gothic style, this was not a plea for revivalism; it simply impressed him as more truthful than the fashionable "Italian." In general, he thought honesty all too rare in his age, as he bemoaned the tricks of builders and the obtuseness of their clients. It was only too characteristic of modern work, he wrote, to be less than the best; the most "contemptible" violation of architectural truth was the widespread use of one material to sham the look of another.[19]

Ruskin was no Manet, but he could see the value of being of one's time. The yeast of modernist hostility to tradition was working in him, surreptitiously but effectively. "There is no law, no principle, based on past practice," he wrote in a memorable paragraph of The Seven Lamps of Architecture, "which may not be overthrown in a moment, by the arising of a new condition, or the invention of a new material."[20] It was the engineers, deaf to the caveats of conservatives, who had all along been constructing bridges and, later, office buildings with whatever seemed useful and safe: cast iron, wrought iron, steel, and, toward the end of the century, reinforced concrete. They made it plain, even to aestheticians, that efficiency and beauty need not be sharply segregated. The French in particular, goaded on by Eugène Emmanuel Viollet-le-Duc—superb scholar and historian, notorious restorer, trained architect, and encyclopedic author—built churches and libraries out of iron and, after 1900, apartment houses with concrete.

The Eiffel Tower, completed in 1889 for an international exhibition in Paris, offered living testimony to the impact that engineers were bound to have on taste in architecture. It also proved a pawn in the wars over taste; 984 feet high, for many years the tallest structure in the world, it was an immediate and immense popular success. Tourists from Paris and elsewhere enjoyed the splendid views it commanded, liked the food in its restaurants, or simply took in its monumental presence as they picnicked under it. By the time the exposition closed, more than three and half million people had visited it and paid a stupefying six million francs for the privilege.[21] Contemporary photographs show that many in these crowds were well-dressed bourgeois.

Even so, the Eiffel Tower scandalized writers and artists, who signed a protest against it—in vain. As so often, advanced spirits were on every side of the question. Pissarro waxed sarcastic about it, and Huysmans denounced it almost incoherently as a "wickered bottle," a "solitary suppository" and "gravy-colored ironmongery."[22] But Seurat painted it in 1889, with no sign of disapproval, showing its reddish rustproofing gleaming in the sun. Some twenty years later, Delaunay, who had long been preoccupied with Eiffel's masterpiece, gave it the Cubist treatment. He lent it a pinkish color and flanked it with imaginary skyscrapers; partly exploding and partly collapsing the tower, he made the solidly anchored structure dance a little drunkenly—an accolade to modernity.

At times, architects engaged in self-criticism sounded like full-fledged bourgeoisophobes. In 1869, in a lecture to the Royal Institute of British Architects,
Kerr linked the deceptive practices common among architects to those rampant in society as a whole. "If we architects are guilty of so much that is spurious in artistic principle, there must be for this effect a corresponding and
equivalent cause. Is there not here and there, in matters besides architecture,
and in perhaps, much more important matters, a good deal of more or less spurious sentiment? Do we not live in the very age of spurious sentiment? History, philosophy, law, politics, poetry—is there not but too much of spuriousness
in every one of these? Faith, hope, even charity, are they not conventional to
the core? And if we, as custodians of an art whose essential attribute it is to
reflect the character of the time, reflect this character all too faithfully, what less
than this and what else than this, could we be expected to do?"[23] True, architecture advertised the glories of culture, he thought, but it just as visibly
unmasked its defects.

In time the sport of denouncing architectural mendacity degenerated into
a platitude equally available to all parties. Each polemicist singled out his
favorite style for its sincerity. The Victorian architect J. J. Stevenson held, with
no sense of incongruity, that England's eclectic Queen Anne style had "the
merit of truthfulness; it is the outcome of our common modern wants pic-
turesquely expressed," a "common vernacular style" with "some new life from
Gothic added."[24] True modernism did not lie that way. But the campaign for
honest construction with honest materials retained its appeal. In the right
hands it was heartfelt and specific enough to inspire efforts at rethinking the
principles of architecture literally from the ground up.

With severe reservations about the past, antihistoricist critics argued that
although many of the famous buildings strewn across Europe were admirable
enough in their way, one could learn mainly from their shortcomings. In 1891,
Mackintosh visited Italy, equipped with a sketch pad and trained judgment, and
in the following year he reported his findings to his countrymen. The much
visited cathedral of Siena, he sternly told them, was "a fine example of the
beauties and peculiarities of Italian Gothic," with its front "one of those frauds
as often seen in Italy, having evidently been considered quite independent &
apart from the rest of the church."[25] He was preaching one of the weightiest
lessons that modernists were beginning to acquire: good architecture means
marrying the inside and the outside of a building.

In his lectures, Mackintosh strung together the commonplaces favored by
antibourgeois artists confronting an obtuse and reactionary society. He called
attention to "the great struggle that must always . . . continue to be waged by
the advocates of individuality, freedom of thought and personal expression on

the one hand and the advocates of tradition and authority on the other." The
latter, many of them prominent architects, "imagine they are helping on the
cause of our art whereas they are retarding it by feebly imatating some of the
visable and superficial features of beautiful old works and neglecting the spirit, the intention, the soul that lies beneath." He lamented "the bad taste, want
of thought, lack of appreciation—the vulgarity of the public—of the ordinary
man in the street," and called on his listeners to be "independant—independant—independant."[26] However derivative his rhetoric, in a decade of feverish
creativity around the turn of the century, Macintosh left his mark on Glasgow.

He could do so because he got what he needed: discriminating and risk-
taking clients. In the late 1890s, he was the architect for the Glasgow School of
Design, strongly supported against local opposition by its principal, Francis
("Fra") H. Newbery, who, with justice, trusted the young Mackintosh's gifts.
The school Mackintosh designed was as practical, as clearly articulated, as any
in his time, at once severe and playful, making barely a concession to neoclassical or Gothic touches. Mackintosh's much admired tearooms for Catherine
Cranston came soon after. Working closely with his wife, Margaret Macdonald, he designed interiors for them that still command admiration. The name
for these establishments was too modest for their scope: they included lunch
and billiard rooms and were frequented as much by gentlemen as by ladies.[27]
Featuring Art nouveau wall decorations and much copied chairs with narrow,
elongated backs, these stylish rooms were an eloquent expression of the independence their designer had called for. There is no evidence that Miss
Cranston lost customers by her courageous choice of architect. She made a discovery that other, equally open-minded clients were making: startling designs
and profitable returns were compatible.

The patrons who gave modernist architecture its opportunity resembled
each other only in their ability to finance costly projects. Before the First World
War, Walter Gropius recalled much later, architects were limiting their practice
mainly to "the small circle of the affluent."[28] But they differed in everything
else, whether in politics or religion. Gaudí's late-nineteenth-century patrons,
clustered in fast-growing Barcelona, were bankers, industrialists, and shipping
magnates anxious to revive Catholicism in an age of rampant unbelief throughout Spain's urban centers. In close rapport with the local clergy, they called for
nothing less than a Catalan Renaixença, an intellectual, artistic, and religious
renaissance. The villas, apartment houses, and gardens that Gaudí designed for
these millionaires, bizarre and unforgettable with their boldly curved façades,
irregular floor plans, and flamboyant tiled decor, were all highly personal creations. They may remind viewers of neo-Gothic, Art nouveau, medieval Spanish, or primitive African architecture, but above all they proclaimed Gaudí's

unique genius. His best-known religious building in Barcelona, an astonishing cathedral, begun in 1884 and still not completed, stands as a tribute as much to his imagination as to the Sagrada Familia it so devoutly celebrates.

Industrialists elsewhere underwrote modernist originality for more secular reasons. In 1907, Germany's largest supplier of electrical equipment, the Allgemeine Elektrizitäts-Gesellschaft (AEG) appointed Peter Behrens, much sought after for private houses and public buildings, as its artistic adviser.* In this capacity, he designed typefaces and light bulbs for AEG and, more conspicuously, factories. The most distinguished of these, an impressive synthesis of steel, concrete, and abundant glass surfaces, was a turbine factory of 1909, much admired and often published as a pioneering experiment in honest, sparsely ornamented functionalism.

For the apprentice architect Walter Gropius, then working in Behrens's studio, the monumentality of that important structure, emphasized in the bulky corners of its façade, was an impurity to be eradicated. All his life he acknowledged Behrens as his teacher, but in his own designs he aimed at what he called "floating lightness."[29] The Fagus shoe-last factory at Alfeld-an-der-Leine, designed in 1911 after he had left Behrens, was the consummate exemplar of this pure modernism.† Gropius achieved unprecedented transparency in the Fagus building through the freest possible use of glass, extreme simplification of floor plans, and structural experiments such as internal weight-bearing piers that left windows to meet at the corners unobstructed.

It bears repeating that this rebuff of tradition required the cooperation of an enthusiastic client with his designer. And, unless the client was an obstinate, intrusive amateur architect like Alfred Krupp, he and the architect had to conduct a dialogue that subtly made the artist the senior partner. There were enough late Victorians to feed the impetus for an architectural revolution. We have the correspondence of Cecil Fitch, an English barrister, with his architect Voysey. He candidly discussed the program for his house and freely offered suggestions, which for the most part Voysey rejected, giving his reasons in brusque sentences but satisfying detail. "All artistic questions you must trust me to decide," he wrote Fitch in November 1899. "No two minds ever produced an artistic result."[30] And his client understood, nor did he try to subvert, this proud declaration of primacy. Plainly, Fitch was the client of every architect's dreams—ideal but not unique.

One historic innovator who for some years enjoyed such gratifying junior

---

* It remains uncertain whether Emil Rathenau, the president of AEG, or Paul Jordan, his director, were chiefly responsible for this imaginative appointment, but it hardly matters: both were men of modern industry.

† We must not omit to mention his partner Adolf Meyer.

partners was Frank Lloyd Wright. Born in 1867, at twenty-one he joined the firm of Adler and Sullivan, two trailblazing architects whose skyscrapers were arousing interest well beyond Chicago. It was a time of valuable apprenticeship for Wright, but in 1893 he struck out on his own and for the next two decades had more commissions, mainly for private houses, than even he, proverbial for his energy, could easily handle. In his "prairie houses" Wright rarely repeated himself, but a distinct look bore his unmistakable signature. They were, to use one of his favorite epithets, "organic," strongly related to their surroundings and articulating inner spaces that opened into one another.*

The midwesterners who entrusted themselves to this iconoclast have been subjected to exhaustive scrutiny, and the results are extremely interesting.[31] Wright would gain notoriety for his unbourgeois way of life—in 1909, he deserted his wife and six children and fled to Europe with a client's wife—and, in later years, for his pose of grandiloquent cultural critic who liked to sound off about decadent American culture. But for nearly twenty years his clients found him accessible, charming, prompt, and, what mattered even more to them, careful with their money. In short, he was businesslike to a fault, the kind of person his clients liked to deal with. He rarely ran over budget.

The cost of Wright's houses ranged from $4,500 to $35,000, calling for modest to considerable affluence, but the leading Chicago millionaires turned to more conventional architects for their mansions. A survey of forty among Wright's early clients shows them to have been virtually all Protestants and businessmen and, a smaller number, in the liberal professions. Almost all were Republicans. Though for the most part relatively progressive in their politics— many of them supported woman suffrage—they were not tempted by Democratic liberalism, and strongly preferred Theodore Roosevelt to Woodrow Wilson. Inventive, usually enthusiastic about modern machinery, they liked to tinker and had no inhibitions about Wright's untraditional designs. He in turn would accommodate them by making a workshop part of their house. Though they preferred golf to strenuous reading, many of them were musical; the sizable living rooms (if one may speak of a "room" in Wright's flowing floor plans) were stages for domestic violin, piano, or voice recitals, often by the lady of the house.

Unlike other self-proclaimed geniuses among architects, Wright did not condescend to such clients; on the contrary, he found them far more appealing

---

* As he later summed up his credo, he aimed to make rooms flow into one another, thus getting away from old-fashioned boxlike enclosures and flooding them with light; harmonize the inside of his houses with their exterior; reduce the variety of their materials to the fewest possible; stress their horizontality with wide overhanging roofs; integrate furnishings with the architecture, and thus manage to get away from interior decorators.

than the highly educated gentlemen whom one might suppose—wrongly—to have been his ideal supporters. The businessman with whom he liked most to work, Wright wrote in 1908, had "unspoiled instincts and untainted ideas" and "the faculty of judging for himself." While "the 'cultured' are still content with their small châteaux, Colonial wedding cakes, English affectations or French millinery," he added drily, his typical client "prefers a poor thing but his own. He errs on the side of character, at least." History would show, he predicted, that this "man of business" had aided the progress of architecture in America. As far as Frank Lloyd Wright could see in 1908, this conventional, prosperous bourgeois was the true champion of modernism—at least his modernism.

An intriguing thought, but apparently valid only for a time. After literally scores of striking successes, Wright found his commissions drying up. His support had been wide but not deep; mixtures of styles reclaimed the terrain they had lost, and it took decades before Wright, sadly neglected, reestablished his reputation and became the grand old man of American architecture. And if the vicissitudes of Wright's seesaw career were more spectacular than those facing other modernists, they were typical enough for their time.

We may conclude that the course of true modernism, like that of true love, never did run smooth. Its victories were nullified by defeats, its defeats erased by victories, its sharp contours evened out by the truces we call eclecticism. The anxiety of bourgeois triumphant in their time, as caricatured in plays, novels, and paintings, has helped to confuse history and historians. In one of his wise aphorisms, Degas once said, "There is a sort of success that is undistinguishable from panic."[32] But not all bourgeois panicked all of the time. Doctrinaire modernism, resolute antimodernism, unstable compromises: the Victorian bourgeoisie was vitally implicated in all three—enduring, even enjoying, modernist earthquakes not least of all. Authors of specialized monographs on individual painters or composers schools have recognized that Victorian bourgeois were active on all sides in the making of twentieth-century art, music, and literature. But the perception of bourgeois as the unreconstructed, philistine champions of ossified taste, as antimodernists incarnate, has retained its prestige to this day.

One memorable exemplar of this persistent misreading is a novel by Frans Coenen, curator of the museum that Abraham Willet and Louisa Holthuysen had left to their city of Amsterdam late in the nineteenth century.* Looking back at that Victorian couple and their world in a transparent roman à clef deceptively titled *Impersonal Recollections,* Coenen reiterated the reigning view

---

* We have met them before; see above, p. 157.

of the mid-nineteenth-century middle class: "All these stiff and stately bourgeois ladies and gentlemen lived very formal, very conformist lives: they did
the things it was proper to do, thought the thoughts it was proper to think.
Their desires, too, conformed to rule, as did their pleasure and their pain, their
happiness or unhappiness. Thus it was the right thing to do to think highly of
art and culture and to 'have a hand' in them—in proportion to one's means."[33]

As the preceding pages have abundantly shown, this verdict is far too mean-
spirited, far too partisan, far too mechanical to capture the rich diversity of
bourgeois experience in the pleasure wars roiling the Victorian and post-Victorian arts. Bourgeois contributed many a stone to that vast and colorful mosa-
ic we call modernism, and a good number of them, though prone to attacks of
mixed feelings, exemplified what Baudelaire once called, without irony, the
heroism of modern life.

CODA

A Bourgeois Experience

Historical explorations have a way of setting their own agenda, dragging the historian along with them. True, the psychology of research has established that all too often historians, like other scientists, start with their conclusions already settled in their minds. But they must be aware of, and at best they obey, their professional ideal of respecting the pressure of the material they have unearthed. This calls for rethinking, perhaps rejecting, their premature judgments. The past, in short, holds its surprises, unwelcome only to the lazy or the doctrinaire. When, literally a quarter century ago, after concentrating for almost twenty years on the Enlightenment, I turned my attention to nineteenth-century high culture, I had no idea that my new commitment would last so long and bulk so large.

More important, I did not foresee the shape that the series would assume, even the topics it would cover. My collective title, *The Bourgeois Experience: Victoria to Freud,* states with fair accuracy the intentions I gradually clarified for myself: I was trying to understand a distinct class in a specified age with particular emphasis on its passions and its prejudices, its self-scrutinies and its tastes embedded in its economic, political, and social world. But that title forced itself on me only in the mid-1970s, after years of drastic revisions and unexpected reversals. The first outlines I had drawn up became virtually unrecognizable. At the outset, I failed to foresee not only the answers I would eventually reach but the questions I would find it necessary to ask. Now, with the task done—I am, with this volume, declaring it done—I look back on the history of this history with some astonishment.

In 1971, having decided to exchange the eighteenth century for the nineteenth, I assigned myself an agreeable, downright self-indulgent project: I would commit myself to several years with the late-Victorian icons who led Western culture into modernism. The protagonists elected themselves with ease: Henry and William James, Edouard Manet and Paul Cézanne, William Morris and Walter Gropius, Henrik Ibsen and Bernard Shaw, Emile Zola and James Joyce, Gustav Mahler and Richard Strauss, perhaps even Arnold Schoenberg. My researches would compel me to count as work reading and rereading great novels and going to serious concerts, exhibitions, or plays. To be sure, I planned to subject these giants of the arts and thought to the discipline of rigorous and skeptical investigation, to discard anecdotes or plot summaries in favor of the strenuous study of an evolving culture. It was to be work, no doubt, but the process of detection, analysis, and presentation would be uninterrupted pleasure; my self-critical qualifying epithet, "self-indulgent," was deserved.

Then, after three or four years of writing lectures and leading seminars on my new specialty, my research drove me to alter my course. I would eventually make room for my favorite painters or novelists, but in a strikingly different context. I came to recognize that rereading Dickens or mastering Mahler's symphonies was actually keeping me from seeing a splendid historical subject right before my eyes, the bourgeoisie, which had been insufficiently mapped and tendentiously treated. Not that I acquired overnight a political perspective on the role of the middle classes in Victorian culture. That came later, although even then I did not conceive of these volumes as a rescue operation. All that first dawned on me was that the inner life of the Victorian bourgeoisie needed its historian. In a characteristic, overworked paradox—I quoted it in 1984, in the first volume of this series, *Education of the Senses*—Lytton Strachey said, "The history of the Victorian Age will never be written: we know too much about it." Quite the contrary, I found that we really knew too little about that age, and often the wrong things.

Shortly after the end of the Second World War, social history garnered enormous prestige, and would enjoy an exceptionally long run. One impetus was the assimilation among English-speaking historians of the *Annales* school, principally through the publications of Marc Bloch, whose grasp on medieval society in all its manifestations and whose unsurpassed ability to synthesize the most diverse phenomena—religious movements and place-names, politics and geography, the role of play and of passing time—became models to the profession.

Another impulse was if anything stronger still: a kind of populist mentality often (though not necessarily) married to a left-wing political persuasion. Many historians entering the craft in the late 1940s were impatient with the narrow perspective—they called it the elitism—of their elders, who by and large singled out the leading actors in history for study. In stark contrast, the postwar generation valued the neglected and the despised—women, peasants, working people, religious and racial minorities—quite as much as the famous and the powerful, quite as worthy to be preserved for the collective memory. In their view, there had been astonishingly little expansion of historians' horizons since 1860, when Jacob Burckhardt published his pathbreaking *Civilization of the Renaissance in Italy,* and Burckhardt, though impressively imaginative in raising hitherto invisible topics to what was called "historical dignity," had confined his researches to a literate minority. For their part, then, social historians focused on the poor and the inarticulate, and elevated the unemployed, children in orphanages, strikers, and, best of all, revolutionaries into their folk heroes; it almost seemed to their old-fashioned colleagues that the poorer the poor or the more rebellious the rebels, the higher the status of the historian deciphering often barely legible messages. The social historian made himself— and, more and more often, herself—into an anthropologist of the past.

I am not offering this sketch in order to minimize the contribution of the new social historians to the mastery of the past. Much of the history they wrote was highly original in choice of subject and methods of analysis and thus widened the boundaries of research in remarkable ways. But one consequence of their deliberate self-limitation was a relative disregard of the bourgeoisie. There was no antibourgeois conspiracy of silence; the supply of solid volumes dealing with the middle classes did not dry up. But the main expenditure of social historians' talents and energies led distinctly away from a class that had been problematic all the way back to Aristotle and that, the legend went, had taken power in the nineteenth century.

Here, then, was my opportunity. It beckoned me to inquiries bound to be less easy than reading, seeing, or listening to masterpieces, but the gain to historical knowledge seemed to me potentially sizable. As I had done all my professional life, once again I responded to the promptings of blank spaces or puzzling notations on the map to which the extant literature offered few, or few satisfactory, clues.

My sense, inchoate at first, that a study of the Victorian bourgeoisie was the right path to follow, only intensified as I surveyed historical commentaries on Victorian bourgeois sexuality. Until a handful of specialists entered the lists in the mid-1970s, opinion on respectable erotic life had gone through three distinct phases: a shamefaced silence among contemporary social observers broken only in fairly outspoken but esoteric and largely inaccessible treatises by medical specialists. This was followed among the Edwardians by disdainful, implicitly self-praising exposés of Victorian middle-class hypocrisy and revelations about lecherous husbands, frigid wives, and flourishing bordellos.

Then, after the Second World War, exploiting a newly licensed freedom of expression, historians simply reiterated their predecessors' contempt for what they were pleased to call nineteenth-century middle-class cant and materialism, if in far franker language and far more scurrilous detail. In their tracts about "madonnas and magdalens" or about "other Victorians," at once solemn and spicy, they gleefully embroidered the harshest lampoons of the uncultivated and lustful bourgeois but kept them essentially unchanged. Yet, as I sifted through the nineteenth-century literature on which these modern judgments were presumably based, I could not evade the conclusion that most recent publications were poorly researched and poorly argued, antibourgeois clichés dressed up as scholarship. These commentators largely, it seemed, read one another.[1] Something more—or, better, something else—was needed.

Finding my subject, the bourgeoisie, was a vital step in the direction of what was to become *The Bourgeois Experience*. And, since I had been interested in Freud from the early 1950s on, his angle of vision commended itself for a probe of the bourgeoisie's inner life, especially since proper Victorians were taciturn about matters that meant the most to them. Hence the problem of unearthing enough intimate material was not so quickly solved.

Then two things happened that eased my difficulties. The first was a fortunate accident waiting to happen. One evening my wife, then an archivist at the Yale Archives and Manuscripts, came home with a photocopy of the first page of a mid-nineteenth-century American diary. It was certain, she said, to interest me. And it did, immensely: it was the opening of a retrospective journal that Mabel Loomis Todd, a writer and lecturer living at Amherst with her husband and daughter, had composed, beginning with the moment that David Todd had impregnated her. Not even a French novel would have been this circumstantial. The next morning, I rushed to the archives to inspect Mabel Todd's papers to have a treasure spread out before me: her pocket diary, her journal for longer entries, her letters, all striking in their lack of reserve, enriched by no less explicit and no less detailed documentation by her husband, an astronomer at Smith College, and her lover, Austin Dickinson, Emily Dickinson's brother. The whole made it possible for me to reconstruct the erotic activity, and to recover much of the emotional entanglements, of this triangle.

Since such rich, personal evidence from generally reticent bourgeois really did exist, I told myself, there must be other instances of it, and from then on I searched for them in libraries and archives at home and abroad, and enlisted colleagues in my explorations. And I located more than I had ever hoped for. The first volume of my series, *Education of the Senses* (1984), which details and analyzes these discoveries, now stood before me in my mind, as did the closely related follow-up volume, *The Tender Passion* (1986), on love. All I needed to do was to write them.

The second event was having a friend persuade me in the mid-1970s to register as a candidate in the Western New England Institute for Psychoanalysis. The lengthy and intensive training on which I then embarked would make me, as it were, a professional in a field in which I had been a fairly well-read amateur for more than twenty years. My venture in adult education proved to be exciting, informative, and wholly satisfactory. Controlled by my historian's regard for the weight of the outside world (a point to which I shall return), psychoanalytic training gave me the framework for this series, directed me at last to the questions I must ask, and even suggested some of the answers.

It is this aspect of my work that has aroused the most persistent criticisms of the *Bourgeois Experience*. With some delightful exceptions, the reviews of its several volumes have fallen into a repetitive pattern: a measure of praise for the "straight" history they contain and an expression of vexation at my apparently heavy reliance on the ideas of Freud.* I say "apparently," because I have always rejected reductionist explanations and insisted on the causal significance of the external world for historical events or epochs. And it seems to have escaped these critics that in my work the two, conventional history and psychoanalytic interpretations, are inextricably intertwined and that there would not have been the first without the second.

I should, I suppose, take wry comfort in being the target of two extremes: of "ordinary" historians for being too committed to Freud and of psychohistorians for not being committed enough. But while such an exposed position was a temptation to seek refuge in the illusion of being a brave, lonely pioneer, rather like an avant-garde artist feeling persecuted by conventional powers that be, I continued to find psychoanalytic thought illuminating on strictly pragmatic grounds: it worked for me and thus eventually, I trust, would work for my readers. It shed light into obscure corners of grounds for action and for complex responses, and thus resolved perplexities that other auxiliary disciplines had left unexplained.

Apart from some currently fashionable assaults on Freud's character, most of the controversies that have swirled around him for a century have focused on his clinical practice. The old (and groundless) charge dating back to the 1920s that Freud was Dr. Sex who advocated libertinism as a cure for every mental

---

* I should note that when I say "Freud," I do not mean his writings alone. Much has happened since his death, and much has been modified, even by "orthodox" psychoanalysts. This cannot be the place where I defend the substantial validity of psychoanalytic propositions. I have done so with special regard to their value to historians, in *Freud for Historians* (1985). Two careful and detailed surveys will help: Paul Kline, *Fact and Fantasy in Freudian Theory* (1972; 2nd ed., 1981), and Seymour Fischer and Roger P. Greenberg, *The Scientific Credibility of Freud's Theories and Therapy* (1977).

distress has faded. But the analyst as clinician remains a source of inconclusive debate. This is perfectly understandable. The countless cartoons showing the analyst listening to his patient lying before him have established a public perception in which troubled humans necessarily take a strong interest.

Actually Freud's ambition was far grander than to assuage the sufferings of neurotics. Of course, the psychoanalytic situation remained at center stage for him, the source and the test of hypotheses. The couch was Freud's laboratory. But he aspired most of all to a general psychology that would apply to "normal" people as much as to neurotics, men as much as women, ancient Greeks as much as contemporary Trobrianders. That is why he wrote his first major book not on the neuroses, on which he was an expert, but on dreams, a common occurrence for every human being throughout history. He was aiming at nothing less than a theory of human nature.

It was this theory—or, perhaps more modestly, this inspired sketch—that has made Freud so congenial to me. No doubt he did not fully succeed, burdened as he was with the inescapable limitations of a single lifetime, and with certain time-bound attitudes, like his indefensible notions about female sexuality. No doubt a great deal of research needs to be done to flesh out his hints, to confirm—or disconfirm—his generalizations. Especially the crucial domain of social psychology, which Freud thought practically indistinguishable from individual psychology, demands much further consideration. Freud's system contains, half concealed, a theory of politics, a theory of art, and, even more daunting, a theory of culture. His *Civilization and Its Discontents* is justly famous for its portrait of the individual in perpetual conflict with society, and of the combat between the forces of life and death, but its implications have never been seriously pursued. We may read the little book as a program for future theorists of culture. Yet, for all its unfinished state, the psychoanalytic view of human nature strikes me as far more persuasive than any competing theory of the mind now available to investigators, whether they are historians, social scientists, or literary scholars.

These students of humanity and its works—philosophy, literature, music, art, houses, entertainments, wars, constitutions, treaties, factories, religions, crimes, commercial ventures, sexual mores—consistently act as amateur psychologists. Certainly historians intent on explaining the *experience* of their subjects, as I have been in these volumes, require as firm a grip on motivation, mastery, and inner discord as they can muster. In the introduction to my first volume, I defined experience as "an encounter of mind with world," and can do no better than to repeat it here. Freud has often been accused of fathering a hermetic doctrine from which external realities are screened out; the psychoanalyst's double doors to his consulting room have been made to serve as the ominous symbol of Freudian arcana. But this indictment gravely misreads his thought. In his post-1920 map of the mind, Freud described only one segment of the mental organization, the id, as wholly shielded from outside forces. But the ego and the superego wrestle with their environment as it offers encouragement or resistance, stimuli to be absorbed or anxieties to be warded off.

Freud thought that even the career of that controversial intimate triangle—the Oedipus complex—is shaped by such external powers as schooling or reading. Indeed that complex, he insisted, has a history, a social history: he explained the different behavior of Sophocles' Oedipus and Shakespeare's Hamlet by the "difference in the mental life of . . . two widely separated cultural epochs." Freud wrote no history, but he did not lack the historical imagination; his theory of human nature can accommodate drastic diversity across time and place. Hence my continuing sensitivity to the impact of social, political, economic realities on the mind, even as its defensive operations distort them, is fully warranted by Freud's scheme of things. But it is this sensitivity that has made me hesitate to call myself a psychohistorian; rather, I like to think of myself as a historian informed by psychoanalysis.

After twenty-five years of keeping company with that much maligned class, the Victorian bourgeoisie, I want in conclusion to offer an account of my findings. It goes almost without saying that I have learned a great deal from biographers and other historians, from specialized monographs and syntheses, a debt I have tried to repay with appreciative entries in my bibliographical essays. I am certainly not the first to pry beneath the Victorians' social surfaces—though sympathetically, quite unlike the malicious and misleading way in which Lytton Strachey debunked his parents' and grandparents' generations. True, I have tried to revise dominant twentieth-century views of the Victorian bourgeoisie almost as often as I have presented hitherto unknown or unused texts. But this does not mean that I have written these volumes in a calculated effort at revisionism for its own sake; I offer the tortuous progress of *The Bourgeois Experience* as evidence for just how much I have permitted what I have called the pressure of the material to point me on my way.

I am, then, far from denying that there were hypocrites, exploiters, and philistines among Victorian bourgeois—many of them, and in positions of influence. Erotic catastrophes in bed are only too well documented in the surviving records of physicians and specialists in mental suffering. The struggle of women to emerge from the shadows of legal and social dependency was all too real. The callousness or condescension of powerful Victorian bourgeois toward working hands in mines and factories, living conditions in burgeoning slums, or abandoned children was becoming, and in retrospect remains, a scandal.

Nothing I say in these volumes could be taken as an apology for industrial tycoons or commercial princes. The nostalgic dreamer intent on idealizing the Victorians will find little comfort in these pages.

However, I do deny that deceit, egotism, sexual predatoriness *define* the nineteenth-century middle classes. My aim throughout has been to widen our perception of the spectrum of the Victorian bourgeois experience, to redraw the dominant, distorted monochromatic caricature to put a crowded, colorful, and recognizable portrait in its place. Like a pointillist, I have accounted for local varieties that, once the viewer steps back, should cohere into a whole. The bourgeois of Edinburgh and the bourgeois of Cologne or Boston were very different breeds, but they were recognizable bourgeois just the same.

In this work of revision I have not slighted the indifferent, the self-satisfied, and the cruel, but have attempted to see them, too, as human. The most narrow-minded, most reactionary, most self-centered Victorians have the right, I believe, to claim the privilege of mixed motives. Ambiguity and ambivalence are the lot of everyone, and they had their conflict-ridden unconscious like everyone else. Following this principle—which, the reader can see, owes something to Freud—I diagnosed as hysterical attacks the editorials and sermons of journalists and preachers who in 1848 warned that the feminist demands formulated at Seneca Falls (moderate, even modest, as we now see them to be) were threatening the end of civilization. I found that habit-ridden, rigid critics who maligned the Impressionists as mere daubers were haunted by anxiety before the new. And I refused to adopt the facile identification of manufacturers who built Sunday schools for their employees as cynics intent on social control, and suggested instead that many a magnate really believed in the hell from which he was trying to save them.

This attitude—I like to think of it as a compound of historical rigor and equally tough-minded psychoanalytic charity—governed my interpretations. I want to summarize them briefly here, compressing more than two thousand pages into some five or six. Essentially, my series has persistently aimed at complicating the past, to rise above melodrama to the far subtler drama that is history. No generalization about the Victorian bourgeoisie can claim anything more than the most limited validity. Nineteenth-century societies were reined in by an array of governmental, social, or personal constraints, by censorship, customs, or a bad conscience; even so, more alternative styles of thinking, feeling, and action were available to bourgeois than ever before—in love, in religion, in politics, in art. I cannot emphasize enough that nothing in the Victorian age was free of controversy, much of it civil enough, and this quality in itself helps to define the nature of the Victorian bourgeoisie. When Walter Gropius was a boy, he was once asked about his favorite color, and he replied: "multicolored—*bunt*." That adjective may serve for the class I have had under my microscope for so long.

This diversity shows up in the bewildering miscellany that was middle-class sexual life in the nineteenth century. Bourgeois eros ranged from extreme repression to unabashed libertinism, but for the average couple, there seems to have been far greater sexual pleasure, for both partners, than we have been led to believe. The evidence is by its nature fragmentary, perhaps skewed, and I know that one generalizes at one's peril. But my findings were among the most gratifying moments in my long search: wives of soldiers fighting in the Civil War arousing their husbands with graphic and provocative letters, married women consulting a physician because they regarded their sexual anesthesia not as a natural condition but as an illness to be cured, college-educated women in a simplistic but revealing survey linking the joys of intercourse to the noble condition of conjugal love. Bourgeois took the ideal of privacy seriously and kept the bedroom door firmly closed. But, as I concluded, it would be a grave mistake to assume that Victorian bourgeois did not practice, and even enjoy, what they did not discuss.

It was telling in this connection that the Victorians' attitude toward the body in sickness as in health, toward newborn infants and dying octogenarians, was far more matter-of-fact, far more candid, than has become the practice in our own "liberated" time. People were born, fell ill, and died at home, in full view of their family. Hence all those oft-repeated jokes about bourgeois placing modest doilies around the legs of their grand piano, or guests asking for the "bosom" of chicken at a dinner party, are so many legends, or exceptional displays that most Victorians would have thought ridiculous. A housewife inspecting a wetnurse's nipples for flaws that might bear the germs of disease, a husband prayerfully rubbing his wife's painful breasts as her milk will not flow freely, a woman (not the hired cook but the lady of the house) prying open a turtle to make soup, the adolescent daughter of an English divine castrating sheep on the family farm, an assiduous daughter cleaning up after her incontinent father: respectable Victorians—women as much as men, perhaps even more so—had their faces pushed into real life with all its obtrusive coarseness. The market for smelling salts was far smaller than critics of the bourgeoisie have wanted us to believe.

Bourgeois public activity, too, the subject of the third volume, *The Cultivation of Hatred* (1993), displayed more good sense and humanity than it has been given credit for. Every society must somehow tame, or utilize, the inescapable dose of aggressiveness built into humans—Freud once again—by imposing social, moral, or legal sanctions against them. On that score, the Victorians had as many difficulties in coping as their predecessors, perhaps, in an age of universal, rapid, and drastic change, even more. The ravages and opportunities of industrialization, the unending struggles between the devout and the Darwinians, the loosening (or at least shifting) constraints on moral behavior, the partial decay of religious and political authority, all made the control of aggression imperative. Victorian bourgeois became increasingly aware of this as the costs of modernity grew ever more visible. That is why, like all cultures but in their unique way, they gave themselves permission to be aggressive by preaching manliness, "scientific" racism, Social Darwinism, all of them alibis (I use the word neutrally) to act out their passions.

While Victorian bourgeois cherished certain alibis for aggressiveness, they went even further to control it. They enacted protective legislation against child labor, destitution in old age, illness and accident, often against fierce opposition requiring inordinate expenditures of energy. They drastically reduced the number of crimes calling for the death penalty. They moved beyond, without abandoning, private charities to make the state responsible for the victims of industrial society. They began to clean up their cities and almost put an end to epidemics. They enfranchised more and more citizens, even pariahs like Jews. Theirs was a time of rule changing, but even more of rule making.

Nowhere was this attempt to bring aggression under control more conspicuous than in sports: less weighty, to be sure, than other aspects of social existence, but a token of larger issues. What blows to permit in boxing, what size to regard as appropriate for the goal in soccer or for a tennis court, what was considered to be unfair in sports in which physical contact was inescapable: the Victorian century grew into the century of the umpire. The point was not to deny or end conflict, but to recognize and tame it.

Many of these projects became exceedingly self-conscious as Victorians struggled with their conscience; they enjoyed, if that is the word, a hypertrophy of inwardness. True, the age was an age of stunning objective achievements, of scientific discoveries and technological breakthroughs. Together, and at times the second living off the first, they changed the world; the railroad was quite literally an epoch-making invention. Science recorded one triumph after another and compelled hitherto nonscientific pursuits to acknowledge, and try with their own procedures to deserve, its prestige. Students of society (or so its practitioners hoped) were moving beyond their informed speculations to social science. And it is symptomatic that nineteenth-century concoctions like Christian Science or Theosophy tried to ride on the coattails of physics or biology by claiming to be competent in theology, philosophy, and the natural sciences alike.

Victorian social scientists and in some measure natural scientists, too, retained the humanitarian program they had inherited from the eighteenth-

century Enlightenment—one thinks of Pasteur—but ultimately their achievements required the separation of moral or political agendas from the disinterested pursuit of truth. But while the Victorian age was eminently an objective
age, its subjective side also flourished. This is one of the stresses with which Victorian bourgeois had to come to terms. And that brings me to *The Naked Heart*
(1995). Putting it rather simply, and not overlooking exceptions like Keats,
Byron, and Stendhal, the romantics lamented what they mourned as the disenchantment of the world, which they blamed on the subversive, anti-Christ-
ian, mind-chilling rationalistic campaigns of the eighteenth-century
philosophes. Their supreme assignment was to re-enchant the world, to restore
faith that would nourish starving souls, alone, fatherless, in an indifferent uni-
verse. This meant the reinstatement of graceful lies, which is to say poetry, and
the exaltation of music, which, with its wordless appeal to deeply buried emotions, might repair some of the damage the Enlightenment had wrought.

Not that romantics were emotional primitives who despised all rationality
or believed that a genius, whether playwright, sculptor, or composer, can create without craftsmanship. Few of them thought that inspiration alone was
enough. But their attack on the Enlightenment's secular program put a heavy
emphasis on the inner life. Even those bourgeois who were not explicitly
romantics showed signs of the inward turn the romantics had so eloquently
advocated. Theirs was an age beginning to appreciate revealing (if still in great
measure reticent) biographies and autobiographies, an age of intimate letters
and diaries, of analytic fictions probing the finest stirring of their characters'
soul, of philosophies of subjectivity—in a word, of hearts laid bare. And it
became an age that institutionalized young love: marital choices increasingly
had to satisfy the couple-to-be as much as, perhaps even more than, the lovers'
parents.

This crisis in family life, which naturally generated friction, suggests that
whatever consensus the nineteenth-century bourgeoisie could mobilize was
subject to marked strains in the private and the public domain alike. In France,
secularist heirs of revolutionary ideas battled devout Catholics over education;
in Germany, at least until the mid-1860s, liberals denounced the authoritarian
Bismarck; everywhere, reform-minded bourgeois confronted the champions of
untrammeled free enterprise, and the interests of great capitalists clashed with
those of their less affluent fellow bourgeois. Nothing documents these divisions
more vividly than British usage, which persisted in the telling plural "middle
classes." And yet, for all these and other tensions, there was a certain rough
agreement just what it meant to be a bourgeois.

Middle-class ideals of moderation, probity, and monogamy might be pious
statements of intent rather than secure realities, but they helped to distinguish

bourgeois from their aristocratic or lower-class neighbors. Middle-class pressures for access to the political arena, though they too varied in intensity from society to society, were another mark of shared desires. And the emergence of a politically aware working class, a possible rival for power, lent many (many, but by no means all) bourgeois a widespread defensive identity across national frontiers. Freud believed that the bourgeoisie had a distinct psychological bent, and he was not alone.

But around the 1880s, this fragile consensus showed signs of unraveling, and it was in the domain of taste that fragmentation could no longer be denied, or bridged. This volume ends with an account of that collapse. Somewhat to my surprise, my interpretations turned out to be as revisionist as those in the first volume. Just as I had discovered far more satisfying sexual relations among Victorian bourgeois than generally supposed, I discovered far more modernists among them than earlier historical literature had prepared me for.

The common perception of Victorian bourgeois taste has long been that, with rare exceptions, it was bad. The middle classes, we were told, were addicted to kitsch, to art and music as mere entertainment, to insincere flourishes about masterpieces they did not have the patience or cultivation really to appreciate. And when bourgeois taste was good—that is to say that when the avant-garde could approve of it—this must be explained on nonaesthetic grounds, probably as an adroit display mounted by social climbers. To their articulate and persistent critics, in short, typical nineteenth-century bourgeois were philistines who loved money and hated art. But my researches, supported by excellent monographs, persuaded me that this invidious judgment was far off the mark.

How could this spiteful, insulting travesty have arisen and retained its credibility for a century and more? The question led me to Flaubert, the most gifted and most unrelenting leader of what I have called, borrowing his own epithet, the tribe of bourgeoisophobes. Not that Flaubert invented the phobic response to the bourgeoisie; its modern version goes back at least to the late eighteenth century, to the German Sturm und Drang exemplified by Goethe's Werther, for whom the middle class, strangers to the higher things, embodied stodginess and mediocrity. As I observe in my historical sketch of bourgeoisophobia, it was taken up by the romantics, most amusingly by E. T. A. Hoffmann, and spread by a small if growing army of antagonists to middle-class values and middle-class tastes. With the advent of modernism, the idea of the painter or poet as alienated from, and superior to, bourgeois consumers of the arts grew into something of a commonplace.

It was far from absurd: bourgeoisophobes had ample material to feed their disdain. But as a sweeping characterization it was fatally flawed; by taking lit-

erally the aggressive critiques by self-interested partisans, it managed to overlook the contribution of bourgeois—of industrialists, bankers, merchants—to
high culture in the Victorian era. What is more, the spectrum of bourgeois taste
covered the whole range of possible expressions from the outer edges of conservatism to those of radicalism, from the support of the conventional to the
equally determined support of the unconventional. Bourgeois fought rearguard
actions, and bourgeois were pacesetters in music, painting, architecture.

Once I had grasped this complexity of Victorian taste, I felt obliged to
review the material from a new perspective. At last, in my concluding volume,
I could approach the culture heroes I had originally wanted to write about, but
now in very different ways. My reexamination forced me to develop some
drastic distinctions. Obviously, though by no means always, the range of participation in high culture depended on financial resources, and so the prices of
admission to plays or operas, of original paintings or copies or cheaper reproductions, became essential elements in any attempt to place bourgeois taste.
What is more, I had to differentiate between bourgeois who cultivated and
paid for the arts on their own (Manchester), bourgeois who relied on the ruling house to supply them (Munich), and bourgeois finding themselves in a situation in which self-help and state sponsorship struggled for supremacy (Paris,
Berlin).

I thought it just as important to trace the impact of critics and reviewers on
the formation of taste. The Victorian age boasted more available cash than ever,
and many with disposable income urgently felt the need for guidance in the
realms of beauty; hence guardians of taste, whether well trained or just fluent,
could steer public responses with unexpected authority. Even more significantly—and I naturally gave them detailed attention—there were bourgeois
who expressed, or changed, current tastes as collectors or as donors to local
museums. The only link among the members of this tribe was the passion for
possession and the willingness to hand over their trophies to the public.

Then modernism erupted, and the gulf among bourgeois became more
unbridgeable than ever. There was a modern Maecenas for every style. Some
bought academic paintings, others fancied startling Postimpressionists; some
were content with supremely unoriginal dwellings, others commissioned Frank
Lloyd Wright to give them a breathtaking design; some protested against that
excessively modern composer Brahms, others were willing to absorb the latest
Mahler symphony. Whatever else one might say about the Victorian bourgeoisie, it is not boring. And on this note, I leave my apologia, and to others the
task of undermining or continuing what I have begun. For, much remains to
be done; *pace* Strachey, we still do not know enough about the Victorians.

After Edward Gibbon completed his vast *The Decline and Fall of the Roman Empire,* he registered his feelings in poignant particularity. With his customary precision, he recorded the day and hour of release: "It was on the day, or rather, night of the 27th of June 1788, between the hours of eleven and twelve, that I wrote the last lines of the last page." Usually the cool ironist, he relaxed his self-control to testify to his sense of an ending: "I will not dissemble the first emotions of joy on recovery of my freedom, and perhaps the establishment of my fame. But my pride was soon humbled, and a sober melancholy was spread over my mind, by the idea that I had taken an everlasting leave of an old and agreeable companion." Like other historians faced with the completion of an enterprise that had virtually become second nature, I can understand Gibbon's sentiments. I do not quite share his pathos, but this series has been my bourgeois experience for too long to have left me unscathed. As I put down my pen—or, rather, as I transfer a text for *The Bourgeois Experience* to a floppy disk for the last time—I, too, am moving on with a mixture of relief and regret: it is done at last! and, it is, sadly, done!

NOTES

Introduction

1 Emile Faguet, "Guizot," *Revue des deux mondes,* C (July–August 1890), 375, 385.

2 See Thomas Nipperdey, *Deutsche Geschichte, 1866–1918,* vol. I, *Arbeitswelt und Bürgergeist* (1990), 391; Tilmann Buddensieg, "Einleitung," *Villa Hügel. Das Wohnhaus Krupp in Essen,* ed. Buddensieg (1984), 7.

3 Engels: *The Condition of the Working Class in England in 1844* (1845; tr. Florence K. Wischnewetzky, 1885, ed. 1892), 95n; Heine: *Lutetia,* pt. 1, letter 29 (January 11, 1841), *Sämtliche Schriften,* ed. Klaus Briegleb, 6 vols. (1969–76), V, 341.

4 Michael Chevalier, *Society, Manners, and Politics in the United States: Letters on North America* (1836; 3rd ed., T. G. Bradford, 1838; ed. John William Ward, 1961), 382.

5 John A, Davis, *Conflict and Control: Law and Order in Nineteenth-Century Italy* (1988), 113.

6 Zola to Henry Fouquier, April 26, [18]82. In "Etude" for *Pot-Bouille, Les Rougon-Macquart. Histoire naturelle et sociale d'une famille sous le second Empire,* ed. Armand Lanoux and Henri Mitterand, 5 vols. (1960–67), III, 1633.

7 Burckhardt to Johanna Kinkel, August 23, 1843, *Briefe,* ed. Max Burckhardt, 10 vols. (1949–86), II, 42.

8 Emerson: *English Traits* (1856), in *The Complete Works of Ralph Waldo Emerson,* ed. Edward Waldo Emerson, 12 vols. (1903–4), V, 80 [ch. 5]; typically it was an Englishman, Thomas H. Huxley, who uttered what may be the most quoted tribute to this point of view: "Sit down before fact as a little child." There is something particularly authoritative about this blunt and poignant declaration, made in 1860, for it came in a reply to the muscular Christian Charles Kingsley, who had attempted to console Huxley for the loss of a beloved child by recalling the doctrine of immortality. Huxley could use no such consolation; it offended his scientific conscience. Holmes: *The Common Law* (1881), I [ch. 1]; Bain: quoted in French in Jules Payot, *L'Education de la volonté* (1893), 29; Paulsen: *Geschichte des gelehrten Unterrichts auf den deutschen Schulen und Universitäten vom Ausgang des Mittelalters bis zur Gegenwart* (1885; 2nd ed., 2 vols., 1896–97), II, 445.

9 Edmond and Jules de Goncourt: *Idées et sensations* (1866), 213; Harrison: John Gross, *The Rise*

and Fall of the Man of Letters: A Study of the Idiosyncratic and the Humane in Modern Literature (1969; ed. 1970), 116.

10 George M. Beard, *American Nervousness, Its Causes and Consequences: A Supplement to Nervous Exhaustion (Neurasthenia)* (1881), 138.

11 Van Gogh to his sister-in-law Jo, [middle of February 1890], *The Complete Letters of Vincent van Gogh,* 3 vols. (1954; tr. 1958), III, 467.

12 Otto Graf zu Stolberg-Wernigerode, *Die unentschiedene Generation. Deutschlands konservative Führungsschichten am Vorabend des ersten Weltkrieges* (1968), 264.

13 George and Weedon Grossmith, *The Diary of a Nobody* (1892; ed. 1995), 19 [ch. 1].

14 See Charles C. B. Seymour, *Self-Made Men* (1858), sixty capsule biographies of men who had risen from rags to riches. In 1861, an English doctor of divinity, William Anderson, imparted the same cheerful lesson under the same title; it went into four editions in four years.

15 See Henry L. Finegold, *A Time for Searching: Entering the Mainstream, 1920-1945* (1992), ch. 5, esp. 126–27.

16 Dickens, *Hard Times. For These Times* (1854; ed. David Craig, 1969), 58–60, 277–82 [Book the First, ch. 4; Book the Third, ch. 5].

17 Henry Maudsley, *The Physiology and Pathology of the Mind* (1867; ed. 1876), 163–64.

18 Freud to Martha Bernays, August 29, 1883, *Briefe, 1873–1939,* ed. Ernst L. Freud (1960), 48–49.

19 Zola, *Pot-Bouille* (1882), *Les Rougon-Macquart,* III, 6 [ch. 1].

20 See E. F. Benson, *As We Were* (1930), 111.

21 Charlotte Brontë to her father, June 7, 1851, in Clement Shorter, *The Brontës: Life and Letters,* 2 vols. (1908), II, 215–16. My attention to this letter was drawn by Asa Briggs, *Victorian Things* (1988), 52.

BOURGEOIS EXPERIENCES, V:
Bourgeoisophobes

1. Gustavus Flaubertus

1 Flaubert to Louis Bouilhet, December 26, 1852, *Correspondance,* ed. Jean Bruneau, 3 vols. so far (1973–), II, 217.

2 Flaubert to Louis Bouilhet, [May 30, 1855], ibid., 576.

3 Flaubert to Ernest Chevalier, July 15, 1839, ibid., I, 48; Flaubert to Caroline Flaubert, [July 25, 1842], ibid., 119; Flaubert to George Sand, [May 17, 1867], ibid., III, 642.

4 Flaubert to Caroline Flaubert, [after December 10, 1842], ibid., I, 134; Flaubert to Caroline Flaubert, [June 8, 1843], ibid., 174.

5 Flaubert to his niece Caroline, October 25, 1872, *Correspondance,* ed. Conard, V, 432; Flaubert to Feydeau, October 28, 1872, ibid., 436–37. [Note that for Flaubert's correspondence after 1868, which is the year the definitive Bruneau edition has reached, I have used the Conard edition, *Oeuvres complètes de Gustave Flaubert,* 26 vols., of which 13 are devoted to the correspondence (1910–34). In these notes I shall distinguish it from the Bruneau edition by adding the publisher's name.]

6 Flaubert to George Sand, [ca. (June) 12, (1867)], *Correspondance,* III, 653–54, ibid., 654; Louise Colet, *Lui* (1859; ed. 1963), 340.

7 William Morris to Emma Shelton Morris, July 29, 1855, in Fiona MacCarthy, *William Morris: A Life for Our Time* (1995), 92.

8 See Benjamin F. Bart, *Flaubert* (1967), 7.

9 Jean Pierre Chaline, *Les Bourgeois de Rouen. Une Élite urbaine au XIXe siècle* (1982), 32, 36, 46.

10 Ibid., 134–35, fig. 21.

11 Considering the size of Rouen, attendance was fairly low: in 1898, there were on the average 327 visitors on free Sundays and holidays, and only 14 on fee days. See Daniel J. Sherman, *Worthy Monuments: Art Museums and the Politics of Culture in Nineteenth-Century France* (1989), 230, and 116; François Bergot, "La Donation François Depeaux au musée des Beaux-Arts de Rouen," *Arts, objets d'art, collections. Etudes sur l'art du Moyen Age et de la Renaissance sur l'histoire du gout et des collections* (1987), 205–12.

12 Rouen, session of November 13, 1909, *Bulletin municipal* (October–November 1909), 136–37.

13 See Bergot, "La Donation François Depeaux," 212; Sherman, *Worthy Monuments*, 205, 232–40.

14 Flaubert, *Le Dictionnaire des idées reçues*, in *Oeuvres*, ed. Albert Thibaudet and René Dumesnil, 2 vols. (1951–52), II, 1000.

15 "CONCERT": "Le catalogue des opinions chic," *Dictionnaire des idées reçues. Edition diplomatique des trois manuscrits de Rouen*, ed. Lea Caminiti (1966), 120; "NOVEL": *Dictionnaire des idées reçues*, in *Oeuvres*, II, 1021; "LITERATURE": ibid., 1016; "BOOK": ibid.

16 For Mme Flaubert as "la bourgeoise," see Flaubert to his brother, Achille, April 25, 1844, *Correspondance*, I, 207.

17 Flaubert to Turgenev, [July 27, 1877], *Lettres inédites à Tourgueneff*, ed. Gérard Gailly (1946), 142; Flaubert, *Bouvard et Pécuchet*, in *Oeuvres*, II, 915 [ch. 8].

18 Flaubert to Georges Charpentier and Madame Charpentier, [ca. September 1879], *Correspondance*, ed. Conard, VIII, 292.

19 Flaubert to Ernest Feydeau, 17 [August 1861], *Correspondance*, III, 170; Flaubert to George Sand, [May 17, 1867], ibid., 642.

20 Flaubert to George Sand, [April 29, 1871], *Correspondance*, ed. Conard, VI, 227.

21 Flaubert: to Louise Colet, [November 22, 1852], *Correspondance*, II, 179; Bourget: *Essais de psychologie contemporaine*, Appendix E (1886), in *Oeuvres complètes*, 9 vols. (1899–1911), I, 139–40.

2. Six-Pack Philistines

1 See Goethe to Eckermann, March 14, 1830, Johann Peter Eckermann, *Gespräche mit Goethe in den letzten Jahren seines Lebens* (1836–48), in Goethe, *Gedenkausgabe der Werke, Briefe, und Gespräche*, ed. Ernst Beutler, 27 vols. (1948–71), XXIV, 732–33.

2 Hans von Marées: to Konrad Fiedler, March 5, 1882, in Julius Meier-Graefe, *Hans von Marées. Sein Leben und Werk*, 3 vols. (1910), III, 234; Liliencron: *Der Mäcen* (1889), in *Sämtliche Werke*, 15 vols. (1905–8), V, 220; Treitschke: "Die goldenen Tage der Bourgeoisie" (1868), *Ausgewählte Schriften*, 4 vols. (4th enlarged ed., 1908), III, 165–71, 250, 254, 251.

3 See Nietzsche to Georg Brandes, February 19, 1888, *Werke in drei Bänden*, ed. Karl Schlechta, 3 vols. (1956–66), III, 1279.

4 Hans Mackowsky, "Hans Baluschek" (1902–3), *Kunst und Künstler*, an anthology from this periodical, ed. Günter Feist, with Ursula Feist (1971), 31.

5 Alfred de Musset, *La Confession d'un enfant du siècle* (1836; ed. Claude Roy, 1973), 27 [pt. 1, ch. 2].

6 Heine: *Lutetia*, pt. 2, letter 59 (May 7, 1843), *Sämtliche Schriften*, ed. Klaus Briegleb, 6 vols. (1969–76), V, 481; Gautier: "Henri Monnier" (1855), *Oeuvres complètes*, 11 vols. (1880), IX, 35–36; Maupassant: see *Correspondance inédite de Guy de Maupassant*, ed. Artine Artinian with Edouard Maynial (1951), 123–24.

7 Zola: on Balzac, *Rappel* (May 13, 1870); *Les Rougon-Macquart. Histoire naturelle et sociale d'une famille sous le second Empire*, ed. Armand Lanoux and Henri Mitterand, 5 vols. (1960–67) III, 1601.

8 Zola: "Le Catholique hystérique," *Mes haines. Causeries littéraires et artistiques* (1866), in *Oeuvres complètes*, ed. Henri Mitterand, 15 vols. (1962–69), X, 47; Zola; "La Critique contemporaine" (1880), *Documents littéraires*, ibid., XII, 478–79.

9 Zola: unpublished "note de travail," in Brian Nelson, *Zola and the Bourgeoisie: A Study of Themes and Techniques in "Les Rougon-Macquart"* (1983), epigraph.

10 Anne Distel, *Impressionism: The First Collectors* (1989; tr. Barbara Perroud-Benson, 1990), 148.

11 Georg Brandes: *Moderne fransk Litteratur* (unpublished lecture, 1889), in Henry J. Gibbons, "Georg Brandes: The Making of an Aristocratic Radical," Ph.D. diss. Department of History, Yale University (1980), 207; Brandes to Edvard Brandes, March 31, 1873, ibid., 205; Brandes to G. Noufflard, June 27 [1886], ibid., 206.

12 In the *Communist Manifesto*, Marx of course shared authorship with Engels. My principal sources for my summary of Marx's thinking about the bourgeoisie are the *Communist Manifesto; The Eighteenth Brumaire of Napoleon Bonaparte;* letters, mainly to Engels; and the posthumously published writings of 1844.

13 Alfred de Vigny, "Dernière nuit de travail de 29 au 30 Juin 1834," preface to *Chatterton* (1834), *Oeuvres complètes*, ed. François Germain, André Jarry, and Alphonse Bouvet, 2 vols. (1986–93), I, 759.

14 Leconte de Lisle, "*Les Fleurs du mal*, par M. Ch. Baudelaire," *Revue européenne* (December 1, 1861), in *Articles, Préfaces, Discours*, ed. Edgard Pich (1971), 146; "Avant-Propos" to "Les Poètes contemporains" (1864), ibid., 157.

15 Gautier, "Préface," *Mademoiselle de Maupin* (1835–36, ed. Geneviève van den Bogaert, 1966), 45.

16 Vienna: Hanslick, *Geschichte des Concertwesens in Wien*, 2 vols. (1869–70), I, 67; Paris: Arnold Benedict Perris, "Music in France during the Reign of Louis-Philippe: Art as 'A Substitute for the Heroic Experience,' " Ph.D. diss., Department of Music, Northwestern University (1967), 113.

17 See "Messrs John Broadwood and Sons' Price List, 1st May, 1818," in Rosamond E. M. Harding, *The Piano-Forte: Its History Traced to the Great Exhibition of 1851* (1933), 379–80.

18 Knight, *Cyclopaedia of the Industry of All Nations* (1851), in Cyril Ehrlich, *The Piano: A History* (1976), 40–41.

19 E. D. Mackerness, *A Social History of English Music* (1964; 2nd corrected impression, 1966), 173, 221; Ehrlich, *The Piano*, 221.

3. Confusing Confrontations

1 Vincent van Gogh to Albert Aurier, early February 1890, *The Complete Letters of Vincent van Gogh*, 3 vols. (1954; tr. 1958), III, 257.

2 Nicolas Green, "Dealing in Temperaments: Economic Transformation of the Artistic Field in France during the Second Half of the Nineteenth Century," *Art History*, X, 1 (March 1987), 59.

3 Thomas Mann, *Tonio Kröger* (1903), in *Ausgewählte Erzählungen* (1945), 155, 157, 157–58.

4 Ibid., 195.

5 Baudelaire, "Salon de 1845" (1845), *Oeuvres complètes,* ed. Y. G. Le Dantec, rev. Claude Pichois (1961), 813-14.

6 Ibid., 814; "Salon de 1846" (1846), ibid., 874-76.

ONE: The Political Economy of Art

1. Battles of the Budgets

1 Alfred de Musset, "Salon de 1836" (April 13, 1836, *Revue des deux mondes),* in *Oeuvres complètes,* 10 vols. (1881), IX, 145, 146.

2 Théophile Thoré, "Salon de 1845," in *Salons de T. Thoré, 1844, 1845, 1846, 1847, 1848* (1870), 114, 115.

4 Charles Baudelaire, "Salon de 1846," *Oeuvres complètes,* ed. Y. G. Le Dantec, rev. Claude Pichois (1961), 879.

4 See G[erhard] A. Ritter and J[ürgen] Kocka, *Deutsche Sozialgeschichte. Dokumente und Skizzen,* vol. 2, *1870-1914* (1974), 341-43.

5 Only a major Rembrandt could cost more: in late 1888 and early 1889, Harry Havemeyer bought an important pair of portraits, unquestionably by the master, for $60,000. Alice Cooney Frelinghuysen et al., *Splendid Legacy: The Havemeyer Collection* (1993), 62.

6 Maria Makela, *The Munich Secession: Art and Artists in Turn-of-the-Century Munich* (1990), 161.

2. Affordable Masterpieces

1 Otto von Leixner, *1888 bis 1891. Soziale Briefe aus Berlin, mit besonderer Berücksichtigung der sozialdemokratischen Strömungen* (1891), 172-80. My attention to this budget was first drawn by G[erhard] A. Ritter and J[ürgen] Kocka, *Deutsche Sozialgeschichte. Dokumente und Skizzen,* vol. 2, *1870-1914* (1974), 344-48.

2 See Alice M. Hanson, *Musical Life in Biedermeier Vienna* (1985), 106-8.

3 Heinrich Leo Behncke, *Eine Lübecker Kaufmannsfamilie,* 4 vols. (1913), III, 212.

4 See Christa Pieske, *Bilder für jedermann. Wandbilddrucke, 1840-1949* (1988), 29.

5 Nadar: (pseud. Gaspard Félix Tournachon), *Quand j'étais photographe* (1900), in *Nadar,* ed. Philippe Néagu and Jean Jacques Poulet-Allamagny, 2 vols. (1979), II, 973; Barbey d'Aurevilly: "Petite anthologie des textes sur la photographie," *Le Nain jaune,* January 3, 1867, ibid., 682. As early as 1839 an anonymous journalist had predicted, "We shall soon see beautiful prints that one once found in the salons of rich amateurs alone decorating homes all the way to the humble dwelling of the laborer and the peasant." Ibid., I, 681.

6 "Die moderne Kunstindustrie," in Wolfgang Brückner, *Elfenbeinreigen-Hochzeitstraum. Die Öldruckfabrikation, 1880-1940* (1974), 15.

7 Charles L. Eastlake, *Hints on Household Taste in Furniture, Upholstery and Other Details* (1868; 3rd rev. ed., 1872), 110. Ten years later, Samuel Smiles put it more generally in a letter to his daughter Janet: it is better to have a good etching of a good painting than a second-rate painting. January 31, 1878, in Samuel Smiles Record, SS/A/I/84, Yale University.

8 Rudolf Binding, *Erlebtes Leben. Selbstbildnis und Bild der Zeit* (1927; ed. 1937), 101-2.

9 Charles Blanc, "Le Cabinet de M. Thiers," *Gazette des beaux-arts,* 1st period, XII (April 1862), 289-320, esp. 290-91.

10 *Billroth und Brahms im Briefwechsel,* ed. Otto Gottlieb-Billroth (1935), 480. I owe this passage to Ilsa Barea, *Vienna* (1966), 285-86.

11 Manet as copyist: Theodore Reff, "Copyists in the Louvre, 1850–1870," *Art Bulletin*, XLVI (December 1964) 552–59, esp. 556; Morisot as copyist: see editor's comment in *Correspondance de Berthe Morisot avec sa famille et ses amis*, ed. Denis Rouart (1950), 10.

12 Duranty: in *Réalisme*, I (July 10, 1856), 1–2, in Reff, "Copyists in the Louvre," 553; Pissarro: ibid., 553n.

13 See Reff, "Copyists in the Louvre," 555–56; John Rewald, "Une Copie par Cézanne d'après Le Greco," *Gazette des beaux-arts*, 6th period, XV (February 1936), 118–21; Jack Lindsay, *Gustave Courbet: His Life and Art* (1973), 19; Sara Lichtenstein, "Cézanne and Delacroix," *Art Bulletin*, XLVI (March 1964), 55–67. Cézanne owned three paintings of Delacroix's, two of his lithographs, and six reproductions of his work. Ibid., 55.

14 Rosalie Braun-Artaria, *Von berühmten Zeitgenossen. Lebenserinnerungen einer Siebzigerin* (n.d.), 105. In the end, Schack did not honor his contract with Lenbach, apparently paying him only a total of 1,030 gulden—somewhat less than 2,000 marks. See Siegfried Wichmann, *Franz von Lenbach und seine Zeit* (1973), 30, 34; Franz von Lenbach, *Gespräche und Erinnerungen* (1904), 47; Georg Winkler, "Lenbach als Kopist und Kunstberater des Grafen Schack," *Die Kunst*, XIX (1909), 23–30, 46–54, quotation at 53.

15 Adolphe Jullien, *Fantin-Latour. Sa vie et ses amitiés* (1909), 11, 1.

16 Salee Lawrence, St. Johnsbury, Vermont, personal communication to the author, September 21, 1994.

17 See the full-page announcement by Amsler & Ruthardt, a Berlin firm, in Franz Hermann Meissner, *Adolph v. Menzel* (1902), vol. VII of the series Das Künstlerbuch, for a bound volume of Max Klinger's *Brahms-Phantasie*, which consisted of forty-one engravings, etchings, and lithographs, for 1,500 marks. The advertisement also offered cheaper smaller collections and individual titles ranging from 48 to 150 marks.

18 Otto von Leixner, *Aesthetische Studien für die Frauenwelt* (1880), separate page after the frontispiece, not paginated.

19 Size mattered: around 1880, the Photographische Gesellschaft Berlin offered its photos ranging in five sizes, from one to forty-five marks, the smallest ca. 3 by 6 inches, the largest ca. 23 by 50. Pieske, *Bilder für jedermann*, 30.

20 For these paragraphs see the collection of posters in the Stadtbibliothek (Monacensia) in Munich, and *Nationaltheater München. Festschrift der Bayerischen Staatsoper zur Eröffnung des wiederaufgebauten Hauses* (1963), passim, esp. Franz Trenner, "Bülow, Levi, Strauss und Possart," 61–80.

21 Comment on Courbet: Karl Gutzkow, "Über Idealismus und Realismus in der Literatur," *In bunter Reihe* (1878), in *Liberale Energie. Eine Sammlung seiner kritischen Schriften*, sel. and ed. Peter Demetz (1974), 257; German art in Paris: Fritz Wernick, "Die deutsche Kunst auf der Pariser Weltausstellung," *Gartenlaube*, XXVI (1878), 696.

22 Berlioz, *Mémoires de Hector Berlioz, comprenant ses voyages en Italie, en Allemagne, en Russie et en Angleterre, 1803–1865*, 2 vols. (1870; 2nd ed., 1881), I, 143.

23 Joseph Joachim to Johannes Brahms, March 3, 1855, *Johannes Brahms im Briefwechsel mit Joseph Joachim*, ed. Andreas Moser, 2 vols. (1908), I, 93.

3. Limits and Possibilities

1 See Shirley Bury, "Redgrave and Felix Summerly's Art-Manufactures," in *Richard Redgrave, 1804–1888*, ed. Susan P. Casteris and Ronald Parkinson (1988), 40.

2 See Jennifer Hall, "The Re-fashioning of Fashionable Society: Opera-going and Sociability

in Britain, 1821–1861," Ph.D. diss., Department of History, Yale University (1996), appendix B (p. 421).

3 E. J. Dent, "Music," in *Early Victorian England, 1830–1865*, ed. G. M. Young, 2 vols. (1934), II, 261.

4 See Anthony Trollope, *An Autobiography* (1883; World's Classics ed., 1953), 43, 50 [both ch. 3], 110 [ch. 7].

5 David Robertson, *Sir Charles Eastlake and the Victorian Art World* (1978), 82.

6 Charles L. Eastlake, *Hints on Household Taste in Furniture, Upholstery and Other Details* (1868; 3rd rev. ed., 1872), 201.

7 See A. P. Oppé, "Art," in *Early Victorian England*, II, 116n, 108.

8 Eastlake, *Hints on Household Taste*, 2, 8; Jakob von Falke, *Geschichte des modernen Geschmacks* (1866; 2nd rev. ed., 1880), vii (preface to 1st ed.); xi (preface to 2nd ed.).

9 Falke, *Geschichte des modernen Geschmacks* (1866; 2nd rev. ed., 1880), xi.

10 William Morris, "How I Became a Socialist," *Justice*, June 16, 1894, in *William Morris: Selected Writings and Designs*, ed. Asa Briggs (1962), 36–37; Morris to Andreas Scheu, September 5, 1883, ibid., 34.

11 See Adeline Daumard, *Les Bourgeois et la bourgeoisie en France depuis 1815* (1987), 103–4.

12 Arnold Benedict Perris, "Music in France during the Reign of Louis-Philippe: Art as 'A Substitute for the Heroic Experience,' " Ph.D. diss., Department of Music, Northwestern University (1967), 229; Jean Montgrédien, *Musique en France des Lumières au Romantisme (1789–1830)* (1986), 30.

13 Zola, "Nos peintres au Champ-de-Mars" (1867), *Mon salon* (1866; 2nd ed., 1879), in *Mon salon. Manet. Ecrits sur l'art*, ed. Antoinette Ehrard (1970), 127.

14 See Lionello Venturi, *Les Archives de l'Impressionisme*, 2 vols. (1939), I, 223; Harrison C. White and Cynthia A. White, *Canvases and Careers: Institutional Change in the French Painting World* (1965), 126.

15 Zola, *Mon salon* (1866), in *Mon salon*, 67.

16 Camille Pissarro to Lucien Pissarro, [end of January 1897], *Lettres à son fils Lucien*, ed. John Rewald, with Lucien Pissarro (1950), 430–31.

17 Thoré, "Salon de 1863," *Salons de W. Bürger*, 2 vols. (1870), I, 415.

18 See Camille Pissarro to Lucien Pissarro, [March 10, 1897], *Lettres à son fils Lucien*, 434.

19 Ernest Chesneau, *Les Chefs d'école* (1964), 245–47; on Meissonier's pay: C. H. Stranahan, *A History of French Painting* (1902), 343; White and White, *Canvases and Careers*, 72.

TWO: The Geography of Taste

1. Dividends from Commerce

1 Charles Hallé, *The Autobiography of Charles Hallé, with Correspondence and Diaries*, ed. Michael Kennedy (1973), 119; Hallé to his parents, April 27, 1848, ibid., 146.

2 Ibid., 119.

3 Désirée Hallé (his first wife) to her sister, [September 19, 1848], ibid., 147–48.

4 C. C. Aronsfeld, "German Jews in Victorian England," *Leo Baeck Yearbook*, VII (1962), 318–19.

5 See *Manchester Guardian*, January 29, 1848, 8; ibid., January 26, 1848, 5; ibid., January 8, 1848, 7.

6 *Autobiography of Charles Hallé,* 122–23.

7 Michael Kennedy, *The Hallé Tradition: A Century of Music* (1960), 31.

8 Hans Richter to Marie Richter, November 8, 1883, in Christopher Fifield, *True Artist and True Friend: A Biography of Hans Richter* (1993), 202.

9 *Manchester Guardian,* January 11, 1879, p. 5.

10 Program, "Thursday evening, December 22nd, 1870 and Friday evening, December 23rd, 1870." Henry Watson Music Library, Manchester.

11 Gerald Cumberland, "Choral Works at the Hallé Concerts," letter to the editor, *Manchester Guardian,* October 4, 1905, p. 5. (My attention to this letter was first drawn by Stefan Collini.)

12 Sir William Napier: *The Life and Opinions of Sir Charles James Napier,* 2 vols. (1857), II, 57 (a passage quoted by practically everyone writing about nineteenth-century Manchester); W. Cooke Taylor: *Notes of a Tour in the Manufacturing District of Lancaster* (1841), in Shena D. Simon, *A Century of City Government: Manchester, 1838–1938* (1938), 34.

13 Asa Briggs, "Manchester, Symbol of a New Age," *Victorian Cities* (1963; ed. 1968), 111.

14 Friedrich Engels, *Die Lage der arbeitenden Klasse in England* (1845; ed. Walter Kumpmann, 1973; 2nd ed., 1977), 195.

15 Thomas Carlyle, *Chartism* (1839), in *Selected Writings,* ed. Alan Shelston (1971), 211 [ch. 8].

16 Ibid.

17 Simon, *A Century of City Government,* 39–43.

18 Michael E. Rose, "Culture, Philanthropy and the Manchester Middle Classes," *City, Class and Culture: Studies of Social Policy and Cultural Production in Victorian Manchester,* ed. Alan J. Kidd and K. W. Roberts (1985), 111.

19 Royal Manchester Institute, *Catalogue of the Exhibition of Pictures by Italian, Spanish, Flemish, Dutch and English Masters, with Which the Proprietors Have Favoured the Institution, for the Improvement of Taste in the Fine Arts, and the Gratification of the Governors and the Public* (1831), 3, in C. P. Darcy, *The Encouragement of the Fine Arts in Lancashire, 1760–1860* (1976), 70.

20 Thomas S. Ashton, *Economic and Social Investigations in Manchester, 1833–1933: A Centenary History of the Manchester Statistical Society* (1934), 13.

21 A. J. P. Taylor has observed that the Free Trade Hall, given its final form in 1856, Manchester's most imposing public auditorium before the town hall of the 1870s came to rival it, was the only building in Europe named after a "proposition." ("The World's Cities: Manchester," *Encounter,* VIII, 3 [March 1957], 3–13, esp. 9.) True enough, but the idea was inextricably linked to the pressures of commerce.

22 Tocqueville, *Journeys to England and Ireland,* ed. J. P. Mayer (1958), 105, a passage frequently quoted.

23 Oliver Elton, "Mr. and Mrs. Charrington (Miss Janet Achurch) in 'A Doll's House,'" April 13, 1897, in Elton et al., *The Manchester Stage, 1880–1900* (1900), 196.

24 *The John Rylands Library Manchester: 1899–1924,* ed. Henry Guppy (1924), 13.

25 Ibid., 15.

26 Ibid.

27 Sir Charles Hallé, "The Royal Manchester College of Music," *Strand Musical Magazine,* I (1895), 323.

28 Darcy, *Encouragement of Fine Arts,* 134, 129.

29 Dennis Farr, *William Etty* (1958), 95.

30 See ibid., 66.

31 Joan Allgrove et al., *A Short Guide to the Whitworth Art Gallery* (n.d.), 4.

2. Majestic Dispensations

1 For the toast of 1818, see *Ferdinand Franz Wallraff*, ed. Joachim Deeters (1974), 104; for the king, see Ralf Zerback, "Unter der Kuratel des Staates—Die Stadt zwischen dem Gemeindeedikt von 1818 und der Gemeindeordnung von 1869," in *Geschichte der Stadt München*, ed. Richard Bauer (1992), 276. "Modern Munich as the whole world knows it," wrote the influential local critic Theodor Goering in 1884, "is in essence a creation of Ludwig I." "Entstehung des neueren Münchens unter Ludwig I. und Maximilian II.," *Dreissig Jahre München. Kultur- und kunstgeschichtliche Betrachtungen* (1904), 14.

2 Friedrich Pecht, *Aus meiner Zeit. Lebenserinnerungen* (1894), 101, in York Langenstein, *Der Münchner Kunstverein im 19. Jahrhundert. Ein Beitrag zur Entwicklung des Kunstmarkts und des Aussstellungswesens* (1983), 55.

3 Max Spindler, *Handbuch der Bayerischen Geschichte*, ed. Spindler, vol. IV, pt. I (1974), 211, 215n.

4 Johann Caspar Bluntschli, *Denkwürdigkeiten aus meinem Leben*, ed. Rudolf Seyerlen, 3 vols. (1884), II, 121.

5 Alfred von Mensi-Klarbach, *Alt-Münchner Theater-Erinnerungen* (1923; 2nd ed., 1924), 14–15.

6 Heinrich Bihrle, *Die Musikalische Akademie München, 1811–1911* (1911), 28.

7 Adolf Hildebrand to N. Kleinenberg, September 27, 1889, *Adolf von Hildebrand und seine Welt. Briefe und Erinnerungen*, ed. Bernhard Sattler (1962), 331. Emperor Wilhelm II's musical taste is revealed in a single episode: on March 20, 1889, he took breakfast at the officers' mess in Potsdam and "deigned" to request eight separate selections from the trumpeters' corps, including three marches, overtures, songs, and medleys almost all alluding to military matters. The fact that the orchestra consisted entirely of trumpeters did not mean that it was prevented from doing "civilian" music. *Neue Zeitschrift für Musik*, LXXXV (1889), 179.

8 Hildebrand to the Herzogenbergs, December 9, 1889, *Hildebrand und seine Welt*, 341. For a brief account of the episode, see M. Doeberl, *Entwicklungsgeschichte Bayerns*, vol. III, *Vom Regierungsantritt König Ludwigs I. bis zum Tode König Ludwigs II. mit einem Ausblick auf die innere Entwicklung Bayerns unter dem Prinzregenten Luitpold*, ed. Max Spindler (1931), 383.

9 Theodor Goering, "Das musikalische München zur Zeit Ludwigs II. Münchener Musikzustände und ihre Ursachen. Das Konzertwesen" (1888), *Dreissig Jahre München*, 145, 149.

10 Rosalie Braun-Artaria, *Von berühmten Zeitgenossen. Lebenserinnerungen einer Siebzigerin* (n.d. [ca. 1917]), 99.

11 Ibid., 97.

12 Alfred Lichtwark, *Deutsche Königsstädte* (1898; 2nd ed., 1912), 119.

13 W. Bürger [Théophile Thoré], "Salon de 1864," *Salons de W. Bürger 1861 à 1868*, 2 vols. (1870), II, 7; Th. Thoré (W. Bürger), *Musées de la Hollande*, 2 vols. (1860), II, 6.

14 Eduard Hanslick, *Geschichte des Concertwesens in Wien*, 2 vols. (1869–70), I, 164.

15 When Hanslick was a young music critic on the *Wiener Zeitung*, he read one of his concert reviews aloud to his editor; it included the sentence "Their Majesties the Emperor and Empress appeared in the court box around seven o'clock; enthusiastic applause broke over them"—whereupon the editor irritably and anxiously interrupted the reading to object to "them." Much to Hanslick's disgust, he corrected this neutral pronoun to *"Allerhöchstdenselben,"* a circumlocution (the "all-highest-themselves") that mercifully defies normal English. Hanslick, *Aus meinem Leben*, 2 vols. (1894), I, 197.

16 Hanslick, *Geschichte des Concertwesens*, 139–84 passim.

17 William Dodd: *The Manchester Institution for the Promotion of Literature, Science, and the Arts* (1823), a circular, 9, in Darcy, *Encouragement of Fine Arts*, 66; *Times*, August 19, 1844: in Jennifer

Hall, "The Re-fashioning of Fashionable Society: Opera-going and Sociability in Britain, 1821–1861," Ph.D. diss., Department of History, Yale University (1996).

18 Munich: Peter Böttger, *Die Alte Pinakothek in München* (1972), 20; Birmingham: Asa Briggs, *The History of Birmingham,* vol. II, *Borough and City, 1865–1938* (1952), 100.

THREE: Acknowledged Legislators

1 Henry B. Fuller, *With the Procession* (1895; ed. 1965), 57.

2 Louisine W. Havemeyer, *Sixteen to Sixty: Memoirs of a Collector* (1930; ed. 1961), 203.

1. Guides to Pleasure

1 Hazlitt: "Fine Arts: Whether They Are Promoted by Academies and Public Institutions," (1814), in *The Complete Works of William Hazlitt,* ed. P. P. Howe, 21 vols. (1930–34), XVIII, 48; Anon.: "The Ethics of Art," *Musical Times and Singing-Class Circular,* XXX (May 1, 1889), 265.

2 Gautier: *Les Grotesques* (1844), in *Oeuvres complètes,* 11 vols. (1888), III, 2; Fontane: "Josef Viktor von Scheffels 'Ekkehart' " (1907), *Werke in drei Bänden,* ed. Kurt Schreinert, 3 vols. (1968), III, 868.

3 In the issue of February 13, 1805, the reviewer in the *Allgemeine musikalische Zeitung,* the most prestigious among musical journals, found Beethoven's Third daring, wild, full of "startling and beautiful passages," but lawless, with "too much that is glaring and bizarre." *Thayer's Life of Beethoven,* rev. and ed. Elliot Forbes (1967), 375. For Constable, see Basil Taylor, *Constable: Paintings, Drawings and Watercolours* (1973), 208.

4 *Musical World,* April 2, 1840, p. 208. (I owe this passage to Jennifer Hall, "The Re-fashioning of Fashionable Society: Opera-going and Sociability in Britain, 1821–1861," Ph.D. diss., Department of History, Yale University [1996], 354.)

5 Dennis Farr: *William Etty* (1958), 106–7; W. Gaunt and F. Gordon Roe: *Etty and the Nude: The Art and Life of William Etty, R.A., 1787–1849* (1943), 22; Thackeray: "May Gambols; or, Titmarsh in the Picture Galleries," *Fraser's Magazine* (1844), in *The Works of William Makepeace Thackeray,* Centenary Biographical Edition, ed. Lady Ritchie, 26 vols. (1910–11), XXV, 298. See Peter Gay, *The Bourgeois Experience,* vol. I, *Education of the Senses* (1984), 385–87.

6 Kathryn Moore Heleniak, *William Mulready* (1980), 149.

7 Herr Kall, member of the *Bürgerschaft* of Hamburg, in *Hamburger Fremdenblatt,* September 26, 1888, in *Ein Geschmack wird untersucht. Die G. C. Schwabe Stiftung,* ed. Werner Hofmann and Tilman Osterwold (n.d.), 41.

8 Friedrich Schlegel, "Gespräch über die Poesie" (1800), in *Kritische Schriften,* ed. Wolfdietrich Rasch (1964; enlarged ed., 1964), 527.

9 Friedrich Schlegel, "Kritische Fragmente," the so-called Lyceumfragmente (1797), ibid., 8.

10 See William Weber, *Music and the Middle Class: The Social Structure of Concert Life in London, Paris and Vienna between 1830 and 1848* (1975), 76–78.

11 Ernest Chesneau, *Les Chefs d'école* (1862; 2nd ed., 1864), i (dedication).

12 Shaw, review dated June 14, 1893, in *Music in London, 1890–94,* 3 vols. (1932), III, 5, 3.

13 Camille Pissarro to Lucien Pissarro, July 30, 1886, May 8, 1887, *Lettres à son fils Lucien,* ed. John Rewald, with Lucien Pissarro (1950), 109; 144.

14 Shaw, reviews dated October 4 and October 11, 1893, in *Music in London,* III, 55, 59.

15 See Eduard Hanslick, *Aus meinem Leben,* 2 vols. (1894), II, 292–309.

16 Théophile Gautier: Maxime du Camp, *Théophile Gautier* (1890; tr. Andrew Lang, 1893), 57; Fontane: to Hermann Kletke, August 29, 1870, *Briefe an Hermann Kletke*, ed. Helmuth Nürnberger (1969), 23. Again, on November 24, 1881, he told Kletke that reviews "don't help much and the few that *do* must be born free." Ibid:, 63.

17 Paul Hayes Tucker, *Claude Monet: Life and Art* (1995), 3.

18 W. Bürger [pseud. Théophile Thoré], "Salon de 1864," *Salons de W. Bürger 1861 à 1868*, 2 vols. (1870), II, 22.

19 Tolstoy: John Bayley, *Tolstoy and the Novel* (1966), 11; Daudet: Leon Edel, *Henry James: The Middle Years, 1882–1895* (1962), 100.

20 Henry James, "Criticism" (1891), *Selected Literary Criticism,* ed. Morris Shapira (1963), 167–68.

21 Ibid.

22 Ibid., 169–71.

23 Ursula Eckart-Bäcker, *Frankreichs Musik zwischen Romantik und Moderne. Die Zeit im Spiegel der Kritik* (1965), 21.

24 Matthew Arnold, "On Translating Homer" (1861), a passage that he defended four years later, in "The Function of Criticism at the Present Time," *Essays in Criticism: First Series* (1865; 4th ed., 1884; shilling ed., 1911), 1.

25 Arnold, "Function of Criticism," 3.

26 Charles Baudelaire, "Richard Wagner et 'Tannhäuser' à Paris" (1861), *Oeuvres complètes,* ed. Y. G. Le Dantec, rev. Claude Pichois (1961), 1222.

27 See Hanslick, *Aus meinem Leben,* II, 228, 226.

28 *Wörterbuch der Unhöflichkeit, enthaltend grobe, höhnende, gehässige und verleumderische Ausdrücke, die gegen den Meister Wagner, seine Werke und seine Anhänger von den Feinden und Spöttern gebraucht wurden* (1876; 2nd ed., 1903; ed. 1967), 15, 17, 116, 73.

2. Master Craftsmen

1 Sainte-Beuve, "Madame Bovary, par M. Gustave Flaubert" (May 4, 1857), in *Causeries du Lundi*, 15 vols. (1850–80), XIII, 363. (The bibliographical situation of Sainte-Beuve's publications is a nightmare. His publishers freely reprinted the volumes in which he gathered his reviews, at times enlarged them and at other times left them unrevised. Until the Pléiade edition of Sainte-Beuve is complete—and it is a long time a-coming—one can do no better than to rely on the particular editions in a good university library.)

2 Ibid., 346–47.

3 Sainte-Beuve, "Poésies complètes de M. Théodore de Banville" (October 12, 1857), ibid., XIV, 71; "De la tradition en littérature et dans quel sense il la faut entendre," inaugural lecture at the Ecole Normale (April 12, 1858), ibid., XV, 368.

4 Sainte-Beuve, Pensée no. 20, "Pensées," *Portraits littéraires*, 3 vols. (1862–64), III, 546.

5 Sainte-Beuve, "Qu'est ce qu'un classique?" (October 21, 1850), *Lundis*, III, 40.

6 Sainte-Beuve, "M. Joubert" (1839), *Portraits contemporains*, 5 vols. (1876–89), I, 365; "De la poésie et des poètes en 1852" (February 9, 1852), *Lundis*, V, 303–4; Pensée no. 19, *Portraits littéraires*, III, 546.

7 Sainte-Beuve to Charles Didier, [June 8, 1834], *Correspondance générale,* ed. Jean Bonnerot and Alain Bonnerot, 19 vols. (1935–83), I, 440.

8 "Who then were his discoveries? Hugo (under Dubois' impulsion); Sénancour (single-handed); Louis Bertrand (at least for the critical justice accorded him); Maurice de Guérin (like-

wise); Marceline Desbordes-Valmore (not alone, but his was the advocacy that kept her in the public eye before Verlaine)." A. G. Lehmann, *Sainte-Beuve: A Portrait of the Critic, 1804–1842* (1962), 289.

9 See Peter Gay, *The Bourgeois Experience,* vol. IV, *The Naked Heart* (1995), 138–39.

10 "Le Vicomte d'Arlingcourt, *L'Etrangère*" (January 15, 1825), *Lundis,* I, in *Oeuvres,* ed. Maxime Leroy, 2 vols. so far (1956–66), I, 81.

11 "Mémoires du marquis d'Argenson, ministre sous Louis XV, *publiés par René d'Argenson,*" *Le Globe* (July 16, 1825), ibid., 109.

12 "Joseph de Maistre," *Revue des deux mondes,* July 15–August 1, 1843, in *Oeuvres,* II, 466.

13 Though little known to the general educated public, Thoré remains an icon to art historians. Francis Haskell has called him "the archetypal hero of this book." *Rediscoveries in Art: Some Aspects of Taste, Fashion and Collecting in England and France* (1976), 86; Wilhelm von Bode recalled in his autobiography that as a young man he knew Thoré's book on Dutch art "almost by heart." Bode, *Mein Leben,* 2 vols. in 1 (1930; begun in 1907), I, 26.

14 Thoré to his mother, December 15, 1835, in *Thoré-Bürger peint par lui-même. Lettres et notes intimes,* ed. Paul Cottin (1900), 22–24.

15 "Bürger," *Salon de 1848,* in *Salons de T. Thoré, 1844, 1845, 1846, 1847, 1848* (1868; 2nd ed., 1870), 565; ibid., preface, ix; "Salon de 1865," *Salons de W. Bürger, 1861–1868,* 2 vols. (1870), II, 238.

16 "Bürger," "Exposition universelle de 1867," ibid., I, 420.

17 "Bürger," "Salon de 1864," ibid., II, 14.

18 "Bürger," *Amsterdam et La Haye. Etudes sur l'Ecole Hollandaise* (1858), 22. The Rembrandt biography was announced by his publisher in 1858 to be ready soon. (See notice appended ibid., p. 3.)

19 See Bürger, *Musées de la Hollande,* 2 vols. (1858–60), II, 67–88.

20 See Gerald Reitlinger, *The Economics of Taste: The Rise and Fall of the Picture Market, 1760–1960* (1961), 140–41. In 1907, the Dutch government bought the magnificent *Woman with a Pitcher* for over £30,000, while in 1931 Andrew Mellon paid around £100,000 for *Girl in a Red Hat.* Ibid., 206.

21 *Monday-Chats by C. A. Sainte-Beuve,* ed. William Mathews (1877), epigraph.

22 Reprinted in full in L. Véron, *Mémoires d'un bourgeois de Paris,* 6 vols. (1853–55), III, 109–12, quotation at 110.

23 See Charles Ledré, *La Presse à l'assaut de la monarchie, 1815–1848* (1960), 244–45; Véron, *Mémoires,* IV, 271.

24 Fontane to Hermann Kletke, December 3, 1879, *Briefe an Kletke,* 59. This tribute comes in the midst of a protest against the intention of the *Vossische Zeitung* to start serializing novels and stories.

3. From Zola to Wilde

1 Zola: "Nos peintres aux Champ-de-Mars" (1867), *Mon Salon* (1866; 2nd ed., 1879), in *Mon salon. Manet. Ecrits sur l'art,* ed. Antoinette Ehrard (1970), 126; Huysmans: see *The Expanding World of Art, 1874–1902,* vol. I, *Universal Expositions and State-Sponsored Fine Arts Exhibitions,* ed. Elizabeth Gilmore Holt (1988), 212; Zola: "Nos peintres aux Champs-de-Mars," 127–28.

2 Shaw on Schubert: March 23, 1892, in *Music in London,* II, 53; on Brahms: June 21, 1893, ibid., III, 12. Shaw was particularly phobic—it is not too strong a word—about Brahms's requiem.

3 Henry James to William Rothenstein, July 13, 1897, *Letters,* ed. Leon Edel, 4 vols. (1974–84), IV, 50.

4 Roger Gard, ed., *Henry James. The Critical Muse: Selected Literary Criticism* (1987), 7.

5 Flaubert to Alfred Le Poittevin, [July 1845], *Correspondance*, ed. Jean Bruneau, 3 vols. so far (1973–), I, 248; Flaubert to Louise Colet, [November 22, 1852], ibid., II, 179.

6 I have explored this defensive technique in some detail in a section titled "The Doctrine of Distance," in *The Bourgeois Experience*, vol. I, *Education of the Senses* (1984), 379–402.

7 Jean Ravenel (pseud. Alfred Sensier): *L'Epoque* (June 7, 1865), in T. J. Clark, *The Painting of Modern Life: Paris in the Art of Manet and His Followers* (1984), 139.

8 "Bürger," "Salon de 1864," *Salons de W. Bürger, 1861–1868*, 2 vols. (1870), II, 98.

9 Peter Gay, *Art and Act: On Causes in History—Manet, Gropius, Mondrian* (1976), 34.

10 Zola, *Edouard Manet*, in *Ecrits sur l'art*, 108–10.

11 Wilde, "The Critic as Artist," *Intentions* (1891), in *The Artist as Critic: Critical Writings of Oscar Wilde*, ed. Richard Ellmann (1969), 355.

12 Ibid., 358.

13 Richard Ellmann, Wilde's most scholarly biographer, has written, "Wilde had always held that the true 'beasts' were not those who expressed their desires, but those who tried to suppress other people's. The society whose hypocrisies he had anatomised now turned them against him. Victorianism was ready to pounce." *Oscar Wilde* (1988), 431; Henry James: to Edmund Gosse, [April 8], 1895, *Letters*, IV, 10; bigots: Lord Alfred Douglas pilloried "the daily press" as "the mouthpiece of Philistinism"; and the progressive drama critic William Archer also thought the British censor "the mouthpiece of Philistinism." Review of Wilde's *Salomé*, in *Spirit Lamp*, IV (May 1893), in *Oscar Wilde: The Critical Heritage*, ed. Karl Beckson (1970), 138; Archer: "Mr. Oscar Wilde's New Play," *Black and White* (May 11, 1893), ibid., 142; Newman: "Oscar Wilde: A Literary Appreciation," *Free Review*, IV (June 1, 1895), ibid., 204.

14 Beerbohm: to "Reggie" Turner, March 3, 1895 [?], Max Beerbohm, *Letters to Reggie Turner* (1964), 100.

15 *St. James Gazette*, "Over-Tolerance," May 27, 1895, p. 3.

16 *Westminster Gazette*, "The End of the Wilde Case: Some Incidents and Morals," May 27, 1897, pp. 1–2.

17 *Reynolds's News*, May 20, 1895, in Ellmann, *Wilde*, 479.

18 For the decisive part of Wilde's testimony, see *The Artist as Critic*, 435–38, and the full treatment by Ellmann, *Wilde*, 435–78.

19 William Butler Yeats: *The Trembling of the Veil* (1922), in Yeats, *Autobiography* (1969), 192; Frank Harris: *Oscar Wilde: His Life and Confession*, 2 vols. (1916), I, 289.

20 This story has aroused much skepticism; it seems too pathetic and too pat to be true. The principal witness was, of course, Frank Harris (*Oscar Wilde: His Life and Confessions*, I, 281), notorious for his egotism as a biographer of Wilde (made still more obvious in his autobiography, *My Life and Loves*, which retails sexual conquests that never took place). But Yeats knew of the offer to spirit Wilde away on a yacht; he had heard the story at the time from Wilde's brother Willie (Yeats, *Autobiography*, 191). Ellmann, whose judgment can be trusted, accepts the story (see *Wilde*, 468); in addition to the sources I have mentioned, he uses Ada Leverson, who was as close to Wilde in those days as anyone (*Letters to the Sphinx from Oscar Wilde and Reminiscences of the Author* [1930], 41), and *Reynolds's News*, June 2, 1895. Philippa Pullar, whose *Frank Harris* (1975) is a model of objectivity and careful research, mentions the story without comment, but, although fully aware of Harris's mendacity, seems not to doubt it.

FOUR: Hunters and Gatherers

1. A Map of Motives

1 Alexandre Dumas fils: preface, Bernard Prost, *Octave Tassaert. Notice sur la vie et catalogue de son oeuvre* (1886), i; William Carew Hazlitt: *The Confessions of a Collector* (1897), 2.

2 Edwin C. Bolles, *Collectors & Collecting* (1898), 11.

3 See *Billroth im Briefwechsel mit Brahms,* ed. Aloys Greither (1964), 28.

4 Anon., untitled, *Musical Times,* XIII (January 1, 1868), 249.

5 Théophile Thoré, "Salon de 1846," *Salons de Théophile Thoré, 1844, 1845, 1846, 1847, 1848* (1868; ed. 1870), 279.

6 A reminiscence by Howard Mansfield, "Charles Lang Freer," *Parnassus,* VII, no. 5 (October 1935), 16, in Thomas Lawton and Linda Merrill, *Freer: A Legacy of Art* (1993), 18.

7 Anon., *Physiologie de l'Opéra, du Carnaval, et de la Cachucha par un Vilain Masqué* (1842), in *Gavarni: The Carnival Lithographs,* ed. Nancy Olson (1979), 6.

8 Freud to Wilhelm Fliess, December 6 [18]96, *Sigmund Freud. Briefe an Wilhelm Fliess, 1887–1904,* ed. Jeffrey Moussaieff Masson with Michael Schröter (1986), 226.

9 Freud, February 19, 1908, in *Protokolle der Wiener Psychoanalytischen Vereinigung,* ed. Herman Nunberg and Ernst Federn, 4 vols. (1976–81), I, 302.

2. Collecting as Autobiography

1 Henri Rochefort, "The Love of Ugliness," *L'Intransigeant,* March 9, 1903, in John Rewald, *Paul Cézanne: A Biography* (1948; ed. 1967, tr. Margaret H. Liebmann, 1968), 185–86.

2 Rewald, *Cézanne,* 183.

3 Ibid., 179; Gerstle Mack, *Paul Cézanne* (1935), 225.

4 Anne Distel, *Impressionism: The First Collectors* (1989; tr. Barbara Perroud-Benson, 1990), 125–26. After Chocquet inherited a good deal of money in 1882, he virtually stopped collecting.

5 See the one-page flier advertising the sale in Yvonne Tiénot, *Chabrier. Par lui-même et par ses intimes* (1965), 143.

6 See Anne Dumas, "Degas as a Collector," *Apollo,* CXLIV, new ser., no. 415 (September 1996), 12.

7 Peter Krieger, "Max Liebermanns Impressionisten-Sammlung und ihre Bedeutung für sein Werk," in Matthias Eberle et al., *Max Liebermann in seiner Zeit* (1979), 60.

8 Distel, *Impressionism,* 75–94.

9 Maupassant, *Bel-Ami* (1885; tr. Douglas Parmée, 1975), 155–57 [ch. 6].

10 Henry James: "The Madonna of the Future" (1873), in *The Novels and Tales of Henry James,* 26 vols. (1907–17), III, 458 [sec. 3]; Theodor Fontane: *Frau Jenny Treibel* (1892), in *Werke in drei Bänden,* ed. Kurt Schreinert (1968), I, 837 [ch. 1].

11 William R. Johnston, "Introduction," *The Taste of Maryland: Art Collecting in Maryland, 1800–1934,* ed. Johnston (1984), v.

12 Andrew Carnegie to W. N. Frew, October 24, 1894, in Joseph Frazier Wall, *Andrew Carnegie* (1970), 817.

13 Galbraith, "Conspicuous Consumption Illustrated," in Alexis Gregory, *Families of Fortune: Life in the Gilded Age* (1993), 7.

14 Carl-Wolfgang Schümann, " 'Die Pfalz der Stahlkönige'—Das Innere der Villa Hügel im

Wandel," *Villa Hügel. Das Wohnhaus Krupp in Essen*, ed. Tilmann Buddensieg (1984), 285, 291.

15 Commenting on private salons in turn-of-the-century Berlin held by affluent collectors, and contrasting them with those held by Bismarck's banker Gerson Bleichröder, Wolfgang Hardtwig has written, "It makes a significant difference whether one went to the culinary feasts at the house of the banker Bleichröder or to the salon in the house of Bernstein, Arnhold, or Kessler; the politically more influential circles doubtless attended those at Bleichröder's." Indeed, "fostering art especially with the Maecenases among entrepreneurs was nearly always only one element among many and for the most part, expressed in numbers, by no means the most important." Thus Bleichröder, immensely rich, was "evidently aesthetically uneducated, but he collected, supported artists, and, for instance, aided the Germanisches Nationalmuseum with donations; but the sums involved remain vanishingly small compared with the *Stiftungen* to Robert Koch or for other innumerable charitable purposes." "Drei Berliner Porträts: Wilhelm von Bode, Eduard Arnhold, Harry Graf Kessler. Museumsmann, Mäzen und Kunstvermittler—Drei herausragende Beispiele," *Mäzenatentum in Berlin. Bürgersinn und kulturelle Kompetenz unter sich verändernden Bedingungen*, ed. Günter and Waldtraut Braun (1993), 51, 56.

16 *Mäzenatentum in Berlin. Bürgersinn und kulturelle Kompetenz unter sich verändernden Bedingungen*, ed. Günter and Waldtraut Braun (1993), 56.

17 Simon to Bode, January 31, 1885, Nachlass Wilhelm von Bode, letters to Bode, Zentral-Archiv, Stiftung Preussischer Kulturbesitz (henceforth Z-SPK); Simon to von Bode, January 18, 1887, ibid.; April 19, 1887, ibid.

18 Simon to Bode, March 26, 1885, ibid., Z-SPK.

19 Draft of a memorandum by Max J. Friedländer (unsigned but easily identified through the handwriting), Acta betr. Geschenk James Simon zum 18. 10, 1904, Nachlass Simon, Z-SPK.

20 Simon to Bode, February 23 and 27, 1897, Nachlass von Bode, Z-SPK.

21 Simon to Bode, January 14, 1896, Z-SPK; Simon to Bode, December 29, 1904, ibid.; Simon to Bode, October 4, 1891, ibid.; Simon to Bode, November 9, 1891, ibid.; Simon to Bode, August 10, 1920, ibid.

22 See *Eduard Arnhold. Ein Gedenkbuch*, ed. Johanna Arnhold and Adolf Grabowsky (1928), 210.

23 Ibid., 254.

24 Trübner to Arnhold, July 9, 1913, ibid., 230.

25 Ibid., 254.

26 Daumier appreciators: see Jan Rie Kist, *Honoré Daumier, 1808–1879* (1979), 74; the collector: Alice Cooney Frelinghuysen et al., *Splendid Legacy: The Havemeyer Collection* (1993), 74.

3. The Victorian Maecenas

1 Asher B. Durand to John Casilear, June 14, 1835, in Lillian B. Miller, *Patrons and Patriotism: The Encouragement of the Fine Arts in the United States, 1790–1860* (1966), 152–53, quotation at 153.

2 Basil Taylor, *Constable: Paintings, Drawings, and Watercolours* (1973), 225.

3 See Conrad Fiedler to Adolf von Hildebrand, January 19, 1885, *Adolf von Hildebrand und seine Welt. Briefe und Erinnerungen*, ed. Bernhard Sattler (1962), 281.

4 The painter Anselm Feuerbach, Marées's friend and rival, wrote his mother in 1868, "Marées, with his interminable talking about himself is worse than boring." October 15, 1867, *Anselm Feuerbachs Briefe an seine Mutter*, sel. and ed. Hermann Uhde-Bernays (1912), 256.

5 Fiedler to Hildebrand, January 8, 1884, *Hildebrand und seine Welt*, 275.

6 [William Thompson Walters], *Antoine-Louis Barye: From the French of Various Critics* (1885), 6.

7 See M. Jonker et al., "Abraham Willet (1825–1888)," *Antiek*, XXIII, no. 4 (November 1988), 193–259.

8 Jack Lindsay, *Gustave Courbet: His Life and Art* (1973), 107.

9 See the reproduction in Klaus Herding, *Courbet: To Venture Independence* (n.d.; tr. John William Gabriel, 1991), 161.

10 Louisine W. Havemeyer, *Sixteen to Sixty: Memoirs of a Collector* (1930; ed. 1961), 196; on Courbet's greatness, ibid., 180.

11 Havemeyer, *Sixteen to Sixty*, 112.

12 Anne Distel, *Impressionists: The First Collectors* (1989; trans. Barbara Perroud-Benson, 1990), 76.

13 Albert Boime, "Entrepreneurial Patronage in Nineteenth-Century France," *Enterprise and Entrepreneurs in Nineteenth- and Twentieth-Century France*, ed. Edward C. Carter, Robert Forster, and Joseph Moody (1976), 151–54; Jean Bouret, *The Barbizon School and 19th Century French Landscape Painting* (1972; tr. 1973), 123.

14 Klaus Lankheit, "Wissenschaftlicher Anhang," *Der Blaue Reiter*, ed. Wassily Kandinsky and Franz Marc, newly ed. Lankheit (1965), 275.

15 See *Expressionismus und Exil. Die Sammlung Ludwig and Rosy Fischer, Frankfurt am Main*, ed. Georg Heuberger (1990).

16 Albert Kostenewitsch, "Russische Sammler französischer Kunst. Die Familienclans der Schtschukin und Morosow," *Monet bis Picasso. Die Sammler Morosow, Schtschukin. 120 Meisterwerke aus der Eremitage, St. Petersburg, und dem Puschkin-Museum, Moskau*, ed. Georg-W. Költzsch (1994), 41–43.

17 Ibid., 68.

18 Ibid., 69.

19 For one instance, see *Uhde. Des Meisters Gemälde in 285 Abbildungen*, ed. Hans Rosenhagen (1908).

20 See William R. Johnston, ed., *The Taste of Maryland: Art Collecting in Maryland, 1800–1934* (1984), passim.

21 Anon., "Une Collection de tableaux modernes," *Gazette des beaux-arts*, 3rd period, XVII (January 1897), 73

FIVE: Movers and Shakers

1. Founders

1 Harold C. Livesey, *Andrew Carnegie and the Rise of Big Business* (1975), 72; Andrew Carnegie, "The Advantages of Poverty," (1891), *The Gospel of Wealth and Other Timely Essays*, ed. Edward C. Kirkland (1962), 66–67. For a more extended analysis of Carnegie's "scientific philanthropy," see Peter Gay, *The Bourgeois Experience*, vol. III, *The Cultivation of Hatred* (1993), 62–64.

2 Annette Blaugrund, *The Taste of Andrew Carnegie* (1991), unpaginated brochure.

3 Helene von Ledebur-de Bary, "Eine Akademie, das 'Museum' genannt," *Das 'Museum.' Einhundertfünfzig Jahre Frankfurter Konzertleben, 1808–1958*, ed. Hildegard Weber (1958), 27.

4 Hans Sarkowicz, "Vorwort," *Die grossen Frankfurter*, ed. Sarkowicz (1994), 9.

5 See Andreas Hansert, *Geschichte des Städelschen Museums-Vereins Frankfurt am Main* (1994), 11–13; Hansert, *Bürgerkultur und Kulturpolitik. Eine historisch-soziologische Rekonstruktion* (1992), 90–96.

6 See Hansert, *Bürgerkultur und Kulturpolitik*, 71.

7 J. E. Crawford Flitch, *The National Gallery* (1912), 11–12.

8 Nor was it uncontested. To give but one instance, in 1891, in a series of three articles (see *Musical Opinion and Music Trade Review* [January, February, April 1891], 133–34, 173–174, 251–52), Arthur F. Smith offered a reasoned argument in behalf of state support.

9 Ernst Lothar Franck, "Der preussische Kunstetat und die Berliner Museen," *Die Nation,* I (January 12, 1884), 212; anon., "Das neue Leipziger Gewandhaus," *Gartenlaube,* XXXIII (1885), 19.

10 Anon.: "Letters on the Fine Arts. No. 2.—Two Objections against Art Unions," *Pictorial Times* (April 1 and 8, 1843); Lady Elizabeth Eastlake: "Memoir of Sir Charles Eastlake," in Charles Locke Eastlake, *Contributions to the Literature of the Fine Arts,* 2nd ser. (1870), 147.

11 For Tate, see Janet Minihan, *The Nationalization of Culture: The Development of State Subsidies to the Arts in Great Britain* (1977), 154–57; Edward T. Cook, *A Popular Handbook to the Tate Gallery: "National Gallery of British Art"* (1898), 1.

12 Richard Redgrave, *The Sheepshanks Gallery* (1870); David Robertson, *Sir Charles Eastlake and the Victorian Art World* (1978), 256, 208.

13 W[alter] A[rmstrong], "Robert Vernon (1774–1849)," *Dictionary of National Biography,* ed. Sir Leslie Stephen, 21 vols. (1885–90), XX, 281.

14 Vernon Heath, *Vernon Heath's Recollections* (1892), 1–2.

15 In this paragraph I am much indebted to an unpublished paper by David Cannadine, "Joseph Gillott and the Family Firm: The Many Faces of Entrepreneurship."

16 Charles Russell Lowell to John C. Bancroft, May 1857, in M. A. DeWolfe Howe, *The Boston Symphony Orchestra, 1881–1931,* rev. and extended in collaboration with John N. Burk (1931), 8.

17 Henry Lee Higginson to his father, September 1857, ibid., 8–9.

18 Ibid., 9–10.

19 Charles Dickens, *American Notes* (1843; ed. 1961), 43 [ch. 3].

20 Josiah Quincy, *The History of the Boston Athenaeum, with Biographical Notes of Its Deceased Founders* (1851), 32–34.

21 Ibid., v.

22 Michael Broyles, *"Music of the Highest Class": Elitism and Populism in Antebellum Boston* (1992), 25–27.

23 Announcement in the Boston newspapers: "The Boston Symphony Orchestra in the Interest of Good Music," ibid., 24–25; John H. Mueller, *The American Symphony Orchestra: A Social History of Musical Taste* (1951), 81.

24 Henry Adams to Henry James, November 18, 1903, *Letters of Henry Adams,* ed. Worthington Chauncey Ford, 2 vols. (1930–38), II, 414.

25 See Johan H. Giskes, "Opbouw (1881–1888)," in H. J. van Boyen et al., *Historie en kroniek van het Concertgebouw en het Concertgebouworkest,* 2 vols. (1989), I, 14–15, 26.

26 Ibid., 17–19.

27 H. Teding van Berkhout, "Geschiedkundig Overzicht, 1883–1923," catalog for exhibition commemorating the fortieth anniversary of the Vereeniging Rembrandt (1923), 9–12, esp. 12.

28 Hansert, *Geschichte des Städelschen Museums-Vereins,* 33.

29 Ibid., 39–49, esp. 37, 48.

2. Buttresses for the Establishment

1 Wiepke Loos, "Carel Joseph Fodor (1801–1860) and His Collection," *The Fodor Collection: Nineteenth-Century French Drawings and Watercolors from Amsterdams Historisch Museum* (1985), 10.

2 Lutteroth, report to the mayor's office, November 16, 1883, in *Ein Geschmack wird untersucht. Die G. C. Schwabe Stiftung,* a documentation, ed. Werner Hofmann and Tilman Osterwold (n.d.), 29.

3 For the description of the older Wagener's collection, see Paut Ortwin Rave, *Die Geschichte der Nationalgalerie Berlin* (n.d.), 14.

4 Wagener to Hermann Anton Stilke, November 11, 1848, Sammlung Wagener, untitled volume of drafts of letters, Z-SPK.

5 Wagener to Karl Friedrich Lessing, February 8, 1842, ibid; Alfred Rethel to Wagener, November 17, 1838 (a penciled note on the letter remarks that the painting had been returned, and Wagener had only one earlier Rethel, done in 1831, in his collection), Sammlung Wagener, folder "Briefe von Künstlern and Konsul Wagener, L–Z." And see Thomas Ender to Wagener, May 28, 1853, folder "Briefe von Künstlern an Konsul Wagener, A–K," Sammlung Wagener, ibid. And see Christian Köhler to Wagener, January 15, 1852, and Nicaise de Keyser to Wagener, November 27 [18]46, Z-SPK.

6 Rave, *Geschichte der Nationalgalerie,* 14, 18.

7 Sammlung Wagener.

8 *Verzeichniss der Gemälde-Sammlung des am 18. Januar 1861 zu Berlin verstorbenen königlich Schwedischen und Norwegischen Konsuls J. H. W. Wagener, welche durch letztwillige Bestimmung in den Besitz seiner Majestät des Königs übergangen ist* (1873), iv–v.

3. The Perspiring Philistine on Trial

1 Robert Louis Stevenson, "Walking Tours" (1876), *Essays by Robert Louis Stevenson,* ed. William Lyon Phelps (1918), 32.

2 See Carolyn Helen Kay, "Educating the Bourgeoisie: Alfred Lichtwark and Modern Art in Hamburg, 1886–1914," Ph.D. diss., Department of History, Yale University (1994), 50.

3 He received the munificent salary of 8,000 marks, rising in twenty-eight years to 19,000 marks. See ibid., 34, 34n.

4 Alfred Lichtwark, "Der Deutsche der Zukunft," *Der Deutsche der Zukunft* (1905), 24.

5 Lichtwark, *Das Bildniss in Hamburg,* 2 vols. (1898), I, 71; Lichtwark to Bode, December 20, 1897, Bode Nachlass, Z-SPK.

6 Lichtwark, *Das Bildniss in Hamburg,* I, 51–52.

7 See Kay, "Educating the Bourgeoisie," 40, 69.

8 "Success": Lichtwark to Bode, July 27, [18]91, Bode Nachlass, Z-SPK; Petersen's dislike: see the unpublished letter from Petersen to Lichtwark, April 14, 1892, in Kay, "Educating the Bourgeoisie," 116; "feud": Lichtwark to Bode, April 16, 1892, Bode Nachlass.

9 Lichtwark to Liebermann, February 5, 1892, *Briefe an Max Liebermann,* ed. Carl Schellenberg (1947), 87.

10 January 2, 1852, *Journals and Correspondence of Lady Eastlake,* ed. Charles Eastlake Smith, 2 vols. (1895), I, 272–73.

11 Zola, "Deux expositions d'art en Mai," *Le Messager de l'Europe* (June 1876); Emile Zola, "Deux expositions d'art en Mai," *Le Messager de l'Europe* (June 1876), in Russian, tr. Madame Morozov, in Zola, *Mon salon, Manet, Ecrits sur l'art,* ed. Antoinette Ehrard (1970), 279.

12 Kirk Varnedoe, *Gustave Caillebotte* (1987), 187.

13 Bénédite, "La Collection Caillebotte au Musée du Luxembourg," *Gazette des beaux-arts,* 3rd ser., XVII (March 1897), 258; Alexandre Hepp, "Impressionism," March 3, 1882, Varnedoe, *Caillebotte,* 10; *Mon salon,* 279; Pissarro advising the Luxembourg: see his letter to his son Lucien, March

10, 1897, *Lettres à son fils Lucien,* ed. John Rewald with the assistance of Lucien Pissarro (1950), 433.

14 Camille Pissarro to Lucien Pissarro, February 18, 1897, *Lettres à son fils Lucien,* 432.

15 See Varnedoe, *Caillebotte,* 209n; Gérôme in Pissarro, *Lettres à son fils Lucien,* 342n.

16 See Pissarro to his son Lucien, March 10, 1897, *Lettres à son fils Lucien,* 433–34.

17 For the new scholarship, see esp. Marie Berhaut, *Caillebotte: Sa vie et son oeuvre* (1978); Pierre Vaisse, "Le Legs Caillebotte d'après les documents," *Bulletin de la Société de l'Histoire de l'Art français* (1983), 201–8.

SIX: Modernism

1. A Profusion of Alternatives

1 See Igor Stravinsky, *An Autobiography* (1936), 47.

2 Emerson, "Culture," *Conduct of Life* (1860), in *The Complete Works of Ralph Waldo Emerson,* ed. Edward Waldo Emerson, 12 vols. (1903–4), VI, 140.

3 Frederic Harrison, "Picture Exhibitions" (1888), *Memories and Thoughts: Men—Books—Cities—Art* (1906), 329–30.

4 Anon., "An Interview with Mr. Charles F. Annesley Voysey, Architect and Designer," *Studio: An Illustrated Magazine of Fine and Applied Art,* I (April 1893), 234.

5 Elizabeth Aslin, *The Aesthetic Movement: Prelude to Art Nouveau* (1969), 14.

6 Anon., "An Artist's Cottage: Designed by C. F. A. Voysey," *Studio,* IV (November 1894), 34.

7 Liebermann, "Zwei Holzschnitte von Manet" (1905), *Die Phantasie in der Malerei. Schriften und Reden,* ed. Günter Busch (1978), 90.

8 Debussy, *Monsieur Croche the Dilettante Hater,* a collection of articles first published in the *Revue Blanche, Gil Blas,* and *Musica* between 1901 and 1905 (1921; tr. B. N. Langdon-Davies, 1928; ed. *Three Classics in the Aesthetics of Music* (1962), 19 [ch. 3]. Winslow Homer reported a very similar passivity before the scenes he painted.

2. Modernists vs. Modernists

1 Arnold Schoenberg to Karl Wiener, June 29, 1912; the same to the same, February 29, 1910, *Briefe,* sel. and ed. Erwin Stein (1958), 27, 22–23.

2 Richard Strauss to Alma Mahler (1915), in Charles Rosen, *Arnold Schoenberg* (1975), 16.

3 Munch: in conversation with the philosopher Eberhard Grisebach, reported by Grisebach to his favorite correspondent, Helene Spengler, his cultivated mother-in-law, February 25, 1914, in *Von Munch bis Kirchner. Erlebte Kunstgeschichte in Briefen aus dem Nachlass von Eberhard Grisebach,* ed. Lothar Grisebach (1968), 38; Mondrian: "Toward the True Vision of Reality," *Plastic Art and Pure Plastic Art and Other Essays,* ed. Robert Motherwell (1951), 10—see Peter Gay, *Art and Act: On Causation in History—Manet, Gropius, Mondrian* (1976), 179.

4 Guillaume Apollinaire, *La Jolie Rousse,* in *Calligrammes. Poèmes de la Paix et de la Guerre (1913–1916)* (1917). Poggioli uses verses from this poem in *The Theory of the Avant-Garde* (epigraph).

5 Verhaeren: "Le Salon des Indépendants," *La Nation,* repr. in *L'Art moderne,* April 5, 1891, in John Rewald, *Post-Impressionism from van Gogh to Gauguin* (1956; 3rd rev. ed., 1978), 7.

6 Camille Pissarro to Lucien Pissarro, December 28, 1883, *Lettres à son fils Lucien,* ed. John Rewald with the assistance of Lucien Pissarro (1950), 73.

7 See Edward Lockspeiser, *Debussy: His Life and Mind*, vol. I, *1862–1902* (1962; 2nd ed., 1966), 125–26.

8 Debussy, *Monsieur Croche*, 12 [ch. 2], 32 [ch. 10].

9 Franz Marc, "Geistige Güter," *Der Blaue Reiter*, ed. Wassily Kandinsky and Franz Marc (1912; newly ed. Klaus Lankheit, 1965), 22.

10 I have here borrowed from my own studies of Liebermann. See "Encounter with Modernism: German Jews in Wilhelminian Culture," *Freud, Jews and Other Germans: Masters and Victims in Modernist Culture* (1978), 105–8.

11 William Morris to Georgina Burne-Jones, May 13, 1885, in Fiona MacCarthy, *William Morris: A Life for Our Time* (1995), 28.

12 Morris, "The Lesser Arts," ibid., 267.

13 See Susan M. Canning, " 'Soyons Nous': Les Vingt and the Cultural Discourse of the Belgian Avant-Garde," in *Les XX and the Belgian Avant-Garde*, ed. Stephen H. Goddard (1992), 30–31, 40; Malcolm Bradbury and James McFarlane, "Movements, Magazines and Manifestos: The Succession from Naturalism," *Modernism: A Guide to European Literature, 1890–1930*, ed. Bradbury and McFarlane (1976; ed. 1991), 200. Around 1860, the loyal and worried Bostonian Charles Eliot Norton wrote James Russell Lowell an admiring letter extolling the cultural importance of New York: "This is a wonderful city. There is a special fitness in the first syllable of its name, for it is essentially New." Nicolai Cikovsky, Jr., "The School of War," in Cikovsky, Franklin Kelly, et al., *Winslow Homer* (1995); *Les XX*, 18.

14 Daumier and Manet: see Gay, *Art and Act*, 37, 37n; Rops: letter to Henri Liesse, [December 8, 1886], in Robert L. Delevoy et al., *Félicien Rops* (1985), 175; Voysey: *Studio*, I (1893), 234. In 1872, the Belgian poet, novelist, and art critic Camille Lemonnier, folk hero among antibourgeois with his daring ideas and fiery talk, said in reviewing the Brussels salon, "I tell artists, be part of your century." "Salon de 1872," in Sura Levine, "Politics and the Graphics of the Belgian Avant-Garde," in *Les XX*, 69n.

3. Causes and Effects

1 See Roger Price, *A Social History of Nineteenth-Century France* (1987), table 1 (p. 4); Christophe Charle, *Histoire sociale de la France au XIXe siècle* (1991), 190, 220–21.

2 Price, *Social History of France*, table 24 (p. 79).

3 Hamerton: *Portfolio*, XXIII (1892), vii; Henry James: to J. B. Pinker, May 20, 1914, Beinecke Za, vol. III, No. 61, Beinecke Library, Yale University (not in Edel's 4-vol. selected letters); Lichtwark: to Bode, November 22 [18]90, Bode Nachlass, Z-SPK.

4 Wassily Kandinsky, *Über das Geistige in der Kunst* (1910; 8th ed., 1965), 22–23, 64.

5 G. K. Chesterton: *The Man Who Was Thursday: A Nightmare* (1908), 6 [ch. 1]; *New York Times*: Barbara Rose, *American Art since 1900: A Critical History* (1967), 76; Roosevelt: "A Layman's Views of an Art Exhibition," *Outlook* (March 29, 1913), in *The Works of Theodore Roosevelt*, ed. Hermann Hagedorn, 24 vols. (1923–26), XIV, 406.

6 Camille Mauclair, "La Réaction nationaliste en art et l' ignorance de l'homme de lettres," *La Revue*, LIV (January 15, 1905), 162, in James D. Herbert, *Fauve Painting: The Making of Cultural Politics* (1992), 127.

7 See Julie Manet, January 15, 1898, May 7, 1898, *Journal (1893–1899)*, ed. Jean Griot (1979), 148, 157.

8 I agree with Linda Nochlin, "Degas and the Dreyfus Affair: A Portrait of the Artist as an Anti-Semite," *The Dreyfus Affair: Art, Truth and Justice*, ed. Norman L. Kleeblatt (1987), 96–115, esp. 101–3.

9 For Degas, see esp. Daniel Halévy, *My Friend Degas* (1960; tr. and ed. Mina Curtiss, 1964).

10 Ralph E. Shikes and Paula Harper, *Pissarro: His Life and Work* (1980), 308.

11 See the convincing argument in Paul Hayes Tucker, *Claude Monet: Life and Art* (1995), 167–71, 179–80.

12 M. H. Port, *Imperial London: Civil Government Building in London, 1851–1915* (1995), ch. 13 ("The Battle of the Styles"); Sir George Gilbert Scott, *Personal and Professional Recollections*, ed. G. Gilbert Scott (1878), 177–201, a fairly extensive apologia.

13 Judikje Kiers and Fieke Tissink, *The Building of the Rijksmuseum: Design and Message* (1992), 4–8.

4. Against the Need for Probability

1 Thomas von Hartmann: "Über Anarchie in der Musik," *Der Blaue Reiter*, ed. Wassily Kandinsky and Franz Marc (1912; newly ed. Klaus Lankheit, 1965), 88.

2 Marius-Ary Leblond: James D. Herbert, *Fauve Painting: The Making of Cultural Politics* (1992), 28; Gauguin: Emil Gauguin, "Preface," *Paul Gauguin's Intimate Journals* (1918; tr. Van Wyck Brooks, 1936).

3 Wassily Kandinsky, *Über das Geistige in der Kunst* (1910; 8th ed., 1965), 133n.

4 Marc, in *Der Blaue Reiter*, 35.

5 Herbert, *Fauve Painting*, 31.

6 Lothar Grisebach, ed., *Von Munch bis Kirchner: Erlebte Kunstgeschichte in Briefen aus dem Nachlass von Eberhard Grisebach* (1968), 38.

7 Marc to Maria Marc, February 22, 1911, in Rosel Gollek, *Der Blaue Reiter im Lenbachhaus München. Katalog der Sammlung in der Städtischen Galerie* (1974), 212.

8 Paul Vogt, *Expressionism: German Painting, 1905–1920* (1978; tr. Antony Vivis and Robert Erich Wolf, 1980), 7.

9 John Richardson, *A Life of Picasso*, vol. I, *The Early Years, 1881–1906* (1991), 433.

10 Ibid., 95. Richardson captures the (fairly obvious) psychoanalytic implications of this parricidal observation: "This Oedipal maxim lies at the heart of Picasso's creative process." Ibid.

11 Ibid., 334.

12 Ibid., 474.

13 Gertrude Stein, *Fernhurst, Q. E. D., and Other Early Writings*, ed. Leon Katz (1971) 108–9, 77. (My attention to this early work was drawn by Robert M. Crunden, *American Salons: Encounters with European Modernism, 1885–1917* [1993], 172–73.)

14. See *Monet bis Picasso. Die Sammler Morosow, Schtschukin. 120 Meisterwerke aus der Eremitage, St. Petersburg, und dem Puschkin-Museum, Moskau*. ed. Georg-W. Költzsch (1994), passim, esp. 80–81, 111, 118–19.

15 See Frank Elgar and Robert Maillard, *Picasso*, tr. Francis Scarfe (1960), 73–74.

16 John Ruskin, *The Seven Lamps of Architecture* (1849; 2nd ed., 1855; World's Classics ed., 1940), 2.

17 Robert Kerr: *The Gentleman's House; or, How to Plan English Residences, from the Parsonage to the Palace: with Tables of Accommodations and Costs, and a Series of Selected Plans* (1864; 2nd rev. ed., 1865), 66, 340; William Morris: "How I became a Socialist" (1894), in MacCarthy, *William Morris*, 261; Morris to Andreas Scheu, September 15, 1883, ibid., 1.

18 Charles Rennie Mackintosh, handwritten draft, Papers on Architecture (1893), Fine Arts Library, University of Glasgow, Mackintosh Collection; F (t); Kerr, *The Gentleman's House*, 368.

19 Morris: Introduction to Ruskin, "On the Nature of Gothic," Kelmscott edition of a chap-

ter from *The Stones of Venice* (1892), in MacCarthy, *William Morris,* 69; Ruskin, *The Stones of Venice,* vol. III, ch. 2, par. 4.

20 Ruskin, *Seven Lamps of Architecture,* 21, 33, 3.

21 See Charles Rearick, *Pleasures of the Belle Epoque: Entertainment & Festivity in Turn-of-the-Century France* (1985), 121–25.

22 See Robert Baldick, *The Life of J.-K. Huysmans* (1955), 130.

23 Robert Kerr, *Royal Institute of Britain's Architects, Sessional Papers,* 1st ser., XIX (1868–69), 104, in John Summerson, *Victorian Architecture: Four Studies in Evaluation* (1970), 10–11.

24 Robert Macleod, *Charles Rennie Mackintosh* (1968), 15.

25 Charles Rennie Mackintosh, draft of a lecture September 1892, Papers on Architecture, Fine Arts Library, University of Glasgow, Mackintosh Collection, F (b). See also his Diary, Italian Tour, 1891: May 11, ibid., F (a).

26 Mackintosh, draft for "Seemliness" (December 1902), 2, 4, 9, ibid., F (e).

27 For a full description, see Macleod, *Mackintosh,* 61–64.

28 See Gay, *Art and Act,* 118.

29 Gay, *Art and Act,* 157.

30 Voysey to Fitch, November 1899, in Frank Jenkins, *Architect and Patron: A Survey of Professional Relations and Practice in England from the Sixteenth Century to the Present Day* (1961), 196.

31 The following three paragraphs are deeply indebted to Leonard K. Eaton, *Two Chicago Architects and Their Clients: Frank Lloyd Wright and Howard Van Doren Shaw* (1969).

32 Daniel Halévy, *My Friend Degas* (1960; tr. and ed. Mina Curtiss, 1964), 119.

33 Frans Coenen, *Onpersoonlijke herinneringen* (1936; tr. James Brockway under the title *The House on the Canal,* 1965) 25.

CODA: A Bourgeois Experience

1 I comment on these writers in some detail in *The Bourgeois Experience,* vol. I, *Education of the Senses* (1984), esp. 466–68.

BIBLIOGRAPHICAL ESSAY

The massive, burgeoning literature on the Victorian bourgeoisie in general and on the arts in particular has compelled me to focus on the titles I found to be particularly instructive, intriguing, or provocative. Since many are exhibition catalogs, I have placed the letter *c* after the date of publication whenever appropriate. When I refer to the four preceding volumes of *The Bourgeois Experience: Victoria to Freud,* I have abbreviated their titles: *Education of the Senses* (1984) = *ES; The Tender Passion* (1986) = *TP; The Cultivation of Hatred* (1993) = *CH;* and *The Naked Heart* (1995) = *NH.*

For this volume, three essential Freudian ideas have been especially important to me: anxiety, the array of defenses such as projection, and ambivalence. Each provides a key to individual thoughts and collective attitudes often ill expressed, if expressed at all, and go to the heart of the bourgeois experience in the Victorian age. The classic text on anxiety remains Sigmund Freud's *Inhibitions, Symptoms and Anxiety* (1926; tr. James Strachey et al. [1959], vol. XX in *The Standard Edition of the Complete Psychological Works of Sigmund Freud,* tr. and ed. James Strachey et al., 24 vols. [1953–74]). Reversing earlier views, Freud came to view anxiety as a signal of danger, realistic or imagined. Amid publications that have taken Freud's insights further, I single out Anna Freud's much cited and still unsurpassed *The Ego and the Mechanisms of Defence* (1936; tr. Cecil Baines, 1937), which organizes and expands on her father's observations; Rudolph M. Loewenstein, "Some Remarks on Defenses, Autonomous Ego, and Psychoanalytic Technique" (1954), *Practice and Precept in Psychoanalytic Technique: Selected Papers,* intro. Jacob A. Arlow (1982), 40–51; Max Schur's comprehensive survey "The Ego in Anxiety," *Drives, Affects, Behavior,* ed. Loewenstein (1953), 67–103; Hans W. Loewald, "The Problem of Defense and the Neurotic Interpretation of Reality" (1952), *Papers on Psychoanalysis* (1980), 21–32; Ernst Kris, "Danger and Morale" (1944), *The Selected Papers of Ernst Kris* (1975), 451–64; and Isabel E. P. Menzies, *The Functioning of Social Systems as a Defence against Anxiety: A Report on the Study of the Nursing Service of a General Hospital* (1970), a brilliant Kleinian pamphlet that goes far beyond its announced theme.

As we have come to recognize, evidence for ambivalence (a technical term that Freud took over from the Swiss psychiatrist Eugen Bleuler) is as abundant as its origins are hard to track down. A fancy name for mixed feelings, its work has featured prominently in my analysis of the pleasure wars. Freud's most sustained, most vivid discussion of ambivalence is his case history nicknamed "Little Hans": "Analysis of a Phobia in a Five-Year-Old Boy" (1909), *Standard Edition,* X, 5–149. Among Freud's explorations of this matter, two of his metapsychological papers stand out: "Instincts and Their Vicissitudes" (1915), ibid., XIV, 111–40, and "Mourning and Melancholia" (1917), ibid., 239–72. Though steadily referred to, ambivalence has had few papers specifically devoted to it. A welcome exception is Anton O. Kris, "The Conflicts of Ambivalence," in *The Psychoanalytic Study of the Child,* ed. Albert J. Solnit et al., XXXIX (1984) 213–34.

Although he has been (justly) criticized for a paucity of empirical material, the German psychoanalytically oriented sociologist Norbert Elias has left his mark on this book as much as on its predecessors with his immensely suggestive view that "human nature" is dynamic and open to change through the centuries. Elias's fundamental text is *The History of Manners: The Civilizing Process,* 2 vols. (1939; ed. 1968), vol. I, *The History of Manners* (tr. Edmund Jephcott, 1978); vol. II, *Power and Civility* (tr. Jephcott, 1982). Among the secondary literature on Elias, largely inspired by the Dutch sociologist Johan Goudsblom, see esp. Abram de Swaan, "On the Sociogenesis of the Psychoanalytic Setting," *Human Figurations, Essays for/Aufsätze für Norbert Elias,* ed. Peter Reinhart Gleichmann, Johan Goudsblom, and Hermann Korte (1977).

Donald D. Egbert, "The Idea of 'Avant-Garde' in Art and Politics," *American Historical Review,* LXXIII (December 1967), 339–66, is a sweeping introduction to the uses of this term; more research would be welcome.

INTRODUCTION: Definitions

In *ES,* I offered a substantial general introduction (pp. 3–68) designed to define "bourgeois." Since the present volume functions at once as a conclusion and an interpretation that stands on its own, I have provided it with its own definitions, consistent with the earlier effort but adding new titles.

This volume and its four predecessors may be read as a protest against clichés that have long served to caricature nineteenth-century bourgeois as canting hypocrites, money-crazed and philistine, incapable of love, rationalistic and yet irrational, and so forth. (Some of these fictions have recently been revived in Donald M. Lowe, *History of Bourgeois Perception* [1982].) Werner Sombart, *The Quintessence of Capitalism* (1913; tr. M. Epstein, 1915), a once influential account best described by its original title, *Der Bourgeois,* is, though still occasionally referred to, at best a historical curiosity. Charles Morazé, *The Triumph of the Middle Class* (1957; tr. 1966), lively and superficial, is more serviceable. *Bürgertum im 19. Jahrhundert. Deutschland im europäischen Vergleich,* ed. Jürgen Kocka, 3 vols. (1988), collects some forty germane articles on particular themes and individual countries. The nineteenth-century sections of Hartmut Kaelble, *Historical*

Research on Social Mobility (1977; tr. Ingrid Noakes, 1981), address an important issue. Papers in *Shopkeepers and Master Artisans in Nineteenth-Century Europe,* ed. Geoffrey Crossick and Heinz-Gerhard Haupt (1984), examine the petty bourgeoisie in several countries, incidentally showing the need for more scholarship. The same holds for Jacques Godechot, "The Business Classes and the Revolution outside France," *American Historical Review,* LXIV (October 1958), 1–13. See Maurice Halbwachs, *Esquisse d'une psychologie des classes sociales* (posthumously published in 1955), which attempts the virtually impossible—with some admirable results. And see the excellent chapter "The Lower-Middle-Class Thesis," in Richard F. Hamilton, *The Social Misconstruction of Reality* (1996), happily congruent with my own views.

The nineteenth-century French bourgeoisie has been splendidly served. Adeline Daumard's thesis, *La Bourgeoisie Parisienne de 1815 à 1848* (1963), abridged in *Les Bourgeois de Paris au XIXe siècle* (1970), and her recent synthesis, *Les Bourgeois et la bourgeoisie en France depuis 1815* (1987), are indispensable. I owe much to Christophe Charle, *Histoire sociale de la France au XIXe siècle* (1991). Among Charle's prolific output, note also *Les Hautes Fonctionnaires en France au XIX siècle* (1980). See also Roger Price, *A Social History of Nineteenth-Century France* (1987). *Les Capitalistes en France (1780–1914)* (1978), ed. Louis Bergeron, is an imaginative anthology with extensive editorial comments. Mechtild Fischer, *Mittelklasse als politischer Begriff in Frankreich seit der Revolution* (1974), explores the political uses of "bourgeoisie." Two near-classic massive studies, André Jean Tudesq, *Les Grands Notables en France. Etude historique d'une psychologie sociale* (1964), and Jean Lhomme, *La Grande Bourgeoisie au pouvoir (1830–1880)* (1960), have not dated. For further titles, see *ES,* 471–72.

Britain's Victorian middle classes have lately received refreshing (but at times unpersuasive) revisionist treatment. Simon Gunn, in "The 'Failure' of the Victorian Middle Class: A Critique," *The Culture of Capital: Art, Power and the Nineteenth-Century Middle Class,* ed. Janet Wolff and John Seed (1988), rightly laments "the absence of a coherent social history of the British middle class" and "the persistence of representations of the Victorian middle class as provincial Gradgrinds, locked in the dour pursuit of 'Facts' and profit margins" (p. 17). He is a little harsh, but his own essay, Alan White, "Class, Culture and Control: The Sheffield Athenaeum Movement and the Middle Class, 1847–64," ibid., 83–115, Janet Wolff, "The Culture of Separate Spheres: The Role of Culture in Nineteenth-Century Public and Private Life," ibid., 117–34, and Caroline Arscott and Griselda Pollock with Janet Wolff, "The Partial View: The Visual Representation of the Early Nineteenth-Century City," ibid., 191–233, are particularly worthwhile.

In fact Gunn and his colleagues have enjoyed good company for some time. Valuable general treatments include S. G. Checkland's impressive *The Rise of Industrial Society in England, 1815–1885* (1964); Harold Perkin's energetic insistence on England as a class society in evolution, in *The Origins of Modern English Society, 1780–1880* (1969); and Geoffrey Best's terse but highly suggestive *Mid-Victorian Britain, 1851–75* (1971). In contrast, F. M. L. Thompson's revisionist *The Rise of Respectable Society: A Social History of Victorian Britain, 1830–1900* (1988) minimizes conflict in general and class conflicts in particular—brisk, confident, but to be used with some reserve. Asa Briggs, *The Age of Improvement, 1783–1867* (1959), holds up well. Add *The Victorian Family: Structure and Stresses,* ed. Anthony S. Wohl (1978).

For more specialized treatments helping to define British middle-class society, see esp. Gregory Anderson, *Victorian Clerks* (1976); Geoffrey Crossick, *An Artisan Elite in Victorian Society: Kentish London, 1840–1880* (1978), to be read with *The Lower Middle Class in Britain,* ed. Crossick (1977), and the earlier I. J. Prothero, *Artisans and Politics in Early 19th-Century London* (1974), with more sympathy for their subjects than every historian would share; W. J. Reader, *Professional Men: The Rise of the Professional Classes in Nineteenth-Century England* (1966), a brief introduction to a large subject; Zuzanna Shonfield, *The Precariously Privileged: A Professional Family in Victorian London* (1987), which profitably focuses on a single clan; H. L. Malchow, *Gentlemen Capitalists: The Social and Political World of the Victorian Businessman* (1991), rather narrow; Leonore Davidoff, *The Best Circles: Etiquette and the Society Season* (1973), which goes beyond its title; Hartmut Berghoff, *Englische Unternehmer, 1870–1918* (1991), a German contribution; and H. J. Dyos, *Victorian Suburb: A Study of the Growth of Camberwell* (1973), by an astute urban historian who died all too soon. Boyd Hilton, *The Age of Atonement: The Influence of Evangelicalism on Social and Economic Thought, 1785–1865* (1988), a searching analysis, markedly contributes to our understanding of Victorian middle-class ideology in the making. Stefan Collini, *Public Moralists: Political Thought and Intellectual Life in Britain, 1850–1930* (1991), clarifies that ideology by looking at Victorian views on ethics, character, and public service. *The Conscience of the Victorian State,* ed. Peter Marsh (1979), explores whiggish, conservative, imperialist, and other springs of, and rationalizations for, public conduct. Thomas Walter Lacqueur, *Religion and Respectability: Sunday Schools and Working Class Culture, 1780–1850* (1976), satisfactorily demonstrates that middle-class concerns with working-class piety were anything but cynical social control. On middle-class status and attitudes, Theodore Koditschek, *Class Formation and Urban Industrial Society: Bradford, 1750–1850* (1990), ranges beyond a single city. Peter Earle's exemplary *The Making of the English Middle Class: Business, Society and Family Life in London, 1660–1730* (1989), though it deals with the prehistory of Victorian class formation (or, perhaps better, class consolidation), is highly pertinent. As anyone who has read or seen Shaw's *Pygmalion* well knows, speech and class identity are of crucial importance in Britain. See K. C. Phillipps, *Language and Class in Victorian England* (1984).

The German *Bürgertum* is the core of Kocka's collection (cited above, p. 268). Special studies rather than syntheses abound. Note particularly, for the public sector, Otto Hintze, "Der Beamtenstand" (1911), in *Gesammelte Abhandlungen,* vol. II, *Soziologie und Geschichte* (1942; 2nd enlarged ed., 1964), 66–125, which has lost none of its luster; and John R. Gillis, *The Prussian Bureaucracy in Crisis, 1840–1860* (1971). On entrepreneurs, Hartmut Kaelble, *Berliner Unternehmer während der frühen Industrialisierung. Herkunft, sozialer Status und politischer Einfluss* (1972), raises the right questions. At the other end of the scale, Friedrich Lenger, *Zwischen Kleinbürgertum und Proletariat: Studien zur Sozialgeschichte der Düsseldorfer Handwerker, 1816–1878* (1986), analyzes the vexed lot of petty bourgeois on the margin (artisans) in one city. Ernest K. Bramsted, *Aristocracy and the Middle Classes in Germany: Social Types in German Literature, 1830–1900* (1937; rev. ed., 1964), examines bourgeois self-appraisals in the German novel. James J. Sheehan, *German Liberalism in the Nineteenth Century* (1978), astutely surveys an influential political (bourgeois) minority. Useful contributions to *The German Family,* ed. Richard J. Evans and W. R. Lee (1981), demonstrate that sweeping generalizations on this difficult topic are unhelpful. Lothar Gall, *Bürgertum in Deutschland* (1989), follows one bourgeois family—the Bassermanns—through generations.

Sheehan's massive *German History, 1770–1866* (1989), a first-rate account, scrutinizes the *Bürgertum.* Hans-Ulrich Wehler's Weberian *Deutsche Gesellschaftsgeschichte,* 3 vols. so far (1987–96), reaching to 1914, must be consulted. Wehler's dashing, rather one-dimensional *Das deutsche Kaiserreich, 1871–1918* (1973), should be read in conjunction with Thomas Nipperdey's severe critique in *Geschichte und Gesellschaft,* I (1975), 539–60. The historian neglects Nipperdey's encyclopedic volumes, all with detailed attention to the *Bürgertum,* at his peril: *Deutsche Geschichte, 1800–1866. Bürgerwelt und starker Staat* (1983); *Deutsche Geschichte, 1866–1918,* vol. I, *Arbeitswelt und Bürgergeist* (1990), and vol. II, *Machtstaat vor der Demokratie* (1992). Johannes Ziekursch, *Politische Geschichte des neuen deutschen Kaiserreiches,* 3 vols. (1925–1930), is well over a half a century old but, with its consistent, well-grounded liberal stance, remains very much worth reading.

The literature on the United States is vast, and I can offer only a somewhat eccentric list of titles that have been important to me. (For American collectors, see below, p. 288–89.) It goes almost without saying that Tocqueville's *Democracy in America,* 2 vols. (1835, 1840; tr. George Lawrence, 1966), must be the starting point. André Jardin, *Tocqueville: A Biography* (1984; tr. Lydia Davis, with Robert Hemenway, 1988), says the essential. Among many commentaries, George W. Pierson, *Tocqueville and Beaumont in America* (1938), James T. Schleifer, *The Making of Tocqueville's "Democracy in America"* (1980), and Roger Boesche, *The Strange Liberalism of Alexis de Tocqueville* (1980), stand out. Parts 5 and 6 of James Bryce, *The American Commonwealth,* 2 vols. (1893; 2nd ed., 1913), bringing Tocqueville up to date, reflect the liberal vistas of the late nineteenth century.

Even though much of his work dealt with more recent history, everything Richard Hofstadter wrote has given me access to America's class society before the Great War. His early *The American Political Tradition and the Men Who Made It* (1948), his influential, controversial *The Age of Reform from Bryan to F.D.R.* (1955), his *Anti-intellectualism in American Life* (1963), or his *The Paranoid Style in American Politics and Other Essays* (1965), opened doors for me. For urban America, the seedbed of middle-class life, see esp. Kenneth T. Jackson, *Crabgrass Frontier: The Suburbanization of the United States* (1985); Gunther Barth, *City People: The Rise of Modern City Culture in Nineteenth-Century America* (1980); Constance McLaughlin Green, *The Rise of Urban America* (1965), to be read with Karen Halttunen, *Confidence Men and Painted Women: A Study of Middle-Class Culture in America, 1830–1870* (1982), which traces shifts in bourgeois values and conduct at mid-nineteenth century.

Stow Persons, *The Decline of American Gentility* (1973), studies the move from country to city and from gentry to the urban buccaneer. A contrasting picture emerges from Tamara Plakins Thornton, *Cultivating Gentlemen: The Meaning of Country Life among the Boston Elite, 1785–1860* (1989). On shaping cultural styles, there are Edward Chase Kirkland, *Dream & Thought in the Business Community, 1860–1900* (1956); Robert Green McCloskey, *American Conservatism in the Age of Enterprise, 1865–1910: A Study of William Graham Sumner, Stephen J. Field and Andrew Carnegie* (1951); R. Jackson Wilson, *In Quest of Community: Social Philosophy in the United States, 1860–1920* (1968); Thomas C. Cochran and William Miller, *The Age of Enterprise: A Social History of Industrial America* (1942; rev. ed., 1961); Irvin G. Wyllie, *The Self-Made Man in America: The Myth of Rags to Riches* (1954). Thomas Bender, *New York Intellect: A History of Intellectual Life in New York City from 1750 to the Beginnings of Our Own Time* (1987), is stimulating and reaches beyond its title. Burton J. Bledstein, *The Culture of Professionalism: The Middle Class and the Development of Higher Education in America* (1976), discusses the meanings of "middle class" rather more cynically than (I think) necessary. Its attitude recalls the radical sociologist C. Wright Mills's once widely discussed *White Collar: The American Middle Classes* (1951).

The old stark division between the cultured minority and the unwashed many had dissatisfied historians long before it was subjected to some tart cultural criticism by American journalists from the late 1940s on. I recall Russell Lynes, "Highbrow, Lowbrow, Middlebrow" (1949), rev. ed. *The Tastemakers* (1954), 310–33, and Dwight Macdonald's long, spirited essay "Masscult and Midcult" (1960), *Against the American Grain* (1962), 3–75, which, like Lynes's article, proposes a threefold division. The utility of this proposal is evident and has application beyond the twentieth century or the United States (in art history, Albert Boime demonstrated it in a book on French taste in the arts; see below, p. 291). At the same time, a certain cultural snobbery (the middle class is capable only of "midcult," more palatable than masscult, but inferior to real cultivation) limits the uses of these expositions.

For other countries, see John A. Davis, *Conflict and Control: Law and Order in Nineteenth-Century Italy* (1988), in some ways an evasive but serviceable survey. Denis Mack Smith, *Italy: A Modern History* (1959; rev. ed., 1969), should be read with J. A. Thayer, *Italy and the Great War: Politics and Culture, 1871–1915* (1964). Smith, *Cavour* (1985), is fine on Italian reunification. Two essays in *Mélanges de l'Ecole Française de Rome—Moyen Age, Temps Modernes*, XCVII (1965), are particularly informative: Paolo Frascani, "Les Professions bourgeoises en Italie à l'époque libérale (1860–1920)," 325–40; and Paolo Macry, "Notables, professions libérales, employés," ibid., 341–59. For Sweden, Jonas Frykman and Orvar Löfgren, *Culture Builders: A Historical Anthropology of Middle-Class Life* (1979; tr. Alan Crozier, 1987), is an interesting sociological study drawing a profile of the Swedish bourgeoisie between 1880 and 1910; following Norbert Elias, it explores manifestations of the bourgeois style like punctuality, cleanliness, discipline, etc.

Largely because its military and artistic glory had faded long before the Victorians, foreign scholars have slighted the nineteenth-century Netherlands. For the controversy over whether the Netherlands came late to industrialization, see Richard T. Griffiths, *Industrial Retardation in the Netherlands, 1830–1850* (1979); J. J. Brugmans, "Economic

Fluctuations in the Netherlands in the 19th Century," *Essays in European Economic History, 1789–1914*, ed. François Crouzet et al. (1969); and J. G. van Dillen, *Omstandigheten en psychische factoren in de economische geschiedenis van Nederland* (1949).

Russia's middle class was small but vigorously participated in the artistic earthquakes of the time. I have profited from Nicholas V. Riasanovsky, *A Parting of Ways: Government and the Educated Public in Russia, 1801–1855* (1976); Thomas C. Owen, *Capitalism and Politics in Russia: A Social History of the Moscow Merchants, 1855–1905* (1981), about a great political failure; Robert W. Thurston, *Liberal City, Conservative State: Moscow and Russia's Urban Crisis, 1906–1914* (1987). There is still much of interest in W. H. Bruford, *Chekhov and His Russia: A Sociological Study* (1948). Not surprisingly, *The Family in Imperial Russia: New Lines of Historical Research*, ed. David L. Ransel (1976), has little on the bourgeoisie—it was, after all, a small class—but see esp. Barbara Alpern Engel, "Mothers and Daughters: Family Patterns and the Female Intelligentsia," 44–59.

For the varied uses of "Victorian," see esp. the spacious entry in *The Oxford English Dictionary*, ed. J. A. Simpson and E. S. C. Weiner, 20 vols. (12 vols. 1933–1986; 2nd ed., 1989), XIX, 609. To the best of my knowledge, other scholars have not commented on the rather expansive definition I have given in the text. The figurative uses of "Victorian" cited in *The Oxford English Dictionary* would seem to give me license (Mark C. Carnes, *Secret Ritual and Manhood in Victorian America* [1989], is not the only title that comes to mind for its employment in American history). For the "pre-Victorians," any sound history of Britain before 1837 will supply the necessary information. The classic Elie Halévy, *England in 1815* (1913; tr. E. I. Watkins and D. A. Barker, 1924; 2nd ed., 1949), remains unsurpassed. G. Kitson Clark, *The Making of Victorian England* (1972), and Muriel Jaeger, *Before Victoria: Changing Standards and Behaviour, 1787–1837* (1956), are useful brief accounts.

The Great Exhibition of 1851, that curious mixture of royal patronage and bourgeois self-assertion, has been astonishingly slighted by historians. *The Crystal Palace Exhibition Illustrated Catalogue, London* (1851) has been reprinted unabridged (1970), introd. John Gloag. C. H. Gibbs-Smith, *The Great Exhibition of 1851: A Commemorative Album* (1970), has its uses. Whitney Walton, *France at the Crystal Palace: Bourgeois Taste and Artisan Production in the Nineteenth Century* (1992), discovers an emerging bourgeois style of consumption. I have profited from Jeffrey A. Auerbach's "Exhibiting the Nation: The Great Exhibition of 1851 and British National Identity," Ph.D. diss., Department of History, Yale University (1996), which is being readied for publication.

BOURGEOIS EXPERIENCES, V: Bourgeoisophobes

In a characteristically suave essay on Flaubert's *Bouvard et Pécuchet*, Lionel Trilling argued, "For him the bourgeoisie was the bourgeoisie from top to bottom." ("Flaubert's Last Testament," *The Opposing Self* [1955], 183.) As my text shows, precisely the opposite was true: "bourgeoisie" was for Flaubert largely a resounding word of abuse, a virtually meaningless category, since it included the working classes. For any understanding of Flaubert, Jean Bruneau's exemplary edition of his *Correspondance*, 3 vols. so far, reaching to 1868 (1973–91), is mandatory. Among English collections of his priceless letters, the best are *The Letters of Gustave Flaubert*, sel., ed., and tr. Francis Steegmuller, 2 vols. (1979–82); *Flaubert-Sand: The Correspondence*, tr. Steegmuller and Barbara Bray (1993); and *Flaubert & Turgenev: A Friendship in Letters: The Complete Correspondence*, ed. and tr. Barbara Beaumont (1985). I have learned much from Victor Brombert's beautifully annotated anthology of passages from Flaubert, published and unpublished, *Flaubert par lui-même* (1971). Brombert, *The Novels of Flaubert: A Study of Themes and Techniques* (1966), is an elegant survey. Steegmuller, *Flaubert and Madame Bovary: A Double Portrait* (1939), still repays reading. César Graña, *Modernity and Its Discontents: French Society and the French Man of Letters in the Nineteenth Century* (1964; ed. 1967), a sociological essay on alienation in mid-nineteenth-century France, has some important pages on Flaubert. Novelists have played splendid variations on their favorite writer: Mario Vargas Llosa, *The Perpetual Orgy: Flaubert and Madame Bovary* (1975; tr. Helen Lane, 1986), and Julian Barnes, *Flaubert's Parrot* (1984), offer special delights. The *Souvenirs littéraires* by Flaubert's friend Maxime du Camp, editor, pioneering photographer, historian of Paris, gossip (1881–82; ed. 1985) have their moments. Francine du Plessix Gray, *Rage and Fire: A Life of Louise Colet, Pioneer Feminist, Literary Star, Flaubert's Muse* (1994), makes rather too much of Flaubert's mistress and sounding board.

For the "real" Rouen in Flaubert's time, Jean Pierre Chaline's reasonable, substantial *Les Bourgeois de Rouen. Une Elite urbaine au XIXe siècle* (1982) sets out the facts in detail. It should be read with the pages on Rouen in Daniel J. Sherman's excellent monograph, *Worthy Monuments: Art Museums and the Politics of Culture in Nineteenth-Century France* (1989), and François Bergot, "La Donation François Depeaux au musée des Beaux-Arts de Rouen," *Arts, objets d'art, collections. Etudes sur l'art du Moyen Age et de la Renaissance sur l'histoire du goût et des collections* (1987), 205–11.

There were, we know, other articulate bourgeoisophobes. See Rüdiger Safranski, *E. T. A. Hoffmann. Das Leben eines skeptischen Phantasten* (1987), perhaps the most successful among German biographies. Brigitte Feldges and Ulrich Stadler, *E. T. A. Hoffmann. Epoche—Werk—Wirkung* (1986), is an intelligent overview of life, work, and ambiance. On Hoffmann the bourgeoisophobe, see Hans-Georg Werner, "Der romantische Schriftsteller und sein Philister-Publikum. Zur Wirkungsfunktion von Erzählungen E. T. A. Hoffmanns," *Weimarer Beiträge*, XXIV (1978), 87–114. Readers without German could do worse than read H. W. Hewett-Thayer, *Hoffmann: Author of the Tales* (1948), and *The Romantic Period in Germany*, ed. Siegbert Prawer (1970), esp. Brian Rowley, "The Novelle," 121–46. And see Peter Gay, *NH*, 37–102, esp. 42–54. (For Théophile Gautier, see below, in the section on critics.) The beautifully annotated five-volume Pléiade edition of Zola's *Les Rougon-Macquart. Histoire naturelle et sociale d'une famille sous le second Empire*, ed. Armand Lanoux and Henri Mitterand (1960–1967), is indispensable. So is Zola, *Correspondance*, impeccably edited by B. H. Bakker, with Colette Becker, 10 vols. (1978–93). F. W. J. Hemmings, *Emile Zola* (1953; 2nd ed., 1966), dependable, fairly brief, is stronger on the life than the works. Frederick Brown, *Zola: A Life* (1995), is a monumental and impressive biography. Brian Nelson, *Zola and the Bourgeoisie: A Study of Themes and Techniques in "Les Rougon-Macquart"* (1983), addresses the issues central to this volume.

For all the mountains of commentary, the Marxist attitude toward the bourgeoisie deserves more attention. Since class is the central category in its thought, observations on bourgeois pervade the work of Marx, Engels, and their loyal acolytes. Some classic, at least most frequently quoted, statements appear in the *Communist Manifesto* (1848); another key document is Marx's witty, devastating foray into contemporary French history, *The Eighteenth Brumaire of Louis Bonaparte* (1852). Among commentaries Isaiah Berlin, *Karl Marx: His Life and Environment* (1939; 4th ed., 1978), brief and lucid, has survived well. See also George Lichtheim, *Marxism: An Historical and Critical Study* (1961; ed. 1965), esp. pt. 4, "The Theory of Bourgeois Society, 1850–1895," and Robert C. Tucker, *Philosophy and Myth in Karl Marx* (1969; rev. ed., 1972).

In recent years, after decades of enthusiastic or damning overinterpretations, Nietzsche has been fortunate in his readers. Walter A. Kaufmann's *Nietzsche: Philosopher, Psychologist, Antichrist* (1950; 4th ed., 1974) made a sensational difference upon its first appearance, but scholars have modified Kaufmann's passionate rehabilitation. Alexander Nehamas, *Nietzsche: Life as Literature* (1985), is a brilliant assessment consistently carried through. See also Michael Tanner, *Nietzsche* (1996), a veritable tour de force: the whole man in less than a hundred pages. Keith Ansell-Pearson, *An Introduction to Nietzsche as Political Thinker* (1996), bravely tackles Nietzsche's aristocratic-anarchistic social thought. Stephen E. Aschheim, *The Nietzsche Legacy in Germany, 1890–1990* (1992), ably traces Nietzsche's diverse influence.

As I have noted in the text, bourgeoisophobia is a good deal older than the nineteenth century. If a history of that phobia is ever written, Jean V. Alter, *Les Origines de la satire anti-bourgeoise en France. Moyen Age–XVIe siècle* (1966), offers a model for other scholars. Its eighteenth-century origins are particularly interesting since the opposite—the idealized bourgeois trader as a rational, pacific, and tolerant model as he appears in Addison and Voltaire—also flourished. The alienation from the supposedly unimaginative and grasping middle classes makes a vivid appearance in late-eighteenth-century German drama and fiction. Roy Pascal, *The German Sturm und Drang* (1951), a social interpretation, still has much to say; see also Astrid Grieger, *"Etwas zu dem Ruhm und Nutzen meines Vaterlands beizutragen." Die politische Dimension der bürgerlichen Kunstkonzeption in der Sturm-und-Drang-Zeit* (1993), and Alan C. Leidner, *The Impatient Muse: Germany and the Sturm und Drang* (1994). A. Blunden, "J. M. R. Lenz," *German Men of Letters*, ed. Alex Natan and Brian Keith-Smith, vol. VI (1972), 207–40, deals with the best-known *Stürmer und Dränger*. W. H. Bruford, *Germany in the Eighteenth Century: The Social Background of the Literary Revival* (1935), authoritatively explores the social and political context. The youthful Goethe, as everybody knows, went through a Sturm und Drang phase, of which *The Sorrows of Young Werther* (1774; first translated into English in 1779) is the classic expression. Since the literature on Goethe is notoriously vast, I shall mention just two titles, Barker Fairley, *A Study of Goethe* (1947), a penetrating and civilized portrait, and Nicholas Boyle, *Goethe: The Poet and the Age,* vol. I, *The Poetry of Desire (1749–1790)* (1991), a comprehensive, impressive analysis.

For the rise and impact of the piano, I have used three major histories: Rosamond E. M. Harding, *The Piano-Forte: Its History Traced to the Great Exhibition of 1851* (1933); Arthur Loesser, *Men, Women and Pianos: A Social History* (1954), a justly popular work; and Cyril Ehrlich, *The Piano: A History* (1976). To this should be added Richard K. Lieberman, *Steinway & Sons* (1995), which manages to be at once scholarly and gossipy.

ONE: The Political Economy of Art

For the intimate connection between bourgeois taste and the pyramid of bourgeois incomes, Gerald Reitlinger, *The Economics of Taste: The Rise and Fall of the Picture Market, 1760–1960* (1961), is indispensable. On contemporary ideas about taste, see Charles L. Eastlake, *Hints on Household Taste in Furniture, Upholstery and Other Details* (1868; 3rd rev. ed., 1872), and its continental counterpart, Jacob von Falke, *Geschichte des Modernen Geschmacks* (1866; 2nd rev. ed., 1880).

From the literature on German artists and their market, a few titles stand out: *Deutsche Malerei im 19. Jahrhundert. Sammlung Georg Schäfer,* ed. Peter Schäfer (1977-c); William Vaughan, *German Romantic Painting* (1980; 2nd ed., 1994), for an influential school, to be supplemented by Gottfried Riemann et al., *Ahnung & Gegenwart. Zeichnungen und Aquarelle der deutschen Romantik* (1994-c), which publishes many little-known drawings and watercolors. Christa Pieske, *Bilder für jedermann. Wandbilddrucke, 1840–1940* (1988-c), is a superb, extremely well-illustrated survey of the kind of art that "little people" liked to hang on their walls, to be supplemented with Wolfgang Brückner, *Elfenbeinreigen-Hochzeitstraum. Die Öldruckfabrikation, 1880–1940* (1974), at once amusing and informative.

The best book on Caspar David Friedrich, who, around 1900, after decades of obscurity, was elevated into a German icon and has received incessant exposure, is Joseph Leo Koerner's learned, clearheaded *Caspar David Friedrich and the Subject of Landscape* (1990). The Friedrich expert Helmut Börsch-Supan produced (with Karl Wilhelm Jähnig) the gargantuan *Caspar David Friedrich. Gemälde, Druckgraphik und bildmässige Zeichnungen* (1973), which offers literal, unvarying keys to each element in Friedrich's oeuvre; it gives, in my view, symbolic interpretation a bad name. For other major German artists, see Horst Vey et al., *Anselm Feuerbach, 1829–1880. Gemälde und Zeichnungen* (1976-c), thorough and dependable; *Anton von Werner. Geschichte in Bildern,* ed. Dominik Bartmann (1993-c), with a series of essays that capture the painter who was virtually the empire's official artist, to be read with Werner's bulky memoir, *Erlebnisse und Eindrücke, 1870–1890* (1913). Siegfried Wichmann, *Franz von Lenbach und seine Zeit* (1973), is a full life of a major financial success, though Franz von Lenbach's autobiography, *Gespräche und Erinnerungen,* retains a certain charm; Matthias Eberle et al., *Max Liebermann in seiner Zeit* (1979-c), impressively surveys this semi-Impressionist's work. All these texts are copiously illustrated. See also the slim but meaty study by Thomas W.

Gaehtgens, *Anton von Werner. Die Proklamierung des deutschen Kaiserreiches. Ein Historien-
bild im Wandel preussischer Politik* (1990), of Werner's most famous painting; Edit Trost,
Eduard Gaertner (1991), an agreeable survey of Berlin's favorite topographical artist; and,
for comparison's sake, Elisheva Cohen and Ismar Schorsch, *Moritz Oppenheim: The First
Jewish Painter* (1983-c), a deliberately *retardataire* German artist—text in English and
Hebrew.

For the ladder of German income in the Victorian century, see Sheehan, Wehler, and
Nipperdey listed above (p. 271). Two well-chosen anthologies, *Deutsche Sozialgeschichte.
Dokumente und Skizzen*, vol. I, *1815–1870*, ed. Werner Pöls (1973), and vol. II, *1870–1914*,
ed. Gerhard A. Ritter and Jürgen Kocka (1974), are highly serviceable. See also
Sozialgeschichtliches Arbeitsbuch, vol. I, *Materialien zur Statistik des Deutschen Bundes,
1815–1870*, ed. Wolfram Fischer et al. (1982), laden with charts and tables; and Ashok V.
Desai, *Real Wages in Germany, 1871–1913* (1968), a technical survey awash in statistics.
Among contemporary social observers, Otto von Leixner, *1888 bis 1891. Soziale Briefe
aus Berlin, mit besonderer Berücksichtigung der sozialdemokratischen Strömungen* (1891),
includes budgets and observant discussions. Nancy B. Reich, *Clara Schumann: The Artist
and the Woman* (1985), and Alice M. Hanson, *Musical Life in Biedermeier Vienna* (1985),
have valuable material on the income of musicians.

In analyzing incomes in France, I have again drawn on Daumard's magisterial work
and on Price, *Social History of Nineteenth-Century France*, esp. ch. 4 (see above, p. 269);
Michael B. Miller, *The Bon Marché: Bourgeois Culture and the Department Store, 1869–1920*
(1981); Jacques Lethève, *The Daily Life of French Artists* (1968; tr. Hilary E. Paddon, 1971),
passim, esp. ch. 9; Ralph P. Locke, "Paris: Centre of Intellectual Ferment," in *The Early
Romantic Era between Revolutions: 1789 and 1848*, ed. Alexander Ringer (1990); and Jean
Montgrédien, *Musique en France des Lumières au Romantisme (1789–1830)* (1986), for the
pay of singers. *Mémoires de Hector Berlioz, comprenant ses voyages en Italie, en Allemagne, en
Russie et en Angleterre, 1803–1865*, 2 vols. (1870; 2nd ed., 1878; ed. Pierre Citron, 1991),
makes for wonderful reading. And see Jean Fourastié, *Machinisme et bien-être. Niveau de
vie et genre de vie en France de 1700 à nos jours* (1950; 3rd ed., 1962; an earlier edition is
available as *The Causes of Wealth*, tr. and ed. Theodore Caplow, 1960). Theodore Zeldin's
encyclopedic *France 1848–1945*, 2 vols. (1973–77), must be consulted. Harrison C. White
and Cynthia A. White, *Canvases and Careers: Institutional Change in the French Painting
World* (1965), offers precise and pointed information. F. W. J. Hemmings, *Culture and
Society in France, 1848–1898* (1971), is a well-informed survey. James Smith Allen, *In the
Public Eye: A History of Reading in Modern France, 1800–1940* (1991), is an ambitious and
welcome analysis.

The matrix within which Britons bought art is soberly presented in T. S. R. Boase,
English Art, 1800–1870 (1959). John Steegman's informal and selective *Victorian Taste: A
Study of the Arts and Architecture from 1830 to 1870* (first published under the title *Consort
of Taste, 1830–1870*, 1950; ed. 1970) remains worth reading. See also the discussion of
"patterns of consumption" in W. Hamish Fraser, *The Coming of the Mass Market,
1850–1914* (1981). R. K. Webb's brief analysis, "The Victorian Reading Public," in *The
Pelican Guide to English Literature*, ed. Boris Ford, vol. VI (1958; 2nd ed., 1982), 198–219,

is a model of clarity, to be read with David Vincent, *Literary and Popular Culture: England, 1750–1914* (1989), for the low end of the economic pyramid. See also the two introductory essays by G. D. Klingopulos, "Notes on the Victorian Scene," *Pelican Guide*, 13–54, and "The Literary Scene," ibid., 57–113; and John Gloag, *Victorian Comfort: A Social History of Design, 1830–1900* (1961). Jennifer Hall, "The Re-fashioning of Fashionable Society: Opera-Going and Sociability in Britain, 1821–1861," Ph.D. diss., Department of History, Yale University (1996), analyzes the hierarchy of income from the perspective of the audiences.

Historians of arts in American society (which is officially all middle-class) have been chipping away at this idealized portrait. John A. Kouwenhoven, *Made in America: The Arts in Modern Civilization* (1948), cuts a wide swath in a narrow compass. Carl Bode's informative *Antebellum Culture* (originally published in 1959 under the title *The Anatomy of American Popular Culture, 1840–1861;* ed. 1970) is more limited in scope (it covers very similar ground to Halttunen—see above, p. 271). Neil Harris, *The Artist in American Society: The Formative Years, 1790–1860* (1966), is an ample, persuasive study. See also Harris, *Humbug: The Art of P. T. Barnum* (1973). Henry Nash Smith, *Democracy and the Novel: Popular Resistance to Classic American Writers* (1978), slim and masterly, pits "elite" against "popular" audiences. (More recently, and more aggressively, Lawrence W. Levine, *Highbrow/Lowbrow: The Emergence of Cultural Hierarchy in America* [1988], has covered similar ground with a more populist animus.)

While the copying activities of major artists have not had the silent treatment from scholars, more can be done. Meanwhile, we have Theodore Reff, "Copyists in the Louvre, 1850–1870," *Art Bulletin*, XLVI (December 1964), 552–59. Denis Rouart, editor of *Correspondance de Berthe Morisot avec sa famille et ses amis* (1950), comments on Morisot. For Courbet, see Jack Lindsay, *Gustave Courbet: His Life and Art* (1973). Adolphe Jullien, *Fantin-Latour. Sa vie et ses amitiés* (1909), has interesting detail. See also Georg Winkler, "Lenbach als Kopist und Kunstberater des Grafen Schack," *Die Kunst*, XIX (1909), 23–30, 46–54; and Beth Archer Brombert's fine biography, *Edouard Manet: Rebel in a Frock Coat* (1995), esp. pp. 33–39.

For cultivation sought, and at times achieved, through foreign travel, James Buzard, *The Beaten Track: European Tourism, Literature, and the Ways to 'Culture,' 1800–1918* (1993), is exemplary; Alan Sillitoe, *Leading the Blind: A Century of Guide Book Travel, 1815–1914* (1995), is rewarding as well.

That protean, immensely powerful model William Morris has a biography worthy of him in Fiona MacCarthy, *William Morris: A Life for Our Time* (1995). Among earlier still valuable studies, I single out E. P. Thompson, *William Morris: Romantic to Revolutionary* (1955; ed. with new intro., 1976), which stresses his radicalism; Peter Stansky, *William Morris* (1983), remarkable for its compression; and Stansky, *Redesigning the World: William Morris, the 1880s, and the Arts and Crafts,* which covers Morris's influence. See also *William Morris: Selected Writings and Designs,* ed. Asa Briggs (1962), a fine anthology; and *William Morris: The Critical Heritage,* ed. Peter Faulkner (1973), which collects the responses of his contemporaries.

TWO: The Geography of Taste

For Manchester, in addition to finding a rich harvest in the Henry Watson Music Library, the Rylands Library, a copious (if not quite complete) three-volume compendium, *Programmes: Hallé's Concerts* (n.d.), which helped to determine the evolution of Mancunian taste, and the *Manchester Guardian*, I relied on an array of published materials. Michael Kennedy, *The Hallé Tradition: A Century of Music* (1960), proved extremely helpful, to be supplemented with *The Autobiography of Charles Hallé, with Correspondence and Diaries*, ed. Kennedy (1973). Christopher Fifield, *True Artist and True Friend: A Biography of Hans Richter* (1993), has interesting sidelights on music in Manchester.

Asa Briggs's sturdy, pioneering essay "Manchester, Symbol of a New Age," *Victorian Cities* (1963), ch. 3, gives a lively account. A. J. P. Taylor, "The World's Cities: Manchester," *Encounter*, VIII, 3 (March 1957), 3–13, is vigorous as usual. See also *Rich Inheritance: A Guide to the History of Manchester*, ed. N. J. Frangopulo (1962), with brief essays on local personalities and urban issues, and a solid introduction, "The Growth of Manchester," by the editor. For me the most profitable chapters in *City, Class and Culture: Studies of Social Policy and Cultural Production in Victorian Manchester*, ed. Alan J. Kidd and K. W. Roberts (1985), were Michael E. Rose, "Culture, Philanthropy and the Manchester Middle Classes" (ch. 5), and M. Harrison, "Art and Philanthropy: T. C. Horsfall and the Manchester Art Museum" (ch. 6). For a widely copied local initiative, see Thomas S. Ashton, *Economic and Social Investigations in Manchester, 1833–1933: A Centenary History of the Manchester Statistical Society* (1934). Howard M. Wach, "Culture and the Middle Classes: Popular Knowledge in Industrial Manchester," *Journal of British Studies*, XXVII (October 1988), 373–404, offers useful material. Robert H. Kargon, *Science in Victorian Manchester: Enterprise and Expertise* (1977), depicts the shift from amateur to professional science. François Vigier, *Liverpool and Manchester during the Industrial Revolution: Change and Apathy* (1970), gives an interesting comparative account. Shena D. Simon, *A Century of City Government: Manchester, 1838–1938* (1938), is a dependable history. For the city's most famous newspaper, see J. L. Hammond, *C. P. Scott of the Manchester Guardian* (1934); and David Ayerst's detailed *Guardian: Biography of a Newspaper* (1971). On the controversial issue of free trade, there is Arthur Redford et al., *Manchester Merchants and Foreign Trade, 1794–1858* (1934). On high culture, see esp. John Seed, " 'Commerce and the Liberal Arts': The Political Economy of Art in Manchester, 1775–1860," *The Culture of Capital* (cited above, p. 269), 45–81, which energetically contests the malicious caricature of Mancunian philistinism.

For institutions, see Manchester Free Library, *Report of the Proceedings at the Public Meetings Held in the Library, Camp Field, Manchester, on Thursday, September 2nd, 1852, to Celebrate the Opening of the Free Library* (1852; slightly abridged ed., 1902); *The John Rylands Library Manchester: 1899–1924*, ed. Henry Guppy (1924); Joan Allgrove et al., *A Short Guide to the Whitworth Art Gallery* (n.d.), a terse account; Royal Manchester Institute, *Catalogue of the Exhibition of Pictures by Italian, Spanish, Flemish, Dutch and English Masters, with Which the Proprietors Have Favoured the Institution, for the Improvement of Taste in the Fine Arts, and the Gratification of the Governors and the Public* (1831); and Sir Charles Hallé, "The Royal Manchester College of Music," *Strand Musical Magazine,* I (1895), 323–39. C. P. Darcy, *The Encouragement of the Fine Arts in Lancashire, 1760–1860* (1976), is slim but very substantial. See also *Art and Architecture in Victorian Manchester,* ed. John H. G. Archer (1985).

Among contemporary witnesses, a few stand out: Louis M. Hayes, *Reminiscences of Manchester: And Some of Its Local Surroundings from the Year 1840* (1905), which, as it were, walks across the town Hayes lived in all his life; ch. 40 is on the Manchester Art Treasures Exhibition of 1857; ch. 52, on music. *The Diaries of Absalom Watkin: A Manchester Man, 1787–1861,* ed. Magdalen Goffin (1993), enriches entries with connecting commentary. Leon Faucher, *Manchester in 1844, Its Present Condition and Future Prospects,* tr. "with copious notes appended by a Member of the Manchester Athenaeum" (1844), has sensitive observations by a foreigner, as does Alexis de Tocqueville, *Journeys to England and Ireland,* ed. J. P. Mayer (1958). W. Cooke Taylor, *Notes of a Tour in the Manufacturing District of Lancaster* (1841), and Sir William Napier, *The Life and Opinions of Sir Charles James Napier,* 2 vols. (1857), often used—and rightly—offer quotable judgments, as does Thomas Carlyle's famous *Chartism* (1839). Another subjective judgment, still alive with its animus, is Friedrich Engels, *The Condition of the Working-Class in England in 1844* (1845; tr. 1892). There is fascinating material in Gustav Friedrich Waagen, *Treasures of Art in Great Britain: Being an Account of the Chief Collections of Paintings, Drawings, Sculptures, Illuminated Mss &c., &c,* 3 vols. (1854), by the knowledgeable director of the royal gallery of paintings in Berlin, following up on an earlier compendium of 1838. Novels are not social history, but Elizabeth Gaskell's come close (setting aside for a moment their literary value), with their penetrating, affectionate, yet unsentimental evocations. *The Letters of Mrs. Gaskell* (1966) have been authoritatively edited by J. A. V. Chapple and Arthur Pollard. And see Winifred Gérin, *Elizabeth Gaskell* (1976).

Manchester's culturally prominent Jews deserve further research, especially on the early-nineteenth-century German-Jewish immigrants. Meanwhile there is Bill Williams, *The Making of Manchester Jewry, 1740–1875* (1976), which, though generally solid, fails to specify the Jewish share in Manchester's music and philanthropy. C. C. Aronsfeld, "German Jews in Victorian England," *Leo Baeck Yearbook,* VII (1962), 312–29, esp. 318–20, is of some help.

The Bayerische Hauptstaatsarchiv, Bayerische Staatsbibliothek, and that rich local archive the Stadtbibliothek (Monacensia), both in Munich, were almost inexhaustible resources. Among secondary texts the most useful were M. Doeberl, *Entwicklungsgeschichte Bayerns,* vol. III, *Vom Regierungsantritt König Ludwigs I. bis zum Tode König Ludwigs II. mit einem Ausblick auf die innere Entwicklung Bayerns unter dem Prinzregenten Luitpold,* completed by Max Spindler (1931), which, though old, retains much authority. *Handbuch der Bayerischen Geschichte,* vol. IV, pts. 1 and 2, *Das neue Bayern,* ed. Spindler (1974–75), is indispensable, esp. pt. 2. *Geschichte der Stadt München,* ed. Richard Bauer

(1992), a modern collective history, has, above all, Ralf Zerback, "Unter der Kuratel des Staates—Die Stadt zwischen dem Gemeindeedikt von 1818 und der Gemeindeordnung von 1869," 274–306, and Elisabeth Angermair, "München als süddeutsche Metropole—Die Organisation des Grossstadtausbaus 1870 bis 1914," ibid., 307–35. Florian Simhart, *Bürgerliche Gesellschaft und Revolution. Eine ideologiekritische Untersuchung des politischen und sozialen Bewusstseins in der Mitte des 19. Jahrhunderts* (1978) explores bourgeois consciousness, and is drenched in Habermas.

I have consulted with profit civilized reminiscences by Munich's literary and drama critics and observant citizens, notably Friedrich Pecht, *Aus meiner Zeit. Lebenserinnerungen* (1894); Theodor Goering, *Dreissig Jahre München. Kultur- und kunstgeschichtliche Betrachtungen* (1904); Alfred von Mensi-Klarbach, *Alt-Münchner Theater-Erinnerungen* (1923; 2nd ed., 1924); Rosalie Braun-Artaria, *Von berühmten Zeitgenossen. Lebenserinnerungen einer Siebzigerin* (n.d. [ca. 1917]); Hermann Uhde-Bernays, *Im Lichte der Freiheit. Erinnerungen aus den Jahren 1880 bis 1914* (1947; 2nd ed., 1963); and Ernst von Possart, *Hermann Levi,* published a year after Levi's death in 1900, which appreciates this great and tormented conductor with whom he worked closely. See also Peter Gay, "Hermann Levi: A Study in Service and Self-Hatred" (1975), *Freud, Jews and Other Germans: Masters and Victims in Modernist Culture* (1978), ch. 4.

Among monographs I learned most from Heinrich Bihrle, *Die Musikalische Akademie München, 1811–1911* (1911); Peter Böttger, *Die Alte Pinakothek in München* (1972), exhaustive; York Langenstein, *Der Münchner Kunstverein im 19. Jahrhundert. Ein Beitrag zur Entwicklung des Kunstmarkts und des Ausstellungswesens* (1983), thoroughly documented; and Ulrike von Hase's conscientious *Joseph Stieler, 1781–1858. Sein Leben und sein Werk* (1971), on the painter famous for his portraits of Beethoven, Goethe, and the "Gallery of Beauties" commissioned by Ludwig I. *Wilhelm von Leibl und sein Kreis,* ed. Michael Petzet (1974-c), does justice to the most gifted though long underappreciated realist painter working in Munich.

The literature on Bavaria's monarchs, whose direction of high culture was overpowering and whose melodramatic careers invite anecdotal treatment, include, for Ludwig I, Doeberl, *Entwicklungsgeschichte,* III, 3–168, and Spindler, *Handbuch,* pt. 2, pp. 69–227, as the most sober texts. Ludwig Hauff, *Leben und Wirken Maximilian II., Königs von Bayern* ("a book for the people") (1864), is an instance of total subservience and piety, but usefully lists the ways King Max supported Bavarian culture. It must be supplemented by the histories already mentioned, and several articles by H. Rall, esp. "Wie König Maximilian II die Kultur förderte," *Bayerland,* LV (1953), 27–32. For Ludwig II, the source of innumerable rumors, there is (as Spindler puts it, p. 253) no "scientifically satisfactory large-scale biography." Meanwhile, we have Gottfried von Böhm, *Ludwig II. König von Bayern* (1921; 2nd ed., 1924). An early treatment of Ludwig and the arts is Luise von Kobell, *König Ludwig II. von Bayern und die Kunst* (1898), partially superseded by Michael Petzet, *König Ludwig II. und die Kunst* (1968-c), whose author has also contributed a chapter on this subject to Wilfrid Blunt, *The Dream King: Ludwig II of Bavaria* (1970), no doubt the (literally) most colorful biography. The career of Richard Wagner is, of course, indelibly linked to that of Ludwig II. From a vast literature, I single out

Robert W. Gutmann, *Richard Wagner: The Man, His Mind, and His Music* (1968), well informed but implacably hostile. Ernest Newman's great *The Life of Richard Wagner,* 4 vols. (1933–47), is severe yet less adversarial. The Master's wife's exhaustive diaries recording his sayings for posterity, Cosima Wagner, *Die Tagebücher,* ed. Martin Gregor-Dellin and Dietrich Mack, 2 vols. (1976–77), are appalling but certainly essential reading. For Wagner's own show, see Frederic Spotts, *Bayreuth: A History of the Wagner Festival* (1994).

THREE: Acknowledged Legislators

The century of critics has found impressive historians. The first four volumes of René Wellek's *A History of Modern Criticism,* 8 vols. (1955–92), are models of searching analyses of critics from the mid-eighteenth century on. Margaret Gilman, *The Idea of Poetry in France from Houdar de La Motte to Baudelaire* (1958), essentially starts with Diderot, but throws much light on the nineteenth-century critical scene. Though not historical in intent, Northrop Frye's influential *Anatomy of Criticism: Four Essays* (1957) has done much to establish a typology for literary critics. On the literary criticism of the romantics, see esp. Wellek, *History of Modern Criticism,* vol. II. Lothar Pikulik, *Frühromantik. Epoche—Werke—Wirkung* (1992), is an orderly overview. Ernst Behler, a leading Schlegel expert, has written a short life, *Friedrich Schlegel in Selbstzeugnissen und Bilddokumenten* (1966), but (surprisingly) no major biography exists; the best life in English (short) is Hans Eichner, *Friedrich Schlegel* (1970). On the foundations of his literary criticism, there is an excellent article by Heinrich Henel, "Friedrich Schlegel und die Grundlagen der modernen literarischen Kritik," *German Review,* XX (1945), 81–93. See also Klaus Briegleb, *Aesthetische Sittlichkeit. Versuch über Friedrich Schlegels Systementwurf zur Begründung der Dichtungskritik* (1962), and, more general, Lilian R. Furst's very helpful *Romanticism in Perspective. A Comparative Study of Aspects of the Romantic Movements in England, France, and Germany* (1969). Rudolf Haym, *Die romantische Schule. Ein Beitrag zur Geschichte des deutschen Geistes* (1870), remains for all its age a vital resource. See also Peter Gay, *NH,* ch. 1.

For its evolution, Lionello Venturi, *History of Art Criticism* (1936; rev. ed. tr. Charles Marriott, 1964), rushes from ancient Greece to the twentieth century in fewer than 400 pages, but maps its development and raises questions that still bedevil art historians. It should be read with Albert Dresdner, *Die Entstehung der Kunstkritik im Zusammenhang der Geschichte des europäischen Kunstlebens* (1915; ed. 1968); it only reaches Diderot but opens the door to an understanding of later criticism. See also the carefully reasoned study by Michael Podro, *The Critical Historians of Art* (1982), esp. chs. 1 to 5, which cover the period between Immanuel Kant and Alois Riegl. Anita Brookner, *The Genius of the Future: Studies in French Art Criticism: Diderot, Stendhal, Baudelaire, Zola, the Brothers Goncourt, Huysmans* (1971), is lively and (fortunately) opinionated. The Marxist Arnold Hauser's *Philosophie der Kunstgeschichte* (1958) is less dogmatic than some of his other work and remains a contribution to the sociology of art.

So far (unless I have missed it) there is no full history of music criticism. Meanwhile we have Max Graf, *Composer and Critic: Two Hundred Years of Musical Criticism* (1946), and Georgia Cowart, *The Origins of Modern Musical Criticism* (1981). Edward Lippman, *A History of Western Musical Aesthetics* (1992), esp. pt. 4, "The Nineteenth Century," explores the philosophical background. Werner Braun, *Musikkritik. Versuch einer historisch-kritischen Standortbestimmung* (1972), offers a wide-ranging sociological-musicological-historical analysis, all in about 150 pages. Among many histories of nineteenth-century music, Leon Plantinga, *Romantic Music: A History of Musical Style in Nineteenth-Century Europe* (1984), is sensitive to the cultural situation in which music criticism emerged. (See also Plantinga, *Schumann as Critic* [1967], a model for further examination of Victorian creators as critics, an area rather neglected except for the greatest exemplars like Baudelaire or Henry James.) Specialized essays abound: see the slim *Beiträge zur Geschichte der Musikkritik,* ed. Heinz Becker (1965), notably Ursula Eckart-Bäcker, "Der Einfluss des Positivismus auf die französische Musikkritik im 19. Jahrhundert" (pp. 69–103), and Imogen Fellinger, "Das Brahmsbild der *Allgemeinen musikalischen Zeitung* (1863 bis 1882)" (pp. 37–54), to be read in conjunction with Peter Gay, " 'Aimez-vous Brahms?' On Polarities in Modernism" (1977), *Freud, Jews and Other Germans,* ch. 5 (see above, p. 281). I am indebted to Eckart-Bäcker, *Frankreichs Musik zwischen Romantik und Moderne. Die Zeit im Spiegel der Kritik* (1965), esp. 15–36, for her scathing account of corrupt music reviewing in Paris at mid-century. For a narrowly focused view of a respectable periodical, see Katharine Ellis, *Music Criticism in Nineteenth-Century France: "La Revue et Gazette musicale de Paris," 1834–80* (1996).

There is considerable diversion (and useful information) in two dictionaries of uncomplimentary comments on composers, the first about Wagner and the second about the profession as a whole: Wilhelm Tappert, *Wörterbuch der Unhöflichkeit, enthaltend grobe, höhnende, gehässige und verleumderische Ausdrücke, die gegen den Meister Wagner, seine Werke und seine Anhänger von den Feinden und Spöttern gebraucht wurden* (1876; 2nd ed., 1903), and Nicolas Slonimsky, *Lexicon of Musical Invective: Critical Assaults on Composers since Beethoven's Time* (1953; 2nd ed., 1965).

In recent years, since Marcel Proust's much praised critique of Sainte-Beuve's biographical approach, *Contre Sainte-Beuve* (compl. 1909; posthumously publ. 1954; tr. and ed. Sylvia Townsend Warner in *Marcel Proust on Art and Literature, 1896–1919* [1964]), Sainte-Beuve's reputation, long unquestioned, has been severely damaged. José Cabanis, *Pour Sainte-Beuve* (1987), the first and longest essay in a collection, is a voice for the defense. Proust's hostility, though understandable, is overstated. As one might somehow expect, Flaubert had anticipated him, tersely, in a letter to George Sand of February 2, 1869; a little derisively, he called his friend Sainte-Beuve a "historian" and wondered if critics would ever be "artists, nothing but artists, real artists." (*The Selected Letters of Flaubert,* tr. and ed. Francis Steegmuller [1953], 217–18.) Wellek, whose own chapter on Sainte-Beuve (*History of Modern Criticism,* vol. III) is comprehensive, curtly dismisses Proust's assessment with one word, "curious" (p. 281). A. G. Lehmann's exhaustive and responsible *Sainte-Beuve: A Portrait of the Critic, 1804–1842* (1962) has unfortunately not been followed up by a second volume. André Billy, *Sainte-Beuve, sa vie et son temps,* 2 vols. (1952), remains unsurpassed. But see also Nicole Casanova, *Sainte-Beuve* (1995), full, well-informed, informal but solidly documented, as well as Maurice Allem, *Portrait de Sainte-Beuve* (1954), a thoughtful canvass by an expert. W. H. Frohock, "The Critic and the Cult of Art: Sainte-Beuve and the Esthetic Movement," *Romanic Review*, XXXII (December 1941), 379–88; and the response by Edna Fredrick, "The Critic and the Cult of Art: Further Observations," ibid., XXXIII (December 1942), 385–87, raise central questions. Gilman, *Idea of Poetry*, has appreciative, though not uncritical, pages (esp. in chs. 6 and 7). The Pléiade edition of Sainte-Beuve is moving at a halting pace, and for most of his texts the reader must still depend on the old nineteenth-century editions of the *Lundis*, the *Portraits des femmes*, and the rest, which, as I have said in the notes, is a bibliographical nightmare. The *Correspondance générale*, ed. Jean Bonnerot, 19 vols. (1935–83), is an important resource.

Théophile Thoré (in later years he confused identification by presenting himself as "W. Bürger" and at times even had "Bürger" write prefaces for Thoré) has had his partisans. P. Pétroz, *Un Critique d'art au XIXe siècle. Théophile Thoré* (1884), was apparently the first to recognize his greatness. *Thoré-Bürger, peint par lui-même. Lettres et notes intimes* ed. P. Cottin (1900), brings together ample documentation. See also H. Marguery's pathbreaking biographical (but not analytical) articles, "Un Pionnier de l'histoire de l'art: Thoré-Bürger," *Gazette des beaux-arts*, 5th ser., XI (1925), 229–45, 295–311, 367–80. Pontus Grate, *Deux critiques d'art de l'epoque romantique: Gustave Planche et Théophile Thoré* (1959), offers a comparative dimension. A published dissertation by Frances Suzman Jowell, *Thoré-Bürger and the Art of the Past* (1977), learnedly connects Thoré's discoveries of the Dutch with his political views. André Blum, *Vermeer et Thoré-Bürger* (1946), sees Thoré's infatuation with Dutch art as a defense of realism. (Significantly, Thoré is a hero, a "great historian and critic" [p. 85], to Francis Haskell; see his fascinating *Rediscoveries in Art: Some Aspects of Taste, Fashion and Collecting in England and France* [1976], esp. 84–102.)

Henry James's criticism (including the self-explorations in the famous prefaces to the New York edition of his novels) not only of fiction but of fellow reviewers amounts to a telling indictment of his time, even if in his isolation he overstates the triumph of vulgarity. Always the professional, James gathered his occasional criticism into four volumes, notably *French Poets and Novelists* (1878; 2nd ed., 1884), which contains longish, often original reviews of Balzac, Flaubert, Gautier, Baudelaire, Sand, and others. *Partial Portraits* (1888) offers a miscellany of thoughts on Emerson, George Eliot, George du Maurier, et al. A late collection, *Notes on Novelists with Some Other Notes* (1914), contains ripe reflections on, among others, Zola, Sand, D'Annunzio. Henry James, *Selected Literary Criticism*, ed. Morris Shapira (1963), reprints complete essays; in contrast Henry James, *The Critical Muse: Selected Literary Criticism*, ed. Roger Gard (1987), gives snippets, thus permitting a wider but shallower view. See also Morris Roberts, *Henry James's Criticism* (1929). On James as an appreciator, critic, and, in his fiction, user of art, see Viola Hopkins Winner, *Henry James and the Visual Arts* (1970), and Adeline R. Tintner, *The Museum World of Henry James* (1986); both link his taste to his fiction. See also Peter Gay, *NH*, 254–63.

For Baudelaire as critic of art and literature, the commentaries in *Oeuvres complètes,* ed. Y. G. Le Dantec, rev. Claude Pichois (1961), are invaluable. *The Painter of Modern Life and Other Essays,* tr. and ed. Jonathan Mayne (1965), is an appetite-whetting collection of his essays on painting, literature, and music. So is *The Mirror of Art: Critical Studies by Baudelaire* (1956), which concentrates on his salons. Margaret Gilman, *Baudelaire the Critic* (1943), is penetrating. The more recent study by Rosemary Lloyd, *Baudelaire's Literary Criticism* (1982), seeks to boost his reputation as a critic and places him in his world. So, in her own way, does Lois Boe Hyslop, *Baudelaire, Man of His Time* (1980), which shows the poet in persistent conversation with writers, artists, and politicians.

Joanna Richardson, *Théophile Gautier, His Life and Times* (1958), is a major biography of this novelist, critic, journalist, champion of the doctrine of art for art's sake. (On that doctrine, Albert L. Guérard, *Art for Art's Sake* [1936], cast its net widely—too widely.) For his formative years, see René Jasinski, *Théophile Gautier, les années romantiques* (1929), and John Garber Palache, *Gautier and the Romantics* (1926). Maxime du Camp, *Théophile Gautier* (1890), is mainly of historical interest. For his art criticism, see Robert Snell, *Théophile Gautier* (tr. J. E. Gordon, 1893), and Michael Clifford Spencer's more recent, excessively hostile *The Art Criticism of Théophile Gautier* (1969). *Critique d'art: Extraits de Salons, 1833–1872. Théophile Gautier,* ed. Marie Hélène Girard (1994), is a handy edition. *Gautier on Dance,* sel. and ed. Ivor Guest (1987), shows the man's versatility. Richard B. Grant, *Théophile Gautier* (1975), is a short life in English.

Hanslick, the "music czar" of late-nineteenth-century Vienna, deserves more consideration in the English-speaking world than he has had; to most he is little more than the bumbling and ridiculous Beckmesser lampooned in Wagner's *Meistersinger.* Werner Abegg, *Musikästhetik und Musikkritik bei Eduard Hanslick* (1974), is trim. Eduard Hanslick, *Aus dem Tagebuch eines Rezensenten. Gesammelte Musikkritiken,* ed. Peter Wapnewski (1989), is a well-selected anthology, with a searching postscript by the editor. *Eduard Hanslick: Musik Criticisms, 1846–1899* (1950), performs a similar service in English. Peter Gay, "For Beckmesser: Eduard Hanslick, Victim and Prophet" (1976), *Freud, Jews and Other Germans,* (ch. 6), is a rescue attempt. So is Stewart Deas, *In Defence of Hanslick* (1940), a pamphlet by an enthusiast.

Shaw's music and drama criticism have been well collected, recently as *Shaw's Music: The Complete Music Criticism,* ed. Dan H. Laurence, 3 vols. (1981), and *Our Theatres in the Nineties,* 3 vols., for the Constable edition of Shaw (1932). In addition, *How to Become a Musical Critic,* ed. Laurence (1960), brings together uncollected material. The same editor has captured the essence of this entertaining and indefatigable letter writer in his selected *Correspondence,* 4 vols. (1965–88). Of course, Shaw's plays, with their commentaries often longer than the play itself, are also a form of criticism. The most comprehensive modern biography of Shaw is Michael Holroyd, *Bernard Shaw,* 4 vols. (1988–93). For analyses of his drama criticism and fundamental attitudes, see esp. the discussion by Martin Meisel, *Shaw and the Nineteenth Century Theater* (1963), esp. chs. 3 and 4.

The most interesting nineteenth-century German critic after the romantics was the novelist, historian, poet, and travel writer Theodor Fontane. His *Sämtliche Werke* (the so-called Nymphenburg Ausgabe), ed. Edgar Gross, 24 vols. in 30 (1959–75), provides the best access to these texts: two volumes for the literary criticism (vol. XXI, 1–2); three volumes for the drama criticism (XXII, 1–3); two volumes for the art criticism (XXIII, 1–2). For the first, Joachim Biener, *Fontane als Literaturkritiker* (1956); for the second, Bertha E. Trebein, *Theodor Fontane as a Critic of the Drama* (1916); for the third, perhaps the best articles are Wilhelm Vogt, "Theodor Fontane und die bildende Kunst," *Sammlung,* IV (1949), 154–63; V (1950), 275–80. Hans-Heinrich Reuter, *Fontane,* 2 vols. (1968), is very thorough in its details but its (relatively muted) left-wing readings remain controversial. Peter Demetz, *Formen des Realismus. Theodor Fontane. Kritische Untersuchungen* (1964), is a stylish appraisal that links Fontane to Scott.

Lionel Trilling, *Matthew Arnold* (1939), an Arnoldian appraisal, helped in the rediscovery of the critic and poet. He has been succinctly captured in Stefan Collini, *Arnold* (1988). Nicholas Murray, *A Life of Matthew Arnold* (1996), seeks to account for his subject's shift from poetry to prose. Sidney Coulling, *Matthew Arnold and His Critics: A Study of Arnold's Controversies* (1974), lays out the debates the combative Arnold rejoiced in. David J. DeLaura, *Hebrew and Hellene in Victorian England: Newman, Arnold, Pater* (1969), puts him into his intellectual world. For an anthology of first-rate articles, see *Matthew Arnold,* ed. Kenneth Allott (1975).

Richard Ellmann has conveniently collected Wilde's literary essays and observations in *The Artist as Critic: Critical Writings of Oscar Wilde* (1968) and supplied a felicitous introduction. *The Letters of Oscar Wilde,* ed. Rupert Hart-Davis (1962), is indispensable; a few items that had escaped have been captured by the same editor, in *More Letters of Oscar Wilde* (1985). Richard Ellmann, *Oscar Wilde* (1988), is the most authoritative life; though justly covered with praise, I find it a shade too admiring. *Oscar Wilde: The Critical Heritage,* ed. Karl Beckson (1970), is sensibly voluminous. Melissa Knox, *Oscar Wilde: A Long and Lovely Suicide* (1994), has been reviled for its psychoanalytic speculations, but strikes me as a brave effort.

For other critics who, for one reason or another, play secondary roles in this book, vols. III and IV of Wellek, *History of Modern Criticism,* provide essential judgments. See also Dorothy Richardson Jones on that prodigious, once extremely influential *"King of Critics": George Saintsbury, 1845–33* (1992), and the helpful but a little cautious overview by Harold Orel, *Victorian Literary Critics: George Henry Lewes, Walter Bagehot, Richard Holt Hutton, Leslie Stephen, Andrew Lang, George Saintsbury and Edmund Gosse* (1984). John Gross, *The Rise and Fall of the Man of Letters: A Study of the Idiosyncratic and the Humane in Modern Literature* (1969), is less narrow and far more lively. James Kissane, "P. G. Hamerton, Victorian Art Critic," *Burlington Magazine* (January 1972), 22–28, discusses an almost forgotten sensible critic and editor. Hamerton's *Thoughts about Art* (1871; 2nd ed., 1876) makes for interesting reading.

Joseph C. Sloane, *French Painting between the Past and the Present: Artists, Critics, & Traditions from 1848 to 1870* (1951), is an excellent study of art criticism in action.

FOUR: Hunters and Gatherers

Scholars, once indifferent to collecting, are now taking it seriously. Werner Muensterberger, *Collecting: An Unruly Passion* (1993), is a suggestive psychoanalytic exploration. In *Museums, Objects and Collections: A Cultural Study* (1992), Susan M. Pearce, a curator who has written widely on her field, has two fascinating chapters (3 and 4), Kleinian in orientation, on this obsession. Among nineteenth-century collectors' autobiographies, a small specialized genre of its own, William Carew Hazlitt, *The Confessions of a Collector* (1897), and Edwin C. Bolles, *Collectors & Collecting* (1898), are among the most self-aware. Joseph Alsop, *The Rare Art Traditions: The History of Art Collecting and Its Linked Phenomena Wherever These Have Appeared* (1982), resembles a tour through a historical museum with a genial guide intent on making his case that collecting has historically been confined to certain cultures. There is rich material in *The English as Collectors,* ed. Frank Herrmann (1972). Francis Haskell and Nicholas Penny, *Taste and the Antique: The Lure of Classical Sculpture, 1500–1900* (1981), a first-rate history, begins with Renaissance collectors, but illuminates the purposefulness of collectors in general. A little-known novel by Robert Graves, *Antigua, Penny, Puce* (1936), is a deft double portrait of two implacable competitors—brother and sister—with much "wisdom" (many would call it male chauvinist) about collectors male and female along the way. Wilmarth Lewis, the great collector of Horace Walpole's correspondence, has a charming and psychologically astute *Collector's Progress* (1952). There is a fascinating little catalog by Lewis Hall, *The William A. Clark Collection: Treasures of a Copper King* (1989-c), which well illustrates that the passion Clark brought to amassing pictures, sculptures, majolica, and delft ware equaled the passion he had expended accumulating a fortune in copper and influence as a senator.

For Freud as collector, see above all *Sigmund Freud on Art: His Personal Collection of Antiquities,* ed. Lynn Gamwell and Richard Wells, intro. Peter Gay (1989-c). The saga of Freud's private "museum" has spread to popular magazines for the educated: see Helen Dudar, "The Unexpected Private Passion of Sigmund Freud," *Smithsonian,* XXI, 5 (August 1990), 100–108. According to his unsparing biographer Edward Jay Epstein, the buccaneer Armand Hammer called his art collection his "ticket to immortality." See *Dossier: The Secret History of Armand Hammer* (1996).

The first half of Aline B. Saarinen, *The Proud Possessors: The Lives, Times and Tastes of Some Adventurous American Art Collectors* (1958; ed. 1968), a pleasingly written and anecdotal introduction to the field, covers the nineteenth century. The monograph by Lillian B. Miller, *Patrons and Patriotism: The Encouragement of the Fine Arts in the United States, 1790–1860* (1966), is a sober survey. Neil Harris, *The Artist in American Society* (cited above, p. 278), fits well into this section. Mahonri Sharp Young, *The Golden Eye: Magnificent Private Museums of American Collectors* (1983), a rapid, copiously illustrated survey, may serve as supplement. Alexis Gregory, *Families of Fortune: Life in the Gilded Age* (1993), provides glimpses into the habitations of the very rich in several countries. See also the thoroughly documented series of essays on the mansion of Alfred Krupp, *Villa Hügel. Das Wohnhaus Krupp in Essen,* ed. Tilmann Buddensieg (1984). The last three titles, each of them lavishly illustrated, offer at least some justification for the avant-gardes' complaints about bourgeois taste.

Many hunters and gatherers are well documented. Thomas Lawton and Linda Merrill, *Freer: A Legacy of Art* (1993), is exhaustive and satisfying on Charles Lang Freer, outstanding collector of Whistler and of Asian art. For the early admirers of Cézanne, surprising because most of them were far from rich, see, among the lives, Gerstle Mack, *Paul Cézanne* (1935), and John Rewald, *Paul Cézanne: A Biography* (1948; ed. 1967, tr. Margaret R. Liebmann, 1968). Cézanne and his fellows have received ample justice in Anne Distel, *Impressionism: The First Collectors* (1989; tr. Barbara Perroud-Benson, 1990), which authoritatively reports on prices and the art market. (See also Raymonde Moulin, *Le Marché de la peinture en France* [1970]). It has been strikingly supplemented by Anne Dumas, "Degas as a Collector," *Apollo,* CXLIV, new ser., no. 415 (September 1996), 3–72, a comprehensive analysis. For *père* Tanguy, see Emile Bernard, "Julien Tanguy, dit le *père* Tanguy," *Mercure de France,* LXXVI (December 16, 1908), 600–616; John Rewald, "Chocquet et Cézanne," *Gazette des beaux-arts,* 6th period, LXXIV (July–August, 1969), 33–96, conveniently reprinted in Rewald, *Studies in Impressionism,* ed. and tr. Irene Gordon and Frances Weitzenhoffer (1986), 121–87; and Anthea Callen, "Faure and Manet," ibid., LXXXIII (March 1974), 157–78. Yvonne Tiénot, *Chabrier. Par lui-même et par ses intimes* (1965), adds important information. Charles Blanc, "Le Cabinet de M. Thiers," *Gazette des beaux-arts,* 1st ser., XII (April 1862), 289–320, is a pleasant interview with the politician as collector. See also Peter Krieger, "Max Liebermanns Impressionisten-Sammlung und ihre Bedeutung für sein Werk," Matthias Eberle et al., *Max Liebermann in seiner Zeit* (1979-c), 60–71. Wolfgang Hardtwig, "Drei Berliner Porträts: Wilhelm von Bode, Eduard Arnhold, Harry Graf Kessler. Museumsmann, Mäzen und Kunstvermittler—Drei herausragende Beispiele," *Mäzenatentum in Berlin. Bürgersinn und kulturelle Kompetenz unter sich verändernden Bedingungen,* ed. Günter and Waldtraut Braun (1993), 39–71, instructively links the collector Arnhold to the museum director Bode, a significant collector in his own right. And see *Eduard Arnhold. Ein Gedenkbuch,* ed. Johanna Arnhold and Adolf Grabowsky (1928), a generous tribute. On Bode, who also belongs to the section on movers and shakers, three slim volumes published in 1995 by the Staatlichen Museen zu Berlin–Preussischer Kulturbesitz, bring the cultural situation, including the place of collectors, to life: Werner Knopp et al., *Wilhelm von Bode. Museumsdirektor und Mäzen;* Angelika Wesenberg, *Wilhelm von Bode als Zeitgenosse der Kunst;* and Volkmar Enderlein, *Wilhelm von Bode und die Berliner Teppichsammlung.* Bode's autobiography, *Mein Leben,* 2 vols. in 1 (1930), has charms of its own. Munich, a good city for collectors, has been well studied in Robin Lenman, "A Community in Transition: Painters in Munich, 1886–1924," *Central European History,* XV (March 1982), 3–33.

William R. Johnston, "William Thompson Walters," *The Taste of Maryland: Art Collecting in Maryland, 1800–1934,* ed. Johnston (1984-c), 50–60, tersely says the essential, especially read with the whole of the catalog. Walters's (anonymously published) anthology, *Antoine-Louis Barye: From the French of Various Critics* (1885), gives evidence of his enthusiasm. (For Barye, see Stuart Pivar, *The Barye Bronzes* [1974-c], a catalogue raisonné, which treats the artist as conscientious craftsman, at once independent and romantic; Charles Otto Zieseniss, *Les Aquarelles de Barye. Etude critique et catalogue raisonné* [1954-c]; and *Antoine-Louis Barye: The Corcoran Collection,* ed. Lilien F. Robinson and Edward J. Nygren [1988-c], esp. Robinson, "Barye and the French Sculptural Tradition," [ch. 1], "Barye and Patronage," [ch. 9–which includes Walters], and Elizabeth W. Harter and Laurence Pamer, "Individuality: Barye's Aesthetic of the Particular" [ch. 2].) Lillian M. C. Randall, *The Diary of George A. Lucas: An American Art Agent in Paris, 1857–1909,* 2 vols. (1979), throws light on Walters and other American collectors. And see Gertrude Rosenthal et al., *The George A. Lucas Collection of the Maryland Institute* (1965-c). For an articulate defense of the kind of painter they loved in Baltimore, see Gerald M. Ackerman et al., *Jean-Léon Gérôme (1824–1904)* (1972-c).

Splendid Legacy: The Havemeyer Collection, ed. Alice Cooney Frelinghuysen et al. (1993-c), is a magnificent record of a magnificent collection. Louisine Havemeyer, *Sixteen to Sixty: Memoirs of a Collector* (1930; ed. 1961), is artlessly enlightening. A pair of catalogs, Hubert von Sonnenburg, *Rembrandt/Not Rembrandt in the Metropolitan Museum of Art: Aspects of Connoisseurship,* vol. I, *Paintings: Problems and Issues,* and Walter Liedtke et al., vol. II, *Paintings, Drawings, and Prints* (1995-c), at once entertaining and scholarly, incidentally throw light on Harry Havemeyer's Rembrandts. On the Fischer collection, *Expressionismus und Exil. Die Sammlung Ludwig und Rosy Fischer, Frankfurt am Main,* ed. Georg Heuberger (1990-c), is definitive; see esp. Heuberger, "Jüdische Mäzene und Kunstsammler in Frankfurt am Main," 9–15. Paul Arnsberg, *Die Geschichte der Frankfurter Juden seit der französischen Revolution,* 3 vols. (1983), esp. vol. III, *Biographisches Lexikon der Juden in den Bereichen: Wissenschaft, Kultur, Bildung, Öffentlichkeitsarbeit in Frankfurt am Main,* has material on Jewish collectors in the city. Sergei Shchukin and Ivan Morosov, those two unsurpassed Russian collectors of modernist art (and patrons of modernist artists), have been impressively served in *Monet bis Picasso. Die Sammler Morosow, Schtschukin. 120 Meisterwerke aus der Eremitage, St. Petersburg, und dem Puschkin-Museum, Moskau,* ed. Georg-W. Költzsch (1994-c).

As for Britain, Trevor Fawcett, *The Rise of English Provincial Art: Artists, Patrons, and Institutions outside London (1800–1830)* (1974), ably covers the early period. Several titles listed in "Geography of Taste," above, notably Darcy, *Encouragement of the Fine Arts,* are equally applicable to this section. See also *Vernon Heath's Recollections* (1892), with candid memories of his uncle, the collector Robert Vernon, and the brief study by Robin Hamlyn, *Robert Vernon's Gift: British Art for the Nation, 1847* (1993). David Robertson, *Sir Charles Eastlake and the Victorian Art World* (1978), is a splendidly vivid biography, which fully justifies its subtitle. (Dianne Sachko Macleod, *Art and the Victorian Middle Class: Money and the Making of Cultural Identity* [1996], which concentrates in the English as collectors, came to my attention only as this book went to press.)

The literature on patrons who "collected" artists as well as their work is uneven. Henry C. Lunn, "Patronage," *Musical Times,* XVIII (June 1, 1877), 272–73, offers an interesting contemporary opinion. Herbert Weinstock, *Rossini: A Biography* (1968), the best I have seen on Rossini's patron and friend Alexandro María Aguado, suggests the need for further work. Alfred Bruyas holds a prominent place in all Courbet biographies: see esp. Jack Lindsay, *Gustave Courbet: His Life and Art* (1973), and the older Pierre Borel, *Le Roman de Gustave Courbet, d'après une correspondance originale du grand peintre* (1922). The *Letters of Gustave Courbet,* ed. and tr. Petra ten-Doesschate Chu (1992), are a valuable resource. For Bruyas as patron of his city, see *Courbet à Montpellier* (1985-c). A savage little novel by Champfleury (pseud. Jules Fleury), *Les Sensations de Josquin* (1859), mercilessly lampoons Bruyas as an egomaniac. (Incidentally, a brief exchange between the narrator and the stand-in for Bruyas foreshadows the conflict the present volume seeks to elucidate: " 'You argue like a painter,' I tell him. 'And you like a bourgeois.' " [p. 31].)

Two articles by Albert Boime show what a historian can do with the modern Maecenas: "Entrepreneurial Patronage in Nineteenth-Century France," *Enterprise and Entrepreneurs in Nineteenth- and Twentieth-Century France,* ed. Edward C. Carter, Robert Forster, and Joseph Moody (1976), 137–91; and "Les Hommes d'affaires et les arts en France au XIXe siècle," *Actes de la recherche en sciences sociales,* XXVIII (1979), 57–75. A good introduction to the Steins, brother and sister, and to their friends, is James R. Mellow, *Charmed Circle: Gertrude Stein and Company* (1974). In editing *A Stein Reader-Gertrude Stein* (1993), Ulla Dydo has revolutionized Stein scholarship, redating her publications, reinterpreting her significance, and writing "an introduction to her language experiments" (p. 3). Robert M. Crunden, *American Salons: Encounters with European Modernism, 1885–1917* (1993), is good on the background and helpful on the Steins.

Caroline Arscott, "Employer, Husband, Spectator: Thomas Fairbairn's Commission of 'The Awakening Conscience,' " *The Culture of Capital* (cited above, p. 269), 159–90, fruitfully examines the complicated history of one patron and one painting. For Rubens as collector, see Christopher White, *Peter Paul Rubens: Man and Artist* (1987), esp. 67–73, and Michael Jaffé, "Rubens as Collector," *Journal of the Royal Society of Arts,* CXVII (1969), 641–60.

FIVE: Movers and Shakers

I have confined myself to accounts of museums, orchestras, and related institutions I found more or less indispensable. For a broad-gauged overview, though good work has been done since, Nikolaus Pevsner, *Academies of Art Past and Present* (1940; new pref., 1973), retains much authority. William Weber, "The Muddle of the Middle Classes," *19th Century Music,* III, 2 (November 1979), 175–85, helps to clarify (by duly complicating) important issues. Weber, *Music and the Middle Classes: The Social Structure of Concert Life in London, Paris and Vienna* (1975), is a terse and pioneering appraisal. Adam Carse, *The Orchestra from Beethoven to Berlioz: A History of the Orchestra in the First Half of the 19th Century, and of the Development of Orchestral Baton-Conducting* (1948), is an excellent technical but accessible study.

M. A. DeWolfe Howe, *The Boston Symphony Orchestra, 1881–1931* (1914; rev. and extended in collaboration with John N. Burk, 1931), is a virtual anthology of Henry Lee Higginson's letters and similar evidence. Josiah Quincy, *The History of the Boston Athenaeum with Biographical Notes of Its Deceased Founders* (1851), celebrates the institution he presided over for so long and offers lengthy swatches of documentation. For the early days in Boston, see Michael Broyles, *"Music of the Highest Class": Elitism and Populism in Antebellum Boston* (1992). Martin Green's *The Problem of Boston: Some Readings in Cultural History* (1966) makes sense of its Mandarin culture. And see Hilliard T. Goldfarb, *The Isabella Stewart Gardner Museum: A Companion Guide and History* (1995). John Maxon, *The Art Institute of Chicago* (1970; rev. ed., 1977), exhibits the trophies of great collectors and donors. Richard Saunders with Helen Raye, *Daniel Wadsworth, Patron of the Arts* (1981-c), gives a good account of the Wadsworth Atheneum, its founding, and its founder.

John H. Mueller, *The American Symphony Orchestra: A Social History of Musical Taste* (1951), offers a wide perspective with a general introduction, miniature histories of seventeen American orchestras, an account of repertoires, and comparisons with foreign orchestras. Levine and Harris (see above, p. 278) are equally at home here. The first half of John Dizikes's very bulky and authoritative *Opera in America: A Cultural History* (1993) deals with the Victorian age. For Carnegie, philanthropist and donor, see Edward C. Kirkland's introduction to his edition of Andrew Carnegie, *The Gospel of Wealth and Other Timely Essays* (1962), his most significant statements; a leaflet by Annette Blaugrund, *The Taste of Andrew Carnegie* (1991-c), adds a few facts; see also Peter Gay, *CH*, 62–64.

Cultural institutions in nineteenth-century Frankfurt am Main are explored in Andreas Hansert, *Bürgerkultur und Kulturpolitik. Eine historisch-soziologische Rekonstruktion* (1992), and *Geschichte des Städelschen Museums-Vereins Frankfurt am Main* (1994), both extended treatments of local museums. *Das 'Museum.' Einhundertfünfzig Jahre Frankfurter Konzertleben, 1808–1958,* ed. Hildegard Weber (1958), is more chatty but meaty. For Berlin's National Gallery, there is Karl Scheffler, *Die Nationalgalerie zu Berlin. Ein kritischer Führer* (1912), with a brief history from 1861 to 1911, and illustrations of paintings with commentary. Paul Ortwin Rave, *Die Geschichte der Nationalgalerie Berlin* (n.d.), is short but intelligently selective. I have benefited from a study of the Wagener papers and those of other major Berlin collectors in the Zentral-Archiv, Sammlung Preussischer Kulturbesitz, in Berlin. Carolyn Helen Kay has studied the daring director of the Kunsthalle, Hamburg's chief museum: "Educating the Bourgeoisie: Alfred Lichtwark and Modern Art in Hamburg, 1886–1914," Ph.D. diss., Department of History, Yale University (1994). Lichtwark's copious letters to his mother and sister have been edited (not with complete fidelity) by Carl Schellenberg (1972): *Briefe an seine Familie, 1875–1913* (1972). The same editor has brought out Lichtwark's *Briefe an Max Liebermann* (1947). Among the catalogs this museum has published, the one closest to my concerns is Eva Maria Krafft and Carl-Wolfgang Schumann, *Katalog der Meister des 19. Jahrhunderts in der Hamburger Kunsthalle* (1969-c). *Ein Geschmack wird untersucht. Die G. C. Schwabe Stiftung,* ed. Werner Hofmann and Tilman Osterwold (n.d.-c), fully illustrates the collection of English academic pictures that Schwabe donated to Hamburg.

Volker Plagemann, *Das deutsche Kunstmuseum, 1790–1870* (1967), canvasses the history of most German museums in sufficient detail. Nearly all museums in the country's major cities have full catalogs, often with historical introductions. I mention only Munich: Peter Böttger, *Die Alte Pinakothek in München. Architektur, Ausstattung und museales Programm* (1972), very bulky, and Erich Steingräber, *Neue Pinakothek. Erläuterungen zu den ausgestellten Werken* (1981-c), with a historical sketch and lists of holdings.

J. E. Crawford Flitch, *The National Gallery*, with its brevity and age (1912), is as much a historical document as a document about history. A more recent summary account is Philip Hendy, *The National Gallery, London* (1960; 4th ed., 1971), which draws on Sir Charles Holmes, *The Making of the National Gallery* (1924). Edward T. Cook, *A Popular Handbook to the Tate Gallery: "National Gallery of British Art"* (1898), is an early visitors' guide. (Strangely enough, there is no biography of Sir Henry Tate, sugar king, collector, Maecenas. Meanwhile we have Janet Minihan, *The Nationalization of Culture: The Development of State Subsidies to the Arts in Great Britain* [1977].) See also Richard Redgrave, *The Sheepshanks Gallery* (1870). Robertson, *Sir Charles Eastlake* (cited above, p. 289), also belongs here. *The Grosvenor Gallery: A Palace of Art in Victorian England,* ed. Susan P. Casteras and Colleen Denney (1996-c), records the brief (1877–90) and strenuous life of an ambitious gallery that became the home of the English aesthetic movement. For Turner's extremely intricate will, adding excerpts from the report of a select committee of the House of Lords set up in 1861, see Walter Thornbury, *Life of J. M. W. Turner R. A.,* 2 vols. (1862), 409–22; there is a lucid account of the far from perspicuous matter in A. J. Finberg, *Life of J. M. W. Turner, R. A.* (1961).

Reginald Nettel, *The Orchestra in England: A Social History* (1946), starts with Handel but concentrates on the nineteenth century. W. W. Cazalet, *The History of the Royal Academy of Music, Compiled from Authentic Sources* (1854), is awash in documents. For one fine English orchestra, see Robert Elkin, *Royal Philharmonic: The Annals of the Royal Philharmonic Society* (1946). See esp. chs. 5 and 6 of E. D. Mackerness, *A Social History of English Music* (1964).

As for institutions in France, *Music in Paris in the Eighteen-Thirties,* ed. Peter Bloom, vol. IV of *Musical Life in 19th-Century France* (1982), collects a number of papers, for the most part extremely instructive; Jacques Barzun's "Introductory Essay: Paris in 1830" (pp. 1–22) is an elegant preface. We may add Arnold Benedict Perris, "Music in France during the Reign of Louis-Philippe: Art as 'A Substitute for the Heroic Experience' " Ph.D. diss., Department of Art History, Northwestern (1967). Albert Boime's pioneering *The Academy and French Painting in the Nineteenth Century* (1971) has discredited the convenient division of French art into academic and avant-garde painting and suggested a more helpful, threefold division. (Boime, *Thomas Couture and the Eclectic Vision* [1980], substantially elaborates his argument.) On the July Monarchy, see Michael Marrinan, *Painting Politics for Louis-Philippe: Art and Ideology in Orléanist France, 1830–1848* (1988). Two valuable studies by Patricia Mainardi, *Art and Politics of the Second Empire: The Universal Expositions of 1855 and 1867* (1987) and *The End of the Salon: Art and the State in the Early Third Republic* (1993), illuminate the institutional side of French high culture after mid-century. They can be supplemented with Jean Paul Bouillon,

"Sociétés d'artistes et institutions officielles dans la seconde moitié du XIXe siècle," *Romantisme*, LIV (1986), 89–113. Caillebotte's provocative last will, leaving his Impressionists to the French state, and its consequences are brilliantly explored by Kirk Varnedoe, *Gustave Caillebotte* (1987), which also surveys his career as a painter. Marie Berhaut, *Caillebotte: Sa vie et son oeuvre* (1978), a study on which Varnedoe has drawn, and Pierre Vaisse, "Le Legs Caillebotte d'après les documents," *Bulletin de la Société de l'Histoire de l'Art Français* (1983), 201–8, have compelled a full revision of the story—I have relied on both. Jane F. Fulcher, *The Nation's Image: French Grand Opera as Politics and Politicized Art* (1987), pushes its thesis too hard, but remains worth reading. William L. Crosten, *French Grand Opera: An Art and a Business* (1972), is convincing. James H. Johnson, *Listening in Paris: A Cultural History* (1995), is a careful and enjoyable examination of what I have elsewhere called "the art of listening"—see *NH*, 11–35.

R. van Luttervelt, *Dutch Museums* (1960), is a good brief survey. On the origins of the Rijksmuseum in Amsterdam, Judikje Kiers and Fieke Tissink, *The Building of the Rijksmuseum: Design and Message* (1992), is succinct. The beginnings of Amsterdam's Concertgebouw are the theme of Johan H. Giskes, "Opbouw (1881–1888)," in H. J. van Boyen et al., *Historie en kroniek van het Concertgebouw en het Concertgebouworkest*, 2 vols. (1989), I, 11–26. Giskas, "De periode Willem Kes (1888–1895)," ibid., 27–68, and Lydia Lansink, "Het Concertgebouw: 'Een Drang tot Hooger Leven,' " ibid., 69–96, round out the story. *Levende Meesters: De schilderijenverzameling van Carel Joseph Fodor, 1801–1860*, ed. Gusta Reichwein, Ellinoor Bergvelt, Frouke Wieringa (1995-c), is a satisfying exposition of Fodor's collection, to be read with *The Fodor Collection: Nineteenth-Century French Drawings and Watercolors from Amsterdams Historisch Museum*, intro. Wiepke Loos (1985-c). Judikje Kiers et al., *Een eeuw apart: Het Rijksmuseum en de Nederlandse schilderkunst in de 19de eeuw* (1993), richly illustrates academic Victorian Dutch art, to be read with Kiers et al., *"The Age of Ugliness": Showpieces of Dutch Decorative Art, 1835–1895* (1995-c), a fascinating glimpse into the kind of overloaded eclecticism against which the modernists rebelled. For royal patronage in the century, see Ellen Fleurbaay and Mieke van der Wal, *Koning Willem III e Arti: Een kunstaarsvereniging en haar beschermheer in de 19e eeuw* (1984-c), an economical treatment.

I have also profited from a well-documented history of the royal museum in Brussels by Françoise Roberts-Jones-Popelier, *Chronique d'un Musée. Musées royaux des Beaux-Arts de Belgique/Bruxelles* (1987), which takes the history of taste and the evolution of the very concept of a museum into account.

SIX: Modernism

My book, I trust, has left no doubt that as I pursued my researches into the intricacies of high culture in the Victorian era, my reading of the conflicts between avant-gardes and bourgeois increasingly deviated from the purely agonistic interpretation that has so long been standard. Those who have held this view, it seems to me, have uncritically accepted the bourgeoisophobes' accusations against bourgeois hypocrites and philistines. A selective anthology of this prevailing consensus from which I dissent should be useful. Irving Howe stresses the combativeness of the avant-garde: "The modern must be defined in terms of what it is not: the embodiment of a tacit polemic, an inclusive negative. Modern writers find that they begin to work at a moment when the culture is marked by a prevalent style of perception and feeling; and their modernity consists in a revolt against this prevalent style, an unyielding rage against the official order. . . . The usual morality seems counterfeit; taste, a genteel indulgence; tradition, a wearisome fetter." In short, we may speak of "a war between modernist culture and bourgeois society." ("Introduction," *Literary Modernism,* ed. Howe [1967], 13, 14, 24.) Earlier, José Ortega y Gasset had already taken a similar tack: "A new style has not infrequently grown out of a conscious and relished antagonism to traditional styles. . . . [T]he development of art from Romanticism to this day cannot be understood unless this negative mood of mocking aggressiveness is taken into account." (*The Dehumanization of Art* [1948], 44.) The most succinct expression of this interpretation is a throwaway line in Renato Poggioli's near-classic *The Theory of the Avant-Garde* (tr. Gerald Fitzgerald, 1968): "The principle or norm of avant-garde art is to be antibourgeois" (p. 126).

Richard Chase is even more blunt: "After the eighteenth century, the democratization of culture and the new literacy confronted the advanced intelligence with a newly arisen welter of taste and opinion which, left to itself, found no other standards than the conformism, at once aggressive and complacent, of the bourgeoisie. In this situation the dissident intellectual, himself characteristically a bourgeois, found his mission. The mediocrity and, as it were, historical helplessness of his class in matters of art and ideas were an open invitation to his powers of discrimination and foresight." ("The Fate of the Avant-Garde," *Partisan Review,* XXIV [Summer 1957], 363.) Albert L. Guérard has identified his opinions more closely with the avant-garde than has any other critic: "Art for Art's Sake is born of the Philistine, consists only in terms of the Philistine, can be defined only by defining the Philistine." The "guiding principle" of modernists is " 'Epater le bourgeois,' to flabbergast the Rotarian." (*Art for Art's Sake* [1936], 87–88.) Daniel Bell's well-known collection of essays (revised) called *The Cultural Contradictions of Capitalism* (1976) makes the same undifferentiated claim: "What is striking is that while bourgeois society introduced radical individualism in economics, and a willingness to tear up all traditional social relations in the process, the bourgeois class feared the radical experimental individualism of modernism in the culture. Conversely, the radical experimentalists in the culture, from Baudelaire to Rimbaud to Alfred Jarry, were willing to explore all dimensions of experience, yet fiercely hated bourgeois life. The history of this sociological puzzle, how this antagonism came about, is still to be written" (p. 18). I have written this book to offer a first start on that history, and to insist that things were not quite that simple.

Not even the subtle Lionel Trilling was immune to this oversimplification. "The author of *The Magic Mountain* once said that all his work could be understood as an effort to free himself from the middle class, and this, *of course,* will serve to describe the chief intention of all modern literature." ("On the Teaching of Modern Literature," originally titled "On the Modern Element in Modern Literature" [1961], *Beyond Culture*

[1965], 30, italics mine.) I could not verify whether Mann ever made this observation (Trilling does not document it), but if he did, he was being less perceptive than his own creation, Tonio Kröger, whom, the reader may remember, I called as a friendly witness in the text (see pp. 43–44). None of this means that I reject this dominant view altogether. There *were* philistines among the bourgeois, many of them. But I find Howe and company overly susceptible to avant-garde propaganda—in short, unhistorical.

A look at a volume that is not so well known as it deserves to be, Herwin Schaefer, *Nineteenth Century Modern: The Functional Tradition in Victorian Design* (1970), would throw doubt on the all-too-popular notion that nineteenth-century bourgeois taste was epitomized by the extravagant, and to most modern taste absurd, displays at the Great Exhibition of 1851; Schaefer demonstrates that furniture, china, cutlery, and scientific instruments designed in the Victorian era often look as if they had come out of the Bauhaus in the early 1920s. (Incidentally, for the well-known avant-garde slogan "One must be of one's time," see George Boas, "Il faut être de son temps," *Journal of Aesthetics and Art Criticism*, I [1941], 52–65.)

Jerrold Seigel, *Bohemian Paris: Culture, Politics, and the Boundaries of Bourgeois Life, 1830–1930* (1986), is a noteworthy study of Parisian fringe culture and a corrective to facile interpretations. For a general treatment, see the careful and detailed reading by Helmut Kreuzer, *Die Boheme. Beiträge zu ihrer Beschreibung* (1968). Peter Bürger, *Theory of the Avant-Garde* (1974; tr. Michael Shaw, 1984), stresses (I think, overstresses) the radical subversiveness of modernism. The book has aroused considerable controversy; see *"Theorie der Avantgarde." Antworten auf Peter Bürgers Bestimmung von Kunst und bürgerlicher Gesellschaft*, ed. W. Martin Lüdke (1976).

Modernism: A Guide to European Literature, 1890–1930, ed. Malcolm Bradbury and James McFarlane (1976; with new pref., 1991), offers well-informed sketches of the cities and of the movements and genres of modernism without troubling itself much with the bourgeoisie. *The Modern Tradition: Backgrounds of Modern Literature,* ed. Richard Ellmann and Charles Feidelson, Jr. (1965), remains the best anthology of brief, well-selected texts. Two long essays by Samuel Lublinski, *Die Bilanz der Moderne* (1904) and *Der Ausgang der Moderne. Ein Buch der Opposition* (1909), offer contemporary, highly polemical definitions of modernism that capture the flavor of the time; the anthology *Die Berliner Moderne, 1885–1914,* ed. Jürgen Schutte and Peter Sprengel (1987), is a perfect companion piece.

Arthur Symons, *The Symbolist Movement in Literature* (1899; rev. and expanded eds., 1908 and 1919; intro. Richard Ellmann, 1958), remains a classic text for an early appreciation of nineteenth-century French avant-garde literature. For the brighter side of modernism—no apocalypse here!—see *The Spirit of Montmartre: Cabarets, Humor, and the Avant-Garde, 1875–1905,* ed. Phillip Dennis Cate and Mary Shaw (1996-c). Charles Rearick, *Pleasures of the Belle Epoque: Entertainment & Festivity in Turn-of-the-Century France* (1985), is rather relentlessly cheerful. Roger Shattuck, *The Banquet Years: The Origins of the Avant-Garde in France, 1885 to World War I* (1955; ed. 1968), delightfully and seriously elucidates modernism in Paris with essays on Alfred Jarry, Henri Rousseau, Erik

Satie, and Guillaume Apollinaire. Peter Jelavich's, *Munich and Theatrical Modernism: Politics, Playwriting, and Performance, 1890–1914* (1985) and *Berlin Cabaret* (1993) effectively deal with German avant-gardes and with (largely antibourgeois) political satire. Jane Block et al. explore a consequential representative of early modernism in *Les XX and the Belgian Avant-Garde: Prints, Drawings, and Books ca. 1890* (1992-c). Kenworth Moffett, *Meier-Graefe as Art Critic* (1973), analyzes a most influential German critic who championed modernist French art.

Since I have concentrated on painting and architecture, this bibliography will reflect this reluctant self-discipline. Werner Hofmann, *Turning Points in Twentieth-Century Art* (n.d.; tr. Charles Kessler, 1969), analyzes the pioneers of modernist painting and architecture. Theda Shapiro, *Painters and Politics: The European Avant-Garde and Society, 1900–1925* (1976), is an impressive study. For the first "rebels" against academic painting, the Barbizon artists and their allies, see esp. *Jean François Millet*, ed. Robert L. Herbert, with Roseline Bacou and Michel Laclotte (1975-c), a superb overview. Jean Bouret, *The Barbizon School and 19th-Century French Landscape Painting* (1972; tr. 1973), a bit naive about the bourgeoisie, is an extensive monograph. Nicholas Green, *The Spectacle of Nature: Landscape and Bourgeois Culture in Nineteenth Century France* (1990), has good material on the Barbizon artists, but depends on Foucault and the postmodernist notion that landscape is "constructed" and a "commodity." See also *Théodore Rousseau*, ed. Hélène Toussaint (1967-c). Alfred Robaut and Etienne Moreau-Nélaton, *L'Oeuvre de Corot*, 4 vols. (1905), holds up well; for a modern appraisal, see Peter Galassi, *Corot in Italy: Open-Air Painting and the Classical-Landscape Tradition* (1991).

Amid a massive, still rapidly growing, literature on the Impressionists, I am much indebted to Robert L. Herbert's beautifully informed and robustly argued *Impressionism: Art, Leisure, & Parisian Society* (1988), which places the painters into their time and place without vulgarizing the meaning of their art. Lionello Venturi, *Les Archives de l'Impressionisme. Lettres de Renoir, Monet, Pissarro, Sisley et autres. Mémoires de Paul Durand-Ruel. Documents*, 2 vols. (1939), contains correspondence and related materials gathered by the Impressionists' favorite dealer. John Rewald's very substantial *The History of Impressionism* (1946; 4th ed., 1973) remains essential. Rewald, *Studies in Impressionism* (cited above, p. 288), conveniently collects some important essays. *The New Painting: Impressionism, 1874–1886*, ed. Charles S. Moffett et al. (1986-c), conveniently reconstructs the exhibitions of the Independents. (The two companion volumes, *The New Painting: Documentation. Impressionism, 1874–1886*, ed. Ruth Berson, 2 vols. [1996-c], a treasure-house of reviews in their original languages and of every painting illustrated in these reviews, reached me only after the text was in press.) David Bomford, Jo Kirby, John Leighton, and Ashok Roy, *Art in the Making: Impressionism* (1990-c), is a technical (but accessible) examination of Impressionist theories about, and use of, color and other materials.

The biographies, monographs, and catalogs most useful to me for individual Impressionists include Brombert's *Edouard Manet* (cited above, p. 278); among earlier studies, Adolphe Tabarant, *Manet et ses oeuvres* (1947), and Pierre Courthion, *Manet* (1962), stand out. T. J. Clark, *The Painting of Modern Life: Paris in the Art of Manet and His Followers* (1985), is provocative as usual; among its benefits are long quotations from Manet's reviewers. (On that topic, see esp. George Heard Hamilton's valuable *Manet and His Critics* [1954].) Emile Zola, *Edouard Manet. Etude biographique et critique* (1867), is of historical interest. Paul Hayes Tucker's authoritative *Claude Monet: Life and Art* (1995) is to be read with his *Monet in the 90s: The Series Paintings* (1990-c); see also Robert L. Herbert, *Monet on the Normandy Coast: Tourism and Painting, 1867–1886* (1994). Richard R. Brettell has made Pissarro his own. See "Camille Pissarro: A Revision," *Camille Pissarro, 1830–1903* (1980-c), 13–37; *Pissarro and Pontoise: The Painter in a Landscape* (1989); and, with Joachim Pissarro, *The Impressionist and the City: Pissarro's Series Paintings* (1993-c). *Letters to His Son Lucien,* ed. John Rewald with the assistance of Lucien Pissarro (1944; rev. ed., 1972), is revealing; for complete coverage see *Correspondance de Camille Pissarro,* ed. Janine Bailly-Herzberg, 5 vols. (1980–91). *Alfred Sisley,* ed. MaryAnne Stevens (1992), is a satisfying overview of this somewhat underrated artist.

The worshipful *The Art of Renoir,* by Albert C. Barnes and Violette de Mazia (1935), not without influence, has not carried the day. Walter Pach, *Renoir* (1983), has a good introduction and comments on the paintings, and Barbara Ehrlich White, *Renoir: His Life, Art, and Letters* (1984), is solid. Jean Renoir, *Renoir, My Father* (1958; tr. Randolph and Dorothy Weaver, 1962), offers intimate affectionate glimpses. Degas is well summed up in P. A. Lemoisne, *Degas et son oeuvre* (1946). Theodore Reff, *Degas: The Artist's Mind* (1976), is an important study; see also Richard Kendall, *Degas by Himself* (1987) and *Degas beyond Impressionism* (1996-c), an impressive revision that discovers an elderly Degas who was far from burnt out or a hermit. Sue Welsh Reed, Barbara Stern Shapiro, et al., *Edgar Degas: The Painter as Printmaker* (1984), is authoritative. Daniel Halévy, *My Friend Degas* (1960; tr. and ed. Mina Curtiss, 1964), is a painfully honest account by an intimate with whom Degas broke over the Dreyfus affair. Two articles by James Fenton, "Degas in the Evening," *New York Review of Books* (October 3, 1996), 48–53, and "Degas in Chicago," ibid. (October 17, 1996), 14–18, admirably review the recent literature.

Anne Higonnet, *Berthe Morisot* (1990), is a succinct, admiring, yet scholarly life. Charles F. Stuckey and William P. Scott, with Suzanne D. Lindsay, *Berthe Morisot, Impressionist* (1987-c), copiously illustrated, is excellent. See also *Correspondance de Berthe Morisot,* ed. Denis Rouart (1950), and the touching diary of her daughter, Julie Manet, *Journal (1893–1899)* (1979). François Daulte, *Frédéric Bazille et son temps* (1952), says the essential.

John Rewald, *Post-Impressionism from van Gogh to Gauguin* (1956; 3rd rev. ed., 1978), remains the book to start with. David Sweetman, *Paul Gauguin: A Complete Life* (1996), ably sums up the copious recent scholarship, but indulges in fanciful speculations about Gauguin's sexual tastes. We can still read with profit Robert Goldwater, *Gauguin* (1983), with a good introduction and commentary on selected paintings. (To be read with Goldwater's *Primitivism in Modern Painting* [1938; enlarged ed., 1986].) Wayne Andersen, *Gauguin's Lost Paradise* (1971), is a persuasive psychoanalytic biography. There is much to be gleaned from *Lettres de Gauguin à sa femme et à ses amis,* ed. Maurice Malingue

(1946; 2nd ed., 1946), and Gauguin's intimate journal, *Avant et après* (1902–3; tr. Van Wyck Brooks, 1923; ed. 1946). See also, for the early Gauguin, Wladyslawa Jaworska, *Gauguin and the Pont-Aven School* (1972).

Mark Roskill, *Van Gogh, Gauguin and the Impressionist Circle* (1970), puts their tempestuous friendship into a larger ambiance. Meyer Schapiro, *Vincent van Gogh* (1983), Ronald Pickvance, *Van Gogh in Arles* (1984-c) and the sequel, *Van Gogh in Saint-Rémy and Auvers* (1986-c), are extremely informative. *The Complete Letters of Vincent van Gogh,* 3 vols. (1958), is eloquent and essential. (*The Letters of Vincent van Gogh,* ed. Ronald de Leeuw [1996], expertly tr. by Arnold Pomerans, offers a gratifying selection.) J. B. de la Faille, *The Works of Vincent van Gogh: His Paintings and Drawings* (1970), is a monumental catalog.

The unclassifiable Cézanne—Impressionist? Postimpressionist? proto-Cubist?—is being overwhelmed with scholarship. Roger Fry, *Cézanne: A Study of His Development* (1927), was a pioneering rediscovery. Gerstle Mack, *Paul Cézanne* (1935), remains worth consulting, as does John Rewald's compact *Paul Cézanne: A Biography* (1939; ed. 1968). Meyer Schapiro, *Cézanne* (1952; 2nd ed., 1962), offers penetrating comments on selected paintings; Schapiro, "The Apples of Cézanne: An Essay on the Meaning of Still-life" (1968), *Modern Art: 19th and 20th Century: Selected Papers* (1978), 1–38, is a model of an art historian's venture into psychoanalytic criticism. Lionello Venturi, *Cézanne, son art et son oeuvre,* 2 vols. (1936), is an indispensable catalogue raisonné. Fritz Novotny, *Cézanne und das Ende der wissenschaftlichen Perspektive* (1938), an interesting German contribution, stresses Cézanne's originality. *Cézanne: The Late Work,* ed. William Rubin (1977-C), has admirable essays by Theodore Reff, John Rewald, Fritz Novotny, and others.

For Georges Seurat, Paul Signac, Henri Edmond Cross, Charles Angrand, and briefly Camille Pissarro, that loose alliance, see Robert L. Herbert, *Neo-Impressionism* (1968). See also Belinda Thomson, *Vuillard* (1988), and Gloria Groom, *Edouard Vuillard, Painter-Decorator: Patrons and Projects, 1892–1912* (1993). Jean and Henri Dauberville, *Bonnard: Catalogue raisonné de l'oeuvre peint,* 4 vols. (1966–74), does justice to a leading Nabi, and see Robert L. Herbert, *Neo-Impressionists and Nabis in the Collection of Arthur G. Altschul* (1965-c). Debora L. Silverman's highly stimulating essay, *Art Nouveau in Fin-de-Siècle France: Politics, Psychology, and Style* (1989), suggestively explores the psychological dimension, and much else. Robert Schmutzler, *Art Nouveau* (1962; tr. Edouard Roditi, 1964), is exhaustive. For the greatest of the pointillists, see William Innes Homer, *Seurat and the Science of Painting* (1964; corr. ed., 1970), and Henri Perruchot, *La Vie de Seurat* (1966).

John Elderfield, *The "Wild Beasts": Fauvism and Its Affinities* (1976-c), well explores André Derain, Maurice Vlaminck, Georges Braque, and the young Henri Matisse; James D. Herbert, *Fauve Painting: The Making of Cultural Politics* (1992), offers a more political reading and treats Fauvism as a blend of traditionalism and innovation. For the Futurists, see Joshua C. Taylor, *Futurism* (1961), and Anne d'Harnoncourt et al., *Futurism and the International Avant-Garde* (1980).

The secessions roiling German-speaking culture have been stylishly explored by Kirk Varnedoe, *Vienna 1900: Art, Architecture & Design* (1986-c), and Maria Makela, *The*

Munich Secession: Art and Artists in Turn-of-the-Century Munich (1990). For Berlin, see Rudolf Pfefferkorn, *Die Berliner Secession* (1972), and Peter Paret, *The Berlin Secession: Modernism and Its Enemies in Imperial Germany* (1980). Max Liebermann must not be neglected here (see above, p. 276). Bernard S. Myers, *The German Expressionists: A Generation in Revolt* (1957; concise ed., 1966), is an essential text, to be supplemented with Paul Vogt, *Expressionism: German Painting, 1905–1920* (1978; tr. Antony Vivis and Robert Erich Wolf, 1980). *Der Blaue Reiter,* the celebrated almanac edited by Wassily Kandinsky and Franz Marc (1912), has been reissued with a new preface, a history of the publication, and documents by Klaus Lankheit (1965). On the group of painters associated with the editors of the *Blaue Reiter,* including Jawlensky, Macke, the young Klee, and others, Rosel Gollek, *Der Blaue Reiter im Lenbachhaus München. Katalog der Sammlung in der Städtischen Galerie* (1974), has much to say. So does Will Grohmann, *Wassily Kandinsky: Life and Work* (1958). Sixten Ringbom, *The Sounding Cosmos: A Study in the Spiritualism of Kandinsky and the Genesis of Abstract Painting* (1970), focuses on the artist's mysticism. On the other great pioneer of nonobjective art, Michel Seuphor, *Piet Mondrian: Life and Work* (1956), is a comprehensive biography; see also L. J. F. Wijsenbeek et al., *Piet Mondrian: Centennial Exhibition* (1971–c), and ch. 4 in Peter Gay, *Art and Act.*

For the Armory Show, see Milton Brown, *The Story of the Armory Show* (1963); Crunden (cited above, p. 290), passim, esp. 339–82, and Barbara Rose, *American Art since 1900: A Critical History* (1967), ch. 3.

John Richardson's remarkable and exhaustive *A Life of Picasso,* 2 vols. of 4 so far (1991, 1996), reaches to 1917 and will certainly replace all previous biographies, although his verdicts on the meaning of Picasso's art and on his character invite further discussion. Meanwhile, amid a vast literature, see Daniel-Henry Kahnweiler, Theodore Reff, Robert Rosenblum, et al., *Picasso: 1881/1973* (1973). On Cubism, which Richardson handles with panache, see also Douglas Cooper, *The Cubist Epoch* (1970), and Robert Rosenblum, *Cubism and Twentieth-Century Art* (1961). For the commercial side, there is Michael Z. Fitzgerald, *Making Modernism: Picasso and the Creation of the Market for Modern Art* (1995). (Robert Jensen, *Marketing Modernism in Fin-de-Siècle Europe* [1994], is a good companion volume that throws its net more widely.)

Nikolaus Pevsner, *Pioneers of Modern Design from William Morris to Walter Gropius* (publ. 1936 under the title *Pioneers of the Modern Movement;* rev. ed., 1960), has long been an influential text, even if its unilinear perspective—as though modernist architecture culminates in Gropius—is rather problematic. (Pevsner's lectures published as *Some Architectural Writers of the Nineteenth Century* [1972] perform a valuable service.) No less significant than *Pioneers* is Sigfried Giedion, *Space, Time and Architecture: The Growth of a New Tradition* (1941), a powerful analysis of the historical preconditions for a modernist architecture. Julius Posener, *Anfänge des Funktionalismus. Von Arts and Crafts zum Deutschen Werkbund* (1964), is an excellent anthology of architects' writings. The first three hundred pages in the autobiography of the great Belgian designer Henry van de Velde, *Geschichte meines Lebens* (tr. from the French MS, and ed. Hans Curjel, 1962), provides a monumental record. (For William Morris, see above, p. 278.)

For the evolution of French modernism in architecture, see esp. Marc Emery, *Un Siècle d'architecture moderne en France, 1850–1950* (1971), and René Jullian, *Histoire de l'architecture en France de 1889 à nos jours. Un siècle de modernité* (1984). Donald Drew Egbert, *The Beaux-Arts Tradition in French Architecture* (1980), sets out the conservative opposition, to be read with *The Beaux-Arts and Nineteenth-Century French Architecture*, ed. Robin Middleton (1982). Françoise Bercé and Bruno Foucart, *Viollet-le-Duc: Architect, Artist, Master of Historic Preservation* (1988-c), introduces that celebrated architectural theorist and politician. See also Jean-Michel Leniaud, *Viollet-le-Duc, ou, les délires du système* (1994).

Vincent J. Scully, Jr., *The Shingle Style and the Stick Style: Architectural Theory and Design from Richardson to the Origins of Wright* (1955; rev. ed., 1971), is an important examination of the roads to modernist architecture in the United States. Hugh Morrison, *Louis Sullivan: Prophet of Modern Architecture* (1935), amply discusses Frank Lloyd Wright's great predecessor and teacher. It should be obvious from the text that my pages on Wright owe a major debt to Leonard K. Eaton's *Two Chicago Architects and Their Clients: Frank Lloyd Wright and Howard Van Doren Shaw* (1969), a searching survey that persuasively analyzes Wright's early successes among a prosperous midwestern bourgeoisie. Robert C. Twombly, *Frank Lloyd Wright: An Interpretive Biography* (1973), and Henry-Russell Hitchcock, *In the Nature of Materials: The Buildings of Frank Lloyd Wright, 1887–1941* (1942), are both valuable, but largely displaced by Neil Levine's massive and fair-minded *The Architecture of Frank Lloyd Wright* (1996). (With its grandiloquence and "poetic" style, Wright's *An Autobiography* [1943] reveals perhaps more than the author wanted.)

The second half of Frank Jenkins, *Architect and Patron: A Survey of Professional Relations and Practice in England from the Sixteenth Century to the Present Day* (1961), a succinct survey, proved useful. John Summerson has left his mark on the history of architecture in Britain. See esp. *Heavenly Mansions and Other Essays on Architecture* (1963) and *Victorian Architecture in England: Four Studies in Evaluation* (1970). Robert Furneaux Jordan, *Victorian Architecture* (1966), is succinct. Joan Bassin's informative *Architectural Competitions in Nineteenth-Century England* (1984), shows the practice at work. Amid a sizable literature, Phoebe Stanton, *Pugin* (1971), deals succinctly with Britain's most active and eloquent early-Victorian Catholic architect. Thomas Howarth, *Charles Rennie Mackintosh (1868–1928)* (1952; 3rd ed., 1990), is a full biography, which, despite the information it conveys, has done the complexity of modernism a disservice by treating Mackintosh as "a tragically misunderstood innovator who was ultimately destroyed by a philistine society." (I am quoting from an excellent review by Martin Filler, "Big Mack," *New York Review of Books*, XLIV, 3 [February 20, 1997], 7–10, quotation at 7. Filler's essay admirably complements the points I have made in the text about Voysey.) For briefer treatments, see Robert Macleod, *Charles Rennie Mackintosh* (1968), and Andrew McLaren Young, *Charles Rennie Mackintosh (1868–1928)* (1968-c). Janice Helland, *The Studios of Frances and Margaret MacDonald* (1996), insists on the independent contribution of Mackintosh's wife and sister-in-law. Elizabeth Cumming, *Glasgow 1900: Art & Design* (1992-c), ranges more widely to encompass the Glasgow school of painting. Several recent studies have rediscovered Voysey. See David Gebhard, *Charles F. A. Voysey, Architect* (1975), an anthology of Voysey's writings; Duncan Simpson, *C. F. A. Voysey: An Architect of Individuality* (1979), which stresses his fundamental convicitions; and Wendy Hitchmough, *C. F. A. Voysey* (1995).

The celebrated story of George Gilbert Scott's "flexibility" in submitting designs for the British Foreign Office is a staple in all histories of modern architecture. His own apologetic account (G. G. Scott, *Personal and Professional Recollections* [1878]) occupies many pages. Ch. 13, "The Battle of the Styles," in M. H. Port, *Imperial London: Civil Government Building in London, 1851–1915* (1995), tells the story well and relates it to public architecture in Victorian London. The equally "unprincipled" designs for Amsterdam's Rijksmuseum are reported and well illustrated in Kiers and Tissink, *The Building of the Rijksmuseum* (cited above, p. 293). For Antoni Gaudí, that remarkable eccentric of Barcelona, G. R. Collins, *Gaudí* (1960), is essential. Conrad Kent and Dennis Prindle, *Park Güell* (1993), places him into his religious-political context.

The emergence of modernist architecture in Germany is brilliantly chronicled in Julius Posener, *From Schinkel to the Bauhaus* (1972). For the remote early-nineteenth-century "founder" of German modernism, much written about, see esp. *Karl Friedrich Schinkel: A Universal Man,* ed. Michael Snodin (1991-c), and Pevsner, "Karl Friedrich Schinkel," *Studies in Art, Architecture and Design,* vol. I, *From Mannerism to Romanticism* (1968), 175–95, which justly stresses the modernity of Schinkel's ideas and work. Fritz Schoeber, *Peter Behrens* (1913), sums up the early work of an architect in whose studio the young Gropius worked. Gropius's breakthrough to uncompromising modernism in 1913 is well covered in Helmut Weber, *Walter Gropius und das Faguswerk* (1961). For a sweeping biography, see Reginald R. Isaacs, *Gropius: An Illustrated Biography of the Creator of the Bauhaus* (1983; 1991); and Peter Gay, *Art and Act,* ch. 3.

Acknowledgments

As usual, I have incurred many and diverse debts; I could not have sustained my invasions of art history, music history, and literary criticism without experienced and considerate guides.

Also as usual, I have enjoyed ample opportunities to try out my ideas—and occasionally to revise them—before a range of academic audiences often appreciative but never uncritical. I shall list only lectures dating from 1996, when I was completing this book. I spoke on bourgeoisophobes at Dickinson College, Ohio Wesleyan University, the University of California at Santa Cruz, and at a Yale conference on modernism. My sharp distinction between the Manchester and Munich bourgeoisies served as a topic at Brandeis University and the Humanities Research Centre of the Australian National University at Canberra. I presented a summary of my argument at a stimulating lunch meeting at the Institute for the Humanities of New York University.

Now that this series is complete, I want to express my warmest thanks to the late Iza Erlich, who died as this volume was going to press, a psychoanalyst and friend who first advised me to undertake psychoanalytic training and thus helped to change my life.

To canvass ideas and speculations with friends, as I have done for more years than I care to ponder, has been invariably pleasurable and, more than that, immensely profitable. As I have through the years, I have once again exploited my old, trusted companions: Gladys Topkis and Gaby Katwan, Vann Woodward and Bob Webb, John Merriman and Stefan Collini, Dick and Peggy Kuhns and Leon Plantinga. Nor should I forget the exhilarating lunches at the "club" with Doron Ben-Atar and David Bell. Old friends in Amsterdam whom I see only too rarely—Maarten Brands, Frouke Wieringa, Herman Beliën—eased my access to the intriguing themes of Dutch collecting and Dutch patronage, while Arthur Mitzman's firm grasp on French literary culture proved most helpful. My former students, and now my friends, Robert Dietle and Mark Micale have been valued lunch companions and correspondents. Carolyn Kay, Jennifer Hall, George Williamson, and Jeffrey Auerbach, my last Ph.D. students, have taught me much as they completed their apprenticeship. I owe much to Egbert Begemann.

I count my hosts in Australia in the summer of 1996 among my most gratifying, and intellectually most rewarding, acquisitions. I gratefully single out Tom and Mary O'Brien in Brisbane, Iain McCalman in Canberra, and Peter McPhee in Melbourne, all of whom made real contributions.

I am grateful, too, for concrete information and concrete gestures. Eleanor Alexander sent interesting thoughts on Charles Freer. Albert Boime, whose publications have made a difference to this book, supplied information about artists at work in museums as copyists. Prof. John Breuilly set me on the track of elusive information about Manchester Jewry (as did Simon Gunn). Esther DaCosta Meyer and I talked about C. F. A. Voysey. Peter Demetz clarified the Futurists for me. Pascal Dupuy supplied me with important material on Rouen's culture. I have enjoyed, and considerably profited from, discussions with Cyrus Hamlin, a most knowledgeable student of German culture. Prof. Wolfgang Hardtwig of the Humboldt University, Berlin, and I discussed significant local patrons. Joan D. Hedrick (as well as Laura Wexler and Diana Royce) did detective work on the mysterious "rich Mr. Stowe." My former colleague Bob Herbert, a brilliant student of French Impressionism, impressively prompt and forthcoming as is his way, gave me excellent advice on Millet and other French artists. Monique van Hoogstraten did indispensable research on Dutch institutions of high culture. William R. Johnston, associate director of the Walters Art Gallery, answered inquiries. Salee Lawrence of the St. Johnsbury Athenaeum corresponded with me about copies of old masters in the museum. Busy as he is, John Nicoll, who directs the Yale University Press in London, went out of his way to secure illustrations for me. Lawrence Rainey helpfully criticized my lecture on bourgeoisophobes. Daniel Sherman patiently took me through bureaucratic thickets to secure the rights to his photograph of the art museum at Rouen. Debora Silverman sent me her important article on van Gogh. My friend Wim Smit clarified Dutch salaries. Frau Dr. Annette Weber gave me information about art books published in Frankfurt. And Sarah Elliston Weiner corresponded with me about copies at Columbia University.

I assembled the archival material on which much of this argument rests through the years, and want above all to thank the unfailingly well-informed and courteous archivists at the Kunsthalle, Hamburg; the archives of the Staatliche Museen, Preussischer Kulturbesitz, Berlin; the Monacensia and the Bayerische Staatsbibliothek, both in Munich; the Rare Book Department, Cambridge University Library; the Henry Watson Music Library, the Manchester Public Library, and the Rylands Library, Manchester; and Manuscripts and Archives, Yale University.

As I had every right to expect, my editor, Don Lamm, efficiently and graciously aided by Chelsea Vaughn, proved congenial and imaginative—in short, solidly helpful. My copy editor Otto Sonntag, who had already shown his light hand and keen eye with volume IV of this series, considerably improved this one, too.

Two readers of the manuscript deserve particular thanks: David Cannadine and my wife, Ruth. David went beyond the single chapter he so effectively read for volume IV to take on the manuscript of the present volume as a whole, much to its benefit. As she has done since 1959, Ruth Gay took time out from her own work, meticulously commented on my prose, and went over each chapter twice, at times more often than that, clarifying my presentation, tightening my argument, and thus (the reader will be grateful) shortening the text.

PETER GAY

INDEX